IBM® PC SHAREWARE

PC-FILE™, PC-WRITE™ PC-TALK® AND EXPRESSCALC™

JOHN R. OTTENSMANN

TAB BOOKS Inc.
Blue Ridge Summit, PA 17214

To Jan and Sandy

FIRST EDITION
SECOND PRINTING

Library of Congress Cataloging in Publication Data

Ottensmann, John R.
IBM PC Shareware.

Includes index.
1. IBM Personal Computer—Programming. 2. PC-File (Computer program) 3. PC-Write (Computer program) 4. PC-Talk (Computer program) 5. ExpressCalc (Computer program) I. Title.
QA76.8.I2594088 1987 005.36′5 86-30167
ISBN 0-8306-0241-0
ISBN 0-8306-2841-X (pbk.)

Questions regarding the content of this book should be addressed to:

Reader Inquiry Branch
Editorial Department
TAB BOOKS Inc.
P.O. Box 40
Blue Ridge Summit, PA 17214

Contents

Trademarks

Ashton Tate, dBASE II, dBASE III, dBASE III Plus are trademarks of Ashton Tate.
AT&T is a trademark of American Telephone and Telegraph Corporation.
Borland and Turbo Pascal are trademarks of Borland International.
CompuServe is a trademark of CompuServe Incorporated.
Compaq is a trademark of Compaq Computer Corporation.
CrossTalk XVI and Microstuf are registered trademarks of Microstuf, Inc.
Dac, Dac Easy Accounting, and Dac Easy Word are trademarks of Dac Software.
Epson is a registered trademark and Equity is a trademark of Epson America, Inc.
ExpressCalc, ExpressGraph, File Express, and ExpressWare are trademarks of ExpressWare.
Farsight is a trademark of Integrated Technologies Corporation.
Generic CADD and Generic Software are trademarks of Generic Software, Inc.
Hayes is a registered trademark and SmartModem is a trademark of Hayes Microcomputer Products, Inc.
IBM is a registered trademark and IBM PC, IBM PC XT, IBM PC AT, IBM PC*jr,* and PC-DOS are trademarks of International Business Machines Corporation.
Leading Edge and Model D are trademarks of Leading Edge Corporation.
Lotus and 1-2-3 are registered trademarks of Lotus Development Corporation.
Microsoft is a registered trademark and MS-DOS, SYLK, and Word are trademarks of Microsoft Corporation.
Mirror and Softklone are trademarks of Softklone Distributing Corporation.
PC-File, PC-Dial, PC-Style, PC-Type, and Buttonware are trademarks of Buttonware, Inc.
PC-Outline is a trademark of Softworks Development.
PC-SIG is a trademark of PC-Software Interest Group.
PC-Talk and Freeware are trademarks of the Headlands Press.

PC-Write and Quicksoft are trademarks of Quicksoft.

Practibase and Practicorp are trademarks of Practicorp.

Radio Shack is a registered trademark and Tandy 1000 is a trademark of Tandy Corporation.

Source is a trademark of Source Telecomputing Corporation.

SuperCalc is a registered trademark of Computer Associates International, Inc.

Thinktank and Living Videotext are trademarks of Living Videotext, Inc.

Twin and Mosaic are trademarks of Mosaic.

VP-Planner, Executive Filer, Executive Writer, and Paperback Software are trademarks of Paperback Software International.

WordStar and MailMerge are registered trademarks of MicroPro International.

Acknowledgments

PC-TALK III screens reproduced with written permission from The Headlands Press, Inc. Copyright (c) 1983, 1984, 1985 The Headlands Press, Inc.

Screen images from ExpressCalc have been reproduced with the permission of ExpressWare Corporation. (c) Copyright ExpressWare Corporation, 1986. ExpressCalc is a registered trademark of ExpressWare Corporation.

Screen images from PC-Write have been reproduced with the permission of Bob Wallace, Quicksoft. (c) 1986 by Bob Wallace, Quicksoft. All rights reserved.

Screen images from PC-File III, version 4.0, reproduced with the permission of Buttonware.

I wish to acknowledge the support of the Indiana University School of Public and Environmental Affairs in Indianapolis for the resources made available for the writing of this book. I also wish to thank Computing Services at Indiana University-Purdue University at Indianapolis for their assistance in obtaining some of the software used.

To my daughter, Sandra, and my wife, Jan Neuenschwander, go special thanks for their special encouragement and support.

Introduction

Personal computers continue to fall in price, making these systems increasingly affordable to ever larger numbers of people. Complete computer systems compatible with the popular IBM Personal Computer can now be purchased for under $1000. This virtually guarantees that large numbers of new users will be acquiring personal computers for use at work, at school, and in the home.

It is the software—the programs that run on the personal computers—that give these machines the power to perform useful work. Word processing programs are required to use personal computers for writing. Data management programs give the machines the capabilities to store and retrieve information. Electronic spreadsheets turn personal computers into powerful analytical tools. Effective use of personal computers requires the appropriate software.

While the prices of the personal computers themselves have steadily fallen, traditional commercial software continues to be quite expensive. The most popular word processing, data management, and electronic spreadsheet programs all cost at least several hundred dollars apiece. When the cost of the computer system alone stood at several thousand dollars, the additional cost for the software was perhaps not unreasonable to most buyers. As the computers fall in price, however, high software prices can pose a genuine problem for many new personal computer purchasers. A user on a budget purchases a new personal computer system for less than $1000, only to find out that the cost of purchasing a few of the most popular pieces of software will be nearly as great as the cost of the computer system itself.

A low-cost alternative for personal computer users on a budget is user-supported software. Individuals write these programs and then encourage users to copy and share the programs with others. (This is in direct contrast to traditional commercial software, where such copying is forbidden and would be a violation of copyright laws.) Each copy of a program includes a request that the user send a contribution to the program's author if the user likes the program and finds it to be useful. The requested contributions are modest, typically ranging from $25 to $75, and entitle the user to a copy of the most current version of the program, and often a printed copy of the complete documentation and the right to acquire further updates at a reduced cost. Perhaps surprisingly, the user-supported concept has worked. Many users have made the requested contributions, generating significant profits for the developers of the software. The software authors have responded in turn by continuing to upgrade their programs and by offering additional programs. New software developers have produced even more programs that are being distributed as user-supported software.

User-supported software is a reasonable option for personal computer users on a budget only to the extent that the programs are fairly easy to use and sufficiently powerful to accomplish significant work. Poor-quality software is no bargain, no matter how low the price. Fortunately for those concerned with the cost of software, many of the user-supported programs are first-rate. Of course, the user-supported programs are not going to have all of the features of the most expensive commercial programs selling for five or six hundred dollars. Many of the user-supported programs do, however, compare favorably with commercial software costing several hundred dollars.

Acquiring the appropriate software is just the first step in making effective use of a personal computer. The owner then has to learn how to use the software. The documentation accompanying very many programs—both commercial and user-supported—is frequently insufficient for new users attempting to learn to use the software. This book shows how to use the most popular user-supported programs, with step-by-step instructions and numerous examples.

The most popular user-supported programs for IBM Personal Computers and compatible systems are covered in this book. The four programs encompass the most common applications of personal computers, and together they constitute a low-cost, comprehensive set of software tools for basic personal computing. PC-File is a program for the storage and retrieval of information. It is very easy to use and has a wide variety of features for effectively managing information and generating reports in various formats. PC-Write is a word processing program that is very quick and responsive, allowing easy editing of text. It also provides for the flexible formatting of text for printing. PC-Talk is a communications program that enables your personal computer to communicate with remote computers, such as computer bulletin boards and electronic information services. Finally, ExpressCalc is an electronic spreadsheet program for use in data analysis. It has most of the standard features of most electronic spreadsheets and is more than adequate for most applications.

This book is made possible by the existence of high-quality user-supported software. The first chapter provides background on user-supported software and gives information on how to obtain the programs addressed in this book. New users of personal computers must first learn to use the operating system, so the second chapter explains the use of DOS, the operating system for IBM Personal Computers and compatibles. It describes how to prepare the disks for using the various programs. Following this are the four major chapters describing the use of PC-File, PC-Write, PC-Talk, and ExpressCalc. This collection of user-supported programs will be sufficient to meet all of the computing needs of many users. Their utility is further enhanced by the ability to share information among the various programs. The seventh chapter of this book explains these procedures for using the programs as an integrated package. The final chapter concludes with further suggestions for pursuing low-cost computing.

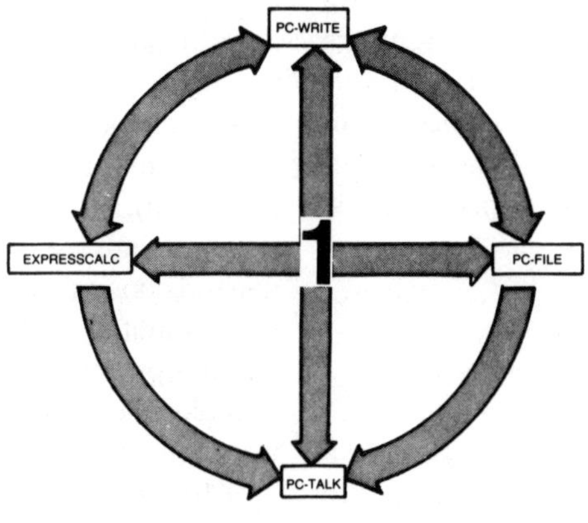

Introducing User-Supported Software

The IBM Personal Computer was first offered for sale in the latter part of 1981. For the first year or so following its introduction, the amount of software available for this new machine was quite limited. One particular problem for some users was the lack of an effective communications program that would allow the IBM PC to communicate with other computers over the telephone lines.

The late Andrew Fluegelman, publisher of *PC World* magazine, saw this need and wrote a communications program for the IBM PC which he called PC-Talk. The program was good, and he wanted to make it available to other users of the IBM Personal Computer. He could have released the program into the public domain, relinquishing all rights to it. Users could have freely copied and shared the program, but Fluegelman would have received nothing for the considerable amount of time he invested in developing the software. Alternatively, he could have sought to market the program as conventional commercial software. Copies of the disk and accompanying printed documentation would have been sold either in computer stores or by mail order. In this case, the costs of distribution and advertising would have required that a fairly substantial price be charged for the program.

Instead of pursuing either of these two options, Fluegelman decided to try an experiment in distributing PC-Talk. He put documentation for the program in a file on the PC-Talk disk, a file which could be printed out by anyone who had a copy of the disk. The program was copyrighted, but Fluegelman granted users the right to make copies of the disk and share the program with others. Included in the documentation of PC-Talk is a simple request: "If you have received this program from another user and find it of value, your $35 contribution will be appreciated." (Early versions requested a smaller contribution.)

Fluegelman called his experiment in distributing software in this way *Freeware*. (Freeware was used as a trademark, and thus cannot properly be employed to refer to any other user-supported software.) He argued that users should be encouraged to copy and share programs, and that users could only determine the value of a piece of software by actually using it for a period of time. Undoubtedly many observers thought Fluegelman to be naive in expecting users to send in contributions for a program they already had. Fluegelman's judgments about human nature proved to be correct, however. Large numbers—very large numbers—of users sent in their contributions for PC-Talk. This initial experiment in user-supported software proved to be a success.

THE NATURE OF USER-SUPPORTED SOFTWARE

The programs distributed in the manner of PC-Talk—with copying and sharing encouraged and a voluntary contribution requested—are referred to as *user-supported software* or *shareware*. A large variety of programs are now available as user-supported software. They provide an economical alternative to the more expensive commercial programs for personal computer users on a budget.

While there are variations from one program to another, the distribution of user-supported software generally follows a fairly standard pattern. The program is recorded on a disk along with a documentation file providing instructions on its use. This documentation file can be printed out by the user to serve as the manual for the program's operation.

Users of the shareware programs are given the permission to freely copy the programs and give copies to others. While some of this sharing takes place among individuals, a great deal of the distribution of user-supported software is handled by computer users groups. The users groups typically maintain libraries of software—both public domain software and user-supported software—and allow members to make copies. Another distribution channel is via computer bulletin boards. Users can *download* the software to their own systems over the phone lines, making copies on disk for their own use.

The distinguishing feature of user-supported software is the request for a contribution to the programs' authors from users who find the programs to be of value. The size of the requested contributions vary, but generally range between about $25 and $75, depending upon the complexity and sophistication of the program. Making such contributions is entirely voluntary, of course, but many users honor these requests and make the contributions. User-supported software might be termed "software on the honor system" (paraphrasing a slogan from a local public television membership campaign).

Although the nature of user-supported software depends upon the willingness of the users to make their voluntary contributions, many of the program authors provide additional incentives to the users to make their contributions and register the software. In many cases, paying the fee entitles the user to receive a copy of the most current version of the program with all of the latest updates and added features. This is a significant benefit, because in many instances users may have received earlier versions of the software that have been circulating. Payment of the contribution may also entitle the user to receive notification of new versions of the programs as they are developed in the future, with the option of acquiring these new versions free or at a reduced price. Many of the shareware authors will also send printed copies of the complete documentation for the program when the software is registered and the contribution made. Not only is the printed manual more convenient than the print-outs of the documentation files on the program disks, but it may also be more complete. Some authors of user-supported software deliberately delete some of the details on the finer points of the software from the documentation on the disks as an incentive to make the contribution and register the program. Limited space for documentation on the disk with the program may also make it impossible for a program's author to include the complete documentation.

Quicksoft, the distributor of the PC-Write program, has gone a step farther in encouraging contributions by turning the registration and distribution of the program into an entrepreneurial opportunity for the users. When a user registers PC-Write and pays the contribution of $75, he or she is sent a program disk with a unique identifying serial number. If other users later register copies of PC-Write made from that copy, the person originally registering the copy receives a "commission" or bonus of $25. Thus, users who register have an incentive to make copies of the program, share the copies with others, and encourage them to register the program as well.

Another notable characteristic of user-supported software is the frequent provision of updates and enhancements to the programs. Programs that began as relatively basic tools have evolved into far more sophisticated pieces of software with a wide range of features. The development and release of enhanced versions of the software is easier than with commercial software, because the program developers do not have large volumes of inventory and copies of programs at the distributors and computer stores that will be made obsolete by the release of a new version. For commercial software developers, the release of a new version of a program is a major event, costing a great deal of money. For the authors of user-supported software, release is as easy as putting the new version on computer bulletin boards and sending out the new version to those who register the program. This has meant that many of the user-supported programs have been continuously updated, with new features being regularly added. As a result, they have matured into flexible, well-crafted, easy-to-use programs.

THE MAJOR USER-SUPPORTED PROGRAMS

PC-Talk, PC-Write, and PC-File are the most prominent user-supported programs for the IBM Personal Computer and compatibles. Each was one of the earliest user-supported programs in its category. Each has received widespread attention and favorable reviews in the computer magazines. The *Whole Earth Software Catalog*, which attempts to identify the best software for personal computers, recommended all three of these programs. Probably more people use these programs than any other user-supported software.

PC-Talk was one of the first communications programs available for the IBM PC and has gained an early, loyal following. Reviews of IBM PC communications software continue to identify PC-Talk as one of the more popular programs. The program is menu-driven and relatively easy to use (for communications software). PC-Talk can store lists of phone numbers in a directory and automatically dial the number chosen. The capabilities are included for file transfer using the popular XMODEM protocol. While PC-Talk cannot do all the work for you—it cannot automatically log on to remote computers like some communications programs—it is a relatively full-featured, capable program.

PC-Write was written by Bob Wallace and is the most popular user-supported word processing program. The strength of PC-Write has always been as a text editor. The program is extremely fast, responding almost instantaneously to most commands. Learning to use PC-Write can take some time, as commands are assigned to virtually every key on the IBM PC keyboard. Once the commands have been learned, however, most functions of PC-Write are just a single keystroke away. New features for formatting text for printing out have been added with every revision, so that PC-Write is now able to do nearly anything most writers could desire, such as justification, printing of headers and footers, and so forth. Unlike most word processing programs, PC-Write stores documents on the disk as standard text files without the use of special codes. This makes it easy to use PC-Write with other personal computer software.

PC-File, written by Jim Button, is the premier user-supported file management program. The program is menu-driven and is so easy to use that one hardly needs a manual. The user defines a database by entering names for the fields of information into blanks on the screen. The entry of the data is accomplished in the same way. PC-File allows the user to search a database for information in a variety of ways. The reporting capabilities of PC-File are easy to use yet surprisingly powerful. Users can generate anything from tabular reports to mailing labels with minimal effort. For basic file management, this program is nearly as versatile as any available for the IBM PC.

ExpressCalc is a user-supported electronic spreadsheet program available from ExpressWare.

ExpressCalc is newer than the other three shareware programs and thus has received less attention. It is included here because the electronic spreadsheet is one of the basic types of personal computer software. ExpressCalc is a powerful and versatile tool for data analysis. It is a fairly standard electronic spreadsheet program, with most of the capabilities common to such programs. Operation of the program is quite similar to SuperCalc, one of the more popular of the commercial electronic spreadsheets.

THE GROWTH OF USER-SUPPORTED SOFTWARE

When Andrew Fluegelman began his Freeware experiment with PC-Talk, no one could have imagined the growth that would take place in user-supported software. From beginnings as small, individual operations, the distributors of user-supported software have grown into significant enterprises. The numbers of authors of user-supported programs continues to grow, and the number and variety of programs offered continually increases. New channels are being developed for the distribution of user-supported software.

As private businesses, the providers of user-supported software do not reveal the numbers of users who have made their contributions and registered the programs. Some published reports have estimated that the revenues of the major shareware producers may well be in the six-figure range. Certainly the growth in these enterprises can be seen in some of the outward manifestations. What began as operations run by the individual authors are now businesses employing numbers of persons. Buttonware, the firm distributing PC-File and other shareware programs, has a toll-free telephone number for ordering the programs and registering the software. Buttonware, Quicksoft, and ExpressWare accept MasterCard and VISA for making the voluntary contributions.

Both Quicksoft and Buttonware have begun advertising their programs in computer magazines. Jim Button has indicated that he intends to begin the distribution of his software through computer stores as well as by mail. While such developments make such user-supported software look more and more like commercial software, they are still distinguished by their very low prices in comparison with most of the other programs currently on the market.

One area in which the user-supported programs are rapidly increasing in popularity is in colleges and universities. Many schools have been making personal computers available for use by students, only to face the problem of providing appropriate software for their use. Under special arrangements, colleges and universities have been making available to their students copies of PC-Write, PC-File, and ExpressCalc, along with printed copies of the documentation, at very nominal prices. Each student wishing to use personal computers can purchase these programs and have a very usable collection of software for basic personal computing tasks.

New user-supported software is being released on a regular basis. In addition to PC-File, Buttonware is distributing several additional shareware programs, including a word processor and a communications program. The success of the user-supported concept is encouraging new program authors to distribute their programs in this fashion. As a result, user-supported software is becoming a viable option for users to accomplish many of their personal computing tasks.

ACQUIRING THE PROGRAMS

The four user-supported programs described in this book—PC-File, PC-Write, PC-Talk, and ExpressCalc—can be obtained in a variety of ways. Many personal computer users groups have copies of these programs in their libraries, and members can obtain copies of the disks. Most cities have computer users groups. Computer stores can often provide information on these groups, and tell you when they meet and how to contact them. The memberships dues are generally very modest. In addition to serving as a source for copying user-supported and public domain software, computer users groups provide valuable assistance and information on the use of personal computers.

The user-supported software may also be

downloaded over the telephone lines from various computer bulletin boards and other sources. There is a catch-22, however, with respect to PC-Talk. One has to have a communications program first in order to contact the bulletin boards and download the software. Obtaining PC-Talk in this fashion would require the use of another communications program; perhaps a friend could help out.

In looking for a copy of the ExpressCalc electronic spreadsheet program, some confusion is possible. Until the middle of 1986, this program was distributed under the name PC-Calc by Buttonware. Users groups and electronic bulletin boards may have their copies of the program with the name PC-Calc. The current version of the program is named ExpressCalc and is distributed by ExpressWare. Registration of the program is with ExpressWare.

The most direct approach is to request the programs directly from the publishers. Headlands Press, the distributors of PC-Talk, will send a copy of the program to anyone sending in a blank formatted disk and a postage paid return mailer. Quicksoft will provide an evaluation copy of PC-Write for $16. ExpressWare will also send a copy of the ExpressCalc disk for $10. In both cases, registration of the software and payment of the contribution are voluntary and can be done later after the user determines he or she is satisfied with the software. To obtain PC-File from Buttonware, one must pay the full registration fee for the programs.

No matter how you obtain copies of the shareware programs, I would strongly encourage those of you deciding to use the software to register the programs and make the voluntary contributions to the developers. This will enable you to obtain the most current versions of the programs, put you on the list for future updates, and provide you with printed copies of the complete documentation. The manuals will be important if you are to make the most effective use of all of the features of the programs. This book provides an introduction to the use of the programs. It cannot cover every feature and in no way is intended to replace the comprehensive documentation.

In addition to these very practical advantages, there is one other important reason for registering the user-supported programs and making the contributions. You will feel good about yourself. It is the right thing to do. The authors of these programs have all worked hard to develop high-quality pieces of software. They are distributing the programs as user-supported software, which gives you the opportunity to try the programs out before making a decision about whether or not they meet your needs. They are asking in return only that you make a modest contribution, far less than the prices for comparable commercial software, and that you contribute only if you decide to use the programs. Please support the authors and the concept of user-supported software.

Complete information on the sources of the four programs is provided below. Please note that the prices are current as of the time this is being written and are subject to change.

PC-File III

Jim Button
Buttonware, Inc.
P.O. Box 5786
Bellevue WA 98006
Telephone: 800-JBUTTON
Price: $59.95 plus $5.00 shipping and handling
Accepts MasterCard and Visa

PC-Write

Quicksoft
219 First N #224
Seattle WA 98109
Telephone: 202-282-0452
Evaluation copy price: $16.00
Registered copy price: $89.00
Accepts MasterCard and Visa

PC-Talk

Freeware
The Headlands Press, Inc.
Post Office Box 862
Tiburon CA 94920

Requested contribution: $35.00

ExpressCalc

ExpressWare
P.O. Box 230
Redmond WA 98073

Disk Set Price: $10.00
Registered Set Price: $49.00
Telephone: 206-643-3503
Accepts MasterCard and Visa

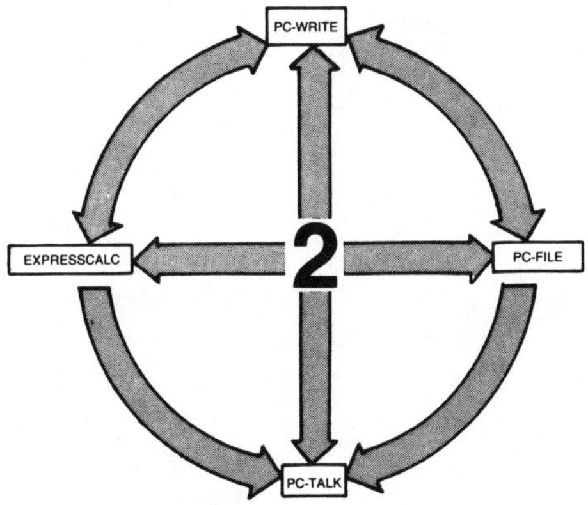

Getting Started With DOS

Using PC-File, PC-Write, PC-Talk, and ExpressCalc requires some basic knowledge about using the personal computer and DOS—the *disk operating system.* DOS is the basic program that must be used along with each of the other programs to provide necessary background support. The user must also employ DOS as a utility to perform basic housekeeping functions, such as making copies of disks and managing files of information on those disks. This chapter outlines the various procedures necessary to get started using the personal computer, and provides specific instructions for preparing working copies of disks with the user-supported programs.

THE "STANDARD" SYSTEM

If you have already purchased a personal computer system, you have undoubtedly learned that there is a bewildering variety of machines and an equally bewildering variety of options that can be selected for any specific computer system. The existence of such a wide range of possible configurations contributes to the complexity and confusion of many of the instruction manuals for personal computers and computer software. The manuals are forced to address every possible combination, explaining how to proceed in each situation. The user finds himself or herself faced with a large number of possibilities and must confront the difficulties of figuring out what applies to his or her unique situation.

Things need not be this difficult. The vast majority of computer systems purchased for basic personal computing are quite similar. This section will define a basic, minimum "standard" system that readers of this book will be assumed to be using. All instructions for operation will be given for this standard system. In only a few instances will it be necessary to provide optional instructions to cover differences among the standard systems. In this way, the presentation can be simplified while still remaining appropriate to nearly all users.

Users of personal computer systems that depart from our "standard" need not despair, however. Appendix B provides additional information regarding the use of the operating system and the four shareware programs with different systems. The documentation for the programs also gives further suggestions for use on various types of computers. Finally, the manuals that accompany the computer system will have additional helpful information.

In addition to serving as a point of reference for this book, the "minimum standard system" serves as a useful guideline for those considering the purchase of a personal computer. Certain users may have specific requirements that require deviations from these recommendations, but the standards should prove useful as a point of departure in comparing various alternatives.

The standard system is assumed to be an IBM Personal Computer or a compatible computer capable of running virtually all programs written for the IBM PC. These are by far the most popular types of personal computers. The four user-supported programs were written for the IBM PC and will perform best on these kinds of machines. The programs can also be made to operate on some of the other machines that run the MS-DOS operating system.

The IBM PC, however, is the standard that is assumed, for a very important reason: In addition to running the four user-supported programs described in this book, IBM Personal Computers and compatible machines can run a wider variety of other software than any other personal computer. Purchasing an IBM PC or compatible leaves one with the widest range of options for future applications. It is no accident that manufacturers who once made computers that were not completely IBM-compatible have either modified their machines or have introduced new systems so that users would have the benefits of compatibility—the capability of running the vast array of IBM PC software.

Second, the standard system is assumed to have two double-sided floppy disk drives. Some of the earliest IBM PCs and some other systems came with single-sided drives. Double-sided drives store twice the information of single-sided drives and are now virtually standard. The user-supported programs come on double-sided disks, so double-sided drives are required to use the programs. Many personal computers can be purchased with a single floppy disk drive, and it is possible to use the four user-supported programs with only one drive. Using a single drive requires a large amount of disk swapping—taking one floppy disk out of the drive and putting another one in. Copying files and disks, including the making of backup copies, is difficult and time-consuming. If at all possible, purchase a personal computer with two floppy disk drives to make operation easier. All instructions in this book will assume the system has two drives. If not, consult Appendix B for suggestions on operation with a single drive.

An alternative to a system with two floppy disk drives is a system with a hard disk drive. Hard disks have far higher storage capacities than floppy disks and operate much more rapidly. They certainly make personal computing more convenient. Because this book is devoted to low-cost computing and hard disks are a more expensive option, most readers will probably not have hard disks. Nevertheless, some suggestions for the use of the four programs on hard disk systems are also given in Appendix B.

The standard system must have at least 256K bytes of random access memory (RAM) in order to use all four of the programs effectively. Some of the programs can make use of additional RAM for certain purposes, but the additional memory is not required for any of the operations described in this book. The price of memory chips has declined so dramatically that acquiring the minimum of 256K of RAM should not pose any problems for users. Additional RAM is always useful and enables the running of a wider range of programs, so those purchasing new systems should seriously consider getting more memory.

Selecting the video display system involves a range of choices. The only assumption being made here is that the video monitor can display 25 lines of text with 80 characters per line. The use of color television sets as monitors, which can display only 40 characters per line, would work with some of the programs, but this is not a reasonable option for serious personal computing. No further assumptions are being made about the video display system, because different users have very different needs. The user-supported programs will operate effectively with virtually all 80-column video display systems. With an IBM PC, the monochrome display adapter used with the IBM monochrome monitor will provide the best text display, but does not support the display of graphics. The color/graphics display adapter card provides the graphics capabilities. This may be used either with appropriate monochrome monitors, which are relatively inexpensive, or with more costly color RGB monitors. Several of the user-supported programs make effective use of color if it is available, but color or graphics display capabilities are not required. The selection of video display options may be slightly different with IBM PC compatible machines, but again, any 80-column system should work fine with the four programs being described here.

The standard system should have a printer, which is assumed to be connected to the parallel printer port. Using the software described here does not make much sense without being able to print out the results. Parallel port connection is being assumed because this is the standard, easiest, and most direct way of interfacing a printer to IBM PCs and compatibles. Printers connected to serial ports may be used, but they require users to provide several operating system commands to set up the port properly and to direct output to the printer. Virtually any printer can be employed.

The only area in which the selection of a printer and its specific features becomes much of an issue is in the use of PC-Write, the word processing program. The ability to format output in certain ways will depend both upon the capabilities of the printer and on the support provided for that printer by PC-Write. The section on the installation of PC-Write in this chapter explains how to determine which printers are supported by that program. For personal computer users on a budget, a low-cost dot matrix printer is likely to be a good choice. These printers have declined in price, and the quality of their output has steadily been improved. The most popular of these printers have been made by Epson, so the purchase of either an Epson or Epson-compatible printer increases the chances that the printer will be supported by any other software you later wish to acquire.

Finally, the standard computer should run PC-DOS (for IBM Personal Computers) or MS-DOS (for compatible machines), version 2.0 or later. As new, updated versions of software are released (including operating systems), they are given higher version numbers. Several of the user-supported programs being used here require at least version 2.0 of DOS.

A summary of the characteristics of the standard system that is being assumed is provided in Table 2-1. Users of systems varying from these standards should see Appendix B for suggestions on modifications to operating procedures to accommodate the differences.

DOS DISK OPERATIONS

This section describes the most basic operation of the personal computer—getting DOS started, copying disks, and formatting new disks. In order to follow the procedures described below, you will need the standard system outlined above, a copy of the PC-DOS or MS-DOS diskette appropriate for your system, and a number of blank double-sided, double-density floppy disks.

What Is DOS?

DOS—the disk operating system, pronounced "doss"—is a special program that must be loaded

Table 2-1. Characteristics of Standard System.

1. IBM Personal Computer or compatible system capable of running IBM PC software
2. Two double-sided floppy disk drives
3. Minimum of 256K bytes of random access memory (RAM)
4. Any video display system capable of displaying 25 lines with 80 characters per line
5. Printer connected to the parallel printer port
6. PC-DOS or MS-DOS operating system, version 2.0 or later

into the memory of the computer first in order to start the computer system. At times, you will be using DOS directly to make copies of disks, prepare new disks for use (formatting), and otherwise perform housekeeping functions on your computer system. You will give DOS the instructions to load and begin the operation of other programs, such as PC-File. At that point, you can forget about DOS; you will be dealing with PC-File or whatever program you are running. DOS remains in the memory of the computer, however, performing a variety of tasks for PC-File. All this takes place automatically without your having to worry about it, but this is why it is always necessary to begin operation of the computer system by loading DOS.

The disk operating system for IBM Personal Computers and compatibles was written by the Microsoft Corporation. When it is sold by IBM for their personal computers, it is called PC-DOS (for Personal Computer Disk Operating System). Versions of this disk operating system provided for other computers, including IBM PC compatibles, are called MS-DOS (for Microsoft Disk Operating System). PC-DOS and MS-DOS are essentially the same operating system and work in the same way. This book will refer to both of them together simply as DOS.

The term *DOS* is commonly used in two different ways; this can sometimes produce confusion. On the one hand, DOS is used to refer to the program that is loaded into the computer when it is started. This DOS program gives the user the ability to perform certain basic functions and works in the background for other programs that are used. Procedures will be given for transferring DOS (this specific program) to other disks so that they can be used to start up the system as well.

DOS also is used to refer to the entire disk labeled PC-DOS or MS-DOS that comes with the machine. With this disk, users have additional capabilities, provided by other programs, for such tasks as copying and formatting disks. These additional features of DOS can only be used when the disk drive contains the original DOS disk, a copy of that disk, or a disk to which the appropriate files have been transferred. These additional programs are not loaded into the memory of the computer when it is started up and will not always be available for your use.

Handling Floppy Disks

The programs you acquire and the information you produce with a personal computer are stored on floppy disks. You will need to become comfortable with the correct handling and storage of these disks.

Floppy disks contain thin circular pieces of plastic coated with magnetic material, much like the tape in an audio or video recorder. Inside the disk drives in the computer, these disks are rotated at high speed, and a movable recording head records information on concentric tracks on the disk and reads information that has been recorded on those tracks. With double-sided disk drives, this recording takes place on both sides.

The circular disk is permanently encased in a thin square plastic or cardboard carrier, often black, to protect it. It is this entire package—the thin plastic disk plus its protective carrier—which is called the floppy disk. A large circular hole in the center allows the disk drive to spin the disk inside the envelope. Two oval-shaped cutouts on either side are provided to allow the recording heads to make contact with the flexible disk inside the envelope. Do not touch the surface of the disk through these cutouts. Oil, perspiration, or dirt from your fingers can damage the disk and cause the loss of information recorded on the surface.

Floppy disks come inserted in protective sleeves. You take the disk out of this sleeve in order to insert it into the disk drive. When you remove a disk from the drive, be careful to replace it back into its protective sleeve. Keeping the disks in these sleeves when not in use helps protect them from dust and damage, and helps keep the information stored on the disks from being damaged.

You cannot tell from looking at the surface of a floppy disk what information has been recorded on the disk. Boxes of new, blank disks come with press-on labels that may be used to identify disks. The labels may be placed on the disk next to or on top of the manufacturer's label. It is best to write the information on the label before placing the label on the disk. If you must write on a label after it is on the disk, use only a soft, felt-tip pen. Do not use pencils or ball-point pens, as the pressure may damage the disk.

Also inside boxes of new disks is a small sheet of little rectangular stickers, called *write-protect tabs.* Floppy disks have a small rectangular notch on one side. This notch must be uncovered for the computer to write information on the disk. If the notch is covered up with one of the write-protect tabs, the computer will refuse to write, erase, or otherwise change information on the disk. Using write-protect tabs is an effective way to protect the information on disks—such as program disks—that you only need to read from and do not need to write on.

Handle your floppy disks carefully. It is best to store them in boxes or files designed for the purpose, but keeping them filed upright in a shoe box should be fine. Do not bend floppy disks or attempt to force them into the disk drive. Do not expose the disks to extreme temperatures by leaving them in direct sunlight or near a radiator. Finally, do not expose floppy disks to magnetic fields that could scramble the information recorded on them. Lest you think this is an unlikely occurrence, note that when a telephone rings, it creates a magnetic field sufficient to damage disks stored adjacent to the phone.

Do not remove floppy disks from a disk drive when the red activity light on the disk drive is on, indicating the drive is running. Doing so can easily damage the disk and corrupt the data already stored on the disk.

The most important rule is to make backup copies of all floppy disks and store the backups in another location. In that way, the spilling of a single cup of coffee or a comparable catastrophe cannot destroy all of your valuable programs and data. Floppy disks are quite reliable for the storage of information when handled carefully, but the information stored on disks can sometimes be lost. Keeping backup copies is the best protection.

Starting the Computer and DOS

To start the computer, use the disk labeled PC-DOS or MS-DOS. Open the door or the lever on the left-hand disk drive. Holding the disk by the label, take it from its protective sleeve and slide it into the slot on the disk drive, label side up. The disk should slide all the way in without being forced. After the disk has been inserted, close the disk drive door or turn the lever. (If your computer is not an IBM PC and has the disk drives one above the other, the top drive is probably the one you should use in starting the system, but check the documentation that came with the computer; this is not always the case.)

Turn on the monitor and turn on the printer before turning on the computer. Then turn on the computer itself. On IBM PCs, the on-off switch is a large red switch on the right-hand side of the machine, near the back. On other machines, the switch may be on the front, the side, or the back. The computer will first appear to be doing nothing; it is running a test program to check itself out before starting operation. After a period of time, the red light on the left-hand drive will come on and the disk drive will begin to make its customary noises, indicating it is operating. The computer is loading DOS into its memory.

The first thing DOS does when it is started is ask the user to enter the current date and time. The date and time will be stored with every file you create, which may assist you in distinguishing different versions of files. First DOS displays its arbitrary starting date and asks you to enter a new date. Type in the current day's date using the format displayed by DOS, and press the Return key to enter this date.

The Return key is to the right of the letters on the keyboard. If it is not labeled "Return," it will have a symbol with an arrow going down and to the left to symbolize a carriage return on a conventional typewriter. The Return key must be pressed after most commands or lines of information have been typed to indicate that you are through and the computer should process the information. Some programs give instructions to press "Enter" instead of "Return." On IBM PCs and compatibles, this means the same thing. Note that in addition to the Return key located directly to the right of the keys for the letters, IBM PCs and many compatibles have an additional key labeled "Enter" at the far lower right-hand corner of the keyboard, next to the numeric keypad. This Enter key functions in the same way as the Return key next to the letter keys.

In this book, the pressing of the Return key (or any special key) will be indicated by placing the name of the key in "brackets" like this: <Return>. This means you should press the key indicated; do not type out the characters. Thus, your response to the DOS date prompt should look something like this:

9-30-86<Return>

Any time you make a mistake when typing in something in DOS, pressing the Backspace key—the key with the arrow pointing left above the Return key—will erase the last character entered and move the cursor back one space. In the same manner as the date, DOS will display its arbitrary starting time and ask you to enter the new time. Enter the time, remembering that DOS uses a 24-hour clock. Follow the format used by DOS in displaying the time, but feel free to omit the seconds. An appropriate response for a time of 2:30 P.M. would be this:

14:30<Return>

After you have completed this process, DOS will display its prompt symbol A> on the screen; this indicates that DOS is ready and awaiting your command. Sometime during this process, the name and version of DOS being used will be displayed, either before or after the date and time prompts. The entire startup process described thus far is illustrated in Fig. 2-1, which displays exactly what would appear on the screen. Note that if you do not care about whether or not the correct date and time are used, you can just press the Return key in response to either of the requests. In this event, DOS just continues to use the arbitrary starting date and time that were displayed. For the sake of consistent file marking, you probably should always enter the time, or never enter it.

Occasionally, you may want to restart personal computer operation from the beginning, reloading DOS and starting over from scratch. You may need to do this when problems occur and you get stuck, or restarting may just be the quickest way to move to some other task. It is not necessary to switch the computer off and then on again, and doing so is not the best thing for the machine. IBM PCs and compatibles provide a reset operation that causes such a restart to occur. To reset the computer, be sure a copy of a disk with DOS is in the startup drive and simultaneously depress the Control, Alternate, and Delete keys, which are typically labeled Ctrl, Alt, and Del. The disk drive will operate, DOS will be loaded, and you will start over with the date and time prompts. Use the reset procedure with care, however, because any information stored only in computer memory (and not on disk) will be lost.

The two disk drives on your computer are referred to by DOS as the A: and B: drives (the colons are parts of the names). The left-hand or startup drive is the A: drive; the second drive is the B: drive. The DOS prompt A> that appears indicates

```
Current date is Tue  1-01-1980
Enter new date: 9-30-86
Current time is  0:00:19.11
Enter new time: 14:30

The IBM Personal Computer DOS
Version 2.10 (C)Copyright IBM Corp 1981, 1982, 1983

A>
```

Fig. 2-1. DOS startup display, including the date and time prompts.

not only that DOS is ready to process commands, but also that the A: drive is to be considered the *default* drive. This means that, in interpreting commands, DOS will assume that you are referring to the A: drive unless you specifically indicate otherwise.

Copying Entire Disks

The first DOS procedure to be covered is the making of copies of entire disks. This is initially important for making backup copies of DOS and the various programs you will be using. Later on, you may want to make copies of disks on which you have stored information. The procedures will be outlined for making copies of the DOS disk and the original program disks for the user-supported programs.

After you have started DOS and the A> prompt is displayed on the screen, and the DOS disk is still in the startup drive, enter the following command:

DISKCOPY A: B:<Return>

DOS commands can be typed in either uppercase or lowercase letters; DOS does not distinguish between them. This command instructs DOS to run the DISKCOPY program to make a copy of whatever disk will be placed in the A: drive onto the disk placed in the B: drive. DOS will instruct you to place your source disk—the disk you are copying from—into the A: drive and to place your destination disk into the B: drive. Since you are first going to be making a copy of DOS, you do not have to do anything to the A: drive; the DOS disk is already in it. Place a new disk into the B: drive and press Return. Both disk drives will operate as the contents of the disk in the A: drive are copied exactly onto the disk in the B: drive.

After the procedure has been completed, DOS will ask if you want to make another copy. Whenever you want to stop, simply press N for no and you will be returned to the DOS A> prompt. Suppose you also want to make a copy of your PC-File disk for backup purposes at this time. Respond by pressing Y and DOS will again direct you to place the source disk in A: and the destination disk in B:. This time, place the PC-File disk in the left-hand, or A: drive, and another new, blank disk in the right-hand, or B: drive, and press Return. It is a good idea to make copies of all software disks before using them. In that way, if you should inadvertently damage a disk, you have not lost the program. When you have finished making copies of all of the disks you wish to copy, enter N in response to the question about copying another. The DOS A> prompt will reappear. An illustration of what appears on the screen as copies are made of two disks is shown in Fig. 2-2.

Several suggestions and cautions regarding the making of disk copies will be offered. In making a copy of a disk, any information previously recorded on the destination disk is completely destroyed. Be sure to use new disks or disks that do not have any information that you want to use. Furthermore, be careful not to get the source disk and

```
A>DISKCOPY A: B:

Insert source diskette in drive A:

Insert target diskette in drive B:

Strike any key when ready

Copying 9 sectors per track, 1 side(s)

Copy complete

Copy another (Y/N)?Y
Insert source diskette in drive A:

Insert target diskette in drive B:

Strike any key when ready

Copying 9 sectors per track, 2 side(s)

Copy complete

Copy another (Y/N)?N
A>
```

Fig. 2-2. Using the DISKCOPY procedure to make copies of two disks.

the destination disk mixed up, or you could end up making a copy of a blank, useless disk on to a valuable program or data disk, destroying that information. Several precautions might be taken to guard against these possibilities. It is a good idea to place a write-protect tab over the notch on the program or data disk you are copying. By doing this, if you accidentally make a mistake, the computer will refuse to write anything on the disk, protecting it from damage. Another suggestion is to always follow the same procedure every time you make copies of disks. The instructions given above provide for copying from the A: drive to the B: drive. It is possible to copy in the other direction, but if you always make your disk copies in the same direction, you decrease the chances of making a mistake and placing a source disk into the destination drive.

Formatting New Disks

Before information can be stored on brand-new disks, the disks must be prepared for use with a formatting procedure. Formatting new disks involves writing special information on the disks so they are ready for the storage of information. In general, this means that you must go through a separate formatting process for all new disks. The only exception comes with the copying of entire disks, described above, because the DISKCOPY procedure automatically formats the disk as part of the disk copying process.

Formatting new disks for the storage of data is a simple process. With the DOS disk in the A: drive and the A> prompt appearing on the screen, simply enter the following command:

```
FORMAT B:<Return>
```

This command instructs DOS to format a disk in the B: drive. B: is being used so that the DOS disk does not have to be removed from the A: drive. The FORMAT program will be loaded and will instruct you to place a new disk in the B: drive and press Return. The B: drive will begin to operate and the disk will be formatted. The procedure takes a while, as the disk drive has to write information to every track on the disk. When the formatting has been completed, you will be asked if you want to format another disk. You can continue to format as many disks as you want, or you can stop at any time. The process of formatting a blank disk for the storage of information, as it would appear on the screen using PC-DOS, is shown in Fig. 2-3. Other versions of MS-DOS may show slightly different information, but all will operate in a similar fashion.

The disks prepared in this formatting process will work for storing information created by your programs. They cannot be used to start the computer, however, because they do not have DOS on the disks. You will probably want DOS on the disks that will contain the working copies of your programs, such as PC-File. Then you can just put the working copy of PC-File containing DOS into the A: drive and turn on the machine. DOS will be loaded and you can begin operation immediately. This is easier than using a separate DOS disk to start the machine and then taking this disk out and replacing it with the program disk.

The copy of DOS is placed on the disk during the formatting process. To format disks with DOS so that they can be used to start the computer, enter this command:

```
FORMAT B:/S
```

The /S indicates that the operating system is to be placed on the newly formatted disk. The process proceeds as before, with an additional message at

```
A>FORMAT B:
Insert new diskette for drive B:
and strike any key when ready

Formatting...Format complete

    362496 bytes total disk space
    362496 bytes available on disk

Format another (Y/N)?N
A>
```

Fig. 2-3. Using the FORMAT procedure to format a new disk.

the end that the system has been transferred. Again, you can repeat the process as often as desired. The process is illustrated in Fig. 2-4. You will want to prepare formatted disks containing the operating system for the working copies of each of your user-supported programs. The instructions for creating those working copies, in the last section of this chapter, assume that you have prepared your blank disks in this manner.

These formatted disks with the operating system can be used to start up the computer. To prove this to yourself, take the DOS disk out of the A: drive and replace it with one of the disks you have just prepared. Press the Control-Alternate-Delete reset combination, and DOS will restart in the usual fashion. The formatted data disks without the operating system cannot be used to start the computer. If you try to start the system with such a disk without a copy of DOS, you will get an error message telling you that the disk is not a system disk.

If you examine the directory of a disk you have formatted with DOS, using the DIR command described below, you will see a file named COMMAND.COM. This file is a *part* of DOS that has been transferred to the disk, but it is not all of DOS. Other parts of DOS are in several "hidden" files that do not appear in the directory listing. You cannot transfer all of DOS to a disk simply by using the COPY command to copy the COMMAND.COM file from the original DOS disk

```
A>FORMAT B:/S
Insert new diskette for drive B:
and strike any key when ready

Formatting...Format complete
System transferred

    362496 bytes total disk space
     40960 bytes used by system
    321536 bytes available on disk

Format another (Y/N)?N
A>
```

Fig. 2-4. Using the FORMAT procedure to format a new disk with a copy of DOS.

(though there are times when you may need to copy COMMAND.COM to another disk). Instead, you must format the disk with DOS, using the FORMAT B:/S command.

DOS FILE OPERATIONS

The operations covered thus far have dealt with entire disks. Information is stored on the disks in files, and it is now necessary to learn the fundamentals of DOS operations required for dealing with these files of information on the disks.

Files, File Names, and the Directory

The information recorded on a floppy disk—both programs and the data that you create and use with those programs—is stored in files. Each file contains a single program or a single set of data, such as a database used with PC-File or a text document used with PC-Write. Each file has a unique file name that is used to refer to the information stored in that file. The arrangement is not unlike a filing cabinet filled with labeled file folders, with each folder containing a different collection of related information.

DOS has a special command to display the directory of a disk, which is a listing of all of the files stored on that disk. To see an example of a directory, place a copy of the DOS disk in the A: drive, be sure you have the DOS A> prompt on the screen, and simply enter the following command:

DIR <Return>

A listing of all of the files on the DOS disk will appear on the screen; the listing will look something like the directory shown in Fig. 2-5. (Your version of DOS may have some different files, but that is not important here.) The directory listing may be too long to fit on the screen; in this case the first part of the directory scrolls off the top of the screen. To see the first part of the directory or to pause any output going to the screen, you can use the DOS pause output command, which is Control-S. The Control key, often labeled Ctrl, is located on

```
A>DIR

 Volume in drive A has no label
 Directory of  A:\

COMMAND  COM     17792  10-20-83  12:00p
ANSI     SYS      1664  10-20-83  12:00p
FORMAT   COM      6912  10-20-83  12:00p
CHKDSK   COM      6400  10-20-83  12:00p
SYS      COM      1680  10-20-83  12:00p
DISKCOPY COM      2576  10-20-83  12:00p
DISKCOMP COM      2188  10-20-83  12:00p
COMP     COM      2534  10-20-83  12:00p
EDLIN    COM      4608  10-20-83  12:00p
MODE     COM      3139  10-20-83  12:00p
FDISK    COM      6369  10-20-83  12:00p
BACKUP   COM      3687  10-20-83  12:00p
RESTORE  COM      4003  10-20-83  12:00p
PRINT    COM      4608  10-20-83  12:00p
RECOVER  COM      2304  10-20-83  12:00p
ASSIGN   COM       896  10-20-83  12:00p
TREE     COM      1513  10-20-83  12:00p
GRAPHICS COM       789  10-20-83  12:00p
SORT     EXE      1408  10-20-83  12:00p
FIND     EXE      5888  10-20-83  12:00p
MORE     COM       384  10-20-83  12:00p
BASIC    COM     16256  10-20-83  12:00p
BASICA   COM     26112  10-20-83  12:00p
        23 File(s)     28672 bytes free

A>
```

Fig. 2-5. Directory of the files on the PC-DOS disk.

the left-hand side of the keyboard and is used to issue special commands to the computer. The Control key works like a Shift key: pressed by itself, it does nothing, but when it is depressed in combination with another key, a special control code is sent to the computer. To pause output going to the screen, such as a directory listing, hold down the Control key and press S. The display of new output and the scrolling of the screen will stop. Pressing any key on the keyboard will cause the listing to resume. You may have to practice issuing the DIR command and pressing Control-S a few times to get the output to pause where you want it.

The directory listing for the DOS disk contains five columns of information. The first column contains the main part of the file name and the second column contains an optional three-character extension. Together these two elements constitute the file name that identifies a particular file that has been stored on the disk. For example, in the directory shown in Fig. 2-5, the main part of the first file name is COMMAND and the extension is COM. Together these constitute the file name, which is written as COMMAND.COM, with the two parts separated by a single period and no spaces. The directory is about the only place where the two parts are displayed separately. The third column in the directory gives the number of bytes of information stored in the file. The last two columns list the date and time the file was created. At the conclusion of the directory listing is a count of the total number of files on the disk and the number of unused bytes of storage that are currently available for the storage of additional information.

Users need to understand the rules for naming files because it will be necessary to give names to files of information created during the operation of various programs. The main portion of a file name can consist of one to eight characters. The first character in a file name must be a letter. Any additional characters can be letters, numbers, and some (though not all) of the special symbols on the keyboard. Rather than attempting to remember which symbols are allowed and which are not, I always follow this very simple rule when creating file names: use a letter, followed by up to seven more letters or numbers, and forget about the special symbols. The second part of the file name, the extension, can consist of up to three additional characters. If a file name includes an extension, the file name is written with a period separating the two parts, as in COMMAND.COM. If a file name does not have an extension, the file name is simply the main part, without a period. CHAP2 would be an example of a file name without an extension. When selecting a name for a file, try to select a descriptive name that will indicate the contents of the file.

During the operation of programs, you will be asked to provide file names to identify files of information. CHAP2 is a more useful name for the word processing file containing the contents of this chapter than something like DF4YUS7. Some programs want you to provide only a main part for the file name (of eight characters or less) without an extension. The programs will then add their own extensions to the file names. These extensions are used by the program to identify the types of file. Extensions are often used in this manner to identify file types. For example, you might wish to use an extension like .DOC (for document) or .TXT (for text) to help you recognize the files you create with a word processing program. Some extensions have special meanings to a particular program like PC-File or to DOS itself. You will begin to recognize these special extensions as you look at a variety of disk directories. For example, you will find the extensions .COM, .EXE, and .BAT for files on your DOS disk and your various program disks. These extensions designate program files that DOS is able to load and execute. Such files can be run simply by typing the main part of the file name at the DOS prompt. This is how you ran the DISKCOPY and FORMAT programs earlier.

Entering the directory command in response to the DOS A> prompt gave the directory of whatever disk was in the default drive A:, which was indicated by the prompt. To obtain the directory of the disk in the B: drive, simply indicate that you wish to use the B: drive when entering the directory command:

DIR B:<Return>

Be sure you have a disk in the B: drive before giving this command. This will produce a directory listing of the files stored on the disk in the B: drive. Suppose you had put a newly formatted data disk without DOS in the B: drive and requested the directory. In that case, you would get the results shown in Fig. 2-6—the message "File Not Found." This is DOS's rather backhanded way of indicating that the directory of the disk is empty and that no files of information are currently stored on the disk.

```
A>DIR B:

 Volume in drive B has no label
 Directory of  B:\

File not found

A>
```

Fig. 2-6. Response to the request for the directory of disk in B: drive with no files.

The directory command and all of the other DOS commands discussed in this section are called *internal* DOS commands. Once DOS has been loaded when the computer is started, these commands are always immediately available for your use whenever you see the DOS prompt. These commands are internal to that part of DOS that remains in the computer. To prove this, take the DOS disk out of the A: drive, place any other disk into the drive, and give the DIR command. The computer will display a directory listing of whatever disk you have inserted.

In contrast to this, the DISKCOPY and FORMAT commands discussed in the previous section are *external* DOS commands. The information required to carry out these operations is stored on separate files on the DOS disk. You can see the files DISKCOPY.COM and FORMAT.COM in the directory listing in Fig. 2-5. When these commands are entered, DOS must first load the appropriate files from the disk. This means that if the file is not on the disk that is currently in the drive, these procedures cannot be executed.

Copying Files

You will have many occasions when you will want to copy files from one disk to another. The need will arise when you are creating working copies of program disks, making backup copies of information stored on data disks, and transferring information from one application to another. DOS provides a COPY command that can be used for all these purposes.

Like the DIR command the COPY command is an internal DOS command that is available for use whenever the DOS prompt, A>, appears on the screen. Use of the command is basically simple: you enter COPY followed by the name of the file you are copying from (the old file) and the name of the file you are copying that information to (the new file), in that order. The COPY command has a variety of options and defaults that increase its flexibility but also means there is more to learn.

Insert the DOS disk into the A: drive and in the B: drive place a formatted disk on to which DOS has been transferred using the FORMAT B:/S command. Be sure you have the A> prompt on the screen. Enter following command:

```
COPY FORMAT.COM B:<Return>
```

This is a command to copy the file FORMAT.COM (the old file) from the disk in the A: drive to a new file on the B: drive that will be given the same name. The disk drives operate as the copying process is under way, DOS indicates that a file has been copied, and the prompt reappears. Obtain a directory of the disk in the B: drive using the command DIR B:. The file COMMAND.COM appears first, having been copied to the disk by the FORMAT B:/S command. You will also see the file FORMAT.COM, which has indeed been copied to that disk. Figure 2-7 illustrates how the screen appears after the copy and directory commands.

While the COPY command used here is typical of those you will use most often, it is actually an abbreviated form of the command. The full command specifies the disk drive and file name of both the source (old) file and the destination (new) file. Instead of the above command, you could have entered the following copy command and produced exactly the same results:

```
COPY A:FORMAT.COM B:FORMAT.COM<Return>
```

Because the A: drive is considered to be the default drive, as indicated by the A> prompt, placing A: in front of the first FORMAT.COM is unnecessary in this case. If it is omitted, DOS automatically assumes that FORMAT.COM is to be found on the default A: drive. Furthermore, because the name of the new file is to be exactly the same as the name of the old file, the name need not be specified. If

```
A>COPY FORMAT.COM B:
        1 File(s) copied

A>DIR B:

 Volume in drive B has no label
 Directory of  B:\

COMMAND  COM     17792  10-20-83  12:00p
FORMAT   COM      6912  10-20-83  12:00p
        2 File(s)    314368 bytes free

A>
```

Fig. 2-7. Copying the file FORMAT.COM to the disk in the B: drive, with the subsequent directory listing.

the name of the new file is not given, the copy command automatically assumes that you want it to have the same name as the old file. Thus, the abbreviated form of the command used above is sufficient to do to copying desired.

Of course, in other cases more information will be needed. If a file named LETTER1 is on the B: drive and you wish to copy this file to the A: drive, you will need to specify the drive when indicating the source file, as follows:

```
COPY B:LETTER1 A:<Return>
```

In some cases, you might want to give a different name to the new copy of the file. For example, you might want to append the extension .BAK to the copied version of the LETTER1 file to indicate that it is for backup purposes. Then the copy command would take the form:

```
COPY B:LETTER1 A:LETTER1.BAK<Return>
```

The copy command is even more powerful and flexible, allowing the copying of multiple files with a single command. This is accomplished by using the wildcard character * (the asterisk), which directs DOS to copy any and all files with any characters appearing where the * is entered. Examples will illustrate the process. The command

```
COPY *.COM B:<Return>
```

will copy all files on the A: drive with the extension .COM to the B: drive. The wildcard character can likewise be used to specify the copying of files with any extension. For example, the command

COPY B:ADDRESS.* A:<Return>

would copy all files on the B: drive with ADDRESS as the main part of the file name, with any extension, to the A: drive. One situation in which this might be useful is in backing up files from PC-File. In creating a database to which you give the main file name ADDRESS, PC-File creates several related files with different extensions that it uses to keep track of its information. This command would automatically copy all of those files from the B: drive to the A: drive. The wildcard can also be used to designate a part of the main file name or extension. Put a copy of the DOS disk in the A: drive and a formatted disk in the B: drive and enter the following command:

COPY D*.COM B:<Return>

The file name specification D*.COM identifies all files with the letter D as the first character of the main portion of the file name, any other characters following for the main portion of the file name, and the extension .COM. Thus, all .COM files on the A: drive beginning with the letter D will be copied. As a wildcard copy proceeds, DOS lists each of the files that are copied. The files actually copied will be DISKCOPY.COM, DISKCOMP.COM, and any other .COM files you might have on your version of DOS that begin with D. A directory listing of the files on the B: drive will list these new files that have been copied and added to the disk in the B: drive. The entire process is illustrated in Fig. 2-8.

```
A>COPY D*.COM B:
DISKCOPY.COM
DISKCOMP.COM
        2 File(s) copied

A>DIR B:

 Volume in drive B has no label
 Directory of  B:\

COMMAND  COM    17792  10-20-83  12:00p
FORMAT   COM     6912  10-20-83  12:00p
DISKCOPY COM     2576  10-20-83  12:00p
DISKCOMP COM     2188  10-20-83  12:00p
        4 File(s)   308224 bytes free

A>
```

Fig. 2-8. Wildcard copying of .COM files beginning with the letter D to the B: drive, with the subsequent directory listing.

These basic procedures for copying files will be sufficient for most situations. The DOS manual provides further explanations on the various options associated with the COPY command, including possibilities that have not been covered here.

Renaming and Erasing Files

Occasionally you may wish to rename files or erase files from the disk. The commands to do this are straightforward, involving the specification of the proper file names.

To change the name of a file, simply type the RENAME command followed by the current name of the file and the name you want it changed to. If you still have the disk in the B: drive onto which you copied the files beginning with D in the last section, you can experiment with this command. Suppose you want to change the file named DISKCOPY.COM to COPIER.COM. Just enter this command:

RENAME B:DISKCOPY.COM COPIER.COM<Return>

The drive designation B: must be specified in this case because the file is on the B: drive and A: is the default drive. It is never necessary to designate the drive for the new file name, because the file is only being renamed and will obviously remain on the same drive.

You may also wish to erase files from a disk because they are no longer of use and you wish to eliminate them from the directory and free the space for other files. Continuing with the same disk in the B: drive, erase the file DISKCOMP.COM with the following command:

ERASE B:DISKCOMP.COM<Return>

This permanently erases the file from the disk. If you now obtain a directory of the disk in the B: drive, you will see the results of the renaming and erasing operations. Instead of the file name DISKCOPY.COM you see the new file name COPIER.COM. The file DISKCOMP.COM does not appear and has been deleted from the disk. The RENAME and ERASE commands and the results of this process as they would appear on the screen are illustrated in Fig. 2-9. Instead of the ERASE command, DOS also allows the use of the DEL command, which stands for delete and works the same way. The choice is purely a matter of personal preference.

You can use the wildcard character * with the RENAME and ERASE commands to deal with multiple files. Be especially careful, however, when using wildcard characters when erasing files, because you can eliminate a large number of files at one time. The following command

ERASE *.*

will erase all of the files from the default disk drive. When you try to do this, DOS will actually ask you if you really want to do this. When you issue any other command to erase files using wildcard characters, however, DOS will not give you this second chance. The files will be immediately erased as soon as you press the Return key.

```
A>RENAME B:DISKCOPY.COM COPIER.COM

A>ERASE B:DISKCOMP.COM

A>DIR B:

 Volume in drive B has no label
 Directory of  B:\

COMMAND   COM     17792   10-20-83   12:00p
FORMAT    COM      6912   10-20-83   12:00p
COPIER    COM      2576   10-20-83   12:00p
        3 File(s)     311296 bytes free

A>
```

Fig. 2-9. Use of the RENAME and ERASE commands, with the subsequent directory listing.

ADDITIONAL FEATURES AND CHARACTERISTICS OF DOS

Several additional features of DOS are useful in certain circumstances. Several of the most common DOS error messages also are described so that you know how to proceed when encountering them.

The default drive that will be assumed for all DOS operations is indicated by the DOS prompt. When the system is started from the A: drive, this automatically becomes the default drive and the prompt is the familiar A>. The default drive may be changed if desired. To change the default to the B: drive, simply give the command B:<Return>. A new DOS prompt of B> is displayed to indicate the change. Now the B: drive is assumed if nothing else is specified. The command DIR will give a directory of the contents of the B: drive. To obtain a directory of the disk in the A: drive, you would now need to make your desires explicit with the command DIR A:. The default affects all DOS commands.

In describing the directory command, the Control-S command for pausing output to the screen has already been described. This command will temporarily halt output so that you can read information before it scrolls off the top of the screen. The command is entered by holding down the Control key and then depressing the letter S. After output has been paused, pressing any key will resume output to the screen.

A similar command, Control-C, will halt most DOS operations in progress and return you to the DOS prompt. This can be helpful for interrupting lengthy operations, such as a long directory listing, which you do not wish to complete. Control-C is entered by holding down the Control key and then depressing the letter C.

Occasionally useful is the DOS TYPE command, which allows you to display the contents of files on the screen. To use the command, simply enter TYPE followed by the name of the file, with a disk drive specification if needed, and press Return. The file will be listed on the screen. The TYPE command is only useful with files of text information, such as those created using PC-Write. You can try the TYPE command with a program file, but the random characters displayed will be totally meaningless.

A handy feature of the system is the Print Screen command, which sends a copy of the information displayed on the screen to the printer. Check to be sure that the printer is turned on and that it is ready to print. The printer will have a button labeled something like "On Line" and a light indicating "On Line" or "Ready." If necessary, press the button so the ready light comes on. To print the contents of the screen, hold down the Shift key and press the Print Screen key (often abbreviated Prt Sc) below the Return key. The screen will be printed out. This feature can be used at any time, when you are working with DOS or when you are using another program. Many of the figures in this book were created using this screen printing function.

No explanation will be provided on the use of DOS batch files, but you should at least know they exist. A series of DOS commands can be placed in a file with the extension .BAT. Typing the main part of the file name will cause the commands to be executed automatically. A particularly important case of a batch file is a special file given the name AUTOEXEC.BAT. The DOS commands in this file will be automatically executed (hence the name AUTOEXEC) whenever the computer is started (or restarted) and DOS is loaded. This is very useful for accomplishing a number of routine tasks when starting the computer. Information on the creation and use of batch files is provided in the DOS manual and in books explaining DOS.

When you are using DOS, occasionally things go wrong and you receive an error message. A typical example arises when you misspell a command or type in nonsense after the DOS prompt and press Return. DOS comes back with the message "Bad Command or File Name" and provides another DOS prompt. This message simply means that DOS could not find a command or a file name matching what you have typed. Nothing needs to be done in response to such an error. Just proceed, entering a valid DOS command. This error is shown at the top of the screen in Fig. 2-10.

A more serious DOS error occurs when a command is issued involving a disk drive and DOS is unable to successfully use the drive. This could happen when an attempt is made to write on a disk with a write-protect tab or when a disk has somehow been damaged. In this case, DOS concludes its error message by asking "Abort, Retry, Ignore?" Pressing A terminates (aborts) the attempted operation. Pressing R for retry causes DOS to attempt the operation a second time. If the problem has been corrected, the operation may be successful. Otherwise, you are likely to get the same error message again. Pressing I causes DOS to attempt to ignore the problem, which may or may not produce any results. Unfortunately, in many situations you may have little choice but to abort the operation. The error obtained when attempting to erase a file from a write-protected disk is also shown in Fig. 2-10, with the operation aborted.

PREPARING WORKING PROGRAM DISKS

This final section outlines the procedures for using DOS to create the working copies of the program disks you will be using to operate PC-File, PC-Write, PC-Talk, and ExpressCalc. The original disks you acquired for these four programs, or copies made of these disks, are not appropriate for

```
A>FORMT
Bad command or file name

A>ERASE FORMAT.COM

Write protect error writing drive A
Abort, Retry, Ignore? A

A>
```

Fig. 2-10. Typical DOS errors: Invalid command and attempt to alter a write-protected disk.

use as working program disks for two reasons. First, these disks do not include copies of DOS and cannot be used to start the computer. It is far more convenient to have working copies with DOS recorded on them. Then you can insert the program disk into the computer, start the machine by loading DOS, and begin working immediately without having to change disks. The second reason for making working copies is that it is sometimes necessary to make modifications to files in order to make the program work properly with your particular computer system. This process is called *installation of the programs* and is required for most personal computer software. It is best to make such changes on a working copy, leaving your original and backup copies of the program disks intact. In that way, if you make a mistake or if the configuration of your system changes, you can go back to the copy of the original disk and start over from scratch. Nothing is permanently lost or damaged.

Before beginning this process, it is important to have the appropriate disks at hand, ready to go. You should have copies of each of your program disks, made with the DISKCOPY command. It is always best to work from copies, retaining the original as a backup to be used only for making additional copies in the event the copy you are using is somehow damaged. Place a write-protect tab over the write-protect notch of each of these copies to provide additional protection against the accidental erasure of information on the disks. In addition, for each working program copy to be created, you will need a new disk that has been formatted with DOS on the disk. This is accomplished by using the FORMAT B:/S command. You can check to make sure these disks have been correctly formatted with DOS by placing the disk in the A: drive and resetting the computer by pressing the Control-Alternate-Delete combination. DOS should load and start operation in the normal fashion. A directory listing of the disk will show a single file, COMMAND.COM. If you need further information on accomplishing either of these tasks, refer back to the section on DOS Disk Operations.

This book describes the use of the most current versions of the four user-supported programs available at the time this is being written. These are PC-File III, version 4.0; PC-Write, version 2.6; PC-Talk III, and ExpressCalc, version 3.10. The information on the versions is summarized in Table 2-2. The installation procedures described below are correct for these versions of the programs. They may work with some earlier versions of the programs and with later versions as well. If you have a different version and the installation procedures do not produce working copies of the program disks that perform correctly, it may be necessary for you to consult the documentation for your versions of the programs in order to determine proper installation procedures.

The PC-File Working Disk

If you have not already done so, load DOS from any disk containing the operating system and proceed through the date and time prompts until the DOS A> prompt is displayed on the screen. Place a copy of your original PC-File disk into the A: drive and place a formatted disk with DOS in the B: drive. Copy the files needed for program operation from the disk in the A: drive to the working copy you are creating in the B: drive by entering the following command:

```
COPY *.EXE B:<Return>
```

A total of twelve files will by copied with this command. One further file must be copied to provide configuration information to the PC-File program. Enter this command:

```
COPY *.PRO B:<Return>
```

Only a single file will be copied with this command.

Table 2-2. Program Versions Used in Book.

Program Name	Version Number	Date
PC-File III	4.0	1985
PC-Write	2.6	1986
PC-Talk III	—	1983
ExpressCalc	3.10	1985

The wildcard is used for the main part of the file name because version 4.0 uses the file name PCFILE.PRO, while the previous version used the file name PC-File.PRO. Using the wildcard in the copy command guarantees the correct file will be copied for either version. This completes the initial preparation of the working copy of PC-FILE. Issuing a directory command to list the files on the B: drive will show the contents. Figure 2-11 illustrates the entire process as it would appear on the screen, including the directory listing.

For those using the "standard system," PC-File will be ready to run properly on your computer. The program will not, however, make use of color if you have a color monitor, and it will not make use of compressed printing features of your printer unless you have an Epson or IBM dot matrix printer or a printer compatible with these. For learning to use PC-File, it is not necessary to do anything about either of these two things immediately. You can change these and certain other characteristics of PC-File at any time. To modify PC-File, place the new working disk in the A: drive and type PCSETUP (PC-SETUP on earlier versions) and press Return. This runs a special setup program that asks a series of questions about how you want PC-File configured. If you have a color monitor, you can select both the background and text colors. You can provide specifications on how PC-File is to work with your printer, but you must know something about printer control codes in order to do this. A variety of other PC-File options can also be selected. The setup program then writes a special "profile" file, named PCFILE.PRO on the disk that stores your specific configuration instructions. This file is read by PC-File each time it is started to set up the program to meet your specific requirements. If you are a new personal computer user, it is probably best not to bother with this procedure for a while. If you have some experience with personal computers and want to install PC-File for color display with a color monitor, go ahead and try running the setup program. If you get hopelessly confused at this time, you can always go back and recopy the original version of PCFILE.PRO from your original disk to your working disk for PC-File.

```
A>COPY *.EXE B:
PCDEF.EXE
PCDOC.EXE
PCEXPOR.EXE
PCFILE.EXE
PCFIX.EXE
PCIMPOR.EXE
PCLABEL.EXE
PCOVL.EXE
PCPRINT.EXE
PCSETUP.EXE
PCSORT.EXE
PCUTIL.EXE
        12 File(s) copied

A>COPY *.PRO B:
PCFILE.PRO
        1 File(s) copied

A>DIR B:

 Volume in drive B has no label
 Directory of  B:\

COMMAND  COM     17792  10-20-83  12:00p
PCDEF    EXE     15744   1-01-86   4:03a
PCDOC    EXE      4599   1-01-86   4:01a
PCEXPOR  EXE     23136   1-01-86   4:00a
PCFILE   EXE     44592   1-01-86   4:05a
PCFIX    EXE     16560   1-01-86   4:00a
PCIMPOR  EXE     17536   1-01-86   4:01a
PCLABEL  EXE      8464   1-01-86   4:00a
PCOVL    EXE     22656   1-01-86   4:00a
PCPRINT  EXE     36656   1-01-86   4:09a
PCSETUP  EXE     13616   1-01-86   4:02a
PCSORT   EXE     21872   1-01-86   4:01a
PCUTIL   EXE     20656   1-01-86   4:00a
PCFILE   PRO       128   1-01-86   4:00a
        14 File(s)     66560 bytes free

A>
```

Fig. 2-11. Preparing a working copy of PC-File.

Further information on the use of the PC-File setup program to alter the way the program operates is provided at the end of the PC-File chapter. Instructions on using PC-File with nonstandard systems and with other printers is provided in Appendix B. The PC-File documentation serves as your reference for these questions.

The PC-Write Working Disk

With the DOS A> prompt displayed on the screen, once again place a copy of your original PC-Write disk in the A: drive and place a formatted disk with DOS in the B: drive. Enter the following command to create a working copy of PC-Write on the disk in the B: drive:

```
WORKDISK B:<Return>
```

A series of DOS commands appear on the screen as files are automatically copied from the disk in the A: drive to the disk in the B: drive, as shown in Fig. 2-12.

The WORKDISK procedure then automatically runs a program allowing you to select the printer for which PC-Write is to be configured. This is important for any word processing program, as the program must have specific instructions on how to get the printer to perform various functions to format the printed output correctly. PC-Write supports a very large number of different printers.

The printer selection program displays a list of brand names of many different printers on the screen. Enter the letter for the brand of printer you are using. For example, I am using an IBM Proprinter, so I entered P for IBM. If a number of different printers from a single manufacturer are supported—as is the case for IBM—an additional listing of specific models is displayed on the lower half of the screen. This list begins with "A. Color," for the IBM Color Printer. The screen appears as shown in Fig. 2-13. If you cannot find your brand of printer on the first screen, select the final choice of other printers, and a list of additional printer models is displayed on the lower half of the screen, just like the list of different models from IBM. Enter the appropriate choice from the second list. For my IBM Proprinter, I entered E. This completes the specification of the printer type. The routine for the chosen printer is installed automatically, and the PC-Write working disk has been created.

```
A>WORKDISK B:

A>ECHO off

A>COPY ED.EXE B:ED.EXE
        1 File(s) copied

A>COPY PR.EXE B:PR.EXE
        1 File(s) copied

A>COPY ED.HLP B:ED.HLP
        1 File(s) copied

A>COPY ED.DEF B:ED.DEF
        1 File(s) copied

A>MENUPRT B:PR.DEF
```

Fig. 2-12. Preparing a working copy of PC-Write.

Finally, if you have a color monitor, enter the following command to allow PC-Write to operate in full color:

```
COPY ED.COL B:ED.DEF<Return>
```

This copies a special file with the information for using a color monitor; this file is used as the definition file (ED.DEF) for the PC-Write editor program.

Earlier versions of PC-Write did not have the automatic procedure for creating working disks. Instead, DOS commands have to be used to copy the appropriate files to the working disk, including a file for your printer. The procedure will be summarized briefly for those with earlier versions of PC-Write. First, enter the following COPY commands:

```
COPY ED.EXE B:<Return>
COPY PR.EXE B:<Return>
COPY HELPE.DEF B:<Return>
```

If you have a monochrome display (not a color display), enter the following command:

```
COPY RULER.DEF B:<Return>
```

Alternatively, if you have a color display, enter this command:

```
COPY COLOR.DEF B:RULER.DEF<Return>
```

```
Printer Picker.  Press letter or digit for your printer (Esc: pick group):
A. Anadex                    M. Epson                    Y. Radio Shack
B. Anderson-Jacobson         N. Genicom                  Z. Roland
C. AT&T                      O. Hewlett-Packard          1. Silver Reed
D. Brother                   P. IBM                      2. Smith Corona
E. Canon                     Q. IDS                      3. Star Micronics
F. Centronics                R. Juki                     4. Tally
G. C.Itoh                    S. NEC                      5. Texas Instruments
H. Comrex                    T. Okidata                  6. Toshiba
I. Dataproducts              U. Olivetti                 7. Transtar
J. Datasouth                 V. Olympia                  8. Xerox
K. Diablo                    W. Panasonic
L. Digital                   X. Printek                  9. Other
A. Color
B. Compact Thermal
C. Graphics
D. Jetprinter
E. Proprinter
F. Quietwriter
G. old w/o graftrax
H. 5216/5218 Wheelprinter
I. 7436, 1403 (fortran)
```

Fig. 2-13. Menu for printer selection when preparing a working copy of PC-Write.

The earlier versions of PC-Write have a large number of files with the extension .PRT that provide instructions on the use of many different printers. Begin the printer setup procedure by examining the file that lists the various print files and the printers supported by each. Enter this command:

TYPE PRINTER.DOC

The document that appears on the screen lists the names of each of the print files (in capital letters), followed by the specific printer models supported by that file (in upper and lowercase letters). The name of each print file is an abbreviation for the name(s) of the printers supported. For example, the IBM PC Graphics Printer and the Epson MX-80 and MX-100 printers are handled by the file named IBMEPSON. Once you have selected the printer file to be used, enter a command to copy that file to a file named RULER.PRT on your working disk in drive B:. For example, if you will be using the IBMEPSON printer file, enter the following command:

COPY IBMEPSON.PRT B:RULER.PRT<Return>

For any other printer file, substitute the name of that file for the name IBMEPSON in the above command. This completes the creation of a working copy of PC-Write for earlier versions of the program.

The PC-Talk Working Disk

Begin with the A> prompt from DOS on the screen, place a copy of your original PC-Talk disk in the A: drive, and place a formatted disk with DOS in the B: drive. The working copy of PC-Talk needs to have only one file copied to the disk. Enter this command:

COPY PC-TALK.EXE B:<Return>

This is the only action required. The copy command

```
A>COPY PC-TALK.EXE B:
        1 File(s) copied

A>DIR B:

 Volume in drive B has no label
 Directory of  B:\

COMMAND  COM     17792  10-20-83  12:00p
PC-TALK  EXE     82148   5-02-85   3:54p
        2 File(s)     238592 bytes free

A>
```

Fig. 2-14. Preparing a working copy of PC-Talk.

and the resulting directory of the working PC-Talk disk are shown in Fig. 2-14.

The ExpressCalc Working Disk

With the DOS A> prompt displayed on the screen, place a copy of your original ExpressCalc program disk in the A: drive and place a formatted disk with DOS in the B: drive. Copy the files needed for the operation of the program by entering the following command:

```
COPY *.* B:<Return>
```

This command will copy all the files on the ExpressCalc program disk to the working disk in the B: drive. Listing the directory of the disk in the B: drive will show the files that have been copied to the working ExpressCalc disk. The entire process, including the directory listing, is illustrated in Fig. 2-15.

This is the extent of the initial installation for ExpressCalc. The choice of the video display option is made at the time ExpressCalc is started, and the few additional configuration options are handled within the program itself. These matters will be covered in the ExpressCalc chapter.

This completes the process of making working copies of the four programs. If you wish to be cautious, you could place write-protect tabs on the PC-File, PC-Write, and ExpressCalc disks. In normal operations, you will not be writing information to these disks or changing them in any way. If you choose to make some modifications to the installations of these programs, however, these will require making changes on the disks and the write-protect tabs will have to be removed. This will be necessary when you run the PCSETUP program for PC-File, when you attempt to change the RULER.DEF or PRINTER.DEF files in PC-Write, and when you use the /CONFIGURE command within ExpressCalc,.

```
A>COPY *.* B:
CALC.EXE
CALC2.EXE
CALC3.EXE
CALC4.EXE
CALC5.EXE
CALC.MSG
EXAMPLE
BW.PRO
40.PRO
BW40.PRO
SL.PRO
        11 File(s) copied

A>DIR B:

 Volume in drive B has no label
 Directory of  B:\

COMMAND  COM     18128   2-22-85   1:16p
CALC     EXE     29056   7-09-86   3:10a
CALC2    EXE     99584   7-09-86   3:10a
CALC3    EXE     61312   7-09-86   3:10a
CALC4    EXE     69504   7-09-86   3:10a
CALC5    EXE     22656   7-09-86   3:09a
CALC     MSG     30336   7-09-86   3:09a
EXAMPLE            768   7-09-86   3:09a
BW       PRO       128   7-09-86   3:09a
40       PRO       128   7-09-86   3:09a
BW40     PRO       128   7-09-86   3:09a
SL       PRO       128   7-09-86   3:09a
        12 File(s)          0 bytes free

A>
```

Fig. 2-15. Preparing a working copy of ExpressCalc.

PC-Talk, on the other hand, routinely writes information on the program disk during the course of normal operations. The program creates several files to store your function key and default menu information. When you use PC-Talk to create a directory of remote computers and their phone numbers, this information is stored in yet another file on the PC-Talk disk. Thus, you must *not* place a write-protect tab over the notch on the PC-Talk disk.

Printing Out the Program Documentation

You will want to have copies of the documentation available for each of the programs you are using. Should you have printed copies of the documentation obtained by registering the program, you are ready to proceed. If you obtained only the disks, however, you will need to print out the documentation provided on the disks.

The procedures for printing out the documentation files vary from program to program and from version to version. As a general rule, you can identify various documentation files by looking at the file names in the directory. The extension .DOC is frequently used for documentation files. You can examine the contents of various files by using the DOS TYPE command to find either instructions for printing out the documentation or the documentation itself.

This section describes the methods to be used for printing out the documentation files on the versions of the four programs used in this book. In each case, DOS must be loaded and a copy of the original program disk must be in the A: drive. The working program disks created above do not include the documentation files and cannot be used.

Beginning with PC-File, an examination of the directory of a copy of original disk shows the first file is named READ-ME. Simply follow instructions and enter the following command:

TYPE READ-ME <Return>

The contents of the file will be displayed on the screen. You will be informed that the disk includes two files associated with the documentation. The file PCFILE.XXX contains the documentation in compressed form, and the file PCDOC.EXE is a program that will uncompress that file and print it out. To get a printed copy of the documentation, be sure your printer is ready and enter the command:

PCDOC <Return>

Follow the instructions given and the documentation will be printed out.

The PC-Write directory begins with the file GO.BAT. Simply enter this command:

GO <Return>

This batch command issues the command to TYPE the file READ.ME. You could have issued the DOS TYPE command to do this directly. The file READ.ME gives complete instructions on how to print out the documentation. Just enter this command:

PRINTMAN <Return>

The PC-Write documentation will be printed. In addition, you can enter the command

TYPE QUICKS.ME <Return>

to get a summary of basic information on how to quickly get started with PC-Write. This file provides instructions on how to make a working disk and begin editing a document.

The original PC-Talk disk has a file named README.DOC. Follow the instructions and enter this command:

TYPE README.DOC <Return>

This file provides instructions on how to run PC-Talk and how to print out the documentation. To print the PC-Talk manual, enter the following command:

PRINTDOC <Return>

The documentation file, PC-Talk.DOC, is printed out. The PC-Talk disk also has another file, COPY-Talk.BAT to automatically make copies of PC-Talk to share with others. To use this procedure, just enter the command

COPYTALK<Return>

and you will be instructed on how to proceed to make additional copies of the PC-Talk disk for others.

The documentation files for ExpressCalc are contained on the second, supplementary disk that comes in addition to the program disk. This disk includes a batch file, PRINTDOC.BAT, to print out the documentation, and four separate documentation files, CALC1.DOC through CALC4.DOC. To print out the documentation, enter this command:

PRINTDOC<Return>

The complete ExpressCalc documentation will be printed out.

Earlier versions of these programs may have slightly different arrangements for the documentation. Documentation files will generally be identified with the extension .DOC. You can examine the contents of these files by using the DOS TYPE command. If no batch procedure or program is provided to print out the documentation, you can use DOS directly to print it out. The procedure is to use the DOS COPY command to copy the contents of a documentation file to the printer, which DOS refers to as PRN, rather than to another file. For example, to print out a copy of a file named CALC1.DOC, enter the following command:

COPY CALC1.DOC PRN<Return>

The contents of the file will be printed out on the printer.

With the working copies of the PC-File, PC-Write, PC-Talk, and ExpressCalc disks and the accompanying documentation at hand, you are ready to begin learning how to use these programs.

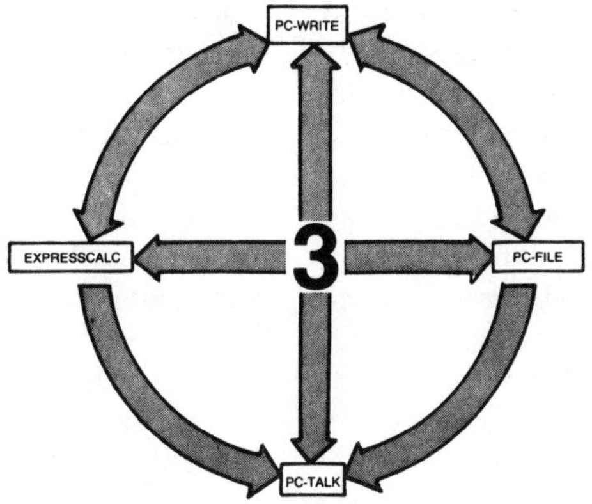

Using PC-File

Tasks involving lists of information, tables of data, or files of cards are potential candidates for personal computer database applications. Possible uses range from a personal address book to an extensive mailing list, from a simple file of household possessions to an inventory for a small business. Managing information on a personal computer with appropriate database software provides many advantages for all types of applications. The computer can quickly search for and display any information contained in the database, relieving the user of the need to manually search through rows of entries or stacks of cards. Updates and corrections can be immediately entered without having to erase entries, retype cards, or otherwise go through a difficult manual procedure. The information can be quickly sorted or resorted in any order desired. Good data management software allows the user to print out the information in a variety of formats ranging from mailing labels to traditional tabular reports. Such printouts can include all of the information in the files or just a portion of the information, with selection based on a variety of criteria.

PC-File is an easy-to-use, flexible, reasonably powerful program for the management of files of information on a personal computer. The program includes the capabilities for performing all of the tasks described above and more. PC-File is menu-driven; the user operates the program by making choices from lists of options. You can start out simply and learn to perform basic functions quickly. As you continue to use PC-File, it is easy to learn to use additional features, increasing your level of proficiency in the use of the program.

PC-File is perhaps the easiest of the four user-supported programs to learn and use. For this reason, it is the first of the programs addressed in this book. Learning to use personal computer software is best accomplished by working through actual applications, learning what is involved in each step of the process. This chapter and each of the following chapters proceed in this manner. Specific problems are identified, and the chapters describe each of the steps involved in using the software to produce solutions. Numerous figures illustrate the information appearing on the screen and the information that is printed out by the programs. You can most effectively learn from these examples by actually using PC-File and the other programs to follow along. Enter the commands and the data. Produce and print out the same results that are presented here. By going through several applications, you will become familiar with the basic operation of the programs and will be able to readily move on to your own applications.

This chapter presents two different applications of PC-File: an address book and an inventory of household possessions. Both are simple, yet realistic and useful. By working through two very different applications, it is possible to illustrate the use of a wider range of the capabilities of PC-File than would be possible in addressing just a single problem. In addition, the basic operations are repeated, reinforcing the key elements in the operation of the program.

This chapter uses PC-File III, version 4.0. This version of the program was released in 1985 and is the latest version available at the time this book is being written. In a few instances in which significant changes have been made from earlier versions of PC-File, the differences are noted. The user is encouraged to register PC-File with Buttonware and obtain the most current version, as some of the later enhancements significantly increase the usefulness of the program. By the time you are reading this, there may well be an even newer version, with further updates and enhancements.

CREATING THE ADDRESS DATABASE

The first application of PC-File involves the setting up of a basic address book containing names, addresses, and telephone numbers. This can be used to print out anything from mailing labels to telephone directories. The next three sections of the chapter go through all of the steps involved in creating and using the ADDRESS database, from the initial planning to production of the final reports.

Planning the Database

Most computer data management programs store data in a fairly rigid format that must be specified in detail before any information is entered. PC-File (and most other programs) allow you to later change the format, but this is a fairly elaborate, time-consuming process. It is best to spend some time determining your information needs and planning the database *before* you start to use the program to define the database and enter the data.

You need to first understand the basic way in which information is structured and stored in PC-File. A collection of related information in PC-File is referred to as a *database*. (Other programs may refer to such a collection as a file of information.) The entire name and address list to be created in this first example, containing the names, addresses, and telephone numbers of many different people, is the database. Each database needs to have a name to identify it. The example database will be referred to as the ADDRESS database.

Databases are collections of *records*, with each record containing the information pertaining to a single individual or other entity. In the ADDRESS database, each record refers to a single person and contains the name, address, and telephone number of that person. Each record in the database will have exactly the same format and will contain exactly the same kinds of information.

Records are in turn made up of *fields*, which are pieces of information about the subject of the records. Fields of information in the ADDRESS database include the last name of the person, the first name, and his or her address, city, state, zip code, and telephone number. Every record has exactly the same fields and therefore can contain exactly the same kinds of information.

The organization of a database can be envisioned in two different ways: as a collection of forms and as a table of information. To imagine the ADDRESS database as a collection of forms, think of how it might be set up in a card file. You could have preprinted cards or forms with lines for the name, address, and so forth. Each of the lines on the form would represent a field. A single card containing the information for one person would be a record. The entire collection of these cards making up the address file would be the database.

Alternatively, consider the organization of the ADDRESS database in a tabular format. Begin with large pieces of ruled paper. Draw vertical lines to provide columns for the name, address, and so forth, and enter each person's name and address on a single line. In this case, the columns would represent the fields of information, each row of information on a single line would represent a record, and the entire collection of sheets making up the name and address list would be the database. You will have occasions to display information from the PC-File databases in both of these formats.

The key points are these: the fields contained in a database determine the information that can be stored. Each record in the database has exactly the same fields of information. Thus, the same kinds of information can be stored in each record, for each person or other entity in the database.

Planning the database involves the specification of exactly which fields are to be provided for the storage of information for each of the records. In addition, you must specify the *sizes* of these fields (the numbers of characters of information that can be stored in each field). This information will have to be provided to PC-File before you can proceed to the entry of data, because the program requires this in order to determine how the database will be stored on the disk.

Planning the ADDRESS database is relatively straightforward. You obviously need to have the person's name for each record. The last name and the first name are best designated as separate fields. In that way, you can print out the information with either the first name or the last name first, and you can easily sort the database in alphabetical order by last name. Field names in PC-File can be up to twelve characters long. They can contain upper- and lowercase letters and numbers, but spaces and special characters can cause problems and should be avoided. The ADDRESS database will use the field names Lastname and Firstname for the two fields. How long should each of these fields be? The easy answer is that they should be just long enough to contain the longest names to be entered into the database. In practice, you may not know all of the names in advance, so you have to make a guess as to the field lengths that will be sufficient. Note that the field length determines the amount of storage space on the disk that will be used for each record. If a field length of 20 characters were chosen for the last name, 20 bytes of storage would be used for each record, even for short last names like Jones. This is why those of you with long names sometimes see the final letters missing on computer-generated letters and labels—the database designers were attempting to save storage space. Fifteen characters should be sufficient to hold most last names. The same field length will be used for first names, giving plenty of room for double names and middle initials.

Defining the remaining fields proceeds in the same way. A field will be required for the street address. This will be given the name Address and a field length of 30 characters, to provide plenty of room for long street names and apartment numbers. The next field will be named City, with a length of 15 characters. The state in the State field can be accommodated with a two character field length if the standard abbreviations are to be used. The shift to these abbreviations is another example of the influence of computer databases. The zip code field, to be called Zip, can have a field length of five characters, unless the new nine-digit zip codes are to be used. The field for the telephone number will be named Phone. The standard telephone number in the United States and Canada consists of ten digits with the area code, but if hyphens are to be used to separate the parts of the number in the usual fashion, the field length will have to be increased to twelve characters. The field names and the corresponding field lengths for the ADDRESS database are summarized in Table 3-1.

Defining the Database

Once you have planned the fields of information to be included within a database, you are ready to begin using PC-File. Place the working copy of the PC-File disk in the A: drive and a blank, formatted disk for the storage of your database in the B: drive. Turn on the computer; DOS should load, and you can enter the date and time. (If the computer is already on and you have the DOS A>

Table 3-1. Fields in ADDRESS Database.

Field Name	Field Length
Lastname	15
Firstname	15
Address	30
City	15
State	2
Zip	5
Phone	12

prompt displayed on the screen, you can skip this step.) To start the PC-File program simply enter this command:

PCFILE<Enter>

The title screen will be displayed, and at the bottom will be the question "Which drive (A-Z) for the Data?" followed by a letter, such as A or B. This determines on which disk drive PC-File will look for and store databases and other information. For the standard system with two diskette drives, it is generally easiest to use the A: drive for the program disk and the B: drive for the data disk. If the letter B is not already displayed, type B. Once B is displayed, press Return to move to the next screen. (The final section of this chapter explains how to reconfigure PC-File so the B will always appear when you start.) The next screen asks a question about path names, which are generally used only by those with hard disks. Press Return to skip this and move on.

The next screen displays a list of the databases already stored on your disk, and you can choose work with one of those or choose to define a new database. If this is the first time you are using PC-File, you will not have any existing databases, and the only possibility will be the definition of a new database. The screen will include a blank space for the name of the new database. A database name must be a valid main part for a DOS file name—that is, a letter followed by up to seven additional letters or numbers. Do not provide a file name extension; PC-File provides these automatically to keep track of the different files it creates. For the database being created, use the name ADDRESS. Just type this in and it will appear in the designated area on the screen, as shown in Fig. 3-1.

You can move the cursor (the underline) to the left or right with the cursor-control (arrow) keys to retype information. Pressing the Delete key (often marked Del) deletes the character at the cursor position and moves everything to the right over to close up the space. If you need to insert a character, press the Insert key (marked Ins), and the triangles surrounding the entry field will change to blocks. Now when you type, new characters are inserted at the cursor location and the other characters are pushed over to the right. Pressing the Insert key again returns you to the normal entry mode where a new character is written over the old character at the cursor position. The use of some of the other special keys on the keyboard will be explained in later sections. For now, try moving the cursor and changing the new database name you have typed in to get used to inserting and deleting characters. Once you have finished experimenting and have the database name ADDRESS typed in correctly, press function key 10 (F10) to move on. PC-File can be somewhat confusing about what key to press to move on. Sometimes it is the Return key, which PC-File refers to as "Enter," and other times it is function key F10. When F10 is required, PC-File will usually indicate this with a prompt at the bottom of the screen. You will next be asked whether you want to define this new database. A Y will be displayed; simply press Return.

The next screen is to be used for defining the database. If you need some assistance at this point,

```
Indicate an existing database or give a new database name.
Type a name
 ►ADDRESS ◄
```

Fig. 3-1. PC-File screen for the entry of a new database name.

you can press Alternate-H; that is, hold down the Alternate key and then press H. A screenful of information will be presented describing the procedures for database definition. The database definition screen displays spaces for defining up to 42 fields by entering the field names and their corresponding lengths. Begin by typing in the first field name, Lastname, and pressing Return. The triangles then move to the Field Length column. Type 15 and press Return. The screen should now look like Fig. 3-2. Continue entering the field names and lengths as indicated in Table 3-1 until you have completed the definition of the database. When you have completed the definition of the database, press function key F10 as indicated on the bottom line.

Defining the database is a crucial step, for once the database definition has been entered, making changes is very difficult and time-consuming. For this reason, PC-File redisplays the information you have entered and asks you to check this to make certain it is correct. The screen will appear as shown in Fig. 3-3. If you need to make any changes, move the triangles to the appropriate field by using the tab key to move to the next field. To move backwards, use the reverse Tab, which is obtained by using the shift key with the tab key. Once you have selected the appropriate field, you can use the right and left arrow keys to position the cursor and, if necessary, use the Insert and Delete keys as described above. When you are satisfied that the database definition has been entered correctly, once again press F10. PC-File will then display a message about the use of "field masks." For now, ignore this advanced feature and simply press Return. The definition of the database is now complete.

Entering the Data

Upon completion of the database definition, the main PC-File menu is displayed, as shown in Fig. 3-4. (The menu for earlier versions of PC-File will look quite different, but the major choices will be

```
(Alt)H for help.  Define the database.
 FIELD NAME          LENGTH                 FIELD NAME          LENGTH
[Lastname      ]    [15  ]                 [              ]    [    ]
[              ]    [    ]                 [              ]    [    ]
[              ]    [    ]                 [              ]    [    ]
[              ]    [    ]                 [              ]    [    ]
[              ]    [    ]                 [              ]    [    ]
[              ]    [    ]                 [              ]    [    ]
[              ]    [    ]                 [              ]    [    ]
[              ]    [    ]                 [              ]    [    ]
[              ]    [    ]                 [              ]    [    ]
[              ]    [    ]                 [              ]    [    ]
[              ]    [    ]                 [              ]    [    ]
[              ]    [    ]                 [              ]    [    ]
[              ]    [    ]                 [              ]    [    ]
[              ]    [    ]                 [              ]    [    ]
[              ]    [    ]                 [              ]    [    ]
[              ]    [    ]                 [              ]    [    ]
[              ]    [    ]                 [              ]    [    ]
[              ]    [    ]                 [              ]    [    ]
[              ]    [    ]                 [              ]    [    ]
[              ]    [    ]                 [              ]    [    ]
[              ]    [    ]                 [              ]    ►    ◄

Enter data. Press (F10) when complete.
```

Fig. 3-2. Definition of the first field of the ADDRESS database.

```
Press [Alt]H for help.
 FIELD NAME        LENGTH                    FIELD NAME        LENGTH
[Lastname     ]   [0015]                    [             ]   [    ]
[Firstname    ]   [0015]                    [             ]   [    ]
[Address      ]   [0030]                    [             ]   [    ]
[City         ]   [0015]                    [             ]   [    ]
[State        ]   [0002]                    [             ]   [    ]
[Zip          ]   [0005]                    [             ]   [    ]
[Phone        ]   [0012]                    [             ]   [    ]
[             ]   [    ]                    [             ]   [    ]
[             ]   [    ]                    [             ]   [    ]
[             ]   [    ]                    [             ]   [    ]
[             ]   [    ]                    [             ]   [    ]
[             ]   [    ]                    [             ]   [    ]
[             ]   [    ]                    [             ]   [    ]
[             ]   [    ]                    [             ]   [    ]
[             ]   [    ]                    [             ]   [    ]
[             ]   [    ]                    [             ]   [    ]
[             ]   [    ]                    [             ]   [    ]
[             ]   [    ]                    [             ]   [    ]
[             ]   [    ]                    [             ]   [    ]
[             ]   [    ]                    [             ]   [    ]
[             ]   [    ]                    [             ]   ▶    ◀
Please review for correctness.
Enter data. Press (F10) when complete.
```

Fig. 3-3. Review of the ADDRESS database definition.

```
B:ADDRESS 0 records, disk can hold approx. 3247 more.

  F1 ADD - Add     a record   |  [Alt]F1 BIN - Set binary search on/off
  F2 MOD - Modify  a record   |  [Alt]F2 GLO - Global update or delete
  F3 DEL - Delete  a record   |  [Alt]F3 KEY - Set up the smart keys
  F4 DIS - Display a record   |  [Alt]F4 NAM - Alter field name or mask
  F5 FIN - Find    a record   |
  F6 LIS - List or clone      |
  F7 SOR - Sort the index     |
  F8 UTI - Utilities          |
  F9 MEN - Show smart key menu |  [Alt]F9 END - Quit or change database

Please press the appropriate function key,
or supply one of the 3-character commands ▶FIN◀
```

Fig. 3-4. Main PC-File menu.

the same.) Whenever you work with a database (any time after it has been defined), you invoke the various functions of PC-File from this menu. The most important choices are listed in the left-hand column. Each has an associated function key and three-letter name, for example, F1, ADD. You can invoke a function either by pressing the function key or by typing the three-letter name and pressing Return. Pressing the function key certainly is easiest. The right-hand column lists advanced functions, and the very fundamental function, END. To invoke these, hold down the Alternate key and then press the appropriate function key, or use the three-letter name.

At this point, the ADDRESS database has been defined, but it is empty; the screen displays the message zero records. The first task is to enter some names and addresses into the database. Press function key F1 to add records. The data entry screen will be displayed. You merely need to fill in the blanks. Type in the last name of the first person, "Winter," and press Return. The screen will appear as shown in Fig. 3-5. Continue on down the form, entering the information into each field. You can employ the various keys discussed earlier for editing. For moving from one field to another, you can also use the up and down arrow keys, instead of using the tab key. When you have completed entering the data, press F10 as indicated on the bottom line.

As during data definition, the information entered for the record will be redisplayed for your review, as shown in Fig. 3-6. Pressing N for no takes you back so you can edit the information; pressing Y for yes accepts the data and displays the blank form for the entry of the next record. If you want to skip this step for the remainder of the records to be entered, you can press X.

When the blank form for the second record is displayed, exactly the same procedure is followed for entering the data. Continue this process to enter as many records as you desire. Remember that you can always add more records to the database at any time later. Also, data entry is less critical than database definition, because you can go back and change information in a record at any time. For now, enter at least 10 or 15 records so you have some information in your database to work with. When you are finished entering data, at least for the time being, press F10 immediately when a

```
ADDing at # 1                                                          ADD
---------------------------------------------------------------------------
Lastname    [Winter             ]
Firstname   ►                   ◄
Address     [                                ]
City        [                   ]
State       [  ]
Zip         [     ]
Phone       [                ]




To cancel, press (F10) if no data was entered, or (Esc) if data was entered
Enter data. Press (F10) when complete.
```

Fig. 3-5. Data entry form for the ADDRESS database, with an entry in the Lastname field.

```
Here is the data you entered:                                    ADD
--------------------------------------------------------------------
Lastname        Winter
Firstname       Joseph
Address         2930 Wildwood Way, Apt. 312
City            Buffalo
State           NY
Zip             14213
Phone           716-385-1997









Is this correct?  Y,N,or X(to stop asking)▶Y◀
```

Fig. 3-6. Review of the first record entered into the ADDRESS database.

blank data entry form is presented. This will terminate the function for adding records and return you to the main menu.

You might or might not want to continue working with PC-File and the ADDRESS database at this point. At some time, however, it will be necessary to learn how to conclude a session with PC-File. While at the main menu, type END and Return or press the Alternate-F9 combination. PC-File will ask whether you would like to work with some other database or just quit. Press Q for quit and Return. You will be returned to the DOS A> prompt.

Always leave PC-File in this manner. Do not simply pull out the disks or turn off the computer. Going through the formal quitting process gives PC-File the chance to correctly close up the database files it has been using. Terminating the program without this final housekeeping might result in some data being lost or in the database being damaged. This is not too likely; PC-File is quite careful about such things as it works along. The best practice, however, is not to take any chances.

MANAGING THE ADDRESS RECORDS

Now that some information has been stored in the ADDRESS database, it is time to learn how to get it back out. The first set of procedures involve dealing with the individual records. You will want to find particular records and display the information on the screen. Furthermore, it may be necessary to edit the information contained in some records, or even to delete certain records. These tasks can all be performed using the Find function on the main PC-File menu, although alternative procedures are available and will be discussed briefly.

Finding and Displaying Records

Restart the program by entering PCFILE at the DOS prompt and answering the first few questions as before. When you get to the screen asking you to either indicate an existing database or give a name for a new database, the screen will be different from the first time you ran PC-File, as shown in Fig. 3-7. The top line will still be blank, for a new database name that you might wish to define, but below this will be the name ADDRESS for the database you have just created. Press the down arrow to select the ADDRESS database and press F10. You will be taken directly to the main PC-File

```
Indicate an existing database or give a new database name.
or select with cursor keys
 ▶         ◀
 [ADDRESS ]




Enter data. Press (F10) when complete.
```

Fig. 3-7. PC-File screen for the selection of the database to be used.

menu, since database definition is not required. This is the procedure you will follow each time you wish to use an existing database.

Suppose you wish to look up the address of a friend named Martin. The Find function, displayed on the main menu, performs such tasks. Press F5 to start the Find procedure. PC-File will display a screen that looks like the data entry form, with the fields filled in with asterisks. To find someone with the last name of Martin, just enter the name into the Lastname field, as shown in Fig. 3-8, and press F10. To try out this command yourself, use the last name of anyone you included in your ADDRESS database.

If the database includes a record for someone with the last name of Martin, the record will be found and displayed on the screen, as shown in Fig. 3-9. What if there were records for several Martins in the database? PC-File searches through the records in the ADDRESS database, in the order in

```
The Binary search field is (not specified)                                      FIN
-----------------------------------------------------------------------------------
Lastname     [Martin*********]
Firstname    [***************]
Address      [******************************]
City         [***************]
State        [**]
Zip          [*****]
Phone        ▶************◀



Fill in the data you want to search for.
Examples: SMITH(exact)  ?SMITH(soundex)  >TH(scan across)  ___TH(wildcard)
Enter data. Press (F10) when complete.
```

Fig. 3-8. Using the Find procedure to locate the record for the person with the last name Martin.

```
Record # 8                                                          FIN
------------------------------------------------------------------------
Lastname      Martin
Firstname     Robert
Address       2955 Jackson Boulevard
City          San Francisco
State         CA
Zip           94133
Phone         415-691-4487




Continue finding, Stop, Modify, or Delete? (C,S,M,D)▶C◀
```

Fig. 3-9. The record found for the person with the last name Martin.

which they were entered, and displays the first record with the last name of Martin that it encounters. Note that the prompt on the bottom of the screen gives options for stopping (S) or continuing (C) the search. If the first Martin is the one desired, the search procedure can then be stopped by pressing S. If it is the wrong Martin, continue the search by pressing C. You can continue this searching until you have found the Martin you want, or until the entire database has been searched. When there are no more Martins to be found, PC-File gives a "not found" message with instructions to press Enter (the Return key).

This basic search procedure actually works to find all records with the letters specified (in the example, M-a-r-t-i-n) in the first six positions of the field Lastname. This would include anyone with the last name of Martin, of course. Also included, however, would be persons with the last name Martindale, or any other name that begins with the letters M-a-r-t-i-n.

The capability to find and display multiple records can sometimes be advantageous. Suppose you are taking a trip to California and wish to look up the names and addresses of all friends living in that state. You could begin the Find procedure by entering the abbreviation CA for California in the State field. Then you could browse through the records for all of the persons living in the state to determine whom you might wish to visit.

In other cases, you may have a more specific record in mind and may not want to look through numerous records. Suppose the database had a large number of Smiths, and you wished to look up the address for a Peter Smith. In specifying the record to find, enter Smith in the Lastname field, move the pointers down, and enter Peter in the Firstname field. This instructs PC-File to find and display only those records with a last name beginning with Smith and a first name beginning with Peter. In other words, the search conditions specified in each field must be met. This will result in Peter Smith's record being displayed on the screen. Searching through multiple records would only be necessary in the rare event that you had more than one Peter Smith in the ADDRESS database. The Find procedure is very flexible. By presenting the form with all of the fields to be filled in, the procedure allows you to make any search as general or as specific as you might desire.

PC-File provides another interesting search procedure, called a *soundex search*, that allows you to find entries that sound like a name, even if they are not identical. For example, suppose the AD-

DRESS database had an entry for an acquaintance named "Smythe," but you were not certain whether it was spelled that way or "Smith." Instead of conducting two searches with the two spellings, you can use the soundex search. In the Lastname field on the find screen, first enter a question mark, ?, to indicate a soundex search, and then enter the name Smith. PC-File will find all last names that sound like Smith, including Smythe.

If you have been trying out various searches with the Find procedure, you have noticed that you are always returned to the beginning of the procedure after a search has been completed. When you are finished searching, pressing F10 returns you to the main PC-File menu.

If you are using an earlier version of PC-File, the Find procedure works differently and allows you to search in only a single field. The procedure first asks for the name of the field to be searched, and then asks for the information in the field you are searching for. Options for various types of searches are the same, however.

Editing and Deleting Records

The editing of information contained in records or the deletion of entire records that are no longer needed can be easily accomplished using the Find procedure in PC-File. Just find the record that you wish to modify or delete in the usual fashion, and then select the appropriate option on the screen.

Suppose that Robert Martin has moved, and you wish to put his new address and phone number in the ADDRESS database. From the PC-File main menu, select the Find function by pressing F5. Enter the last name Martin in the appropriate field on the search form and press F10. The record for Robert Martin will be displayed on the screen, as shown in Fig. 3-9. In response to the query on the bottom line of the screen—Continue finding, Stop, Modify, or Delete?—enter the letter M and press Return. The message at the top of the screen changes to MODifying and the fields are displayed within the brackets used when the information was originally entered. You can now move the pointers to the various fields and make changes in the address using the normal editing capabilities of PC-File.

After the new address for Robert Martin has been entered, the screen appears as shown in Fig. 3-10. Press F10 to indicate that you have finished entering the data. The top line of the screen will now indicate that the record has been modified. The

```
MODifying # 8                                                   FIN
--------------------------------------------------------------------
Lastname     [Martin          ]
Firstname    [Robert          ]
Address      ►3311 Van Buren Boulevard         ◄
City         [San Francisco   ]
State        [CA]
Zip          [94138]
Phone        [415-691-4487]




Enter data. Press (F10) when complete.
```

Fig. 3-10. Changing the address for Robert Martin.

bottom line indicates that the modification has been completed and provides the options of finding the next record or quitting the find. Assuming that this is the only modification to be made, enter Q for quit and press Return. (If you had wanted to make changes to the records for several different Martins, you could have continued the search and made the modifications one after the other.)

Deleting a record from the file is equally easy. For example, to delete the record for Peter Smith, begin by entering the Lastname Smith and the Firstname Peter in the normal fashion to search for that record. When the record is displayed on the screen, enter the letter D for delete and press Return. The screen display changes, with the message "Type DELETE or KEEP" at the bottom of the screen, and the word KEEP displayed following this command. To actually delete the record from the database, you must type the word DELETE in place of the word KEEP, as shown in Fig. 3-11, and press Return. The record is then permanently deleted.

PC-File follows this procedure for your protection, to prevent you from accidentally deleting a record by pressing the wrong key. When a record is deleted, it is permanently erased from the database, and the information it contains is forever lost. You do not want to erase important records accidentally. Thus, PC-File forces you to actually type the word DELETE in order to indicate that you really want to get rid of the record that has been displayed. If you decide after viewing the record that you do not wish to delete it, just pressing Return while the word KEEP is displayed will exit the deletion procedure and let you continue with the search in the normal fashion. More importantly, if you make a mistake in entering your search criteria and get the wrong record, you cannot accidentally delete the record simply by pressing the Return key.

When you have completed the record modifications or deletions, you are returned to the main search screen. Pressing F10 terminates the Find procedure and returns you to the main PC-File menu.

Alternative Procedures

The Find procedure allows you to search for and display any record in the database and provides options for the modification and deletion of the records you have found. You will probably use the Find procedure whenever you wish to carry out any of these operations. Given this, you may be wondering why the main PC-File menu includes sepa-

```
Record # 9                                              FIN
-----------------------------------------------------------
Lastname      Smith
Firstname     Peter
Address       One Longhorn Way
City          Houston
State         TX
Zip           77022
Phone         713-682-8625




Type DELETE or KEEP▶DELETE◀
```

Fig. 3-11. Deleting the record for Peter Smith.

```
                                                                  DIS

  To cancel, just press (Enter) with no response.
  Supply the KEY, or #nn, or +(nxt rcd), -(prior), \(last), PgUp, PgDn
  ►Martin          ◄
```

Fig. 3-12. Using the Display procedure to locate the record for a person with the last name Martin.

rate procedures to Modify (MOD), Delete (DEL), and Display (DIS) a record. In earlier versions of PC-File, the Find procedure was less powerful and lacked some of the options described above. The Modify, Delete, and Display procedures are retained in the current version of PC-File, and these procedures provide several options for looking at the information contained within the database that are not available within the Find procedure.

To look at information in the database using the Display procedure, press F4. You will be presented with a cryptic prompt line at the bottom of the screen, as shown in Fig. 3-12. The prompt line indicates the possible options you can use in specifying the record to be displayed. The first is the KEY, which PC-File assumes to be the value in the first field in the database. Thus, if you are looking for someone with the last name Martin, you can enter Martin, as shown in Fig. 3-12, and press Return. The Display procedure can only search for records for which you know the value stored in the first field. It is not as flexible as the Find procedure.

The second option for the Display procedure locates and displays the record in the database with a specified record number. This option is described as #nn on the prompt line. As records are added to the database, PC-File gives each record a unique record number. These have been displayed each time you have entered or examined records. Displaying a record based on the record number might be useful if you were using a printout of the information in the database that included the record number. For example, if you wished to display record number 9, simply type in #9 and press Return. The record would be displayed.

When you are using the Display procedure, pressing + (the plus sign) and Return displays the next record in the database. Likewise, pressing – (the minus sign) displays the previous record. This will be useful only when you know something about the order in which the records are currently stored in the database and suspect that the record of interest is adjacent to the record you are currently displaying. In a similar fashion, pressing \ (the backslash key, not the regular slash on the same key as the question mark) displays the last record in the database. This might be useful if you have been entering data and wanted to see the final record.

The most useful options allow you to browse through the database, looking at 20 records at a time. Browsing is accomplished using the page up (PgUp) and page down (PgDn) keys on the keyboard. To start browsing through the database from the beginning, display the first record by entering #1 and pressing Return. Pressing Page Down will then shift into the browse mode and display the first 20 records, one per line, with the fields as columns down the screen. Figure 3-13 shows the first 20 records for the ADDRESS database. The record number for each record is displayed in the first column, followed by the Lastname, the Firstname, and the Address fields. The records are displayed in the order in which they are stored in the database, and the number of fields that can be displayed at one time is limited by the width of the screen.

To view additional fields, scroll the screen sideways by pressing the Tab key until the desired field is displayed. Scrolling the screen back to the left is accomplished by using Shift-Tab; that is, by holding down the shift key and pressing Tab. Just remember that you are moving from field to field in a record; this movement can always be accomplished by using the Tab and Shift-Tab keys. Pressing Page Down again displays the next twenty records, in effect moving "down" the page on which the database information is being displayed. Page Up reverses the procedure, allowing you to back up and display the preceding twenty records in the browse mode. Thus, you can use the Page Up and Page Down keys to scroll through the database and look for any information.

The Modify procedure, invoked by pressing F2, and the Delete procedure, invoked by pressing F3, operate exactly like the Display procedure. You can locate a record by the key, or by the record number, or you can browse through the database. The only difference is that you are given the opportunity to modify the records or delete the records you have displayed. Modification and deletion work in exactly the same manner as when these options are selected from within the Find procedure.

Should you manage the records in your database using only the Find procedure, or should you employ the Modify, Delete, and Display proce-

RCD.				DIS
1	Winter	Joseph	2930 Wildwood Way, Apt. 312	Buffalo
2	Spring	Andrea	4430 Flower Circle	Chapel Hil
3	Summer	William	7613 Wilson Avenue	Los Angele
4	Fall	Gerald	213 Oak Street, Suite 445	Hanover
5	Smith	Mary	495 Washington Street	New York
6	Williams	George	5698 Cactus Tree Court	Phoenix
7	Johnston	Maria	4340 High Circle Lane	Indianapol
8	Martin	Robert	3311 Van Buren Boulevard	San Franci
9	Smith	Peter	One Longhorn Way	Houston
10	Olson	Sheryl	6499 Wandering Lane	Indianapol
11	Waters	Sally	3890 North Lake Shore Drive	Chicago
12	Starr	Roland	4980 E. Macarthur Boulevard	Indianapol
13	Smith	Abraham	6688 Forthright Lane	Philadelph
14	Peterson	Arthur	4920 Boylston Street, Apt. 7A	Indianapol
15	Apple	Peter	12961 W. Jonathan Way	Irvine
16	Able	Eric	9876 Hightower Court	Indianapol
17	Walters	Sandra	2399 Westview Boulevard	Indianapol
18	Schultz	Samuel	2742 W. 49th Street	Milwaukee
19	Scott	John	4882 Jefferson Street	Two Rivers
20	Stephenson	Roberta	942 Woodward Way	Zionsville

To cancel, just press (Enter) with no response.
Supply the KEY, or #nn, or +(nxt rcd), -(prior), \(last), PgUp, PgDn
▶ ◀

Fig. 3-13. The first twenty records in the ADDRESS database displayed in the browse mode.

```
Lastname          15
Firstname         15
Address           30
City              15
State              2
Zip                5
Phone             12




ALL-  for all flds(column format),  ALL! for all flds(1 rcd per page)
Column = 0.  Field to List, or action:
▶Lastname                                                              ◀
```

Fig. 3-14. Screen for the specification of the report format, with Lastname entered as the first field.

dures? This is completely a matter of personal preference. Use whatever is easiest for you. I find it easiest to do just about everything using the Find procedure, but I use the Display procedure when I wish to browse through the database. On the other hand, you may find the other procedures quicker and easier to use in certain situations.

PRODUCING ADDRESS REPORTS

In addition to looking up individual records, you will want to use the information in a database to print out more elaborate reports containing some or all of the information in the database. The List function in PC-File provides the capabilities for generating such reports in a wide variety of formats that you can specify. In conjunction with such reporting, you will often want to sort the database in order to present the information in a particular order. This section uses these capabilities of PC-File to produce a simple phone list and to print mailing labels from the ADDRESS database.

Simple Reporting: The Phone List

A very simple report that can be produced using the ADDRESS database is a telephone directory listing the last names, first names, and telephone numbers of the persons in the database. From the main PC-File menu, press F6 to select the List function to design and produce this directory. The first screen asks you which report format you wish to use. If this is the first time you are producing a report, no report formats will be listed. The pointers will designate a blank field, which is to be used whenever you create a new report format. Press F10 to indicate you are creating a new report format and wish to proceed.

You will then be asked to specify a title for the report. The title is optional, but it would be nice to have the heading "Telephone Directory" at the top of the report, so type that in (without the quotation marks) and press Return.

The next screen is used to specify the basic format in which the information is to be printed in the report. Listed at the top of the screen are the names of the fields in the database and their lengths, for your reference in specifying the format. At the bottom is the prompt line asking for the field to be listed or for other information. At the beginning of the prompt line is the column number, indicating the number of columns you have used up on the current line of the report. The first field to be listed in the telephone directory is the Lastname field, so enter Lastname. The screen appears as shown in Fig. 3-14. Then press Return. You can actually enter only the first part of the field name—just enough to uniquely specify the field. In this case, entering just L would be sufficient, since no other field begins with L. Now enter the next field to be printed on the line—Firstname—and press Return. Finally, enter Phone as the final field and press Return. To indicate that you have completed defining the format of the report, press Return once more without entering anything.

You will next be asked if you wish to save the report format. Saving the format allows you to recall the format and use it again in producing reports. In general, saving the format is a good idea—you can always delete it later if you have no use for it. Y will be displayed; press Return in response to the question.

Assuming that you have indicated that you desire to save the report format, you will next be asked to give a name for this format. You can select any valid file name, up to eight characters in length. The name should describe the format so that you can recall it easily. Since this is a format to generate a telephone directory, why not name it DIRECT? Enter this name for the format and press Return.

The next question asks whether you wish to list the report on your printer or on the screen (scrn), or whether you want the output stored in a file on the disk (dsk). Listing the report on the screen allows you to preview the report and assure that it is correct before going through the process of printing it. This is often a good idea, so enter S for the screen option and press Return.

Now you are asked about subtotals in the report. Subtotals make no sense for this phone list, so press Return to indicate that no subtotals are desired. Then you are asked whether all records or only selected records are to be listed. The report can include only a portion of the records in the database, selected according to different criteria. For now, choose the option of printing all of the records by accepting the A and pressing Return.

The telephone directory is then listed on the screen. Figure 3-15 shows the first part of the telephone directory listing. First come the headings for

```
press (Esc) to stop
Lastname        Firstname       Phone
--------------- --------------- ------------
Winter          Joseph          716-385-1997
Spring          Andrea          919-273-5488
Summer          William         213-638-7734
Fall            Gerald          603-298-4822
Smith           Mary            212-327-4625
Williams        George          602-567-4945
Johnston        Maria           317-492-8473
Martin          Robert          415-691-4487
Smith           Peter           713-682-8625
Olson           Sheryl          317-583-5822
Waters          Sally           213-348-5294
Starr           Roland          317-873-8264
Smith           Abraham         215-342-5827
Peterson        Arthur          317-492-4687
Apple           Peter           714-335-2649
Able            Eric            317-382-4822
Walters         Sandra          317-563-8244
Schultz         Samuel          414-823-4781
Scott           John            414-981-3376

 Press ENTER ► ◄
```

Fig. 3-15. First part of the telephone directory report listed on the screen.

the three columns, Lastname, Firstname, and Phone. Following comes the information for the individual records, in the order in which those records are currently stored in the database. If the database has not been sorted, this is the order in which the records have been entered into the database. When the screen has been filled, the listing of the database pauses and you are given the instruction to press Enter (the Return key). In this way, the listing of the output is paused so you can examine it before proceeding. This process continues until all of the records in the database have been listed. You will then get the message "End of detail list."

Pressing Return brings up a screen that presents the number of records listed and the total number of records in the database. Figure 3-16 shows this screen. At the bottom of the screen are a series of options concerning where to go next. The options are List (L), Sort (S), PC-File (F), and Quit (Q). The PC-File option (F) takes you back to the main PC-File menu. From there, you can select any of the procedures offered on the menu, including the List and Sort procedures and the option of quitting PC-File. All of the other options listed are simply shortcuts that take you directly to the other parts of PC-File. The List option (L) takes you back to the beginning of the List procedure. The Sort option (S) takes you directly into the PC-File Sort procedure, which is used for reordering the database. The Quit option (Q), of course, allows you to leave PC-File or to switch the database you are using directly. You will see these options displayed at several points during the operation of PC-File. Their use allows you to move directly to the part of PC-File in which you want to work, avoiding the need to go through the main menu and avoiding the necessity of loading some information from the PC-File program disk. For now, just return to the main menu by pressing F and then Return.

```
TOTALS
----------------------------
Printed 25 of the 25 records.




(L)List (S)Sort (F)pc-File (Q)Quit
Enter L,S,F, or Q▶L◀
```

Fig. 3-16. Conclusion of the List procedure.

Sorting the Database and Printing the Directory

The telephone directory listing shown in Fig. 3-15 has a reasonable format for such a report, but the names appear in an arbitrary order. When information is entered into a PC-File database, the records are stored in the order entered. Thus, if the information has been entered in an arbitrary order, the database will be in that same arbitrary order. Any listing of the database will result in the records being displayed in that same order. For a telephone directory, however, the records should be listed in alphabetical order. To accomplish this, it is necessary to sort the records in the database.

Sorting is very easy. From the PC-File main menu, proceed to the Sort procedure by pressing F7. On the screen there will be a listing of all of the field names and a request for you to enter the name of sort field #1. The telephone directory should be in alphabetical order by last names, so enter Lastname. The screen will appear as shown in Fig. 3-17. Press Return. You will then be asked whether the sort is to be ascending (A to Z) order or descending (Z to A) order. An ascending sort is the default option; the A is already displayed. This is the correct choice, so simply press Return.

Next comes the request for sort field #2. Records with the same last names should be in alphabetical order by the first names, so the secondary sorting field is Firstname. Enter that field name and press Return. Once again, press Return to indicate that you want first names to also be sorted in ascending order. When you are then

```
Lastname
Firstname
Address
City
State
Zip
Phone




SORT FIELD # 1 ▶Lastname◀
```

Fig. 3-17. Screen for the specification of a sort of the database.

prompted for sort field #3, indicate that you are through designating sorting fields by pressing Return without entering a field name.

You will next be asked to specify a disk drive that can be used for a work area for the sort. For sorting small databases, such as those used in the examples here, work space on the disk will not be needed. In most instances, you can safely specify that the B: drive, the drive on which the database is stored, be used for the sorting work space. If you have a very large database that very nearly fills the disk in the B: drive, consult the PC-File manual for suggestions on providing a work space for the sort. For now, just enter B and press Return.

You will now get messages regarding the progress of the sort. A small database such as the one being used in this example will be sorted very quickly. Large databases with hundreds or thousands of records can take much longer. When everything is done, you will get a message that the sort has been completed. A list of options for the next activity similar to that at the end of the List procedure is displayed: (F) File, for the main menu; (L) List for the List procedure; (S) Sort to do more sorting; and (Q) Quit. Now that the database has been sorted in alphabetical order, the completed telephone directory can be printed out. This involves the use of the List procedure, so press L and Return.

This time when you begin the List procedure, the name of your existing report format, DIRECT, will be displayed as shown in Fig. 3-18. Use the down arrow key in the cursor control cluster to move the pointers down to select the DIRECT format and press F10 to proceed. Since you are using an existing report format that you had defined earlier, you will not have to enter information on the title or the format of the report. The first question will be whether you want the report listed on the printer, screen, or disk. Since everything should be ready to go, this time select the printer, accepting the P and pressing Return.

You will then be asked to set up your printer. Be sure the printer is turned on, that the paper has been advanced to the top of the page, and that the printer is ready. (The printer should have a light, indicating whether or not it is ready, and a button that you can press to place the printer on line.) PC-File asks if it should print an alignment pattern. The alignment pattern consists of lines of XXXX that show you where printing will start at the top of a page. This is particularly handy for getting mailing labels adjusted just right. For now, do not worry about this; accept the N and press Return.

You have seen before the remaining questions. Indicate that you do not want subtotals by pressing Return. Likewise, accept the default option that all records be printed by pressing Return with the A on the screen. The telephone directory will now be printed out on the printer. The product, as it was printed out by PC-File, is shown in Fig. 3-19.

Producing Mailing Labels

Sooner or later you will want to print mailing labels with the ADDRESS database. The procedure for doing so is not that different from the way the telephone directory was created. Just a few new features have to be employed.

Begin by entering the List procedure with F6. Leave the pointer on the blank report field and press F10 to indicate you are creating a new report format. When the title is requested, simply press Return; a title is not needed with mailing labels.

```
Which report format (blanks if new report)
Type a name or select with cursor keys
 ▶        ◀
 [DIRECT   ]






Enter data. Press (F10) when complete.
```

Fig. 3-18. Opening screen of the List procedure for the selection of the report format.

You then come to the screen where you specify the format for the report. The person's first name comes first on the mailing label, so enter Firstname and press Return. This is followed on the same line by the last name, so enter Lastname and press Return.

So far, this is the same procedure you followed in defining the telephone directory, but now you want the next field of the record, the address, printed on the following line. Entering a slash (/) and pressing Return indicates that you want to start a new line in the listing of the record. Address will be the only field on this second line, so enter that field name, press Return, enter another slash to indicate a new line, and again press Return. The third line of the mailing label will have the city, state, and zip code. Enter the appropriate field names, each followed by a press of the Return key.

The format specified thus far would produce an appropriate looking mailing label three lines long. Spaces will be needed to separate the labels. The most common mailing labels start every inch, or six lines. After entering the Zip field, enter a slash and press Return. This will cause a fourth (blank) line to be printed after the City-State-Zip line. Two more slashes, each followed by Returns, will cause two more blank lines to be printed. Now the mailing label format will print a total of six lines—three lines of information and three blank lines. The printing of the names will start on every sixth line, appropriate for one-inch mailing labels. To complete the format definition, press Return once more without entering anything.

Answer yes (entering Y) to the question about saving the report format, and enter a format name of LABELS. Because this is a multiple line report format, PC-File asks if you want the output printed in report format or labels format. The report format includes the title and field headings at the top of each page, as in the telephone directory, and it allocates the full space for printing the information for each field. If you are printing out Joe Smith, the first name Joe is allocated the full 15 spaces for the Firstname field, and the line looks like this:

```
Joe            Smith
```

The labels format dispenses with the headings and deletes extra spaces between the information printed out from adjacent fields. Now if you are printing out Joe Smith, the last name is moved over so the line looks like this:

```
Joe Smith
```

For printing out mailing labels, you obviously want the labels format (that is what it is designed for), so enter L and press Return.

TELEPHONE DIRECTORY

09-30-86 AT 5:11 p.m. Page 1

Lastname	Firstname	Phone
Able	Eric	317-382-4822
Apple	Peter	714-335-2649
Fall	Gerald	603-298-4822
Hall	Ellen	615-357-8431
Hill	Elizabeth	303-834-2763
Johnston	Maria	317-492-8473
Martin	Robert	415-691-4487
Martindale	Douglas	212-443-9566
Olson	Sheryl	317-583-5822
Peterson	Arthur	317-492-4687
Reilley	Steven	301-337-4352
Schultz	Samuel	414-823-4781
Scott	John	414-981-3376
Smith	Abraham	215-342-5827
Smith	Mary	212-327-4625
Smith	Peter	713-682-8625
Smythe	Audrey	404-283-6287
Spring	Andrea	919-273-5488
Starr	Roland	317-873-8264
Stephenson	Roberta	317-873-3864
Summer	William	213-638-7734
Walters	Sandra	317-563-8244
Waters	Sally	213-348-5294
Williams	George	602-567-4945
Winter	Joseph	716-385-1997

TOTALS

Printed 25 of the 25 records.

Fig. 3-19. Print out of the telephone directory.

Enter P to indicate you want the results printed on the printer, but use plain paper the first time to check out the format. Save your more expensive mailing labels until you are sure you have things right. No subtotals are required, so press Return.

Instead of printing out all of the labels and using up a lot of paper, assume you want to produce labels only for those persons living in your area. (Perhaps you want to invite them all to a party.) When asked whether you want all records or only selected records listed, press S and Return to indicate that you wish to make a selection. The record selection screen will be displayed. You need to enter the field on which the selection will be based and the selection criteria. In this instance, you wish to select records for which the city is Indianapolis.

On the first blank line under the "Field to search on" column, enter the field name City. Pressing Return moves the pointer to the "Compare how?" column. Since you want the value in the City field to equal Indianapolis, the equal sign (=) already in this field is correct, so just press Return. (You can use other comparison operators such as less than (<) and greater than (>) when appropriate.) The next entry comes under the heading "Compare to which field or to what value?" Since you want to determine whether the information in the City field is equal to "Indianapolis," this is the value for the comparison.

Enter "Indianapolis" in this column; since this is a value, it must be enclosed within quotes. The rightmost column is for specifying "And, Or, End." If you are entering two or more conditions on separate lines, you need to specify whether both must be true if the record is to be selected (And, A) or only one or the other must be true (Or, O). After the last or only comparison, you must enter End, E. Since City = "Indianapolis" is the only comparison you are requiring, accept the E that is already entered in this field. The record selection form should now look like the one shown in Fig. 3-20. Indicate that you are done by pressing F10.

The mailing labels for those persons living in Indianapolis are now printed out. The actual output is shown in Fig. 3-21. If you lay a strip of your continuous form mailing labels next to the output you have printed, you can readily make sure that the spacing is appropriate for printing one record on each label. If it is not, you will have to define a new format with more or fewer slashes. When the format is correct, you can place the mailing labels into your printer and print out the actual labels. Just reenter the List procedure and select the LABELS format you have defined. You can choose to have an alignment pattern printed to line up the labels at the correct starting point. Even taking these precautions, you will probably have to fiddle with the alignment, wasting some labels, to get the information printed correctly the first time you try this. I know I did! Once you get the hang of it, you can quickly print out mailing labels any time you want.

PC-File has several additional features that enhance the printing of mailing labels. The labels you

```
Lastname
Firstname
Address
City
State
Zip
Phone
--------------------------------------------------------------------------
                                 Compare to which field     And,
 Field to             Compare    or to what value?          Or,
 search on             how?      (if value, in quotes)      End
[City              ]  [= ]  ["Indianapolis"            ]  [E]
[                  ]  [= ]  [                          ]  [E]
[                  ]  [= ]  [                          ]  [E]
[                  ]  [= ]  [                          ]  [E]
[                  ]  [= ]  [                          ]  [E]
[                  ]  [= ]  [                          ]  [E]
[                  ]  [= ]  [                          ]  [E]
[                  ]  [= ]  [                          ]  [E]
[                  ]  [= ]  [                          ]  [E]
[                  ]  [= ]  [                          ]  ►◄

  Enter data. Press (F10) when complete.
```

Fig. 3-20. Selection of records with City equal to "Indianapolis."

```
Eric Able
9876 Hightower Court
Indianapolis IN 46266


Maria Johnston
4340 High Circle Lane
Indianapolis IN 46213


Sheryl Olson
6499 Wandering Lane
Indianapolis IN 46233


Arthur Peterson
4920 Boylston Street, Apt. 7A
Indianapolis IN 46242


Roland Starr
4980 E. Macarthur Boulevard
Indianapolis IN 46209


Sandra Walters
2399 Westview Boulevard
Indianapolis IN 46239
```

Fig. 3-21. Print out of mailing labels for persons living in Indianapolis.

have been printing thus far have only one label across ("one-up"). You can purchase mailing label stock with two, three, or more labels across. PC-File can print out labels in these formats using a separate program called PCLABEL. You use the List procedure to print the labels to a disk file, exit PC-File, and then run the PCLABEL program to do the printing. The procedure is outlined in the PC-File manual. By using the snapshot label feature, you can make PC-File print out a single mailing label for any record you are currently viewing. To use this, you have to define a snapshot label format using the PCSETUP program. Once this has been done, you can print out a snapshot label by using the Alternate-5 combination (holding down the Alternate key and pressing the 5 at the top of the keyboard). Once again, see the PC-File manual for further details on how this is done.

THE HOME INVENTORY DATABASE

In creating and using the ADDRESS database, you have employed most of the basic features of PC-File and should be well on your way in learning to use this program. The ADDRESS database did not, however, contain any numeric data on which totals or subtotals might be produced. Some of the more advanced capabilities of PC-File have not been used thus far. A second database for keeping records of household possessions will be employed to explore some of these additional features.

Planning the Home Inventory Database

An inventory of major possessions is a useful tool for keeping track of those items, figuring the value of your assets, and providing information for insurance purposes in the event of loss or theft. PC-File is an ideal tool for keeping such an inventory. Not only can information easily be added to and deleted from the database, but the List procedure can be used to produce a variety of useful reports summarizing this information. As in any database application, the first step is the planning of the structure of the database and the information to be included.

The first field in the database will be a description of the item; call this field Item. The field will have to be sufficiently long to allow for a reasonable description. Thirty characters should be sufficient; abbreviations can always be used in describing any item.

The various possessions fall into different categories, such as audio equipment, computers, recreational items, and so forth. In using the information in the database, you will often want to be able to group the items into such categories. A field named Category, with a length of ten characters, should be sufficient. In designating categories for the various items, it is important to settle on a standard set of category names to be entered into this field. If you use "Audio" to describe the category for some items and "Hi-fi" to describe the category for others, it will be very difficult to later group these items and to select all of the audio equipment. Part of the definition of this field will thus be the specification of a standard set of categories within which all your possessions are to be grouped. You can, of course, go back and change the entries in the category field after the database has been created and the data entered. It is far easier, however, to settle on these categories before proceeding to enter any data. For the purposes of the small example being presented here, just three categories will be used—audio, computers, and recreation. A full-scale application will require many more categories.

The inventory should include the date each item was acquired; name this field Date. The format of the information to be entered into this Date field must now be specified. Most convenient is the standard format month-day-year, as in 12-22-85. In order to keep the information in fixed locations for searching and sorting, it will be necessary to always include two digits for the month and the day. Single-digit months and days must have leading zeros, as in 01-01-87. This date field should be eight characters in length to accommodate the month, the day, the year, and the two hyphens. Only numerals and the hyphen character are allowed as entries in this field.

Finally, the inventory database will have a field named Value containing the initial acquisition price of the item. A field length of seven would be sufficient for prices up to 9999.99 (remember to count the decimal point). To allow for larger values, perhaps a field length of eight should be designated. Only numerals and the period (or decimal point) are allowed as entries in this field.

The structure of the simple inventory database is summarized in Table 3-2. In a real application, additional fields of information might well be desired, but the inventory database is being kept simple for this example. The procedure for modifying an existing database to add more fields of information will be explained below.

Table 3-2. Fields in INVEN Database.

Field Name	Field Length	Allowable Characters
Item	30	—
Category	10	—
Date	8	0-9 -
Value	8	0-9 .

Defining the Database

To define the household inventory database, start PC-File in the normal manner. When asked to specify the database, enter the name INVEN and press F10. (INVENTORY exceeds the eight-character limit for database names.) Enter the field names and field lengths as before, with one exception. Fields containing numeric data must be designated so that totals can be computed and the data can be displayed right-justified in the columns in the appropriate fashion. Numeric fields are specified by adding the number sign, #, to the end of the field name. The Value field is a numeric field, so the field name should be entered as Value#. After the database definition has been completed, the screen should look like Fig. 3-22.

After you have completed the database definition and have proceeded to the main PC-File menu, it is time to define edit masks to assure that only the proper characters can be entered into certain fields in the INVEN database. In this way, any attempt to enter letters in the Date field, for example, will be caught and rejected by PC-File. Use the NAM procedure to alter the field name or mask. Enter this procedure either by typing NAM and Return or by pressing the Alternate-F4 combination, holding down the Alternate key and pressing function key 4. A screen will display a list of all field names and will ask which field you wish to change. To enter an edit mask for the Date field, type Date and Return. The field name Date appears after "New Name." You could change this field name by typing over the word Date, but you do not want to do this now. Move the cursor to the mask field and enter the following edit mask:

```
:09 - - :
```

```
(Alt)H for help.  Define the database.
 FIELD NAME       LENGTH                       FIELD NAME          LENGTH
[Item          ]  [30  ]                       [             ]     [    ]
[Category      ]  [10  ]                       [             ]     [    ]
[Date          ]  [8   ]                       [             ]     [    ]
[Value#        ]  [8   ]                       [             ]     [    ]
[              ]  [    ]                       [             ]     [    ]
[              ]  [    ]                       [             ]     [    ]
[              ]  [    ]                       [             ]     [    ]
[              ]  [    ]                       [             ]     [    ]
[              ]  [    ]                       [             ]     [    ]
[              ]  [    ]                       [             ]     [    ]
[              ]  [    ]                       [             ]     [    ]
[              ]  [    ]                       [             ]     [    ]
[              ]  [    ]                       [             ]     [    ]
[              ]  [    ]                       [             ]     [    ]
[              ]  [    ]                       [             ]     [    ]
[              ]  [    ]                       [             ]     [    ]
[              ]  [    ]                       [             ]     [    ]
[              ]  [    ]                       [             ]     [    ]
[              ]  [    ]                       [             ]     [    ]
[              ]  [    ]                       [             ]     [    ]
[              ]  [    ]                       [             ]     ▶    ◀

Enter data. Press (F10) when complete.
```

Fig. 3-22. Definition of the home inventory database, INVEN.

The screen will now appear as shown in Fig. 3-23. The colons indicate that this is an edit mask defining valid characters that may be entered in the field. The 09 indicates that the digits 0 through 9 will be accepted, and the – – indicates that hyphens will be accepted. (Characters must always be entered in pairs, indicating a range; thus, the double hyphens are required.) Press F10 to enter this edit mask.

For the Value# field, only numerals and the

```
                                                                    NAM
--------------------------------------------------------------------------
Item
Category
Date
Value#




New name[Date        ]
    mask▶:09--:                                                  ◀
Enter data. Press (F10) when complete.
```

Fig. 3-23. Entry of an edit mask for the Date field.

decimal point (period) can be entered. Type in Value# and enter the following edit mask:

:09..:

Press Return in response to the request for the name of the field to change in order to exit the procedure. The NAM procedure can be used in a variety of additional ways. Field names can be changed. Provisions can be made to automatically enter certain values into specific fields without requiring any action by the data operator. You can define calculated fields, in which the value is automatically calculated using the values entered into other numeric fields.

Entering the Data

Information is entered into the INVEN database using the ADD function (F1) as before. An example of a typical record that might be entered into the database is shown in Fig. 3-24. The only difference arises when attempts are accidentally made to enter invalid data into the two fields with edit masks. If a letter is pressed when entering data into the Date field, for example, PC-File refuses to accept the character. In this way, the database is protected from the entry of incorrect information.

While entering information into the INVEN database, remember to use the standard categories for each item. Failure to do so will make it difficult to produce reports grouping the items by category.

USING ADVANCED FEATURES WITH INVEN

The household inventory database provides the opportunity to explore a variety of additional advanced features of PC-File. In describing a number of different procedures, additional searching, sorting, and listing capabilities will be employed. The examples outlined below do not exhaust the possibilities of PC-File, but they do provide sufficient exposure to the capabilities of this program so that you should be able to learn and understand the remaining features by using the PC-File manual.

```
ADDing at # 1                                                    ADD

Item        ▶Super GT Personal Computer    ◀
Category    [Computers ]
Date        [09-30-85]
Value#      [1190.00 ]

To cancel, press (F10) if no data was entered, or (Esc) if data was entered
Enter data. Press (F10) when complete.
```

Fig. 3-24. Entry of a record into the INVEN database.

Searching INVEN

With the ADDRESS database, the Find procedure was used to locate individual records based on searches for values stored in particular fields. Several additional types of searches will be used in finding records in the INVEN database.

Suppose you wished to locate the record with the information on the speakers for your stereo system. Obviously the record would have the word "speakers" in the description of the item, but this will not necessarily come first; the brand name may precede the word "speakers." The normal PC-File search will locate a record only if the string being searched for comes first in the field. For fields like Lastname or City, this is not a problem. For the item field in the INVEN database, it can be.

The solution to the problem is the "Scan Across" search mentioned on the Find screen. Invoke the Find procedure by pressing F5 on the main PC-File menu. At the bottom of the screen is a line of examples. The third is >TH(scan across). When the > (greater than) symbol is placed before the information being searched for, PC-File will look for the occurrence of that information anywhere within the field being searched. To search for the record with the word "speakers" somewhere in the Item field, enter the following in that field on the Find screen:

>speakers

The screen will appear as shown in Fig. 3-25. Press F10 to indicate that you have finished specifying the search. PC-File will search for any records with the word "speakers" occurring at any position in the Item field. The record in Fig. 3-26 will be displayed.

The scan across search seems so much more powerful and flexible than the standard PC-File search, which looks only at the beginning of the field. Why not use this procedure for all searches? First, such a search can sometimes locate records you do not want, complicating the search process. For example, suppose in the ADDRESS database you were searching for someone with the last name of Donald. A scan across search would also find the records for those with the last name MacDonald. The record you want would be located eventually, but you might have to go through other records first.

More importantly for large files, the scan across search can take a considerable length of time—far longer than the standard search. PC-File keeps an

```
The Binary search field is (not specified)                                  FIN
--------------------------------------------------------------------------------
Item          ►>speakers********************◄
Category      [**********]
Date          [********]
Value#        [********]




Fill in the data you want to search for.
Examples: SMITH(exact)  ?SMITH(soundex)  >TH(scan across)  ___TH(wildcard)
Enter data. Press (F10) when complete.
```

Fig. 3-25. Specification of a "scan across" search for "speakers" in the Item field.

```
Record # 4                                                              FIN
___________________________________________________________________________
Item         Excelsior Speakers (2)
Category     Audio
Date         12-01-83
Value#       280.00






Continue finding, Stop, Modify, or Delete? (C,S,M,D)▶C◀
```

Fig. 3-26. Record found using the "scan across" search for "speakers" in the Item field.

index to the records that enables it to find records very quickly using the normal search procedure that looks for the information at the beginning of a field. For the scan across search, however, PC-File has no choice but to read each record and search through all of the information stored in the designated field. This can take a very long time for large files. Of course when this is the only way of locating the desired record, using the scan across search is an appropriate choice. PC-File can do the searching far more quickly than you could look through the individual records yourself.

The next search will combine two capabilities of the Find procedure—the ability to find records based upon the values in multiple fields and the ability to specify partial matches in an individual field (the wildcard search). For the example, the search will be for audio equipment acquired in 1986. Begin at the initial screen for the Find procedure. To indicate that the search is to be for audio equipment, enter the word "Audio" (without the quotes) in the Category field in the usual manner.

Indicating the year, however, requires the use of the wildcard search capabilities. The year is stored in the last two columns of the Date field, since all dates have the form 01-01-86. To search for items acquired any time in 1986, you do not care about the month or the day; they can have any values. In a wildcard search, you can enter the special wildcard character _ (the underscore character) for any positions in the search field where you will accept any values—where you do not care what the values are. In the Date field on the Find screen, enter ______86, six underscores followed by 86. This will fill the field. This indicates to PC-File that it should look for records with 86 in the final two positions in the Date field, ignoring the values for the month and day. After you enter the two search criteria, the Find screen will appear as shown in Fig. 3-27. Pressing F10 begins the search; the screen then displays the record shown in Fig. 3-28; this record meets the search criteria specified.

To review, the Find procedure will search for records that match the criteria specified in as many fields as desired. The basic search procedure looks for the records in which the value specified is at the beginning of the field and is the most efficient. Soundex searches, specified with a question mark (?) before the search value, attempt to find records in which the value in the field sounds like the value specified. The scan across search, indicated by the greater than symbol (>) before the search value,

```
The Binary search field is (not specified)                          FIN
________________________________________________________________________
Item        ▶******************************◀
Category    [Audio*****]
Date        [______86]
Value#      [********]





Fill in the data you want to search for.
Examples: SMITH(exact)  ?SMITH(soundex)  >TH(scan across)  ___TH(wildcard)
Enter data. Press (F10) when complete.
```

Fig. 3-27. Specification of the search for audio equipment acquired in 1986.

will locate records in which the value occurs anywhere within the field. Finally, wildcard searches employ the wildcard character (the underscore, __) to indicate that the values in certain positions within a field are to be ignored, enabling searches to be made based on the values in specific locations within the field.

Producing INVEN Reports

In the discussion of generating reports from the

```
Record # 16                                                         FIN
________________________________________________________________________
Item        New Wave Car Stereo
Category    Audio
Date        01-01-86
Value#      190.00





Continue finding, Stop, Modify, or Delete? (C,S,M,D)▶C◀
```

Fig. 3-28. Record found searching for audio equipment acquired in 1986.

INVEN database, examples from the simplest default report to an elaborate summary with subtotals will be covered. Let us begin with the simple listing of the database in the default column format. From the main PC-File menu, press F6 to select the List procedure. Since you are creating a new report format, leave the pointer at the empty field and press F10. Enter the title "Household Inventory Listing." When you press Return, the screen is displayed for the definition of the report format.

PC-File includes two default format specifications that allow you to produce simple reports without going through the tedious process of listing all of the fields desired. ALL! gives a simple listing of the field names followed by the contents of the field, with one field per line. This nicely lists the entire contents of the database. Unfortunately, the format prints one record per page and then skips to a new page. This might be reasonable for databases with many fields per record, but for databases with shorter records, this wastes a lot of paper. If you want to try out this format, print the results to the screen first and be sure that this is what you really want before wasting a lot of paper.

More useful is the ALL- format, which produces a table in column format with all of the fields in the database. As long as the total width of all of the fields in a database does not exceed the length of the line that can be printed on your printer, this is a nice, quick way to produce a report of the contents of a database. To use this format, just type ALL- on the format definition screen. The screen will appear as shown in Fig. 3-29. Press Return to enter this format specification and then press Return once more to indicate that you are done defining the report format. Exactly the same result could have been achieved by entering each of the field names in the order in which they come in the database. Using the ALL- format is certainly easier.

You then proceed through the List procedure in the usual manner. Indicate that you wish to save the report format by entering Y and Return. Enter a name such as INVRPT (for inventory report) and

```
Item                30
Category            10
Date                 8
Value#               8











ALL-  for all flds(column format),  ALL! for all flds(1 rcd per page)
Column = 0.  Field to List, or action:
▶ALL-
```

Fig. 3-29. Specification of the standard column report format using ALL–.

press Return. Choose whether the report is to be listed on the screen or the printer in the usual fashion. For this initial report, do not ask for subtotals; just press Return. List all of the records by pressing Return with the default, A. The completed report will be listed on the screen or on the printer, depending upon the selection made. The printed report listing all of the information in the INVEN database is illustrated in Fig. 3-30. Note that the report includes the total and average for the Value# field. Because this field was defined as a numeric field (the field name was entered as Value#), PC-File automatically produces this summary information for the field unless instructed otherwise.

The second report from the INVEN database will be more complex, requiring the use of a number of additional listing and sorting features of PC-File. The information on the household items is to be grouped by category in the report, with subtotals for the Value field in each category. Within each category, the items are to be listed in order by the date of acquisition. Finally, information is to be included only on items acquired since 1983, and the recreation category is not to be included in the table.

The first task is the sorting of the INVEN database in the appropriate order. Enter the Sort procedure, either by entering S at the conclusion of the List procedure or by pressing F7 at the PC-File main menu. For grouping and subtotaling, a file must be sorted in order on the field being used for the grouping. This is because PC-File accomplishes the grouping and generates the subtotals by keeping track of the data in that field as the records are

```
                    HOUSEHOLD INVENTORY LISTING
09-30-86 AT 6:12 p.m.                                      Page 1
```

Item	Category	Date	Value
Super GT Personal Computer	Computers	09-30-85	1190.00
Telescreen Monitor	Computers	09-30-85	96.00
Audio Deluxe Receiver	Audio	10-10-82	340.00
Excelsior Speakers (2)	Audio	12-01-83	280.00
Ecstacy Turntable	Audio	12-25-82	135.00
SuperLite Tent	Recreation	03-20-84	94.00
SuperWarm Down Sleeping Bag	Recreation	08-15-84	72.00
SuperLite Backpack	Recreation	12-25-84	45.00
SuperPro Dot Matrix Printer	Computers	01-20-86	385.00
Floppy Disk File	Computers	03-30-86	25.00
CommunicationsPro Modem	Computers	05-01-86	235.00
GamePro Home Computer	Computers	11-11-82	490.00
SturdyWood Computer Desk	Computers	02-14-86	93.00
FineSound Compact Audio Player	Audio	12-25-85	260.00
FineSound Equalizer	Audio	12-25-85	189.00
New Wave Car Stereo	Audio	01-01-86	190.00
Waxless X-Country Skis	Recreation	01-20-83	88.00
X-Country Ski Poles	Recreation	01-20-83	19.00
X-Country Ski Boots	Recreation	01-20-83	54.00

```
TOTALS
----------------------------
Value                4,280.00        225.263  AVG.
Printed 19 of the 19 records.
```

Fig. 3-30. Printed report of the contents of the INVEN database using the standard column report format.

retrieved and printed. Each time the data value changes—say from Audio to Computers—PC-File assumes a group has ended and prints the appropriate subtotal. If the Audio and Computers records were in random order in the file, PC-File would identify numerous groups and produce a meaningless report. Thus, the INVEN database must first be sorted in order by Category if that field is to be used for the subtotals and grouping. Enter the field name Category and press Return for the first sort field.

The specifications for the report called for the items to be displayed in order by the date of acquisition within each category, so it is necessary to further sort the INVEN database by date. This is slightly more complex; you cannot simply sort on the Date field. PC-File knows nothing about the way in which dates are stored. The information in the Date field is simply a string of characters, to be sorted like any other string of characters. Simply sorting by Date would cause an item acquired on 01-01-86 to be placed before (earlier than) an item acquired on 12-01-83. The reason is simply that 01 comes before 12. To sort dates correctly, it is necessary to sort first by the year, and then by the month and day. For the second sort field, you wish to sort by the year, which is stored in the final two positions, positions seven and eight, of the Date field. To specify this, enter the following:

```
Date,7,2
```

This command tells PC-File to sort only on the information in the Date field beginning in the seventh position, with a length of two characters. This is the year. Then, to further sort the records by the month and day, enter the following for the third level of sorting:

```
Date,1,5
```

This specifies a sort based upon the information in the first five columns of the Date field, the month and the day. Sorting in this way will correctly order the records by date (within each of the categories).

Once the sorting of the INVEN database has been completed, return to the List procedure and press F10 to indicate the creation of a new report format. Assume that you do not wish the time of day to be printed on the report. When entering the title, first enter 0M (that is a zero followed by the letter M) to indicate this option. Then type in the title, "Selected Inventory Report." The line should look like this:

```
0MSelected Inventory Report
```

The option to not print the time is only one of a number of options available to control the printing of reports that can be entered at the beginning of the title. The PC-File manual contains a complete list of the various options, each of which begins with zero or one.

After pressing Return, you are ready to define the report format. Since the report is being grouped and subtotaled by Category, this field should be the first column. Enter Category and press Return. It might be nice to have a little more space between the columns. To specify an extra five spaces at this point, enter >5 (the greater than symbol and the number 5) and press Return. Continue to enter the remaining fields and the extra spaces to separate the columns as follows:

```
Item<Return>
>5<Return>
Date<Return>
>5<Return>
```

For the Value# field, indicate that you wish to have subtotals and totals printed, but not averages, by following the field name with the letters S and T in brackets. This entry should appear as follows:

```
Value# [ST]<Return>
```

PC-File provides additional options for specifying the information to be computed and reported for each numeric field. One additional Return will indicate the completion of the format definition and take you to the next screen. If you wish to save this report format, indicate Y and provide a name, such as INVRPT2. Choose whether the report is to be listed on the printer or the screen.

Now, when asked for the field to cause subtotal break, enter Category and press Return. This will cause the breaks each time the value in the Category field changes. Group highlighting will make this report easier to read by printing the category value only once for each category. So answer the question with Y and press Return. To the question, "New page after each subtotal break?" accept the N for no and press Return.

Not all of the records are to be included in this report, so next indicate that only selected records are desired by entering S and pressing Return. The record selection screen will then be presented. The report specification called for the Recreation category to be excluded and only items acquired from 1983 forward to be included. Enter the category specification first. In the field to search on, enter Category. In the column headed "Compare how?" enter < >, which stands for "not equal." In the third column, the value "Recreation," enclosed in quotes, should be entered. This specifies that only those records in which the value in the Category field is not equal to Recreation should be selected. In other words, select everything except Recreation.

This is not the end of the selection criteria, however. The report is to select records not in the Recreation category with a year of acquisition that is 1983 or later. Two comparisons must be employed, and both must be true for a record to be selected. Because both criteria must be met, the comparisons are joined with "And"—the first *and* the second must be true. Enter an A in the rightmost column.

Drop down to the second line to enter the comparison for the year. Once again, it is necessary to refer to the final two positions in the Date field to find the year. The specification is exactly the same as for the Sort procedure. Date is followed by a comma, a seven (indicating the starting position within the field of the characters of interest), another comma, and the two (indicating the length of the string of characters of interest). Therefore, specify the comparison of the year, within the Date field, by entering the following in the "Field to Search on" column:

```
Date,7,2
```

For the comparison operator, enter the greater-than symbol (>), since the report is to list the later years. The report is to list the records with the years of 1983 and later, so enter into the third column:

```
"82"
```

The year 1982 must be used because the comparison is greater than, not greater than or equal to. A comparison of "Year greater than 1982" will list all records from 1983 on. This completes the specification for record selection. The screen should appear as shown in Fig. 3-31. If it does not, it can be edited in the usual fashion. Press F10 when it is completed.

The report is now ready to be listed to either the screen or to the printer, depending upon the selection made earlier. The printout of the report generated using this procedure is shown in Fig. 3-32. All of the records selected in each category are listed together, in order by date. The category value is listed only once, for the first record, to emphasize the grouping (this is what is referred to as *group highlighting*). Subtotals for the value field are reported after each group of records, and the total value is reported at the end of the report.

Note that the subtotaling and the record selection criteria are not part of the report format stored under the name INVRPT2. This means that the report format can be used to produce a variety of different reports. Each time the report format is reused by selecting INVRPT2 at the beginning of the List procedure, you will be asked if subtotals are desired and if records are to be selected. If you wish to make a selection of records from the database, it will be necessary to again define the record selection criteria at this time.

Modifying the INVEN Database

Despite the best planning, it is sometimes

```
Item
Category
Date
Value#

─────────────────────────────────────────────────────────────────────────────────
                                   Compare to which field     And,
 Field to               Compare    or to what value?          Or,
 search on               how?      (if value, in quotes)      End
[Category          ]  [<>]  ["Recreation"                 ]  [A]
[Date,7,2          ]  [> ]  ["82"                         ]  [E]
[                  ]  [= ]  [                             ]  [E]
[                  ]  [= ]  [                             ]  [E]
[                  ]  [= ]  [                             ]  [E]
[                  ]  [= ]  [                             ]  [E]
[                  ]  [= ]  [                             ]  [E]
[                  ]  [= ]  [                             ]  [E]
[                  ]  [= ]  [                             ]  [E]
[                  ]  [= ]  [                             ]  ▶◀

Enter data. Press (F10) when complete.
```

Fig. 3-31. Specification of the selection of records not in the recreation category with year of acquisition 1983 or later.

necessary to change the structure of a database, by adding or deleting fields or changing the lengths of fields. PC-File allows such changes to be made by creating a new database that is a modified copy of the original database. The procedure is referred to as *cloning* the database.

Assume that you wish to change the INVEN database in two ways: the Category field is to be increased in length to 15 characters to accommodate larger category names, and a new field is to be added for miscellaneous comments about the items in the database. This comment field could be used to enter such information as warranty terms or dates on which the item has been repaired. PC-File allows the last field in a database to be a longer "super field" with more space than the standard maximum of 65 characters. The PC-File manual indicates the maximum lengths for super fields, which depend upon the number of fields in the database. A field to be named Comment, with a length of 150 characters, will be added to the database.

The List procedure is used to clone a database to produce a new, modified database. Enter the List procedure from the main menu by pressing F6. Indicate that you wish to define a new report format by pressing F10 with the pointers selecting the blank report field. Do not type in a title; simply press Return.

In defining the report format, you will be specifying the fields to be contained in the new, cloned database. Begin by entering each of the field names in the original database, followed by Return. (You could change the order of the fields in the new database by entering the field names in a different order.) To add the new Comment field, type >150 (the greater than symbol followed by the width of the new field) and press Return. The new field will be named >150 in the cloned database; you can change this later. Press Return once more to indicate completion of the format definition for the new database.

Do not save the report format; type N and press

```
                          SELECTED INVENTORY REPORT
09-30-86                                                                Page 1

Category          Item                                  Date          Value
----------        ------------------------------        --------      --------
Audio             Excelsior Speakers (2)                12-01-83        280.00
                  FineSound Compact Audio Player        12-25-85        260.00
                  FineSound Equalizer                   12-25-85        189.00
                  New Wave Car Stereo                   01-01-86        190.00
..Subtotals.. 4 records, Category = Audio
Value                   919.00

Computers         Super GT Personal Computer            09-30-85       1190.00
                  Telescreen Monitor                    09-30-85         96.00
                  SuperPro Dot Matrix Printer           01-20-86        385.00
                  SturdyWood Computer Desk              02-14-86         93.00
                  Floppy Disk File                      03-30-86         25.00
                  CommunicationsPro Modem               05-01-86        235.00

..Subtotals.. 6 records, Category = Computers
Value                 2,024.00

TOTALS
-----------------------------
Value                 2,943.00
Printed 10 of the 19 records.
Records were selected as follows:
Category       <> "RECREATION"                AND
Date           >  "82"                        END
```

Fig. 3-32. Print out of the final report from the INVEN database.

Return. When asked where the report is to be listed, select D for disk and press Return. You will be asked if you wish to clone the database or print the report to the disk. Select the clone option by entering C and pressing Return. The next question asks whether you wish to change any field lengths. Since you do, enter Y and Return. Enter the field name Category and press Return; type in the new field length of 15 and press Return. Pressing Return once more indicates completion of the field length changes.

Now you will be asked for the disk drive on which the new database is to be stored. Press B and Return to place the new database on the same disk with the old. (Note that if you have a very large database that fills up most of the disk, you will have to create the cloned database on a new disk in the A: drive.) For the new database name, enter INVEN2 and press Return. Select all records by accepting the A and pressing Return. Finally, the procedure for cloning the database has been specified. The cloned database is created, various messages are displayed, and the task is complete. Press Return to get back to PC-File to work with the new database.

When you reenter PC-File, the new database name INVEN2 will be displayed on the list of databases. Select this database and press F10. The first thing to do when the main PC-File menu is displayed is to change the name of the new field to Comment. Press the Alternate-F4 combination to enter the Name procedure. The list of the fields contained in the INVEN2 database will be displayed, including the newly-created field with the name >150. Since this is the field you wish to change, type in >150 and press Return. The bottom of the screen now contains a line labeled New Name, with the original field name >150 following in brackets. Type in the new field name Comments over the old field name. The screen will now look like Fig. 3-33. Press F10 to indicate that the changes are complete, and press F10 once more to return to the main menu.

At this point, you will probably want to add comments to some or all of the records in the new database. If you wish to go through all of the records, using the Modify procedure is the easiest. Enter Modify by pressing F2. To start with the first record, type in #1 and press Return. The information will be displayed in the new record format, with the lengthened Category field and the new Comment field. Move the pointers down to the Comment field and enter any information you wish. The screen will now appear as shown in Fig. 3-34. Press

```
                                                                 NAM
--------------------------------------------------------------------
Item
Category
Date          :09--:
Value#        :09..:
>150




New name[Comments      ]
    mask ►                                                  ◄
Enter data. Press (F10) when complete.
```

Fig. 3-33. Changing the field name to "Comments" in the cloned INVEN2 database.

```
MODifying # 1                                                    MOD
--------------------------------------------------------------------
Item         [Audio Deluxe Receiver          ]
Category     [Audio          ]
Date         [10-10-82]
Value#       [340.00  ]
Comments     ▶Purchased at Ace Super Stereo Store.  Repaired, power supply
problems, 6-30-85.  Right channel bass control noisy.
   ◀

Enter data. Press (F10) when complete.
```

Fig. 3-34. Modifying the first record in the cloned INVEN2 database, adding a comment.

F10 when you are finished. If you wish to go through the records in the database to add comments, proceed to the next one by entering + and Return.

When you are certain that the new database is correct and that none of the information from the original INVEN database has been lost, you may wish to delete the original. This can be done using the DOS ERASE command. A PC-File database has three files on the disk, with the extensions .DTA (data), .INX (index), and .HDR (header). Thus, the INVEN database has the three files INVEN.DTA, INVEN.INX, and INVEN.HDR. The DOS wildcard can be used to erase all of these files at once using a single command:

```
ERASE INVEN.*
```

Similar commands can be used to copy PC-File databases to make backup copies.

Instead of using DOS, it is possible to delete, copy, and rename databases and perform other functions within PC-File by using the Utilities procedure. From the main PC-File menu, press F8 to enter the Utilities procedure. The list of options shown in Fig. 3-35 will be displayed. To erase the INVEN file, select the delete file option and enter the file name.

CONFIGURING PC-FILE

PC-File includes the capability for customizing the operation of the program to most effectively utilize the system you are using and to match your preferred style of operation. The PCSETUP program accomplishes this customization. It is menu-driven and quite easy to use. The most important configuration options for most users will involve the video display and the printer.

To change the configuration of PC-File, place the program disk in the A: drive. Be sure there is no write protect tab on the disk, as the setup procedure writes information to the PC-File program disk. At the DOS prompt type PCSETUP and press Return. The first question asks about the compatibility of your system with the IBM Personal Computer. If you are using an IBM PC compatible (the standard system described in Chapter 2), enter 1 and Return. If you are using a noncompatible system, refer to Appendix B for further instructions.

```
DATABASE UTILITIES                                                UTI

                    1. Copy (backup a database)

                    2. Rename a database

                    3. Delete a database

                    4. Delete a report format

                    5. Export a database

                    6. Import a database

                    7. Merge 2 databases together

                    8. Return to PC-File

Select a number from the menu▶8◀
```

Fig. 3-35. Options available in the Utilities procedure.

The next question asks whether you are using a monochrome monitor or a color monitor. Select the appropriate option. With a color monitor, the setup program then allows you to select the colors used for the background and the text. PC-File can be run displaying any color combination desired.

The next series of questions relate to the printer. If your printer has the capability, PC-File can automatically switch to narrow, compressed text when printing reports too wide to fit on the paper using the normal text. Thus, with the common dot matrix printer that allows 80 normal characters to be printed on a line, compressed characters can be used to fit up to 132 characters on a line. PC-File comes configured to do this switching for IBM and Epson dot matrix printers. If you have one of these—or a compatible printer—just indicate that you do not wish to change this. On the other hand, if you have another printer, you will have to change the setup.

If the printer cannot vary the number of characters printed per inch (like many daisy wheel printers), make that choice and that is it. Most dot matrix printers can vary the width of characters and the number of characters printed on a line under software control. If you pick this option, you will have to enter the printer control codes to produce normal and compressed print. The printer manual will contain such codes. For a C.Itoh ProWriter, for example, the code for normal text is Escape N and the code for compressed text is Escape Q. The printer manual should also have the decimal values for these codes. For the ProWriter, these are 27 78 for normal and 27 81 for compressed. The setup program will ask for the number of characters that can be printed on a line with normal and compressed text and will ask for the decimal values of the control codes. Once these have been entered, PC-File can automatically use this information to fit reports on the printed page in the most appropriate fashion. You will then be asked about the number of characters per line and the number of lines per page printed by your printer.

The remaining questions are relatively straightforward. Defining the "snapshot mailing labels" requires reference to the PC-File manual if that feature is desired. Using a system with two floppy disk drives, the B: drive will generally contain the databases. If you always use the same database for a major application, you can have PC-File start that database directly.

The final choices allow you to speed up operation of PC-File. Normally, after each record has been changed, PC-File automatically writes the changes to the disk, resulting in a slight delay. This can be changed so that disk access occurs only when needed, but selecting this option slightly increases the risk of losing some data if power is lost or other problems occur. Also, when entering a command, such as the Y or N for a yes-or-no question, PC-File normally requires that you then press Return. This can be changed so that operation continues as soon as the command is entered, without pressing Return. This is quicker, but makes it easier to make mistakes. The option would make sense for a more experienced user.

After you have answered all of the questions, the PCSETUP program writes a special file with all of the information on the PC-File disk. PC-File uses this file to establish appropriate operating procedures. You can run the PCSETUP program as often as you like to change the configuration. Unfortunately, each time you run the program, you have to go through and give the answers to each question. There is no way to conveniently change just a single option with the setup program.

CONCLUSION

The ADDRESS and INVEN databases are representative of the applications for which most users will employ PC-File. The examples have covered most of the functions of PC-File that will be needed for such applications. If you have gone through these examples, you should be well on your way to becoming a proficient PC-File user.

PC-File does, however, include a host of additional features that can come in handy in specialized circumstances. Even more options are available in the List procedure than have been covered in the examples. A global update and delete procedure can be used to make wholesale changes to a database (with disastrous results, if you are not careful!). You can immediately print a mailing label for any record displayed on the screen using the snapshot mailing label feature. Searches of large files can be speeded using the binary search option. "Smart keys" can be defined to have special meanings to expedite commonly used procedures. The PC-File manual provides information on all of these features and others. With the experience gained thus far in using PC-File, it will be much easier to go through the manual and learn how to use these additional capabilities of PC-File.

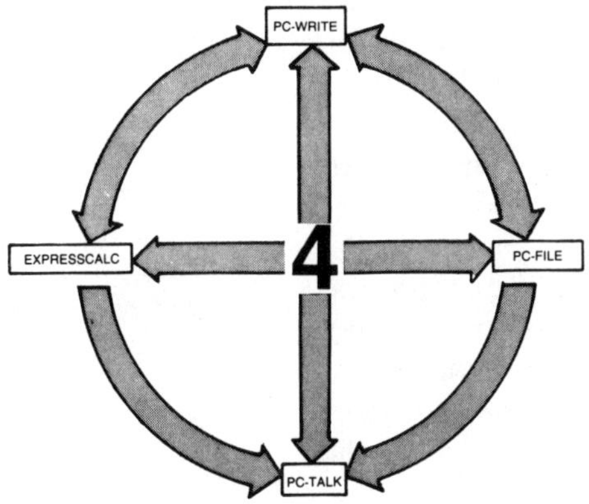

Using PC-Write

Word processing is one of the most widely used applications for personal computers. Word processing programs allow text to be entered just once. The text can then be edited, corrections can be made, and formats can be varied, all without having to retype a page. The document is stored in a file on the disk, and a copy of the document can be printed out at any time. Revisions can be made to the document, and it can be printed out again. Word processing can be useful for tasks ranging from one-page letters to long documents. For anyone who writes, word processing makes the task far easier and more convenient.

PC-Write is a surprisingly powerful word processor. Virtually all commands are entered with single keystrokes or keystroke combinations. The most amazing feature of PC-Write is its speed. Enter most commands, and the task is completed almost instantaneously. PC-Write operates more quickly than many commercial word processing programs costing hundreds of dollars. The files created by PC-Write are in a standard format, making the interchange of information with other programs very easy.

PC-Write is not without limitations. The length of documents is limited by the requirement that they be contained in the memory of the computer while editing. PC-Write does not include a spelling checker, a very handy feature. Documents can be checked with a variety of separate spell-checking programs, however. PC-Write does not provide every exotic formatting feature found in the most expensive word processing programs. On balance, however, PC-Write is an excellent program. A person might well choose to use PC-Write even if he or she could afford a far more expensive program.

The power, flexibility, and responsiveness of PC-Write come at a price. Learning to use the program effectively takes some time and effort. Commands are entered with keystrokes. PC-Write makes use of virtually every key on the keyboard, and most of the two-key combinations, to perform its tasks. The number of commands can seem overwhelming to a beginning user. Help screens can be used to jog one's memory, however, and the newest version includes some limited menus as well.

The key to learning to use PC-Write is to take things a step at a time. Only a small number of commands need be learned to begin entering, editing, and printing documents. As you continue to use the program, you will acquire more commands that provide access to additional features and to quicker ways of accomplishing the standard tasks. Learn these gradually, as you use the program.

This chapter begins with an introduction to the basic operation of PC-Write, going through the process of entering and editing text and printing out the document. This takes you through the first level, giving the fundamentals needed to begin word processing. The following sections of the chapter take you to the second level, providing more details on the various facets of the program. You can go straight through, learning each aspect of PC-Write, or you can refer to these sections as you come across tasks that require the advanced capabilities. Even these sections cannot cover every feature of operation of this powerful and complex program. The PC-Write reference manual provides the information for the third level of learning about the remaining details of the program.

This chapter uses version 2.6 of PC-Write, released in 1986. This version represents a substantial improvement in the program. Many new features were added. Automatic paragraph reformatting will be the most obvious enhancement for the casual user. The help menus have been greatly expanded, and a limited menu capability has been added. The documentation has been vastly improved. The improvements definitely make it worthwhile to register the program and obtain the latest version.

Nevertheless, the basic operation of PC-Write has remained consistent from one version to the next. Most of the instruction provided in this chapter is equally applicable to older versions of the program, including the widely distributed version 2.4.

BASIC OPERATIONS: GETTING STARTED

This section introduces PC-Write, covering the basic operations needed to start using the program for word processing. Upon finishing this section, you will be able to create a document and enter text, edit the document to make changes and corrections, and print out the document. With this knowledge of the fundamentals, you will be able to begin using PC-Write for actual word processing.

Creating a Document

Insert a working copy of the PC-Write program disk in the A: drive and a blank, formatted disk for the storage of document files in the B: drive. Turn on the computer; DOS should load, and you can enter the date and time. (If the computer is already on and you have the DOS A> prompt displayed on the screen, you can skip this step.) PC-Write is started by entering ED (for editor) followed by the name of the file you wish to edit. If you are creating a new document, enter a file name for the new document. The file name can be any valid DOS file name, with up to eight characters optionally followed by a period and a three-character extension. To have the file stored on the disk in the B: drive, prefix the file name with that drive identifier. Begin by creating your first document, to be named FIRST.DOC, on the B: drive, by entering the following command:

```
ED B:FIRST.DOC<Return>
```

The PC-Write editing program is loaded and the title screen is displayed. At the top of the screen is the message "File not found," which indicates that no file by that name was located on the B: drive. This is what you want—you are creating a new document. On the other hand, were you attempting to edit an existing file, this message would indicate a problem. Either the file was not on the disk in the B: drive, or perhaps you misspelled the file name. Pressing the Escape key would provide the opportunity to retype the file name.

In this case, you want to create a new file. The final prompt on the top line indicates that you must press F9 (function key 9) to create the file. Press F9, and you are presented with the PC-Write display for editing documents, shown in Fig. 4-1. The line across the top of the screen is the status line, providing information on the current operation of PC-Write. The remainder of the screen is the area

```
Esc:MenuPush Reform-. 99% Free.  0% Thru. Read "B:FIRST.DOC"
_
```

Fig. 4-1. Initial PC-Write display for the entry of a new document.

in which text is entered and displayed as you use the word processor. The cursor, a blinking underline, appears on the far left hand side of the second line. The cursor indicates where text will be entered.

A few of the entries on the status line will be explained now so the information does not appear completely foreign. On the far right is the message

```
Read "B:FIRST.DOC"
```

This tells you that the name of the file being edited is B:FIRST.DOC, and that the file has just been read from the disk. Since this is a new file, there was actually nothing to read, which is why the screen is empty. As soon as a single character is entered or changed, the message will change to

```
Edit "B:FIRST.DOC"
```

This means that the file has been modified since it has last been read from the disk. It is also a warning that you will have to save the document if you wish to permanently retain those changes.

The entry to the left on the status lines describes memory usage and the current position in the file. Right now, this entry reads

```
99% Free.  0% Thru.
```

This means that 99 percent of the memory available for the creation of a PC-Write document is empty. (It is actually 100 percent right now, but the maximum value displayed is 99 percent.) As text is entered, some of that memory is used to store the document, and the amount of free memory is reduced. As the amount of memory free approaches zero percent, memory is filled, and you are reaching the limit of the size of the document that can be edited by PC-Write. The second value, 0% Thru, indicates the relative position of the cursor in the current document. With no text, the indication is meaningless, but when you are moving around in a long document, this provides a useful indicator of your relative position. For example, an indication of 33% Thru tells you that the cursor is approximately one-third of the way into the document. The other entries on the status line will be discussed later, when these entries become relevant to a feature being used.

Now begin typing in text. You can type in the text used in the example shown in Fig. 4-2, or you can type in your own text. It will be easy enough to use your own text to practice the editing described below. If you make a mistake while entering the text, you can use the backspace key to move the cursor back and erase the preceding letter. The backspace key can be pressed as many times as needed, moving back and erasing as many characters as necessary. Do not worry too much about errors now, however, as you will have the opportunity to go back and edit the document, making as many corrections as needed. In fact, most users of word processors enter text as fast as they can type, not worrying about errors at all. It is faster to keep on going and make all of the corrections later.

The major difference between using a typewriter and a word processor is that you do not press the Return key at the end of the line. Just keep typing. When more text has been entered than will fit on a line, the extra word will be quickly moved down to the start of the next line and text entry will continue there. This feature of word processing programs is called *word-wrap;* the words of text wrap around to the next line automatically.

Press the Return key twice at the ends of paragraphs. This will indicate the start of a new paragraph and place a blank line between the two

```
Esc:MenuPush Reform-. 96% Free.  0% Thru. Edit "B:FIRST.DOC"
PC-WRITE is a word processor that is low in cost and is easy to use.  PC-WRITE
combines a fast editor with extensive capabilities for formatting documents in
a variety of ways.  Most personal computers users find this program has all
the features they could want in a word processor.

PC-WRITE has fine formatting capabilities that allow documents to be printed
with different fonts and enhanced text, making maximum use of the features of
most printers.  Text can be readily positioned anywhere on the page.  Multiple
line headers and footers can be printed.  PC-WRITE supports more different
printers than most other word processing programs.

The PC-WRITE editor has a wide seliction of commands for moving the cursor and
for inserting and deleting text.  Features of the editor include block
operations for copying, moving, and deleting text, and good search and replace
capabilities.  The latest version of PC-WRITE includes automatic reformatting
of paragraphs as text is inserted and deleted, a welcome addition.

PC-WRITE can merge data files with documents.  A typical application would be
the production of form letters.  The merge procedure in PC-WRITE is one of the
most flexible of all word processors in terms of the types of data files that
can be used.  This flexibility allows PC-WRITE to be used as a flexible report
generator for many data base programs.

With the tremendous variety of features, nearly all invoked by keyboard
```

Fig. 4-2. Text entered into the document FIRST.DOC.

paragraphs. For now, accept this as a reasonable format. Methods for producing different paragraph formats will be discussed later.

Several paragraphs of text will be sufficient to explore the editing capabilities of PC-Write. Common sense says you should not entrust a long piece of original work—say the first chapter of your novel—to the computer on your first attempt. Practice a little first.

Even though the current document is just for experimentation, now is the time to develop good habits to protect your work. As you enter text or otherwise edit documents, the changes that are made are stored only in the memory of the computer. If the power goes out for an instant, if you forget and turn off the computer, or if you make some other mistake, the information can be lost. A good practice is to regularly save the document on the disk. In that way, if disaster strikes, you will only lose the information entered or changes made since your last save. Saving the document on the disk is easy: Press F1 and then F3. When you press F1, a menu of choices appears across the top of the screen. If you use the cursor control key to move the highlighted box over to F3.Save, a description of this function appears on the second line, as shown in Fig. 4-3. (You do not have to move the highlighted box over here in order to save the document, however.) After pressing F1 to get this menu, you can press F3 to save the document on the disk.

You are returned to your document. The message on the right end of the status line has changed from Edit to Read, indicating that the document being displayed is currently identical to the file on the disk. As soon as you enter a single character or make any other change to the document, the message again changes back to Edit.

Enter another sentence or two of text for good measure. It would be possible to immediately begin the editing of the text, but you will need to learn how to finish an editing session with PC-Write sooner or later. The sequence F1, F2 saves the document if necessary and exits PC-Write, returning to the DOS prompt. Pressing F1 brings up the same menu as before. When you move the highlighted area to F2.Quit, you receive the message that this command will save the document if it has been changed since the last save and then exit from the program to DOS. Pressing F2 does the save and exit. The file FIRST.DOC is stored on the disk in the B: drive, which you can confirm by typing DIR B: and pressing Return. Since PC-Write files are standard text files, you can even examine the contents of the file by using the TYPE command. Enter this command,

TYPE B:FIRST.DOC <Return>

and the document you have just created will be displayed on the screen.

Editing the Document

The next step is the editing of the new document, making any changes, insertions, or deletions required. Begin by restarting PC-Write, telling it to edit the document with the file name FIRST.DOC in the B: drive. Again, start the editing program with this command:

ED B:FIRST.DOC <Return>

This time, PC-Write is being instructed to read in an existing document for further editing. You first see the message that the program is reading B:FIRST.DOC. The title screen appears with a new set of options on the top line. Pressing the Escape key will take you directly into the editor, while pressing function key F9 first makes a backup copy of the file. Each time you enter an existing file, PC-Write allows you to create a backup copy that has the same name as the file except for an & (amper-

```
Esc F1:Help F2.Exit F3.Save F4.Command F5:Name F6:File F7:Print F8:Dir F9:Unsave
Save text to disk (even if not changed), then continue editing
combines a fast editor with extensive capabilities for formatting documents in
a variety of ways.  Most personal computers users find this program has all
the features they could want in a word processor.

PC-WRITE has fine formatting capabilities that allow documents to be printed
with different fonts and enhanced text, making maximum use of the features of
most printers.  Text can be readily positioned anywhere on the page.  Multiple
line headers and footers can be printed.  PC-WRITE supports more different
printers than most other word processing programs.

The PC-WRITE editor has a wide seliction of commands for moving the cursor and
for inserting and deleting text.  Features of the editor include block
operations for copying, moving, and deleting text, and good search and replace
capabilities.  The latest version of PC-WRITE includes automatic reformatting
of paragraphs as text is inserted and deleted, a welcome addition.

PC-WRITE can merge data files with documents.  A typical application would be
the production of form letters.  The merge procedure in PC-WRITE is one of the
most flexible of all word processors in terms of the types of data files that
can be used.  This flexibility allows PC-WRITE to be used as a flexible report
generator for many data base programs.

With the tremendous variety of features, nearly all invoked by keyboard
```

Fig. 4-3. Saving FIRST.DOC on the disk.

sand) before the first two letters of the extension. The backup file for FIRST.DOC will be FIRST.&DO. This is for protection in case the original copy somehow gets damaged or in case you just want to go back and start over. Unless disk space is at a premium, it is a sensible precaution to make these backup copies, so press F9. The backup file is written to the disk, and the beginning of the text of the file FIRST.DOC is displayed on the screen with the status line at the top. You are ready to begin editing.

The cursor can be moved around the screen by using the four arrow keys. Press the right arrow once to move the cursor over one space. Hold the key down and it repeats, moving the cursor a longer distance. Press the down arrow and the cursor moves down. If the document is longer than a single screen, pressing the down arrow after the cursor has moved to the bottom of the screen moves the cursor down through the document, scrolling the text upwards on the screen.

First correct the spelling error in the word "selection" on the first line of the third paragraph by changing the first letter i to e. Move the cursor to the letter c, the letter following the one you wish to change. Press the backspace key to move the cursor back to delete the letter. Notice that the remainder of the text on the line moves over to the left as the character is deleted. The cursor is in the space where the character was deleted, which is now occupied by the following character. Now press the e key to enter the correct letter. The letter is inserted at the location of the cursor, and the remaining text on the line has been pushed back over to the right. The word is now correct.

Now try inserting a word into the text, adding the word "powerful" before "word processor" on the first line of the text. Move the cursor to the first letter in "word," the word following the location where the insertion is to be made. With the cursor

```
Esc:MenuPush Reform-. 96% Free.  1% Thru. Edit "B:FIRST.DOC"
PC-WRITE is a powerful word processor that is low in cost and is easy to use.  P
combines a fast editor with extensive capabilities for formatting documents in
a variety of ways.  Most personal computers users find this program has all
the features they could want in a word processor.

PC-WRITE has fine formatting capabilities that allow documents to be printed
with different fonts and enhanced text, making maximum use of the features of
most printers.  Text can be readily positioned anywhere on the page.  Multiple
line headers and footers can be printed.  PC-WRITE supports more different
printers than most other word processing programs.

The PC-WRITE editor has a wide selection of commands for moving the cursor and
for inserting and deleting text.  Features of the editor include block
operations for copying, moving, and deleting text, and good search and replace
capabilities.  The latest version of PC-WRITE includes automatic reformatting
of paragraphs as text is inserted and deleted, a welcome addition.

PC-WRITE can merge data files with documents.  A typical application would be
the production of form letters.  The merge procedure in PC-WRITE is one of the
most flexible of all word processors in terms of the types of data files that
can be used.  This flexibility allows PC-WRITE to be used as a flexible report
generator for many data base programs.

With the tremendous variety of features, nearly all invoked by keyboard
```

Fig. 4-4. Document after the insertion of the word "powerful" on the first line.

```
Esc:MenuPush Reform-. 96% Free.  1% Thru. Edit "B:FIRST.DOC"
PC-WRITE is a powerful word processor that is low in cost and is easy to use.
PC-WRITE combines a fast editor with extensive capabilities for formatting
documents in a variety of ways.  Most personal computers users find this
program has all the features they could want in a word processor.

PC-WRITE has fine formatting capabilities that allow documents to be printed
with different fonts and enhanced text, making maximum use of the features of
most printers.  Text can be readily positioned anywhere on the page.  Multiple
line headers and footers can be printed.  PC-WRITE supports more different
printers than most other word processing programs.

The PC-WRITE editor has a wide selection of commands for moving the cursor and
for inserting and deleting text.  Features of the editor include block
operations for copying, moving, and deleting text, and good search and replace
capabilities.  The latest version of PC-WRITE includes automatic reformatting
of paragraphs as text is inserted and deleted, a welcome addition.

PC-WRITE can merge data files with documents.  A typical application would be
the production of form letters.  The merge procedure in PC-WRITE is one of the
most flexible of all word processors in terms of the types of data files that
can be used.  This flexibility allows PC-WRITE to be used as a flexible report
generator for many data base programs.

With the tremendous variety of features, nearly all invoked by keyboard
```

Fig. 4-5. Results of reformatting the document after the insertion.

on the first letter of "word," type in the new word, "powerful," followed by a space. The word is properly inserted into the text and the remaining text on the line is pushed over to the right. The results are shown in Fig. 4-4.

There is only one problem. By inserting the word "powerful," the line was lengthened and the remaining text was pushed over, past the right margin and off the screen. PC-Write indicates that more text is contained on this line by highlighting the last character on the line, P. You can use the right arrow key to move over and examine this additional text, the word "PC-Write." As you do so, the entire display scrolls over to the left. All of the text is still there, but the format, or arrangement, of the text is certainly not the way you want it to be. To reformat the paragraph and rearrange the text so it is displayed within the margins, move the cursor to the beginning of the paragraph and press F7, the reformat key. The extra text is moved down to the next line, and further adjustments are made throughout the paragraph to complete the reformatting. The text now appears as shown in Fig. 4-5.

Many popular word processing programs require that the text be manually reformatted in this fashion, by issuing a separate command whenever insertions or deletions alter the arrangement of the text. The obvious question is, "Why can't the computer do this automatically?" With PC-Write, it can. Version 2.6 of PC-Write includes an automatic reformatting capability. It is just turned off when the program is started. The status line includes the entry Reformat –. The minus sign indicates that automatic reformatting is currently not in effect. To turn on automatic reformatting, press Shift-F7, holding down the Shift key and pressing function key F7. The minus sign changes to a plus; the entry on the status line reads Reformat +, indicating that automatic reformatting is now turned on.

To observe the automatic reformatting in operation, insert another word in the text, placing the word "program" after the word "editor" in the first line of the third paragraph. Move the cursor to the first letter of "has," and type in the word "program" plus a space. Notice how the final words on the line, "cursor" and "are," are automatically shifted down to the next line, and how further changes are made throughout the paragraph. With automatic reformatting, it is no longer necessary to issue the reformat command to shape up the paragraph.

Automatic reformatting also occurs when characters are deleted, making a line shorter. Delete the word "data" in the first line of the fourth paragraph. Move the cursor to the space following the word and press the backspace key five times. As the characters are deleted, the line is shortened, leaving space for additional text on the line. With the automatic reformatting, text from the following line is moved up to the end of this line automatically, and appropriate changes are made in the remainder of the paragraph.

For most documents, you will probably want to turn the automatic reformatting feature on as soon as you start working with the document. If automatic reformatting is so convenient, why should it ever be turned off? For text entered in complex formats, such as tables, automatic reformatting can wreak havoc. You may not want each line automatically filled with text. In such cases, the automatic reformatting feature should be turned off, and manual reformatting, using the F7 key, can be used when needed. To turn the automatic reformatting off, just press the Shift-F7 combination again. This command turns reformatting on if it is off, and turns it off if it is on. The status line will always show whether this feature is off or on.

The next step in the editing will be changing the word "fine" in the first line of the second paragraph to "good." The same procedure could be used as before: you could delete the word with the backspace key and then type in the new word, which will be inserted in the line. However, since the new word is exactly the same length as the old word, the new word could be typed in right over the top of the old. If you attempt this now, the new word is inserted in the line, and the old word is pushed over to the right. PC-Write is currently in its "Pushright" mode, which causes new characters to be inserted at the cursor while the existing text is pushed over to the right. Most programs refer to this as the *insert* mode. PC-File has an insert mode that can be selected, allowing text to be inserted on a line in this manner, while the remaining text is pushed over to the right. The word "Push" on the status line indicates that PC-Write is operating in the pushright, or insert, mode.

The alternative is to enter text in the "Overtype" mode, in which characters are inserted at the cursor and replace the current text. Any text that is typed "overtypes" the existing text. To shift to the overtype mode, press the scroll lock key once. The word "Push" on the status line is changed to "Over." The scroll lock key *toggles* between the pushright and overtype modes. Pressing scroll lock again shifts back to the pushright mode. The current status is always displayed on the top line.

With PC-Write in the overtype mode, move the cursor to the first letter in the word "fine," and simply type in the new word "good." The new text is placed on top of the old, replacing it.

Remaining in overtype mode, replace the word "good" with the word "excellent." Move the cursor to the beginning of the word and start typing. After typing the first four letters, "exce," you have replaced the old word, but you still have letters left to type. Continued typing would replace the first part of the next word. Press the Insert (Ins) key about eight times to insert spaces for the remaining letters. The Insert key inserts a space at the cursor and pushes the remaining text on the line over to the right, opening up a space on the line. The screen will appear as shown in Fig. 4-6, with the newly-opened space on the line. Now type in the remainder of the word. After finishing the typing of the word, several extra spaces remain where you did the insertion. To delete these spaces, press the Delete (Del) key three times. The Delete key deletes the character at the cursor and pulls the remainder of the line back to close up the space.

Think of the Insert and Delete keys as a pair, one inserting spaces at the cursor and pushing the remainder of the line over to the right, and the other deleting characters at the cursor and pulling the re-

```
Esc:MenuOver Reform+. 96% Free. 14% Thru. Edit "B:FIRST.DOC"
PC-WRITE is a powerful word processor that is low in cost and is easy to use.
PC-WRITE combines a fast editor with extensive capabilities for formatting
documents in a variety of ways.  Most personal computers users find this
program has all the features they could want in a word processor.

PC-WRITE has exce         formatting capabilities that allow documents to be
printed with different fonts and enhanced text, making maximum use of the
features of most printers.  Text can be readily positioned anywhere on the
page.  Multiple line headers and footers can be printed.  PC-WRITE supports
more different printers than most other word processing programs.

The PC-WRITE editor program has a wide selection of commands for moving the
cursor and for inserting and deleting text.  Features of the editor include
block operations for copying, moving, and deleting text, and good search and
replace capabilities.  The latest version of PC-WRITE includes automatic
reformatting of paragraphs as text is inserted and deleted, a welcome
addition.

PC-WRITE can merge files with documents.  A typical application would be the
production of form letters.  The merge procedure in PC-WRITE is one of the
most flexible of all word processors in terms of the types of data files that
can be used.  This flexibility allows PC-WRITE to be used as a flexible report
generator for many data base programs.
```

Fig. 4-6. Replacing the word "good" with "excellent" in the Overtype mode, using the insert key to open up spaces.

mainder of the line back to the left. Try it. With the cursor anywhere in the document, press Insert a number of times and a space is opened up. Pressing Delete the same number of times eliminates these spaces, closing up the hole that had been created.

The backspace key and the Delete key both erase a single character and close up the space. The difference is that the backspace key erases the character before the cursor, while the Delete key erases the character at the cursor.

Several options have been presented for performing the basic editing functions. Text can be entered in either the pushright (insert) or overtype modes. Insertions can be made by typing in the pushright mode or by using the Insert key. Characters can be erased with both the backspace key and the Delete key. The various options produce the same results. As you learn to use PC-Write, certain combinations will become more comfortable. Use whichever options make the editing easiest for you.

Continue to edit the document, making any changes you wish. With a little practice, these editing operations will become very easy and familiar. Editing the document on the screen is certainly easier than making the changes on paper and retyping the document.

Remember to save your document on the disk occasionally to record the changes you have made and protect against the loss of your work in the event of a problem. Pressing F1 and then F3 saves the document and returns you to PC-Write so you can continue editing.

Printing the Document

The final objective of word processing is the printing of a document on paper. With the current version of PC-Write, you can either print the document while you are editing it, or you can print the document from the DOS prompt after you have exited from the editor. Both operations will be described here.

To print the document while you are editing, press F1 and F7. Pressing F1 presents the two-line menu of your next options, shown earlier in Fig. 4-3. If you move the highlighted area to F7.Print, the message on the second line will inform you that this option saves the document if the text has been changed and then prints a file using the print program.

Pressing F7 changes the top line to ask for the name of the file to be printed. The name of the file you are currently editing is displayed. You can change this to print out any file, but the assumption is that you probably want to print the current file. Accept this by pressing Return. The top line now changes to present three more options. Escape allows you to change your mind, and F9 directs the output to a file on the disk. F10:Printer is ready, it is the option to print out the document on the printer. Be sure the printer is turned on and is ready, and press F10.

The main menu for the PC-Write printing program is now displayed on the screen. The commands assigned to the function keys are identified on the second and third lines from the top. The highlighted selection box is on F1, and the message on the fourth line provides additional information concerning this option. Use the cursor control keys to move the highlighted area over and down to F10.Continuous. This displays the message that this option starts continuous printing, which is the choice desired. The screen will now appear as shown in Fig. 4-7.

Press F10 to begin printing the document. The document will be printed out, and you will be returned to the editor to continue work. The printout of the sample document is shown in Fig. 4-8.

As the document is being printed, if you decide you wish to stop, press the Escape key. The list of your next choices will be displayed across the top

```
Waiting.   Print from "B:FIRST.DOC" to "PRN", ready to begin.
 F1.Help-screen  F3.Finished     F5:Input-end     F7:Repeat-pages F9.Page-stop
 F2.Exit-to-DOS  F4.DOS-command  F6:User-input    F8:Skip-pages   F10.Continuous
Start continuous printing of all pages (stop if Esc pressed)

 These keys are active when printing has been stopped for a command:
   F1: Show help screen with Dot lines and font characters.
   F2: Exit to DOS, even if printing was started from edit program.
   F3: Exit to DOS or back to edit program, whichever one started printing.
   F4: Stay resident, but do a DOS command shell until DOS "exit" command.
   F5: Force end of current input file (if last input file, end printing).
   F6: Enter input text or Guide lines (like .U, enter lines typed by user).
   F7: Repeat a page then stop, or repeat each page to print multiple copies.
   F8: Skip pages then stop, or skip pages each time to print every Nth page.
   F9: Print one page, then stop for another one of these commands.
   F10:Start continuous printing of pages (but stop if Esc key pressed).
 These keys are active when you are entering text on the Top Line:
   Esc key: no more user input lines (end input file).
   Enter (Return key): finish this line, enter another.
   Left/right Arrows: move cursor left or right one character.
   Home/End keys: move cursor to the beginning or end of the line.
   Bksp/Del keys: delete one character on the left or the right.
   Ins key: insert one space pushing the rest of the line right.
   Scroll Lock: toggle between Pushright and Overwrite typing mode.
```

Fig. 4-7. Main menu for the PC-Write printing program.

PC-WRITE is a powerful word processor that is low in cost and is easy to use. PC-WRITE combines a fast editor with extensive capabilities for formatting documents in a variety of ways. Most personal computers users find this program has all the features they could want in a word processor.

PC-WRITE has excellent formatting capabilities that allow documents to be printed with different fonts and enhanced text, making maximum use of the features of most printers. Text can be readily positioned anywhere on the page. Multiple line headers and footers can be printed. PC-WRITE supports more different printers than most other word processing programs.

The PC-WRITE editor program has a wide selection of commands for moving the cursor and for inserting and deleting text. Features of the editor include block operations for copying, moving, and deleting text, and good search and replace capabilities. The latest version of PC-WRITE includes automatic reformatting of paragraphs as text is inserted and deleted, a welcome addition.

PC-WRITE can merge files with documents. A typical application would be the production of form letters. The merge procedure in PC-WRITE is one of the most flexible of all word processors in terms of the types of data files that can be used. This flexibility allows PC-WRITE to be used as a flexible report generator for many data base programs.

With the tremendous variety of features, nearly all invoked by keyboard commands, learning to use PC-WRITE effectively takes some time. However, novices can learn the fundamentals required to do useful work with the program with only brief instruction. The more elaborate features of the program can then be learned gradually as they are needed. The key to getting started is not to be intimidated by the program. Do not panic at the large numbers of commands in the manual, on the quick reference card, or on the help screens. You will never have to learn all of the commands if you do not wish to. PC-WRITE provides options. Learning to use the program involves learning which of these options are best for you.

Fig. 4-8. Printout of FIRST.DOC.

of the screen: Escape to stop at once, F9 to finish printing the current page first, and F10 to continue printing. When you choose to stop, the menu of printing options is again displayed. Pressing F3 returns you to the editing program.

Alternatively, you can print out the document from the DOS A> prompt after exiting the editor. PC-Write prints out all documents using a separate printer program named PR. In the printing procedure described above, you were using this program from within the editor. To print out a document from DOS, enter PR followed by the file name. For the example, enter the following at the DOS A> prompt:

```
PR B:FIRST.DOC<Return>
```

Then follow exactly the same procedure as before. The first prompt provides the options to exit (Escape), print to a file on the disk (F9), and print to the printer (F10). Get the printer ready and press F10. The main menu for the PC-Write printing program is displayed, as illustrated earlier in Fig. 4-7. Press F10 to begin continuous printing and print out the document. When printing is completed, you are returned to the DOS prompt rather than to the editor.

Earlier versions of PC-Write do not allow the printing of documents while they are being edited. The printing program must be used from the DOS prompt. The printing menu is also different, though the major functions are the same.

This section has taken you through the entire cycle of creating, editing, and printing a document using PC-Write. The basic techniques required to begin word processing have been covered. The commands described in this section are summarized in Table 4-1.

ADVANCED EDITING PROCEDURES

Once the basic operations of PC-Write have been learned, increasing your capabilities involves learning how to use new features. The new features allow you to perform operations more efficiently and to accomplish new tasks not possible with the basic operations. This section describes additional features that can be used in editing documents with PC-Write. Each part is self-contained. You can use the information on block operations, for example, without reading the earlier parts.

Cursor Movement

The four arrow keys allow you to move the cursor to any location in a file. Making long moves with the arrow keys, especially in a long document, can be very time consuming. PC-Write includes a very large number of commands for moving the cursor

Table 4-1. Basic PC-Write Operations.

Function	Command
Begin editing document (from DOS)	ED filename
Save document and continue editing	F1 F3
Finish editing	F1 F2
Print document while editing	F1 F7
Print document from DOS	PR filename
Shift between pushright and overwrite text entry modes	Scroll lock
Shift between manual and automatic reformatting	Shift-F7
Reformat paragraph (manual reformatting)	F7
Delete character to left of cursor	Backspace
Delete character at cursor	Delete
Insert space at cursor	Insert
Move cursor one space	Arrow keys

around more expeditiously. Few, if any, users should attempt to learn every one of these commands. A basic set of cursor movement commands will allow you to move around in longer documents quickly and easily.

Most of the cursor movement commands use the keys on the cursor control keypad, often in combination with other keys. You have already used the arrow keys to move around the file a character or line at a time. To move the cursor to the beginning of a line, press the Home key, and to move the cursor to the end of the line, press the End key. These are fairly intuitive and speed the movement of the cursor back and forth on a line.

The cursor can be moved to the edge of the screen—top, bottom, left, and right—by using the four arrows in conjunction with the Shift key. Hold down the Shift key and press the up arrow. The cursor will jump to the top of the screen. These commands are relatively easy to remember. The arrow keys alone move the cursor one position. With the Shift key, the arrow keys move the cursor to the edge of the screen.

With longer documents, you will often wish to scroll through the document to examine different portions. The Page Up (PgUp) and Page Down (PgDn) keys scroll the document up or down one line at a time. Page Down moves *down* the page of the document, so the text scrolls *up* on the screen. Some people find this counter-intuitive, but this is hardly a problem. If pressing one of the keys moves the document in the wrong direction, press the other.

To scroll the text a screenful at a time, use the Shift key in conjunction with the Page Up and Page Down keys. Shift-Page Down displays the next screenful of text in the document, and Shift-Page Up displays the preceding screenful. The Shift key works here as it does with the arrow keys. By themselves, the arrow keys and the Page Up and Page Down keys move a single line at a time. The Shift key extends the range of all of these cursor control keys, causing screen-sized moves.

In longer documents, it is often handy to be able to jump to the beginning or the end of the text. To jump to the beginning of the file, hold down the Shift key and press the plus key on the far right-hand side of the keyboard, next to the cursor control keys. PC-Write refers to this key as Grey+, because these keys are a darker shade of grey on the IBM PC keyboard. The plus sign on the top row of the keyboard is a distinct key and will not work with this command. Shift-Grey–, using the minus key on the right-hand side of the keyboard moves the cursor to the end of the document.

While moving through a longer document, you may wish to find out just where the cursor is located in the file. Press Shift-F9, and the top line changes to display the location of the cursor. This line indicates the line on which the cursor is located, out of the total number of lines in the document. It also displays the column in which the cursor is located on the line, the number of the line on the current page, and the current page number, out of the total number of pages in the document. As soon as you begin typing or otherwise editing the text, the cursor position line disappears and is replaced by the status line.

This cursor location feature can be taken one step further, allowing a jump to any specified position in the document. Press Alternate-F9 (hold down the Alternate key and press F9) and a similar cursor location line appears at the top of the screen, as shown in Fig. 4-9. Displayed on this line are not only the cursor location indications but also the function key prompts allowing changes to be made to any of these to set up a cursor jump. In Fig. 4-9, the cursor is currently located on line six of the document, out of a total of 35 lines. To move the cursor to another line, say line 19, press F7. You can now type the number of the line desired over the old line. When you have done this, pressing Return will jump the cursor to that line. In a similar manner, you can jump to a particular column by pressing F8 and entering the column number. F9 allows you to change the line on the page, and F10 allows you to change the page. Used in succession, you can specify a line on a particular page to jump to. In each case, pressing Return causes the jump to be made, moving the cursor to the location specified. You are then returned to the editing mode, with the status line at the top of the screen.

```
F7:Line 6/35 in file.  F8:Column 1/74.  F9:Line 6/35 on F10:Page 1/1
PC-WRITE is a powerful word processor that is low in cost and is easy to use.
PC-WRITE combines a fast editor with extensive capabilities for formatting
documents in a variety of ways.  Most personal computers users find this
program has all the features they could want in a word processor.

PC-WRITE has excellent formatting capabilities that allow documents to be
printed with different fonts and enhanced text, making maximum use of the
features of most printers.  Text can be readily positioned anywhere on the
page.  Multiple line headers and footers can be printed.  PC-WRITE supports
more different printers than most other word processing programs.

The PC-WRITE editor program has a wide selection of commands for moving the
cursor and for inserting and deleting text.  Features of the editor include
block operations for copying, moving, and deleting text, and good search and
replace capabilities.  The latest version of PC-WRITE includes automatic
reformatting of paragraphs as text is inserted and deleted, a welcome
addition.

PC-WRITE can merge files with documents.  A typical application would be the
production of form letters.  The merge procedure in PC-WRITE is one of the
most flexible of all word processors in terms of the types of data files that
can be used.  This flexibility allows PC-WRITE to be used as a flexible report
generator for many data base programs.
```

Fig. 4-9. Menu for moving the cursor to a specified position.

The cursor movement, location, and scrolling commands covered here are summarized in Table 4-2. These should be sufficient for most users of PC-Write. A large number of additional cursor movement commands are available. You can move through the document word by word, sentence by sentence, and paragraph by paragraph. The PC-Write documentation provides complete information on all of the possible ways to move around through a document. Pick the commands that make the most sense—the ones that are easiest for you to learn and use. Few users of PC-Write will use all of the many commands.

Deleting Text

The backspace and Delete keys allow text to be erased from the document a character at a time. With patience, these can be used to delete anything. In many instances, however, commands to make deletions in larger units are very useful.

Many times you will want to delete an entire word. PC-Write includes two commands for deleting words. Like backspace and Delete, they work in different directions from the cursor. Control-Backspace deletes all characters in the word to the left of the cursor (like backspace, it works to the left). Control-Escape deletes all characters in a word from the location of the cursor to the right. If the cursor is located on the space between two words, Control-Backspace deletes the entire word to the left. Control-Escape only deletes the space.

To delete an entire line of text, use Shift-Control-Return. Hold down both the Shift and Control keys—using the Shift key on the left, below the Control key, is easier—and press Return. The entire line on which the cursor is located is deleted. To delete only the text on a line from the position of the cursor to the end of the line, use Control-Return.

Be careful when using the deletion commands, especially those that delete a substantial amount of text. You may find that you have made a mistake

Table 4-2. Cursor Movement Commands.

Function	Command
Move one character or one line	Arrow keys
Move to beginning or end of line	Home, End
Move to edges of screen	Shift-Arrow keys
Scroll one line up or down	PageUp, PageDown
Scroll one screen up or down	Shift-PageUp, PageDown
Move to beginning or end of file	Shift-Grey +, Grey –
Cursor location	Shift-F9
Jump to location	Alternate-F9

and really did not want the text deleted. For the word and line delete operations, PC-Write provides an undelete command, sometimes referred to as an "oops" command. If you have deleted a word or line and wish to restore it, press Control-F4. The deleted text is moved back into the document at the location of the cursor. The text will be marked, or highlighted. Press F5 to remove this marking.

A summary of the text deletion commands described here is provided in Table 4-3. For deleting larger quantities of text, PC-Write has a block deletion operation. Since that works like the other block operations, it is described in that section, below. Further information is also provided there on the undelete function, which is closely related to block deletion.

Block Operations

PC-Write provides direct methods for copying, moving, and deleting blocks of text very easily. All of these block operations work in a similar fashion, using the concept of *marking* a block of text on the screen and then performing the operation with the *marked* block of text. If you understand these ideas, block copy, move, and delete operations will be simple.

Begin by using the block move operation to move the second paragraph in the sample text FIRST.DOC after the third paragraph. Move the cursor to the beginning of the paragraph to be moved, and press F6 to start the block move operation. The first character is highlighted, and the status line displays the message "Marking." This means that you are in the middle of the process of marking a block of text for a subsequent block operation. The screen will appear as shown in Fig. 4-10.

Begin moving the cursor down towards the end of the paragraph by pressing the down arrow. As

Function	Command
Delete character	
To left of cursor	Backspace
At cursor	Delete
Delete word	
To left of cursor	Control-Backspace
From cursor to right	Control-Escape
Delete line	
Entire line	Shift-Control-Return
From cursor to end of line	Control-Return
Undeleting words, lines	Control-F4

Table 4-3. Text Deletion Commands.

```
Esc:MenuPush Marking. 96% Free. 14% Thru. Read "B:FIRST.DOC"
PC-WRITE is a powerful word processor that is low in cost and is easy to use.
PC-WRITE combines a fast editor with extensive capabilities for formatting
documents in a variety of ways.  Most personal computers users find this
program has all the features they could want in a word processor.

PC-WRITE has excellent formatting capabilities that allow documents to be
printed with different fonts and enhanced text, making maximum use of the
features of most printers.  Text can be readily positioned anywhere on the
page.  Multiple line headers and footers can be printed.  PC-WRITE supports
more different printers than most other word processing programs.

The PC-WRITE editor program has a wide selection of commands for moving the
cursor and for inserting and deleting text.  Features of the editor include
block operations for copying, moving, and deleting text, and good search and
replace capabilities.  The latest version of PC-WRITE includes automatic
reformatting of paragraphs as text is inserted and deleted, a welcome
addition.

PC-WRITE can merge files with documents.  A typical application would be the
production of form letters.  The merge procedure in PC-WRITE is one of the
most flexible of all word processors in terms of the types of data files that
can be used.  This flexibility allows PC-WRITE to be used as a flexible report
generator for many data base programs.
```

Fig. 4-10. Beginning of the marking of a block of text for a block move.

you move down, you see the text being highlighted between the current location of the cursor and the point where the marking began. This highlighted area indicates the area you are currently marking. The cursor can be moved around anywhere in the document, changing the area you are marking. To mark the paragraph for moving, move the cursor down to the end of the paragraph, locating the cursor at the beginning of the first line of the following paragraph, on the T. Press F6 again to conclude the marking. The nature of the text highlighting may change, depending upon your video display. The message on the status line will change from "Marking" to "MARKED." The marking process is complete. You now have a marked block of text ready for a block operation. The screen will appear as shown in Fig. 4-11.

The move operation will remove the marked block—the paragraph—from its current location and insert the block in a new location in the document. The location of the insertion is indicated by the position of the cursor. Move the cursor to the beginning of the fourth paragraph, placing the cursor over the first character on the line, on the P. Press F6 one more time to move the block. The paragraph will disappear from its original location and will be inserted at the new location after what had been the third paragraph. The move operation is completed. Move the cursor to the beginning of the document using Shift-Grey+, and the document will appear as shown in Fig. 4-12. One minor step remains: to unmark the marked block, press F5.

Copying works in the same manner as moving, except that the marked block is not removed from its original location. Rather, a second copy of the marked block is inserted at the location of the cursor in the final step. To copy a block, move the cursor to the beginning of the block and press F3 to begin marking. Move the cursor to the end of the block, and press F3 again to freeze the marking, giving a marked block. Move the cursor to the location where the copy is to be inserted, and press

```
Esc:MenuPush MARKED.  96% Free. 32% Thru. Read "B:FIRST.DOC"
PC-WRITE is a powerful word processor that is low in cost and is easy to use.
PC-WRITE combines a fast editor with extensive capabilities for formatting
documents in a variety of ways.  Most personal computers users find this
program has all the features they could want in a word processor.

PC-WRITE has excellent formatting capabilities that allow documents to be
printed with different fonts and enhanced text, making maximum use of the
features of most printers.  Text can be readily positioned anywhere on the
page.  Multiple line headers and footers can be printed.  PC-WRITE supports
more different printers than most other word processing programs.

The PC-WRITE editor program has a wide selection of commands for moving the
cursor and for inserting and deleting text.  Features of the editor include
block operations for copying, moving, and deleting text, and good search and
replace capabilities.  The latest version of PC-WRITE includes automatic
reformatting of paragraphs as text is inserted and deleted, a welcome
addition.

PC-WRITE can merge files with documents.  A typical application would be the
production of form letters.  The merge procedure in PC-WRITE is one of the
most flexible of all word processors in terms of the types of data files that
can be used.  This flexibility allows PC-WRITE to be used as a flexible report
generator for many data base programs.
```

Fig. 4-11. Marked block of text highlighted for a block move.

F3 a third time. The copying is complete. Press F5 to unmark the block.

Deleting a block of text is similar, but it includes one less step because the deleted block is not moved or copied to any location in the document. Move the cursor to the beginning of the block, and press F4 to begin marking. Move the cursor to the end of the block to be deleted. Pressing F4 not only marks the block; it immediately deletes it. The text you were marking disappears.

If you made a mistake or change your mind about the deletion, you can breathe a sigh of relief. The block of deleted text has not disappeared, it has been temporarily placed in a buffer. A special command, Control-F4, exists to undelete the last deletion. This command takes the text in the buffer and inserts it at the location of the cursor. Magically, the deleted text reappears.

The deleted text can be recalled as long as it remains in the buffer, and the text remains in the buffer until another operation places text into the buffer, replacing it. When words and lines are deleted with the commands described above, the deletions are also placed in the buffer, and the same Control-F4 undeleted command serves to bring these back. Do not leave text in the buffer, waiting to replace it later. It is too easy to forget and perform another operation that replaces that text. Then you really have lost it.

Certain other PC-Write operations, such as reformatting, make use of marked blocks of text as well. To mark a block of text for any other purposes, you can use either the block move or block copy marking commands; they are equivalent. Press F3 (or F6) to begin marking the block, and press F3 (or F6) again to finish the marking. The product will be a MARKED block displayed on the screen. Just do not give the third command to actually copy or move the block. To mark the entire document, which is occasionally useful, use Control-F5. The usual unmarking command, F5, unmarks these blocks as readily as any others. The com-

```
Esc:MenuPush MARKED.  96% Free.  0% Thru. Edit "B:FIRST.DOC"
PC-WRITE is a powerful word processor that is low in cost and is easy to use.
PC-WRITE combines a fast editor with extensive capabilities for formatting
documents in a variety of ways.  Most personal computers users find this
program has all the features they could want in a word processor.

The PC-WRITE editor program has a wide selection of commands for moving the
cursor and for inserting and deleting text.  Features of the editor include
block operations for copying, moving, and deleting text, and good search and
replace capabilities.  The latest version of PC-WRITE includes automatic
reformatting of paragraphs as text is inserted and deleted, a welcome
addition.

PC-WRITE has excellent formatting capabilities that allow documents to be
printed with different fonts and enhanced text, making maximum use of the
features of most printers.  Text can be readily positioned anywhere on the
page.  Multiple line headers and footers can be printed.  PC-WRITE supports
more different printers than most other word processing programs.

PC-WRITE can merge files with documents.  A typical application would be the
production of form letters.  The merge procedure in PC-WRITE is one of the
most flexible of all word processors in terms of the types of data files that
can be used.  This flexibility allows PC-WRITE to be used as a flexible report
generator for many data base programs.
```

Fig. 4-12. Paragraph moved using the block move commands.

mands for block operations covered here are summarized in Table 4-4.

Table 4-4. Block Operation Commands.

Function	Command
Copy block	
Begin marking	F3
End marking	F3
Copy	F3
Move block	
Begin marking	F6
End marking	F6
Move	F6
Delete block	
Begin marking	F4
End marking, delete block	F4
Insert deleted block	Control-F4
Unmark block	F5
Mark entire document	Control-F5

Margins and the Ruler Line

In the basic example describing the use of PC-Write, the lengths of the lines of text, the margins, and the format of the text of the lines were taken as given. Most often, however, you will want wider margins on the page and shorter lines of text than the default settings of PC-Write provide. Fully justified text might be preferred to a ragged right margin. PC-Write allows control over how the text is displayed on the screen and printed out through the use of a feature called the *ruler line.*

Begin a new document with the file name SECOND.DOC. Prior to entering any text, the margins and justification options will be changed by modifying the ruler line. Press F2, and the ruler line appears on the screen, as shown in Fig. 4-13. The ruler line displays the default settings for the margins and tab stops provided by PC-Write. The left

```
Esc F1:Help F2.Clear F3:To-file F4.Insert F5.Default F6:From-file Grey± Col:1
L---+---T1----+-T--2----T----3--T-+----4T---+---T5----+-T--6----T----7--T-+--R
```

Fig. 4-13. Ruler line showing the default settings.

margin, indicated by the L, is in column 1. The right margin is at column 79, as indicated by the R, which also specifies that the text is to be formatted ragged right—not justified. The locations of tab stops are indicated by the T's.

The print line on narrow-carriage printers is 80 columns wide when using the standard-sized letters. Moving the margins in 10 characters from each side, to columns 10 and 70, would provide nice wide margins. When the ruler line is displayed, the cursor is placed on the ruler line. The left and right arrow keys can be used to move it back and forth. Move the cursor to column 10. The current cursor column is indicated on the far right end of the menu line. Enter an L, for left margin. The original L in column 1 changes to a lowercase l, indicating that it was the previous left margin. Only the capital L affects the text. Suppose a five-space indent is required for paragraphs. Move the cursor to column 15 and enter a P, for paragraph margin. Now move the cursor over the column 70 to set the right margin. To cause the text to be justified to the right margin, enter a J. The ruler line should now appear as shown in Fig. 4-14.

This edited ruler line will now govern the formatting of text as it is entered for your document. Remove the ruler line by pressing F2 again. Now press Return and begin entering text. The text will be located inside the new margins, paragraphs will be indented after the carriage return indicating the end of the previous paragraph, and the text will be justified between the margins. Figure 4-15 shows the first three paragraphs of text entered into this document using the new ruler line.

When you edit a ruler line, the changed ruler line remains in effect for as long as you are editing the document. If you stop editing, the modified ruler line will be lost. When you come back to edit the document later, the default PC-Write ruler line will be used again. This would certainly be a nuisance; so PC-Write allows you to embed the ruler line in the document itself. The ruler line will be saved with the document. When you come back to the document to work on it later, this embedded ruler line will automatically be used. To embed the ruler line in the document being edited, move the cursor to the first line of the document. Press F2 to display the ruler line, F4 to embed the ruler line in the document on the line above the cursor, and F2 to hide the ruler line.

A similar procedure can be used to substitute the current, edited ruler line for the default ruler line used by PC-Write. F2 displays the ruler line, F3 changes the default ruler line in the control file used by PC-Write, and F2 hides the ruler line. If you do this, the new ruler line will be used every time a document is created or edited with PC-Write, unless the document has its own, different ruler line embedded within it.

The ruler line has a variety of options associated with it. In specifying the location of the right margin, using an R indicates that the text is to be formatted ragged right, allowing the lines to end at different locations. Using a J, as was done

```
Esc F1:Help F2.Clear F3:To-file F4.Insert F5.Default F6:From-file Grey± Col:71
l---+---TL----P-T--2----T----3--T-+----4T---+---T5----+-T--6----T----J--T-+--r
```

Fig. 4-14. Modified ruler line with wider margins, paragraph indent, and justification.

```
Esc:MenuPush Reform+. 98% Free.  0% Thru. Edit "B:SECOND.DOC"

          This ·is an example of text entered using ·the ·modified
     ruler line created for SECOND.DOC.  ·Note that the lines ·are
     shorter ·and that the paragraph is indented.  ··Also ·observe
     that the text is right-justified.
          When ·you ·press Return to indicate the start of ·a ·new
     paragraph, ··the cursor automatically moves to the ·paragraph
     indent position.  Paragraphs must begin with that indentation
     or the formatting of the text becomes confused.
          The ·right-justification of the text occurs either ·when
     text ·is manually reformatted or when automatic ·reformatting
     is turned on.  ·When the text is formatted in right-justified
     form, dots appear on the screen at the points where the extra
     spaces are inserted.  ·These dots can be "hidden" ·by ·giving
     the ·Alternate-Space command to hide all formatting commands.
     In any even, ·these dots will not appear when the document is
     printed.
```

Fig. 4-15. Text entered into SECOND.DOC using modified ruler line.

in editing the ruler line above, causes the line to be justified. Spaces are added between words so the lines end at the right margin. You can also have all lines centered by using a C, or flush right by using an F.

If you plan on indenting the first lines of paragraphs, be sure to use the paragraph margin indicator P. This will cause the cursor to automatically indent after you press Return to indicate the end of the previous paragraph. Do not use spacing or the tab key to indent paragraphs instead. In reformatting text, either manually or automatically, PC-Write must determine the end of the paragraphs. The program recognizes a new paragraph by finding a new line that begins at the paragraph margin or by finding a blank line caused by two carriage returns in a row. If such indications are not found, PC-Write would reformat the entire document into a single paragraph, which you undoubtedly do not want to happen.

If you are changing the margins on a document after it has been created, special ruler line options can be used so that the original text will be reformatted to the new margins. In addition to the L and P for the new left and paragraph margins, enter M and Q at the locations of the old left and paragraph margins, respectively. These tell PC-Write that text beginning at these old margins should be reformatted to the new margins. Any other text in the document is not reformatted.

This procedure will be followed to change the margins for the original document, FIRST.DOC. Begin editing B:FIRST.DOC. With the cursor at the top of the document, press F2 to display the ruler line. Type an M in column one to indicate the old left margin. Type L in column 10 for the new left margin. Type R in column 70 for the new, ragged right margin. After the ruler line has been properly edited, press F4 to insert the new ruler line into the document. Then press F2 to hide the ruler line. Move the cursor up. The new, embedded ruler line is now displayed as what PC-Write refers to as a *guideline*. A guideline is a line beginning with the small male symbol (a circle with an arrow). Guidelines help to control the formatting of a document, but they are not printed with the rest of the document.

It is now necessary to reformat the document to the new margins specified by the embedded ruler line. Press Control-F5 to mark the entire document. Press F7 to reformat the document. All of the text is reformatted within the new margins. Finally, press F5 to unmark the document. The document will appear as shown in Fig. 4-16. Any new text entered into FIRST.DOC will be formatted according to the new, embedded ruler line.

The positions of tab stops can be set by placing Ts on the ruler line at the desired locations. These tab stops work exactly like those on a typewriter. Press the tab key, and the cursor moves forward to the next tab stop. You can also use Shift-Tab to move backwards to the previous tab stop.

When entering tables of numbers, you may want to take advantage of the decimal tab stops, which are established by placing the letter D on the ruler line. When you tab over to a decimal tab, the numbers (or other text) that are entered are pushed over to the left from the cursor location until a decimal point is entered. This automatically lines up numbers of different lengths correctly.

A summary of the ruler line commands and options discussed in this section is provided in Table 4-5. PC-Write has additional ruler line options and different ways to use ruler lines. For example, multiple ruler lines can be used to produce different formatting in various parts of a document. The PC-Write manual provides many more details.

Reformatting Text

The basic reformatting of paragraphs when words are added or deleted was covered in the review of the basic operations. To review briefly, with automatic reformatting turned on, the necessary changes are made immediately and automatically. With automatic reformatting off, insertions or deletions can alter the format of a paragraph. Pressing F7 reformats the paragraph. The command Shift-F7 switches back and forth between automatic and manual reformatting, which is indicated on the status line by Reform + and Reform – .

```
Esc:Menu Push Reform-. 95% Free.  3% Thru. Edit "B:FIRST.DOC"
M---+---TL----+-T--2----T----3--T-+----4T---+---T5----+-T--6----T----R--T-+--r
         PC-WRITE is a powerful word processor that is low in cost and
         is easy to use.  PC-WRITE combines a fast editor with
         extensive capabilities for formatting documents in a variety
         of ways.  Most personal computers users find this program has
         all the features they could want in a word processor.

         The PC-WRITE editor program has a wide selection of commands
         for moving the cursor and for inserting and deleting text.
         Features of the editor include block operations for copying,
         moving, and deleting text, and good search and replace
         capabilities.  The latest version of PC-WRITE includes
         automatic reformatting of paragraphs as text is inserted and
         deleted, a welcome addition.

         PC-WRITE has excellent formatting capabilities that allow
         documents to be printed with different fonts and enhanced
         text, making maximum use of the features of most printers.
         Text can be readily positioned anywhere on the page.
         Multiple line headers and footers can be printed.  PC-WRITE
         supports more different printers than most other word
         processing programs.

         PC-WRITE can merge files with documents.  A typical
```

Fig. 4-16. Embedded ruler line with old and new margins, and the reformatted document.

Function		Command
Display ruler line		F2
Hide ruler line		F2
Embed ruler in document		F2 F4 F2
Place ruler line in control file		F2 F3 F2
Ruler line commands:		
Left margin	L - New	
	M - Old	
Paragraph margin	P - New	
	Q - Old	
Right Margin	R - Ragged right	
	C - Centered	
	F - Flush right	
	J - Justified	
Tab stops	T - Normal tab	
	D - Decimal tab	

Table 4-5. Ruler Line Commands.

Reformatting quickly becomes more complex when you are attempting to alter the overall format of all or part of a document. The easiest way to handle this is to include the designations for the old left margin and the old paragraph margin in the new ruler line being created. Then as the old text is reformatted, it will automatically be adjusted to the new left margin and new paragraph margin. The right margin poses no problems. Whenever text is reformatted, it is adjusted using the right margin currently in effect on the ruler line. The reformatting will also follow the currently specified option at the right margin—ragged right, justified, or whatever.

Having changed the ruler line, it is now necessary to reformat the text that has already been entered. With automatic reformatting on, text in a paragraph will be reformatted according to the new ruler line whenever a change is made to the paragraph. This is not a very practical way to reformat an entire document, however.

The reformat command, F7, will reformat the paragraph in which the cursor is located. Even better, if text is marked in the document, the F7 will reformat all of the marked text. Use the block mark commands, F3 or F6, to mark the block that is to be reformatted. If the entire document is to be reformatted, use Control-F5 to mark the entire document. Press F7 and the entire marked block will be reformatted using the specifications on the current ruler line. F5 can be used to unmark the block.

In complex documents with varying left margins, specifying the old left margins and old paragraph margins may not work to reformat all left margins. In such instances, it is necessary to use a more complex procedure to move the left margins to the position desired. Begin by moving the cursor to the beginning of the block to be moved. To move the block to the right, press the Insert key until the first line is moved over to the position desired. Then press Shift-Delete to slide the line back to its original position. Mark the block to be moved using the normal block marking procedures. Finally, press Shift-Insert, and the entire block will be shifted over to the desired position.

Moving the block over to the left uses a similar procedure. With the cursor at the beginning of the block, press Delete until the first line is moved into the proper position. Shift-Insert slides the line back. Mark the block and press Shift-Delete. The block will be moved over to the left.

After either of these moves, you may want to reformat the text in the block to the current right margin. If you do, press F7 while the block is still marked. As usual, F5 unmarks the block.

A document may include sections that you do not want to have reformatted. Tables or lists of names and addresses are examples of such sections. You can prevent the reformatting of a section by entering special guidelines with dot commands before and after the section. Insert a blank line before the section to be protected from reformatting and place the cursor in the first column. Press Alternate-G; then type a period and a minus sign. To indicate the end of the area to be protected from reformatting, add another blank line and enter Alternate-G, period, plus sign. More information on the use of these dot commands is provided in the following section in the discussion of page layout.

One useful command for formatting text does not really fit into any section. To center text on a line, give the command Shift-F8 while the cursor is on the line. The text will be automatically centered. The ruler line has an option for centering, but for individual lines, like titles, this procedure is far easier than fiddling with the ruler. Use this to add a centered title to FIRST.DOC. Place the cursor on the first character in the text. Press the Return key twice to enter two blank lines above the start of the document. Move the cursor up two lines and type in the title "PC-Write." Now press Shift-F8, and this title will be centered, as shown in Fig. 4-17.

Finding and Replacing

PC-Write allows you to find the occurrence of any text in the file. This can be very helpful in locating a particular place in the text that is to be edited. The find procedure can be extended to include the replacement of the text found with other text. If

```
Esc:Menu Push Reform-. 95% Free.  5% Thru. Edit "B:FIRST.DOC"
M---+---TL----+-T--2----T----3--T-+----4T---+---T5----+-T--6----T----R--T-+--r
                                 PC-WRITE

        PC-WRITE is a powerful word processor that is low in cost and
        is easy to use.  PC-WRITE combines a fast editor with
        extensive capabilities for formatting documents in a variety
        of ways.  Most personal computers users find this program has
        all the features they could want in a word processor.

        The PC-WRITE editor program has a wide selection of commands
        for moving the cursor and for inserting and deleting text.
        Features of the editor include block operations for copying,
        moving, and deleting text, and good search and replace
        capabilities.  The latest version of PC-WRITE includes
        automatic reformatting of paragraphs as text is inserted and
        deleted, a welcome addition.

        PC-WRITE has excellent formatting capabilities that allow
        documents to be printed with different fonts and enhanced
        text, making maximum use of the features of most printers.
        Text can be readily positioned anywhere on the page.
        Multiple line headers and footers can be printed.  PC-WRITE
        supports more different printers than most other word
        processing programs.
```

Fig. 4-17. Adding a centered title to FIRST.DOC.

you discover you have misspelled a word throughout a file, for example, the find and replace feature can make correcting the problem very easy.

Begin by searching for the word "fonts" in the file FIRST.DOC. Move the cursor to the beginning of the file by pressing Shift-Grey+. Then press F9 to initiate the find procedure. The top line of the screen changes to the find and replace prompt, with the cursor on the period after the word Find. This is where you type in the text you wish to search for. Type in "fonts." The screen will now appear as shown in Fig. 4-18. Begin the search by pressing the Grey+ key, which instructs PC-Write to search forward through the file. At the first occurrence of the word "fonts" the search stops and the word is highlighted in the text, as shown in Fig. 4-19. If this is where you want to go, eliminate the highlighting by pressing F4—the normal command for unmarking blocks—and proceed with your editing. If you wish to continue to search for additional occurrences of the word "fonts," press the grey+ key again. If PC-Write comes to the end of the file without finding the word "fonts" again, it will display a message that the word has not been found.

Grey+ searches forward from the current cursor position and Grey− searches backwards. Once a word to be searched for has been entered using F9, PC-Write can search for that word any time you are editing; just use Grey+ and Grey− to search forward or backward from the cursor. To change the word to be searched for, press F9 again, and enter the new word in place of the old.

Now try searching for the word "flexible" and replacing it with the word "versatile" in the document. Press F9 so the word to be searched for can be entered. Note that the word "fonts" from the previous search is displayed. Enter the word "flexible" over the old word. Now press F10 to enter the replacement. The cursor jumps over to the period after Replace. Type in the word "versatile."

```
Esc  F9:Find "fonts"  F10:Replace "."
M---+---TL----+-T--2----T----3--T-+----4T---+---T5----+-T--6----T----R--T-+--r
                                     PC-WRITE

          PC-WRITE is a powerful word processor that is low in cost and
          is easy to use.  PC-WRITE combines a fast editor with
          extensive capabilities for formatting documents in a variety
          of ways.  Most personal computers users find this program has
          all the features they could want in a word processor.

          The PC-WRITE editor program has a wide selection of commands
          for moving the cursor and for inserting and deleting text.
          Features of the editor include block operations for copying,
          moving, and deleting text, and good search and replace
          capabilities.  The latest version of PC-WRITE includes
          automatic reformatting of paragraphs as text is inserted and
          deleted, a welcome addition.

          PC-WRITE has excellent formatting capabilities that allow
          documents to be printed with different fonts and enhanced
          text, making maximum use of the features of most printers.
          Text can be readily positioned anywhere on the page.
          Multiple line headers and footers can be printed.  PC-WRITE
          supports more different printers than most other word
          processing programs.
```

Fig. 4-18. Initiating a search for the word "fonts."

```
Esc:Menu Push Reform-. 95% Free. 41% Thru. Edit "B:FIRST.DOC"
M---+---TL----+-T--2----T----3--T-+----4T---+---T5----+-T--6----T----R--T-+--r
                                PC-WRITE

      PC-WRITE is a powerful word processor that is low in cost and
      is easy to use.  PC-WRITE combines a fast editor with
      extensive capabilities for formatting documents in a variety
      of ways.  Most personal computers users find this program has
      all the features they could want in a word processor.

      The PC-WRITE editor program has a wide selection of commands
      for moving the cursor and for inserting and deleting text.
      Features of the editor include block operations for copying,
      moving, and deleting text, and good search and replace
      capabilities.  The latest version of PC-WRITE includes
      automatic reformatting of paragraphs as text is inserted and
      deleted, a welcome addition.

      PC-WRITE has excellent formatting capabilities that allow
      documents to be printed with different fonts and enhanced
      text, making maximum use of the features of most printers.
      Text can be readily positioned anywhere on the page.
      Multiple line headers and footers can be printed.  PC-WRITE
      supports more different printers than most other word
      processing programs.
```

Fig. 4-19. Finding the first occurrence of the word "fonts."

Begin the search forward for the word "flexible" by pressing Grey +. When the word is found, it is highlighted as before. Press F10, and the word will be replaced with the word "versatile." To continue to search and replace, press Grey + again. If you come across an occurrence of the word "flexible" that you do not wish to replace, just press Grey + to continue the search. Searching and replacing works exactly like searching alone, except that you use F10 to do the replacement when desired.

All occurrences of a word in a file can be automatically replaced in one step by using the command Alternate-F10. A new prompt line appears at the top of the screen. Option F9:Repeat-replace provides for the automatic replacement. Press F9, and all occurrences of the word "flexible" are replaced with the word "versatile" throughout the file. Use this option with care, as it is very easy to accidentally make replacements you do not wish to make. It is usually safer to search and replace one occurrence at a time, so the word can be checked before you press F10 to make the replacement. PC-Write includes a number of additional options for the search and replace function that are described in the manual.

FORMATTING TEXT FOR PRINTING

The editing operations described in the preceding section are used to control the entry and changing of text and affect the document displayed on the screen. Additional formatting commands are used to determine the way in which the document is printed. These commands are added to the file, but they do not affect the display of the document on the screen, except for some highlighting. The effect of these commands can be observed only when the document is printed out. This section covers enhancing text, controlling the layout of the pages that are printed, and adding headers and footers.

Enhancing Text

Printing words or phrases in a document in a special manner is often desired to highlight information or to display the information in a special format. For example, text can be underlined and titles can be printed in larger characters. With PC-Write, such enhanced printing is accomplished by entering special characters into the file before and after the words to be printed in a different manner.

Use FIRST.DOC to see the effect of such enhancements by printing the title in double-wide characters and by underlining the first few words in the text. Since the special enhancement characters are to be inserted into the text, be sure that PC-Write is in the pushright (insert) mode by pressing the scroll lock key if necessary. To print the title in double-wide characters, move the cursor to the first character in the title and enter Alternate-D by holding down the Alternate key and pressing D. This enters the double-wide font character, which is displayed on the screen as a little triangle. The title is highlighted. Move the cursor to the space following the title and enter Alternate-D again to indicate the end of the special enhanced text. Another triangle is entered. The letters between the two special symbols are highlighted, indicating that these are to be printed in the special font. Finally, move the cursor to the beginning of the title and delete four spaces before the title. This is necessary to print the title centered with the wider letters.

A similar procedure is used to underline the phrase "PC-Write is a powerful word processor" on the first line of the first paragraph. Place the cursor on the first letter, P, and enter Alternate-U, for underline. The underline symbol is displayed on the screen as a little double arrow with an underline. Move the cursor to the space after the word "pro-

```
Esc:MenuPush Reform-. 95% Free.  0% Thru. Read "B:FIRST.DOC"

M---+---TL----+-T--2----T----3--T-+----4T---+---T5----+-T--6----T----R--T-+--r
                              ►PC-WRITE►

     ↨PC-WRITE is a powerful word processor↨ that is low in cost and
     is easy to use.  PC-WRITE combines a fast editor with
     extensive capabilities for formatting documents in a variety
     of ways.  Most personal computers users find this program has
     all the features they could want in a word processor.

     The PC-WRITE editor program has a wide selection of commands
     for moving the cursor and for inserting and deleting text.
     Features of the editor include block operations for copying,
     moving, and deleting text, and good search and replace
     capabilities.  The latest version of PC-WRITE includes
     automatic reformatting of paragraphs as text is inserted and
     deleted, a welcome addition.

     PC-WRITE has excellent formatting capabilities that allow
     documents to be printed with different fonts and enhanced
     text, making maximum use of the features of most printers.
     Text can be readily positioned anywhere on the page.
     Multiple line headers and footers can be printed.  PC-WRITE
     supports more different printers than most other word
     processing programs.
```

Fig. 4-20. FIRST.DOC with enhancement characters for wide printing of title and underlining in first line of text.

cessor" and enter Alternate-U again. Another underline symbol is entered, and only the text between the two underline symbols remains highlighted. The screen should now appear as shown in Fig. 4-20.

Now print out the document. The title will be printed in double-wide characters, and the words at the beginning of the first paragraph will be underlined. The printout of the file FIRST.DOC with the text enhancement is shown in Fig. 4-21.

```
                    P C - W R I T E

PC-WRITE is a powerful word processor that is low in cost and
is easy to use.  PC-WRITE combines a fast editor with
extensive capabilities for formatting documents in a variety
of ways.  Most personal computers users find this program has
all the features they could want in a word processor.

The PC-WRITE editor program has a wide selection of commands
for moving the cursor and for inserting and deleting text.
Features of the editor include block operations for copying,
moving, and deleting text, and good search and replace
capabilities.  The latest version of PC-WRITE includes
automatic reformatting of paragraphs as text is inserted and
deleted, a welcome addition.

PC-WRITE has excellent formatting capabilities that allow
documents to be printed with different fonts and enhanced
text, making maximum use of the features of most printers.
Text can be readily positioned anywhere on the page.
Multiple line headers and footers can be printed.  PC-WRITE
supports more different printers than most other word
processing programs.

PC-WRITE can merge files with documents.  A typical
application would be the production of form letters.  The
merge procedure in PC-WRITE is one of the most versatile of
all word processors in terms of the types of data files that
can be used.  This flexibility allows PC-WRITE to be used as
a versatile report generator for many data base programs.

With the tremendous variety of features, nearly all invoked
by keyboard commands, learning to use PC-WRITE effectively
takes some time.  However, novices can learn the fundamentals
required to do useful work with the program with only brief
instruction.  The more elaborate features of the program can
then be learned gradually as they are needed.  The key to
getting started is not to be intimidated by the program.  Do
not panic at the large numbers of commands in the manual, on
the quick reference card, or on the help screens.  You will
never have to learn all of the commands if you do not wish
to.  PC-WRITE provides options.  Learning to use the program
involves learning which of these options are best for you.
```

Fig. 4-21. Printout of FIRST.DOC with wide printing and underlining enhancements.

The text enhancement characters are all entered using the Alternate key with a letter; they are displayed on the screen with little symbols. The most commonly used text enhancements are presented in Table 4-6. Other text enhancement characters for special applications are described in the PC-Write manual.

Text enhancement characters are always used in pairs, one at the beginning of the text to be enhanced, to turn the enhancement on, and one at the end of the text, to turn it off. Enhancement only works on a single line of text; the enhancement is automatically turned off at the end of a line, whether or not the second character is encountered. This protects you from the problem that occurs with some other word processors. The second command to turn off a feature, such as underlining, is accidentally omitted and the remainder of the document is printed underlined. If the text to be enhanced falls on two lines, such as the title of a book to be underlined, it is necessary to indicate the enhancement on both lines.

Because the editing of text can require reformatting, which will change where lines are broken, it is often better to enter the text enhancement characters after the text is more or less in final shape. Otherwise, the reformatting of a line may move a section of enhanced text from one line to two lines, causing incorrect results.

The text enhancement characters are inserted into the document, but they are not counted by PC-Write when determining the number of characters that will fit on a line. Thus, a line with enhancement characters may extend beyond the right margin when it is displayed on the screen. The line will, however, be printed correctly. The enhancement characters can be deleted, like any other characters, by using the backspace or Delete keys. The characters will be moved along with the text in block operations.

Text enhancement characters in a document can be "hidden" so they do not distract you while you are editing the document. Holding down the Alternate key and pressing the space bar hides the special characters. Press Alternate-Space again, and the text enhancement characters are again displayed.

The actual printing of text marked by enhancement characters depends upon the capabilities of the printer you are using. Some printers are not able to print all of the different types of text provided for by PC-Write. The original PC-Write disk comes with a file that can be used to test the performance of your printer in producing the various enhancements. With the PC-Write working disk in the A: drive, place the backup copy of the original PC-Write disk in drive B: and give the following command to print out the test file:

```
PR B:PRINT.TST<Return>
```

The printout of this file will show which of the text enhancements are supported by the printer and will illustrate exactly how the enhanced text will be printed. The print out of the test file using the IBM Proprinter is shown in Figure 4-22.

Table 4-6. Text Enhancement Commands.

Enhancement	Command
Boldface printing	Alternate-B
Compressed printing (16 characters per inch)	Alternate-C
Elite printing (12 characters per inch)	Alternate-E
Standard fast printing (10 characters per inch)	Alternate-F
Superscript printing (higher)	Alternate-H
Italics printing	Alternate-I
Subscript printing (lower)	Alternate-L
High quality pica printing (10 characters per inch)	Alternate-P
High quality elite printing (12 characters per inch)	Alternate-Q
Underline printing	Alternate-U

Entering the text enhancement characters in a document is useful only for the special printing of short sections of text because the enhancement must be specified for each line. For printing the entire document or large blocks of the document in an enhanced mode, a different procedure using dot commands can be employed. This is discussed in the following section.

Controlling Page Layout and Printing

PC-Write has a large number of special commands called *dot commands*, which can be used to control the way in which a document is printed out. The dot commands are entered on separate lines in called *guide lines*; these begin with a special character. Each of these commands gives instructions to the printing program, PR, which interprets them and prints the document out accordingly. The lines themselves are not printed.

To print the document FIRST.DOC double-spaced, begin by moving the cursor to the first text column, column 10, on the first line of the document, the title. Press the Return key to add a blank line above the text, and move the cursor up one line by pressing the up arrow key. The cursor is now located at the beginning of the new blank line that has just been inserted. Now you will enter a guide line (a line that guides PC-Write but is not printed) with a dot command to cause the output to be printed with double-spacing. Enter Alternate-G, which indicates that this is a guide line. A small "male" symbol will appear on the screen, representing the Alternate-G character. Then, immediately following, enter this dot command, exactly as shown:

```
.M:2
```

The period indicates this is a dot command; the M: is the command for setting line spacing, and the 2 indicates that the text is to be double-spaced (printed every two lines). The screen should now appear as shown in Fig. 4-23. Print out the file, and the text will be printed double-spaced. Figure 4-24 shows the first several paragraphs of the printout.

The top and bottom margins on the page can be set with the dot commands .XT: and .XB: respectively. The size of the margin is specified in lines, measured at six lines per inch. An extra left margin can be specified with the command .X: with the extra margin specified in character spaces. If you have a document with the left margin in column 1 on the screen, for example, this dot command can be employed to move the text over when it is printed, giving a wider left margin. Be sure the page has room for the lines of text to be printed, however.

Dot commands can be used to specify the style of text to be used in printing the entire document or portions of the document. The same alternate-letter codes used for enhanced printing are used to specify the font in which text is to be printed. Use the dot command .R: followed by the alternate-letter code. For example, to print elite characters at twelve characters per inch, enter Alternate-G (indicating the guide line), .R: (the font selection dot command), and Alternate-E (selecting elite printing). The .Q: command followed by the font character turns off the printing in this font.

Dot commands can be placed anywhere in a document. Each command must be on a separate line beginning with the Alternate-G character followed by a period. Dot commands that affect text take effect immediately, while dot commands that affect the layout of pages take effect on the next page, unless they are on the first lines of the page, before any text. The format in which a document is printed can thus be varied throughout the document.

While discussing the layout of pages, it is appropriate to give consideration to the places at which breaks will occur between pages. When a document is printed, the PC-Write printing program places as many lines on each page as the format specifications allow. Printing then continues on the next page. These page breaks may not always occur in the best places. A single line of a paragraph may be placed at the bottom of one page or the top of the next. A section title could get left at the bottom of a page, separated from its section. You can force page breaks to occur anywhere in the document by entering Alternate-T. This forces

PC-Write PRINTER FONT DEMONSTRATION

STANDARD FONTS:

Bold	**ABCDEFGHIJKLMNOPQRSTUVWXYZ abcdefghijklmnopqrstuvwxyz**
Compressed	ABCDEFGHIJKLMNOPQRSTUVWXYZ abcdefghijklmnopqrstuvwxyz
Double wide	ABCDEFGHIJKLMnopqrstuvwx
Elite	ABCDEFGHIJKLMNOPQRSTUVWXYZ abcdefghijklmnopqrstuvwxyz
Fast	ABCDEFGHIJKLMNOPQRSTUVWXYZ abcdefghijklmnopqrstuvwxyz
Higher	ABCDEFGHIJKLMNOPQRSTUVWXYZ abcdefghijklmnopqrstuvwxyz
Italics	ABCDEFGHIJKLMNOPQRSTUVWXYZ abcdefghijklmnopqrstuvwxyz
Jade Green	ABCDEFGHIJKLMNOPQRSTUVWXYZ abcdefghijklmnopqrstuvwxyz
Lower	ABCDEFGHIJKLMNOPQRSTUVWXYZ abcdefghijklmnopqrstuvwxyz
Marine Blue	ABCDEFGHIJKLMNOPQRSTUVWXYZ abcdefghijklmnopqrstuvwxyz
Overstrike	ABCDEFGHIJKLMNOPQRSTUVWXYZ/abcdefghijklmnopqrstuvwxyz
Pica	**ABCDEFGHIJKLMNOPQRSTUVWXYZ abcdefghijklmnopqrstuvwxyz**
Quality	**ABCDEFGHIJKLMNOPQRSTUVWXYZ abcdefghijklmnopqrstuvwxyz**

Red	ABCDEFGHIJKLMNOPQRSTUVWXYZ abcdefghijklmnopqrstuvwxyz
Second strike	ABCDEFGHIJKLMNOPQRSTUVWXYZ abcdefghijklmnopqrstuvwxyz
Underline	ABCDEFGHIJKLMNOPQRSTUVWXYZ abcdefghijklmnopqrstuvwxyz
Variable	ABCDEFGHIJKLMNOPQRSTUVWXYZ abcdefghijklmnopqrstuvwxyz
W, Double Under	ABCDEFGHIJKLMNOPQRSTUVWXYZ abcdefghijklmnopqrstuvwxyz
Yellow	ABCDEFGHIJKLMNOPQRSTUVWXYZ abcdefghijklmnopqrstuvwxyz
FONT COMBINATIONS:	Bold Higher Italic Lower Over Second Under W-Under
C font	ABCabc ABCabc ABCabc ABCabc ABCabc ABCabc ABCabc ABCabc
D font	Aa Aa Aa Aa Aa Aa Aa Aa
E font	ABCabc ABCabc ABCabc ABCabc ABCabc ABCabc ABCabc ABCabc
F font	ABCabc ABCabc ABCabc ABCabc ABCabc ABCabc ABCabc ABCabc
P font	ABCabc ABCabc ABCabc ABCabc ABCabc ABCabc ABCabc ABCabc
Q font	ABCabc ABCabc ABCabc ABCabc ABCabc ABCabc ABCabc ABCabc
V font	ABCabc ABCabc ABCabc ABCabc ABCabc ABCabc ABCabc ABCabc

PC-Write™, the **Fast**, Friendly, Flexible **Word Processor**

Fig. 4-22. Printout of PRINT.TST using the IBM Proprinter.

```
Esc:Menu Push Reform-. 95% Free.  1% Thru. Edit "B:FIRST.DOC"
♂M---+---TL----+-T--2----T----3--T-+----4T---+---T5----+-T--6----T----R--T-+--r
        ♂.M:2
                                   ►PC-WRITE►

        ↨PC-WRITE is a powerful word processor↨ that is low in cost and
        is easy to use.  PC-WRITE combines a fast editor with
        extensive capabilities for formatting documents in a variety
        of ways.  Most personal computers users find this program has
        all the features they could want in a word processor.

        The PC-WRITE editor program has a wide selection of commands
        for moving the cursor and for inserting and deleting text.
        Features of the editor include block operations for copying,
        moving, and deleting text, and good search and replace
        capabilities.  The latest version of PC-WRITE includes
        automatic reformatting of paragraphs as text is inserted and
        deleted, a welcome addition.

        PC-WRITE has excellent formatting capabilities that allow
        documents to be printed with different fonts and enhanced
        text, making maximum use of the features of most printers.
        Text can be readily positioned anywhere on the page.
        Multiple line headers and footers can be printed.  PC-WRITE
        supports more different printers than most other word
```

Fig. 4-23. FIRST.DOC with the dot command specifying double-spaced printing.

the following text to begin printing on the next page.

To know where to enter the Alternate-T page break characters, however, you have to know where you want to force page breaks to be made. The document can be printed, but this is time consuming, and entering a page break to correct a problem in the printout can produce new problems later in the document. PC-Write allows you to determine where page breaks will occur in a document while you are editing. Move the cursor to the beginning of the file by entering Shift-Grey +, and enter the repage command, Alternate-F7. Page breaks will be determined, taking into account the page format specified by any dot commands. Page breaks will be indicated in the document by small "female" symbols. The lines with the page break symbols will be highlighted. If a page break comes in a bad place, enter a page break a few lines earlier with Alternate-T. Then repage the document and keep checking.

Sometimes you know in advance that certain portions of the text, such as a table, should never be divided between pages. By placing the dot command .E at the beginning and end of such elements, you assure that they will not be split up. When the document is printed, if the block will fit on the current page, it will be printed there. Otherwise it will be printed starting at the top of the next page.

The most commonly used dot commands are summarized in Table 4-7. PC-Write has a large number of additional dot commands to control printing. These are all described in the manual.

Headers and Footers

A header or footer is a line or group of lines printed at the top or bottom of each page in the document. Headers and footers are used for printing running titles that are to appear on each page. They are also used for the printing of page num-

PC—WRITE

PC-WRITE is a powerful word processor that is low in cost and is easy to use. PC-WRITE combines a fast editor with extensive capabilities for formatting documents in a variety of ways. Most personal computers users find this program has all the features they could want in a word processor.

The PC-WRITE editor program has a wide selection of commands for moving the cursor and for inserting and deleting text. Features of the editor include block operations for copying, moving, and deleting text, and good search and replace capabilities. The latest version of PC-WRITE includes automatic reformatting of paragraphs as text is inserted and deleted, a welcome addition.

Fig. 4-24. First several paragraphs of printout of FIRST.DOC double-spaced.

bers for a document. Dot commands are used to specify the printing of headers and footers.

As an example, a header will be added to FIRST.DOC to print the text "First Document" at the top of each page at the right margin, and a footer will be used to print the page number centered at the bottom of each page. If headers and footers are to be printed throughout the document,

Table 4-7. Commonly-Used Dot Commands.

Function	Command
Indicate the beginning and end of a block of text to be kept on one page	.E
Print a footer	.F:text
Print a header	.H:text
Multiple line spacing	.M:number
Page number for current page	.N:number
Stop printing text in given font	.Q:font
Start printing text in given font	.R:font
Add extra characters to left margin	.X:number
Bottom margin	.XB:number
Top margin	.XT:number

the dot commands should be at the beginning of the file, before any of the text. Move the cursor to the beginning of the .M:2 dot command and add four blank lines at the top by pressing Return four times. Move the cursor to the first line and enter Alternate-G to indicate this is a guideline. Then enter the following dot command:

```
.H:...First Document
```

The .H: is the header command; the information following specifies the header to be printed. "First Document" is the text. Preceding the text with the three dots indicates that the text is to be right justified—lined up with the right margin. A single header is printed on the line immediately above the text. One would obviously want at least one blank line separating the header from the text. This is accomplished by adding a second header line to print a blank line of text. On the second line, enter Alternate-G followed by the header command, .H:, and leave the rest of the line blank.

The page number will be printed in a footer at the bottom of the page. A blank footer line will be required to separate the page number footer line from the text. On the third line from the top, enter Alternate-G followed by the footer command, .F:, and leave the rest of the line blank. The fourth line will have the footer that prints the page number. Begin with Alternate-G. Then enter the following:

```
.F:...$$$...
```

The three dollar signs, $$$, instruct PC-Write to print the current page number. The printing program will keep track of page numbers as it prints out the document. By placing three periods on each side, the page number will be printed centered between the left and right margins. With these four dot commands entered, the screen should appear as shown in Fig. 4-25. When the document is printed out, the header and the page number in the

```
Esc:MenuPush Reform-. 95% Free. 10% Thru. Edit "B:FIRST.DOC"
♂M---+----L----+-T--2----T----3--T-+----4T---+---T5----+-T--6----T----R--T-+--r
          ♂.H:...First Document
          ♂.H:
          ♂.F:
          ♂.F:...$$$...
          ♂.M:2
                                  ►PC-WRITE►

          ↥PC-WRITE is a powerful word processor↥ that is low in cost and
          is easy to use.  PC-WRITE combines a fast editor with
          extensive capabilities for formatting documents in a variety
          of ways.  Most personal computers users find this program has
          all the features they could want in a word processor.

          The PC-WRITE editor program has a wide selection of commands
          for moving the cursor and for inserting and deleting text.
          Features of the editor include block operations for copying,
          moving, and deleting text, and good search and replace
          capabilities.  The latest version of PC-WRITE includes
          automatic reformatting of paragraphs as text is inserted and
          deleted, a welcome addition.

          PC-WRITE has excellent formatting capabilities that allow
          documents to be printed with different fonts and enhanced
```

Fig. 4-25. Dot commands for printing headers and footers in FIRST.DOC.

First Document

PC-WRITE

PC-WRITE is a powerful word processor that is low in cost and is easy to use. PC-WRITE combines a fast editor with extensive capabilities for formatting documents in a variety of ways. Most personal computers users find this program has all the features they could want in a word processor.

The PC-WRITE editor program has a wide selection of commands for moving the cursor and for inserting and deleting text. Features of the editor include block operations for copying, moving, and deleting text, and good search and replace capabilities. The latest version of PC-WRITE includes automatic reformatting of paragraphs as text is inserted and deleted, a welcome addition.

PC-WRITE has excellent formatting capabilities that allow documents to be printed with different fonts and enhanced text, making maximum use of the features of most printers. Text can be readily positioned anywhere on the page. Multiple line headers and footers can be printed. PC-WRITE supports more different printers than most other word processing programs.

PC-WRITE can merge files with documents. A typical application would be the production of form letters. The merge procedure in PC-WRITE is one of the most versatile of all word processors in terms of the types of data files that

1

Fig. 4-26. Print out of first page of FIRST.DOC with headers and footers.

footer will be printed on each page. Figure 4-26 shows the first page that is printed.

To have page numbering begin with some number other than one, perhaps for the second part of a long document, use the .N: dot command to specify the page number for the current page. Using the procedures described here, most types of headers and footers can be printed, but additional dot commands are available to print different headers and footers on the left and right pages of a document that is to be bound after printing.

HELP AND MENUS

The PC-Write editor program provides two types of assistance to users while they are operating the program. The help function displays capsule summaries of most PC-Write operations and commands. Menus can be displayed for the selection of most PC-Write commands. These features can be helpful for looking up and using infrequently used commands.

The main help screen can be displayed anytime during the editing of a document by pressing F1 twice. The help screen can be displayed with a single press of F1 from prompt lines, or submenus can be displayed at the top of the screen. The help screen contains a list of the help topics in five columns on the top half of the screen, with a highlighted selection bar for the selection of a topic. When the help screen is first displayed, the first topic, "Basics," is highlighted. The bottom half of the screen provides the help information on the topic selected. For example, Fig. 4-27 shows the help screen as it initially appears, with the "Basics" topic selected and some basic information on the operation of PC-Write displayed on the bottom half of the screen.

The four cursor control arrows are used to move the highlighted area through the list of topics to make a selection. As each topic is highlighted and selected, the corresponding help information is displayed on the bottom half of the screen. To

```
Esc: Help off, cancel.  F1: Help off, continue.  Arrows: Select a Help topic:
Basics          DOS commands     Footnotes        Merge: input     References
Auto-numbering  Dot lines I      Guide lines      Merge: template  Ruler lines
Auto-reformat   Dot lines II     Headers/footers  Merging steps    Scroll/jump
Char: foreign   Dot lines III    Locate cursor    Misc. stuff      Shareware
Char: math      Enhance text     Manual reformat  Page breaks      Spaces/hyphens
Copy/move text  Enter text       Margins/tabs     Page layout      System/file
Cursor moves    File management  Mark text        Printing         Windows
Delete text     Find/replace     Merging          Record keys      Glossary

B A S I C S                                          Loading a File and Exiting

 FILE OPERATIONS                                SEE ALSO:
 1. Create or load a file   A>ED filename         CURSOR MOVES: Arrow keys

 2. Enter text              from keyboard         RULER LINES: format (margins)

 3. Save the text to disk   Press F1 F3           DOT LINES: format (printing)

 4. Edit the text           Bksp, Del, Ins        ENTERING TEXT: editing

 5. Close the file          Press F1 F2           MARKING: move, copy, delete

 6. Print the file          Press F1 F7           FIND/REPLACE: text or chars
```

Fig. 4-27. PC-Write help screen with the "Basics" topic selected.

look up the codes to be placed in the text to produce enhanced text, simply move the highlighted area to the "Enhance text" topic. A list of the alternate-letter codes used for text enhancement is displayed. To refresh your memory on the procedures for marking text, select the "Mark text" option. When you have completed using the help function, pressing F1 one more time takes you back to your document.

Especially after you have become familiar with the basic operation of PC-Write, the help function can serve as a very useful reference for looking up information on specific topics. The information is available at the press of a few keystrokes. Finding out what you need to know is often quicker than searching through the PC-Write manual. The manual need be consulted only on those occasions where more detail is needed than is provided on the help screen. It is worthwhile to take some time to browse through the information presented for each of the help topics. In that way, you will not only learn more about PC-Write, but you will have a better idea of the nature of the information available to you with the help function when you have a question or encounter a problem.

The other way PC-Write provides assistance to the user is through menus. You have already seen and used the system menu displayed when you press F1 to save documents, exit PC-Write, or print a document. This menu is displayed earlier in this chapter in Fig. 4-3. A list of the commands available from the menu, each associated with a function key, is displayed on the first line. A highlighted area can be moved back and forth with the left and right arrow keys to select a command. A line of information describing the command selected is displayed on the line below. Any command can be invoked by pressing the associated function key. Alternatively, you can select the command desired by moving the highlighted area to that command and then pressing Return.

A series of optional menus associated with all of the function key operations can be displayed. At the left end of the status line is the message "Esc:Menu." Pressing the Escape key while editing displays the main menu listing the operations associated with each of the function keys. Once again, a highlighted area can be moved around to select a function. The description of the function selected is displayed on the line below. Pressing Return executes the function selected (or you can press the appropriate function key).

From the main menu, you can select three other menus by pressing the Shift, Alternate, and Control keys. Each of these menus displays the operations associated with the use of the function keys and those keys. For example, the shift menu, shown in Fig. 4-28, displays the commands invoked by pressing the function keys in while holding down the Shift key. Again, a highlighted area can be moved to select a command. An explanation of the command selected appears on the line below. Pressing Return invokes the highlighted command. You can move back and forth among these menus by pressing the Shift, Alternate, and Control keys. The up and down arrows can also be used to scroll through the series of menus; pressing the up arrow is the only way to get back to the main menu. Escape returns you to editing your document from any of these menus.

Experiment with the menus to determine whether they will aid you in the operation of PC-Write. Each user will develop his or her own style. I like being able to access the help screens to look up information and do so frequently. The menus, on the other hand, seem to me to be more trouble than they are worth. To me, it seems that you have to know what the command is in order to be able to find it on the menus. And selecting an option with the highlighted area and pressing Return seems to be a lot more work than just pressing the appropriate function key. But these are just my preferences. You will develop your own. The good thing about PC-Write is that it gives the user a variety of options in the use of the program. Each user is given the opportunity to develop methods for the operation of PC-Write that make sense to him or her.

PRINTING DOCUMENTS

The PC-Write printing program includes a variety of options for controlling what takes place while printing a document. Printing can be started

```
Esc:cancel.  F1-F1:help.  Alt/Shf/Ctl/Arrow:select.  Fn-key/Letter/Enter:action.
sF1.Fn-keys±                                        sF7.Reform±     sF9.Location
sF2:Merging      sF4:Shareware                      sF8.Center
Turn function key reminder on+ or off-

         .F:

         .F:...$$$...

         .M:2
                               PC-WRITE

         PC-WRITE is a powerful word processor that is low in cost and
         is easy to use.  PC-WRITE combines a fast editor with
         extensive capabilities for formatting documents in a variety
         of ways.  Most personal computers users find this program has
         all the features they could want in a word processor.

         The PC-WRITE editor program has a wide selection of commands
         for moving the cursor and for inserting and deleting text.
         Features of the editor include block operations for copying,
         moving, and deleting text, and good search and replace
         capabilities.  The latest version of PC-WRITE includes
         automatic reformatting of paragraphs as text is inserted and
         deleted, a welcome addition.

         PC-WRITE has excellent formatting capabilities that allow
         documents to be printed with different fonts and enhanced
```

Fig. 4-28. Menu showing the commands available using the shift key in conjunction with the function keys.

and stopped, specific pages can be selected for printing, and text or commands can even be inserted from the keyboard while printing.

As explained above in the section on basic operations, the printing of a document can be invoked in two different ways. While editing a document, pressing F1 and then F7 begins the printing procedure. Alternatively, printing can be started from the DOS A> prompt by entering PR followed by the name of the file to be printed. In either case, you are asked whether the document is to be printed to a disk file or to the printer. Most often, you will choose the printer. The main printing menu is then displayed, as shown in Fig. 4-29. This displays all of the commands you can enter either before the printing has started or at any time that the printing has stopped.

The status line at the top of the screen indicates that the printer program is currently waiting for a command to be entered using the function keys or the menu. The printing operation is to read the file FIRST.DOC and direct the results to the file PRN, which is the printer. If printing were to be to a disk file, the name of this file would be specified. Finally, the message is displayed that printing is ready to begin.

To begin printing the document from the first page, without using any of the special features of the printer program, press F10 for continuous printing or F9 for printing that will stop at the end of each page. This would be used for printing on single sheets that have to be individually fed into the printer for each page.

During the actual printing, pressing Escape will

interrupt the printing. You might wish to do this if you have printed as much of the document as desired or if a problem has occurred in printing, such as the paper getting out of alignment. When Escape is pressed, three choices are displayed, as shown in Fig. 4-30. Escape terminates printing at once, F9 completes the printing of the current page, and F10 picks up printing where it was interrupted, as if nothing had happened. Note that after pressing Escape, your printer may keep printing for some time before stopping. Many printers have an internal buffer that receives and holds characters to be printed. Pressing Escape causes PC-Write to stop sending text to the printer and its buffer, but the printer will continue printing until the buffer is empty.

After the printing has been permanently stopped either by pressing Escape to stop immediately or F9 to stop after the end of the current page, the main printer menu is displayed again. You can use F7 to repeat the printing of the current page, which is useful if a problem has occurred in printing. Pressing F3 exits to where you entered the printing program—the editor or DOS. F2 exits directly to DOS, even if you began printing from the editor.

If you wish to begin printing in the middle of the document, pressing F8 at the beginning allows you to specify any number of pages to be skipped. Enter the number of pages to be skipped and press Return. Select the option to skip pages and then stop. Then press F9 or F10 to begin printing at the desired page, shown on the status line. The option to skip pages each time will result in the printing of every other page, every third page, and so on. This is likely to be useful only when you wish to print on both sides of the pages. You can print the odd-numbered pages first, then turn the paper over and print the even numbered pages.

An additional feature of the printer program is the ability to enter lines of text or guidelines into the file to be printed from the printer program. This

```
Waiting.   Print from "B:FIRST.DOC" to "PRN", ready to begin.
 F1.Help-screen  F3.Finished      F5:Input-end     F7:Repeat-pages F9.Page-stop
 F2.Exit-to-DOS  F4.DOS-command   F6:User-input    F8:Skip-pages   F10.Continuous
Show help screen, giving dot commands and other information

  These keys are active when printing has been stopped for a command:
    F1: Show help screen with Dot lines and font characters.
    F2: Exit to DOS, even if printing was started from edit program.
    F3: Exit to DOS or back to edit program, whichever one started printing.
    F4: Stay resident, but do a DOS command shell until DOS "exit" command.
    F5: Force end of current input file (if last input file, end printing).
    F6: Enter input text or Guide lines (like .U, enter lines typed by user).
    F7: Repeat a page then stop, or repeat each page to print multiple copies.
    F8: Skip pages then stop, or skip pages each time to print every Nth page.
    F9: Print one page, then stop for another one of these commands.
    F10:Start continuous printing of pages (but stop if Esc key pressed).
  These keys are active when you are entering text on the Top Line:
    Esc key: no more user input lines (end input file).
    Enter (Return key): finish this line, enter another.
    Left/right Arrows: move cursor left or right one character.
    Home/End keys: move cursor to the beginning or end of the line.
    Bksp/Del keys: delete one character on the left or the right.
    Ins key: insert one space pushing the rest of the line right.
    Scroll Lock: toggle between Pushright and Overwrite typing mode.
```

Fig. 4-29. Main menu for PC-Write printing program.

```
Esc:Stop immediately  F9:Stop after page printed  F10:Continue printing



These keys are active when printing has been stopped for a command:
  F1: Show help screen with Dot lines and font characters.
  F2: Exit to DOS, even if printing was started from edit program.
  F3: Exit to DOS or back to edit program, whichever one started printing.
  F4: Stay resident, but do a DOS command shell until DOS "exit" command.
  F5: Force end of current input file (if last input file, end printing).
  F6: Enter input text or Guide lines (like .U, enter lines typed by user).
  F7: Repeat a page then stop, or repeat each page to print multiple copies.
  F8: Skip pages then stop, or skip pages each time to print every Nth page.
  F9: Print one page, then stop for another one of these commands.
  F10:Start continuous printing of pages (but stop if Esc key pressed).
These keys are active when you are entering text on the Top Line:
  Esc key: no more user input lines (end input file).
  Enter (Return key): finish this line, enter another.
  Left/right Arrows: move cursor left or right one character.
  Home/End keys: move cursor to the beginning or end of the line.
  Bksp/Del keys: delete one character on the left or the right.
  Ins key: insert one space pushing the rest of the line right.
  Scroll Lock: toggle between Pushright and Overwrite typing mode.
```

Fig. 4-30. Interrupting the printing of a document with the escape key.

might be useful for printing the current date at the top of a document or for inserting one or more guidelines to control the way in which the text is printed. For example, a document could be produced without specifying the font to be used in printing. When drafts are produced, printing automatically takes place in the fast, lower-quality draft mode of the printer. Then when printing out the final copy, a guideline could be added to the beginning of the file to direct the printing to take place in the higher-quality, but slower print mode of the printer. Begin printing FIRST.DOC by entering the following command from the DOS prompt:

PR B:FIRST.DOC<Return>

Be sure that the printer is ready, and press F10 to indicate that the document is to be printed to the printer. The main printer program menu is displayed. Press F6 to indicate that you wish to enter a line of text or a guideline at the beginning of the file. The prompt will indicate that the printer program is ready to do this, and that you should press any key to continue. Press any key, and you are returned to the main menu. Now press F10 to instruct the print program to begin continuous printing. At this point, the printer program will prompt you for the text to be inserted. Type in the following guideline, with the dot command indicating that you want the text printed in the high-quality pica (10 characters per inch) font:

<Alternate-G>.R:<Alternate-P>

This line will appear at the top of the screen with the Alternate-G and Alternate-P characters displayed as graphics symbols as if you had entered these while editing a document. The screen will appear as shown in Fig. 4-31. Press Return to enter this line. Since this is all the text to be entered, press Escape to indicate that you have completed entering text from the keyboard. Printing of the document will then begin in the high-quality character set selected.

The PC-Write printing program also allows you to specify in your document files points at which information is to be entered from the keyboard. The dot command .U must be inserted into the document. When the printer program encounters this command during printing, printing is paused and you are given the opportunity to enter text or guidelines into the document. These and other features of the printer program are explained in the PC-Write manual.

CUSTOMIZING PC-WRITE

The most important aspects of configuring PC-Write to work with your particular system are taken care of during the installation procedure. At that time, users with color displays can set up the program to operate (very effectively) using color. During installation, PC-Write is also set up to work with your particular printer, which you select from a long list of printers supported by this word processor.

For most beginning users, these options will be sufficient to accommodate their needs. PC-Write does include edit and print control files that specify virtually all aspects of the operation of PC-Write. The edit control file can be modified to reassign keys on the keyboard, adjust the appearance of the screen, and change the operation of the editor and the various defaults. Virtually any aspect of the way in which the printer program controls the printer can be modified by changing the printer control file. Thus, PC-Write can be configured to use an exotic feature provided by your printer. Furthermore, custom control files can be created and tailored to specific situations or even individual documents.

The control files reside on the PC-Write disk with the names ED.DEF and PR.DEF. When the editor or printer programs are run, they read the information in these (or sometimes other) control files to determine their operating configurations.

The editor and printer control files are modi-

```
"♂.R:♣"
Enter input text line or Guide line in line above.  Press Enter at end of line.
Press F1 for Help screen.  Press Esc after all lines entered to end input file.

These keys are active when printing has been stopped for a command:
  F1: Show help screen with Dot lines and font characters.
  F2: Exit to DOS, even if printing was started from edit program.
  F3: Exit to DOS or back to edit program, whichever one started printing.
  F4: Stay resident, but do a DOS command shell until DOS "exit" command.
  F5: Force end of current input file (if last input file, end printing).
  F6: Enter input text or Guide lines (like .U, enter lines typed by user).
  F7: Repeat a page then stop, or repeat each page to print multiple copies.
  F8: Skip pages then stop, or skip pages each time to print every Nth page.
  F9: Print one page, then stop for another one of these commands.
  F10:Start continuous printing of pages (but stop if Esc key pressed).
These keys are active when you are entering text on the Top Line:
  Esc key: no more user input lines (end input file).
  Enter (Return key): finish this line, enter another.
  Left/right Arrows: move cursor left or right one character.
  Home/End keys: move cursor to the beginning or end of the line.
  Bksp/Del keys: delete one character on the left or the right.
  Ins key: insert one space pushing the rest of the line right.
  Scroll Lock: toggle between Pushright and Overwrite typing mode.
```

Fig. 4-31. Entering a guideline from the keyboard prior to the printing of a document.

fied by using PC-Write itself to add or change commands included in these files. The list of options is long, and the process for making changes is fairly complex. You should have a fair amount of experience in the use of PC-Write before attempting to modify these files. When you wish to try, carefully study the detailed information provided in the PC-Write manual for instructions on how to proceed.

CONCLUSION

PC-Write is a very powerful word processor. The key to learning to use this program is to take it one small step at a time. First learn the basics involved in creating, editing, and printing out documents. Then, as you wish to do more complex things, learn about new features of the program one at a time. In this way, you will not be overwhelmed by very large numbers of commands to be mastered at one time. You learn the operation of the program step by step.

With PC-Write, you can do nearly anything in editing and formatting text that can be accomplished with expensive commercial word processors. With any of these programs, however, it is necessary to take the time to learn about the various features and how they can be used to make the word processor work for you.

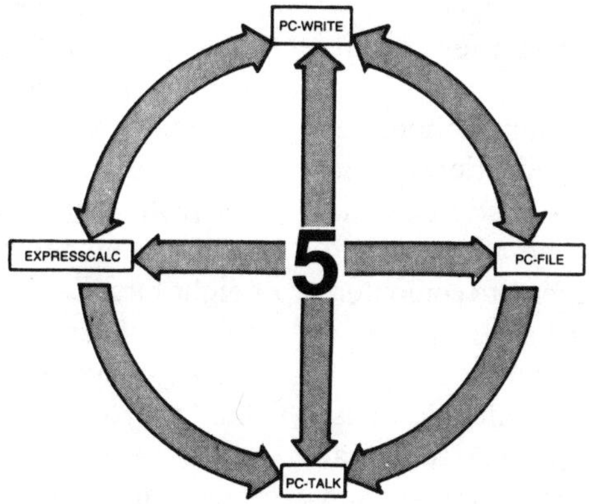

Using PC-Talk

A personal computer with a modem and communications software can be used to explore the fascinating world of computer communications. The range of possible activities is nearly endless. With computer information services such as CompuServe and The Source, you can do many different things: chat via computer with others who share specific interests, play complex multiple-player games, read the latest information on the news wires, check current stock prices, look up airline schedules and make reservations, pay bills, obtain computer programs to use on your system, and even go shopping. Huge online databases can be consulted to perform sophisticated research. If your company or university has one or more large computers offering timesharing services, a personal computer can be employed to access these computers. Finally, literally hundreds of small computer bulletin board systems can be contacted to share software and communicate with other personal computer users. Indeed, many public-domain and user-supported computer programs—including those described in this book—can be obtained from these bulletin board systems.

Personal computer communications requires the use of communications software to manage the process of communicating with remote computers. PC-Talk is a very fine, useful communications program. In addition to supporting the basic communications functions, PC-Talk can capture information received from remote computers, including program and data files, and can transmit such files to the remote computers. The program incorporates a telephone directory and the capabilities for automatically dialing remote computer systems. Strings of text can be stored for reuse, for example, for logging on to remote computer systems. PC-Talk can be easily configured for specific personal computer systems, for various communications needs, and for individual operating preferences.

As communications programs for personal computers go, PC-Talk is easy to use. Help is provided by the program, displaying all available commands on the screen, and clear prompts are provided for various functions. Compared with a word processing program, for example, communications programs like PC-Talk have far fewer commands to learn.

Unfortunately, computer communications remains one of the more complex applications. A variety of technical matters such as baud rates and communications protocols must be addressed to successfully communicate with a remote computer. Many new users find the process difficult and frustrating.

In learning personal computer communications, two procedures might be followed. The technical terms and the rules for configuring the program and modem for communications can be learned by rote. More effective, however, is learning the basic fundamentals involved in computer communications to understand what is actually going on. The latter procedure provides a more effective foundation for computer communications. For this reason, the current chapter proceeds in a somewhat different fashion than those dealing with the use of the other programs. The first section provides an introduction to communications fundamentals. With this foundation, the use of PC-Talk for basic communications can be introduced. This is followed by sections addressing additional features of PC-Talk, including the use of the dialing directory, the receiving and transmitting of files, keyboard input strings, and advanced functions of the program.

COMMUNICATIONS FUNDAMENTALS

To understand the process of computer communications, you must first understand the nature and format of the information being communicated. Then comes learning about the actual hardware—the communications port and the modem—used in transmitting and receiving this information. Finally, the role of the communications software in managing the information and the hardware must be considered. This section addresses each of these areas.

Information: Bits, Bytes, and Baud Rates

The smallest unit of information in a computer is a *bit*, which has just two values, conventionally referred to as zero and one. A switch can be on or off, a circuit can have a high voltage or a low voltage, a spot on a floppy disk can be magnetized in one direction or the other. Each of these can be used to represent a single bit of information, whether a value is zero or one.

One bit cannot convey very much information, so it is common to refer to *bytes*, which are groups of eight bits. Each of the bits in the byte can have either the value of zero or one, making for 256 possible combinations of zeros and ones in a byte. Thus, a byte can represent 256 possible states.

One of the most common uses of bytes is to store characters of information, such as letters, numbers, and special symbols. For example, this sequence of zeros and ones in a byte can be used to represent the capital letter M:

```
01001101
```

Similar combinations can be used to represent all of the letters, numbers, and special symbols. Virtually all personal computers and many larger computers use a standard code to represent the characters, called the American Standard Code for Information Interchange, abbreviated ASCII and pronounced "AS-key." The ASCII code includes 128 combinations for representing all of the letters, numbers, symbols, and a variety of control codes (such as the carriage return). With the ASCII code, one bit in the byte is not used.

Most often, the information communicated between computers will be text made up of characters represented in the ASCII code. In some cases, such as when program files are transmitted, the collections of bits in the bytes will have different meanings. When such binary files are transmitted, all eight of the bits in each byte will have significance.

To communicate with other computers, these bytes of information must be transmitted over the telephone lines. Accomplishing this requires that the bits be transmitted one at a time, in sequence. The signal for each bit will be varied depending upon whether its value is zero or one. This is referred to as *serial data transmission*. Thus, the information sent over the line is nothing more than a long string of bits, each having the value zero or one.

With all of these bits of information being sent out one after the other, the receiver has to have some means of determining where one byte or character of information ends and the next begins. In the form of communications nearly always used with personal computers (technically called *asynchronous* communication), signals are provided to mark the beginning and end of each byte or character. The transmission of a byte or character begins with a special start bit and ends with one or more stop bits. These mark off an individual unit of information for the receiving computer.

These information packages can be assembled in a variety of ways. First, the number of data bits, the actual bits of information being transmitted, can be varied. A full eight bits of information can be sent, and this is necessary if program files or other binary files using all eight bits in the byte are being transmitted. If text is being transmitted, however, only seven data bits are actually required, since the ASCII code requires only seven bits for its 128 code combinations. Some highly specialized applications involve even fewer data bits.

An additional bit of information, called a *parity bit*, can be added as an option to serve as a check on the accuracy of the transmission. With even parity, which is most common, the value of the parity bit is set so that the total number of bits with the value one is even. Thus, if the data bits include an even number of ones, the parity bit is set to zero, and if the data bits include an odd number of ones, the parity bit is set to one, making the total even. The receiver of the information can do a test upon receiving the information to determine whether the total number of ones is even. If an error has occurred in transmission, altering the value of one of the bits, the total will come out odd, indicating the error. Odd parity can also be used, which just reverses the procedure. Once in a while systems will use mark or space parity, in which the extra parity bit is always set to either a one or a zero, respectively. This obviously provides no error checking, but is sometimes used to get two systems to communicate in a compatible manner. If no extra parity bit is added, the data transmission is referred to as having no parity.

Finally, varying numbers of stop bits can be added to the end of the package. One stop bit is most common, but sometimes two are used. The most common parameters for personal computer data communications are seven data bits, even parity, and one stop bit, often used for text transmission, and eight data bits, no parity, and one stop bit, required for the exchange of program files and other binary information. The sequence of bits used to transmit the character M with seven data bits, even parity, and one stop bit is illustrated in Fig. 5-1.

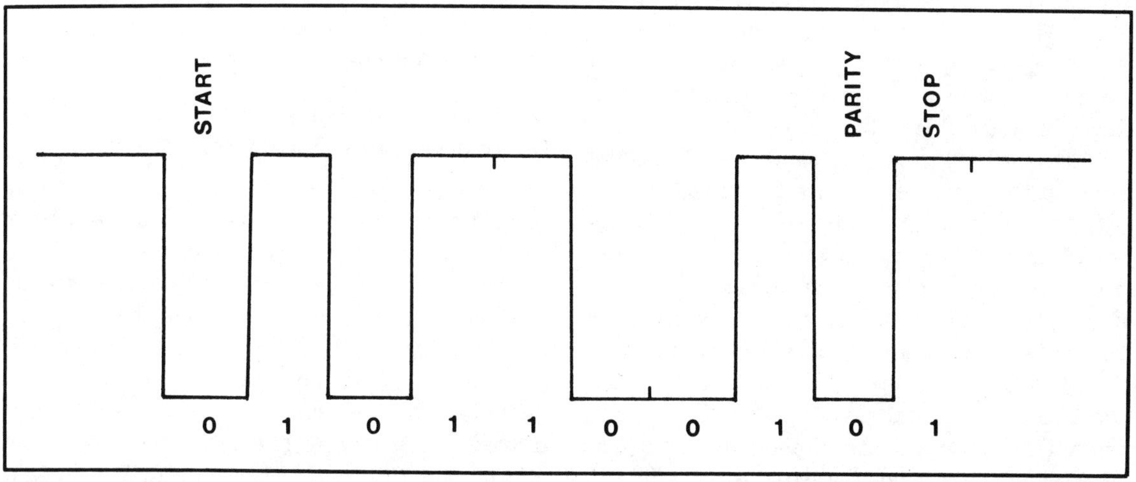

Fig. 5-1. Sequence of bits to transmit the ASCII character "M" with seven data bits, even parity, and one stop bit.

Understanding the formats used for the communication of information is important. For two computers to communicate with one another, they must agree on the format used for the transmission of the information. Without such agreement, the receiving computer does not know how to interpret the information sent by the the sending computer. As a practical matter, this means that a personal computer user attempting to communicate with a remote computer must adopt the format used by the remote computer.

Another element affecting the interpretation of information transmitted between computers is the speed of transmission. The two computers must agree on the rate at which bits of information are to be transmitted, so that the receiving computer knows when to look for another bit. Speed is measured in the number of bits transmitted per second, which is frequently referred to as the *baud rate*. The most common speeds for data communications over telephone lines are 300 bits per second, or 300 baud, and 1200 bits per second, or 1200 baud. The transmission of one character or byte of information requires start, stop, and possibly parity bits in addition to the seven or eight data bits, typically resulting in ten bits per character. Thus, data transmission at 300 baud is approximately 30 characters per second, and data transmission at 1200 baud is approximately 120 characters per second. If two computers do not agree on the baud rate at which information is to be transmitted, the result is garbage. Many systems you may contact, however, will have the capability of sensing whether your computer is transmitting at 1200 baud or 300 baud and will adjust themselves accordingly.

One final aspect of information transmission is whether the computer receiving a character of information will automatically send that character back (echo the character) to the sending computer. Such echoing back of the information is done in *full-duplex* communication, which is by far the most common arrangement, especially in communications with large computers. When you press the letter A on the keyboard of your personal computer, the letter A is sent to the remote computer. The remote computer sends the letter A back. The A is received by your personal computer and displayed on your screen. The advantage of this procedure is that you have an automatic check on the accuracy of the transmission. If you press A and some other character appears on the screen, you know that an error has occurred somewhere in the process.

Sometimes, however, *half-duplex* communication, in which the characters are not echoed back, is employed. Your computer receives nothing from the remote computer when a key is pressed. Therefore, if you wish to see what you are typing—which you undoubtedly do—your computer will have to display the character on the screen itself, as the key is pressed. A communications program will provide options for handling either situation, and the correct one must be selected. If you are set up to directly display characters on screen for half-duplex communications and the remote computer echoes the character back in full-duplex mode, each character will be displayed twice. The character is displayed the first time as you press the key and the second time as the same character is received back from the other computer. The solution is to change so that the character is not displayed directly as a result of typing. On the other hand, if you are set up for full-duplex communications but communicating with a computer in half-duplex mode, nothing that you type will appear on the screen. The character is not displayed as you type, and it is not echoed back. The information is being transmitted, but you cannot see it. Once again, it is necessary to switch, this time so the character is displayed as it is typed.

Hardware: Communications Ports and Modems

Specific hardware is required to enable a personal computer system to communicate with other computers over the telephone lines. To transmit information, a *serial communications port* converts the bits in a byte of information inside the computer into the string of ones and zeros, with the associated start, parity, and stop bits. A *modem* then converts the pulses from the serial port into tones that can be transmitted over the telephone lines. To receive information, this process is reversed. The modem converts the tones into serial pulses, which the serial port then converts into a byte of information that can be used inside the computer.

The basic IBM Personal Computer does not come standard with any serial ports. They must be added to the machine using boards that plug into the slots inside the machine. The serial port can be the only function provided by a board. IBM calls its board providing one serial port the *asynchronous communications adapter*. Alternatively, the serial port can be one of the functions provided by a multifunction board, along with other functions such as added memory, a parallel printer port, and a clock/calendar. Many IBM PC compatible machines include at least one serial port as standard. An additional serial port can be added using a plug-in board.

Within the computer, communications with the serial ports is managed by the operating system. DOS can support two serial ports, which are referred to as COM1: and COM2: (the colons are part of the names). When a serial port is added to a computer, it must be configured as either COM1: or COM2: by setting switches or changing jumpers on the board. Instructions with the plug-in boards explain this procedure. When you wish to communicate with one of these serial ports, it is then necessary to specify whether you will be using COM1: or COM2:. When a computer has only a single serial port, it is invariably configured as COM1:, and an added port will then be configured as COM2:. If your computer has two serial ports, it is necessary to know which one the modem is connected to in order to properly communicate with that port and the modem.

An external modem is plugged into the serial port using a cable between the socket for the port on the back of the computer and the modem. Two general types of modems are available: *acoustic* and *direct-connect*. Acoustic modems are no longer widely sold, but many are still in use. An acoustic modem has cups in which a telephone handset is placed. Communication with the phone is via a small microphone and speaker—hence, acoustic. Far more common now are direct-connect modems, which are directly connected to the telephone line using standard modular phone jacks. The direct connection is more reliable, especially at higher baud rates.

An alternative is an *internal modem board* that plugs directly into one of the slots inside the computer. The connection is made directly to the telephone line from a modular phone jack on the back of the computer. The internal modem boards combine the circuitry for the serial port with the modem itself. This means that the modem board is viewed by the computer and the operating system as a serial port and must be configured as either COM1: or COM2: like any other serial port.

Internal modem boards are often less expensive than external modems because they do not require a separate case, power supply, and serial port. The disadvantage is that they cannot be readily moved from one computer to another. The case would have to be opened and the modem board removed.

Most direct-connect modems—external and internal—include a variety of features to simplify communications. They can dial the telephone number, "hang up" the phone when you are through, and even answer the telephone when it rings. To accomplish such functions, commands must be sent to the modem instructing it concerning the tasks to be done. This means that the modem must understand a set of these commands. The SmartModem, made by Hayes Microcomputer Products, was one of the first very popular direct-connect modems providing these functions. The commands recognized by the Hayes modems have become a de facto standard. Many of the modems manufactured by other companies are Hayes-compatible and recognize the same set of commands. To use a "smart" modem with these added features, you will need to know what commands are required to accomplish the various functions.

Software and Communications

The final element in personal computer communications is the communications software. The computer must be running a program that manages the communications function. Optionally, a communications program provides a variety of support functions to make communications easier.

The central function of any communications program involves taking characters entered at the keyboard and sending them to the serial port to transmit information. Reversing the process, the program must accept characters received by the serial port and display them on the screen.

An important feature of a communications program is a facility allowing the user to set up the serial port for the desired communications parameters. This would include setting the baud rate, the number of data and stop bits, and the parity bit.

With a "smart" direct-connect modem, the communications program could include features for controlling the modem. The most obvious of these is dialing telephone numbers automatically.

Finally, the communications program can tie the communications process in with the rest of the personal computer system. Procedures can be provided for printing information as it is received, saving information in files on the disk, and transmitting information contained in files on the disk.

Perhaps one of the most confusing aspects of personal computer communications is keeping straight what you are communicating with. When you are in communications with a remote computer, you are most often sending information to that remote computer and receiving information back from that computer. Once in a while you will be sending commands to the modem, and you will receive short responses back from the modem. Occasionally you will be issuing commands to the communications program and receiving feedback from that program. These latter interactions take place within your personal computer system, unbeknownst to the remote computer. By realizing that at different times you are communicating with different entities, it should be easier to keep clear about what is actually happening. The instructions on the use of PC-Talk for communications are designed to make these differences clear.

BASIC COMMUNICATIONS WITH PC-TALK

The first step in using PC-Talk to communicate with remote computers is learning to configure the program, make the connection, and then terminate the connection. Once you have become proficient in accomplishing these basic tasks, you can learn to use the additional features of the program one at a time.

Note that this chapter cannot provide much information on how to interact with the remote computer once you are connected and in communication. Each computer system accessed by remote terminals or computers has its own unique procedures for communicating. If you are using a service such as CompuServe or The Source, instructions can be obtained from the service. Business and university computer systems will provide their own instructions to authorized users. With computer bulletin board systems, some instructions will be given when you establish a connection. Read the information carefully and determine what is required to get further assistance from the system. Most online computer systems have some sort of built-in help facility to provide assistance to users with questions on how to proceed. Learn how to access and use whatever help is provided.

Starting and Setting Up PC-Talk

To begin, place a working copy of the PC-Talk disk in the A: drive. Turn on the computer, DOS should load, and you can enter the date and time. (If the computer is already on and you have the DOS A> prompt displayed on the screen, you can skip this step.) To start the PC-Talk program simply enter this command:

```
PC-TALK<Enter>
```

The title screen will be displayed. Press any key to continue. The beginning PC-Talk operating display appears as shown in Fig. 5-2.

At the upper left-hand corner of the screen is the "= = = Proceed . . ." message. Whenever this is displayed, PC-Talk is informing you that it is ready for you to enter a command or to begin or resume communications with the remote computer.

The message in the upper right-hand corner reminds you to have your modem turned on if you wish to proceed with data communications. In the

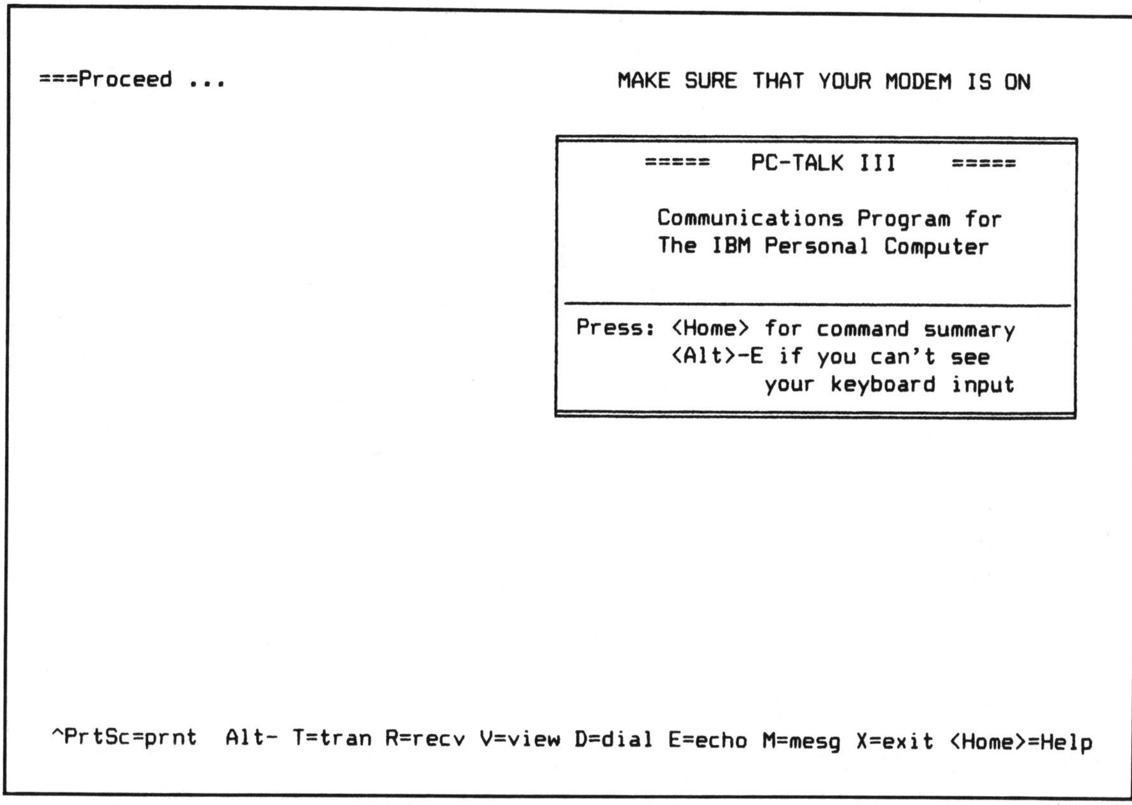

Fig. 5-2. Beginning operating display of PC-Talk.

box is information on two key commands. Pressing the Home key on the cursor control keypad displays a summary listing of all PC-Talk commands. This is the major help function provided by the program. The Alternate-E combinations switches from full-duplex to half-duplex mode and back again as it is pressed. If you do not see your keyboard input as it is being typed, press Alternate-E so the characters are displayed on the screen. This switches from the full-duplex mode, which is standard when PC-Talk is started, to the half-duplex mode. On the other hand, if you ever see characters being repeated on the screen, press Alternate-E again to switch from half-duplex back to full-duplex mode so that characters are displayed only as they are received from the other computer.

Across the bottom of the screen is a list of some of the most commonly used PC-Talk commands. Each of these will be discussed as the functions of PC-Talk are covered in this chapter.

Try the simplest of the PC-Talk commands. Press Home to get help and display the summary of the PC-Talk commands. The screen will appear as shown in Fig. 5-3. As you can see, most of the commands are invoked by pressing some key in conjunction with the Alternate key. The list is not that long. PC-Talk does not have nearly as many commands to learn as the programs covered in the previous chapters. Do not worry about getting rid of the command summary box. It will disappear, be overwritten, or scroll off the screen as you continue operation of PC-Talk.

The first thing to do is to make sure that PC-Talk is set up correctly for your system and your needs. The configuration of PC-Talk at the time it is started is determined by a list of defaults, which may be modified. To examine these defaults to determine whether any need to be modified, enter the command to set the program defaults, which is Alternate-F. The screen will be headed by the mes-

```
===Proceed ...                          ===PC-TALK III  COMMAND SUMMARY===

                                         ↑PrtSc =  print screen contents
                                         ^PrtSc =  contin. printout (or ^PgUp)
                                          Alt-R =  Receive a file  (or PgDn)
                                          Alt-T =  Transmit a file  (or PgUp)
                                        transmit:  pacing '=p'  binary '=b'
                                       tran/recv:  XMODEM '=x'
                                          Alt-V =  View file   Alt-Y = delete
                                          Alt-D =  Dialing directory
                                          Alt-Q =  redial last number
                                          Alt-K =  set/clear Func keys (Alt-J)
                                          Alt-=    set/clear temp Alt keys
                                         Alt-E = Echo toggle  Alt-M = Message
                                         Alt-S = Screendump   Alt-C = Clearsc
                                          Alt-P =  communications Parameters
                                          Alt-F =  set program deFaults
                                          Alt-L =  change Logged drive
                                          Alt-W =  set margin Width alarm
                                          Alt-Z =  elapsed time/current call
                                          Alt-X =  eXit to DOS
                                       Ctrl-End = send sustained Break signal

  ^PrtSc=prnt  Alt- T=tran R=recv V=view D=dial E=echo M=mesg X=exit <Home>=Help
```

Fig. 5-3. Summary of commands displayed by PC-Talk.

sage "Set New Defaults," followed by a listing of all of the present program defaults, as shown in Fig. 5-4.

Only a handful of the defaults are of concern to the new user of PC-Talk. The first four involve the communications parameters, initially set to 300 baud, even parity, seven data bits, and one stop bit. These can be easily altered to common values while using PC-Talk by issuing the Communications Parameters command. Nevertheless, if you regularly plan on 1200 baud communications, it makes sense to change the defaults so that PC-Talk begins at that speed. Likewise, if you anticipate the need to generally communicate with eight data bits and no parity (the most common alternative to the current default) this could be changed as well. The only remaining default of importance initially is the communications port, the fourth item from the bottom in the second column. The initial default is COM1:, but if the serial port for your modem is COM2: this needs to be changed.

For my own use of PC-Talk, I plan to generally communicate at 1200 baud. With a 1200-baud modem, why use the slower 300-baud speed? I will most often use a format with seven data bits, even parity, and one stop bit. The internal modem is configured as serial port COM2:. The applicable modification of the defaults would be accomplished as follows: When the Alternate-F set default command is given, the cursor appears following the current baud rate entry. To change this, type in the new baud rate desired, 1200, followed by Return. None of the following communications parameters need to be changed. To leave an entry unchanged, press Return and the cursor will drop down to the next line. Keep pressing Return until the cursor is finally on the Communications port line, following the COM1: entry. Change this by typing COM2: and press Return.

After entering all of the changes to be made, it is no longer necessary to continue pressing Return to go through the remainder of the list. Press

Escape. (An arrow will appear on the screen at the point where you are stopping.) Then press Return. You will be asked if the changes are correct. If they are, press Y. The screen should now appear as shown in Fig. 6-5. Pressing N will terminate the set-default procedure. You can begin again by issuing the Alternate-F command. After you indicate that the changes are correct, you are then asked whether you wish to make these changes permanent. Answer Y again. The screen changes to reflect the new defaults, and the default information is written to a file on the disk. These defaults are currently in effect, and the next time you start PC-Talk, these defaults will apply in initially configuring the program.

What defaults should you set? The first four communications parameters are not critical, for these can be altered very easily. Nevertheless, if you plan to communicate at 1200 baud, you might as well change the default baud rate. If you do not know what option to select for parity, data bits, and stop bits, leave these alone for now. The most important single thing is setting the proper communications port. If you leave the default at COM1:, and your modem is connected to COM2:, absolutely nothing will happen when you attempt to communicate. What if you do not know which communications port is used by your modem? Start by leaving the default at COM1: and try to proceed. If absolutely nothing happens, then try changing the default to COM2:.

After you finish with the default setting procedure, the PC-Talk prompt "= = = Proceed . . ." appears on the screen, again indicating that PC-Talk is ready to communicate or to accept another command. This would be a good time to learn how to change the basic communications parameters without changing the defaults. The command for this is Alternate-P. Press this and the selection of options shown in Fig. 5-6 will be displayed on the screen. This list covers the most commonly used communications parameters: seven data bits, even parity, and eight data bits, no parity, at both 300 and 1200 baud. Enter the appropriate numbers from 1 to 4 to make a selection and press Return. Pressing F and Return resets the parameters to their default values, which may well be the same as one of the four options listed. X and Return ter-

```
===SET NEW DEFAULTS===

 Present program defaults:

Baud rate       300        Screendump file B:SCRNDUMP.PCT
Parity          E          Redial delay    20
Data bits       7          Connect prompt  CONNECT
Stop bits       1          Line 25 help    Y
Echo            N          Foreground      7
Messages        N          Background      0
Strip #1        0          High inten.     15
Replace #1      0          Print port      LPT1:
Strip #2        0          Print init.
Replace #2      0          Print width     80
Strip #3        0          Comm. port      COM1:
Replace #3      0          Comm. init.     ,CS,DS
Pacing p=                  Modem init.
Logged drive    B:         C/R subst.      }
Margin width    70

 Enter ↵ to leave unchanged - <space>↵ for 'null' value - <ESC>↵ to quit
*** Enter new values
```

Fig. 5-4. Procedure for the setting of defaults, showing the initial PC-Talk defaults.

```
===SET NEW DEFAULTS===

 Present program defaults:

Baud rate        300 1200        Screendump file B:SCRNDUMP.PCT
Parity           E               Redial delay    20
Data bits        7               Connect prompt  CONNECT
Stop bits        1               Line 25 help    Y
Echo             N               Foreground      7
Messages         N               Background      0
Strip #1         0               High inten.     15
Replace #1       0               Print port      LPT1:
Strip #2         0               Print init.
Replace #2       0               Print width     80
Strip #3         0               Comm. port      COM1: COM2:
Replace #3       0               Comm. init.     ,CS,DS
Pacing p=                        Modem init.
Logged drive     B:              C/R subst.      }
Margin width     70

 Enter ↵ to leave unchanged - <space>↵ for 'null' value - <ESC>↵ to quit
*** New values ok (y/n)?
```

Fig. 5-5. Changing the default values.

minates the procedure without changing the baud rate or other communications parameters from what they were before. Enter the desired choice and press Return to get ready to communicate.

Note that in all of the activity undertaken thus far, you have been communicating exclusively with PC-Talk, issuing various commands to the program. If you changed communications parameters in the course of this process, PC-Talk would have sent appropriate signals to the serial port to configure it as specified. This is as far as any communications would have proceeded. Thus far, no communication has occurred either with the modem or with any remote computer.

```
===COMMUNICATIONS PARAMETERS===

Present parameters: 1200,E,7,1

Echo-N Mesg-N Strip-N Pace-N

Options:
   1 -  300,E,7,1  (text)      2 -  300,N,8,1  (binary)
   3 - 1200,E,7,1  (text)      4 - 1200,N,8,1  (binary)
               F - reset params to defaults
               X - exit to terminal
Choose:
```

Fig. 5-6. Changing the basic communications parameters.

Making the Connection

Having made any required changes in the communications parameters or other defaults, you are now ready to make the connection with another computer and begin communications. Different procedures must be followed for acoustic and direct-connect modems. Both will be outlined here.

For beginners, acoustic modems are perhaps easier because there is so little to do. Pick up the telephone and dial the number of the remote computer. When you hear a high-pitched tone, that is the remote computer answering the telephone. Place the handset in the cups on the modem (making sure the cord is at the correct end) and you are ready to begin communicating. Do whatever is required by the remote computer system to begin communications. In many cases, pressing Return is an appropriate way to begin, but this is not always the case. An example of the start of a communications session is presented below, after the discussion of establishing a connection with a direct-connect modem with automatic dialing.

If you are using a direct-connect modem with an automatic dialing feature, you need to first determine the code required to instruct the modem to dial the telephone number. With Hayes and Hayes-compatible modems, the code to dial a number using touch-tone dialing is ATDT (the letters must be capitalized). AT is the command prefix to obtain the modem's attention, D is the command instructing the modem to dial a telephone number, and T indicates the use of touch-tone dialing. Pulse dialing would be accomplished with the command ATDP. If you are using a modem with a different set of commands, you will have to consult the documentation that came with the modem to determine the command to dial a telephone number.

As an example, suppose I wish to dial CompuServe. Their telephone number for 1200-baud service in Indianapolis is 638-2762, and this is a local call. To instruct the modem to dial this number, I enter the following command:

```
ATDT6382762<Return>
```

From the modem's speaker, I should hear the dial tone, the tones as the number is dialed, the ringing of the phone, and then, perhaps, a brief high-pitched tone from the remote computer before the speaker cuts out. A Hayes-compatible modem responds with the message "CONNECT," which is displayed on the screen. Other modems may generate different messages. The screen should now show both the modem dialing command and the connect message. For the example given, using a Hayes-compatible modem, the screen appears as shown in Fig. 5-7.

Up to this point, you have been communicating with your modem, giving the modem the command to dial the number and receiving the response that a connection has been established with a remote computer. Now things change: you are ready to begin communications with the remote computer. At this point, the user of the direct-connect modem has reached the same point that the user of the acoustic modem reaches when the handset is placed in the cups on the modem. Communication with the remote computer has been established, and you are ready to enter your first command to that computer.

CompuServe instructs users to begin communications by entering a Control-C. This is displayed on the screen as ^C. The CompuServe computer responds by requesting your CompuServe User ID Number. In my case, the number is 76167,456. The number is entered and Return is pressed. Next comes the prompt for my password. The purpose of passwords is to restrict access to the authorized user. Needless to say, I will not give you my real password. Suppose my password were BOAT*TOUCH (CompuServe's standard example password). I would type this in, but the characters are not displayed (echoed back) on the screen. Many systems do not echo passwords to prevent someone from determining a password by looking over the user's shoulder. After pressing Return, if the password is correct, I am logged onto the CompuServe system. CompuServe's opening message is displayed. The screen display of this logon to CompuServe is illustrated in Fig. 5-8. This sequence would be identical whether the initial connection were established with an acoustic modem

```
ATDT6382762

CONNECT















 ^PrtSc=prnt  Alt- T=tran R=recv V=view D=dial E=echo M=mesg X=exit <Home>=Help
```

Fig. 5-7. Dialing the CompuServe number and making a connection with a Hayes-compatible modem.

```
ATDT6382762

CONNECT
^C

User ID: 76167,456
Password:

Job 50 on CompuServe Information Service at 19:26 EST 5-Au













 ^PrtSc=prnt  Alt- T=tran R=recv V=view D=dial E=echo M=mesg X=exit <Home>=Help
```

Fig. 5-8. Making the connection and logging onto CompuServe.

or a direct-connect modem.

Note that communications have now been occurring with the remote computer. The commands to log onto the CompuServe system are sent to that computer, and the CompuServe computer responds with the various prompts or messages. Each remote computer system will have its own procedures for logging on and for interacting with the system after you are logged on. You will have to obtain the documentation or in some other way learn the procedure for each computer system with which you will be communicating.

Terminating Communication

Once you have completed communications with a remote computer, you have to go through the proper procedures to terminate the communications. The first task is to tell the remote computer that you have finished. This will require entering the appropriate command required by the computer system with which you are communicating. Either BYE or OFF serves to disconnect you from CompuServe. Enter this command, followed by Return. A disconnect message will be sent by the CompuServe computer, and you will be disconnected from the remote computer. Other computer systems may require different disconnect procedures. In any event, this communication is taking place with the remote computer.

The remote computer has now "hung up" the phone on its end and you are disconnected. Several random characters may appear on the screen. After a few seconds, an automatic direct-connect modem will sense that this has occurred. A Hayes-compatible modem will send back the message "NO CARRIER" and hang up the phone. This logging off of CompuServe and the disconnection by the modem is illustrated in Fig. 5-9. With an acoustic modem, you need to hang up the phone manually, taking the handset out of the modem and replacing it on the telephone.

All this assumes that everything works as planned, and you are able to instruct the remote computer to terminate communications and hang

```
the service you want to use.  For example, if you want to go directly to the
index, you may enter the GO command followed by the page number IND-1 at any !
prompt.

Press <CR> for more !

CompuServe                    CIS-76

  Key digit or H for help !GO IND-1 <CR>
  You may abbreviate the page number by eliminating the dash and the number
after the initial three characters of the page number.  This will take you to
the selected service's first page.  For example, to go to the first page of the
index, you could enter the following command.
  Key digit or H for help !GO IND <CR>
Last page !OFF


Thank you for using CompuServe!

Off at 19:27 EST 5-Aug-86
Connect time = 0:02
<<>>_wT
NO CARRIER
```

Fig. 5-9. Logging off CompuServe and concluding communications.

up the phone at its end. What if you want to terminate communications and hang up the phone but are unable to get the remote computer to respond appropriately? In that case, you will need to hang up the phone and disconnect from your end. With an acoustic modem, just hang up the phone. With a direct-connect modem, a different procedure is required. You have to instruct the modem to hang up the phone.

The first task in terminating a connection with a direct-connect modem is to get the modem's attention. When the connection was initially established with the remote computer, the modem automatically shifted from its command mode, in which it recognized a variety of commands, to its data mode, used for the actual communications. In the data mode, the modem ignores characters that look like commands, passing them, instead, to the remote computer. This is necessary, for what if the information being transmitted included the characters "ATDT?" You do not want the modem to immediately start dialing a number.

While in the data mode, the modem looks only for one special *escape sequence* that instructs the modem to shift back to its command mode. With Hayes-compatible modems, this sequence is a short interval of time followed by three plus signs (+ + +) followed by another short interval of time. This is chosen because it is extremely unlikely that you would ever wish to transmit this sequence to the remote computer. To get the attention of a Hayes-compatible modem, wait a second and enter three plus signs. The modem will recognize this as its escape sequence and respond with its prompt "OK."

You have just "awakened" the modem and told it that anything that follows should be considered to be a command. Then you can issue the command to hang up the phone, which is ATH (H for hang-up, of course) followed by Return. The modem disconnects itself from the telephone line, hanging up the phone and returns another OK response. You are now back to where you started. In giving the + + + escape sequence and the ATH hang-up command, you are communicating with the modem, which is responding with the OK prompts. Other modems that are not Hayes-compatible will require different procedures and commands to disconnect the modem from the telephone line ("hanging up" the phone).

What do you do if you cannot figure out how to terminate communications in an orderly fashion? If the problem arises in communicating your desire to end the session to the remote computer, you can just hang up. Eventually the computer will notice that you have left and disconnect by itself. If you are paying for the time you are connected, however, this could result in extra charges until the remote computer gets around to disconnecting. Just hanging up is also discourteous, even for computers, so try to disconnect yourself from the remote system in an orderly manner. If you cannot figure out how to do so, however, nothing really catastrophic is likely to happen.

What if you cannot figure out how to disconnect your modem from the telephone line? The phone will remain "off the hook," the line will remain busy, and no one will be able to call you. You are going to have to learn how to disconnect the modem and hang up the phone eventually. If you encounter some problems the first few times you try data communications, however, you can just take the drastic approach of turning off the modem or, if the modem is internal, turning off the entire computer system. This will hang up the phone and restore service.

USING THE DIALING DIRECTORY

The remaining features of PC-Talk involve issuing commands to the program itself to undertake special functions. One of the most useful features of PC-Talk for users with "smart" modems is the dialing directory. This allows the storage of the name, phone number, and communications parameters required for communication with remote computers and the automatic dialing of those computers.

Making Entries in the Directory

PC-Talk's dialing directory is accessed with the command Alternate-D. This brings up the dialing directory. The first time you use this feature, the directory will be empty, and the screen will appear as shown in Fig. 5-10. To use the directory feature for automatically dialing numbers, it is first necessary to make entries into the directory.

Automatic dialing requires the use of the appropriate modem dialing command. The first line of the screen shows the current command that will be used by PC-Talk. With a new directory, the command is ATDT, the Hayes-compatible command for touch-tone dialing. If this is correct for your system, nothing needs to be done. If another command is needed for instructing your modem to dial a number, however, you will need to change the command. To do so, enter R to revise the directory and press Return. Then enter M to indicate your wish to change the modem dialing command and press Return. Enter the correct command and press Return. The change will be made and displayed on the top line.

As an example, the CompuServe number dialed above will be entered into the dialing directory as the first entry. Begin by entering R and Return to revise or add to the directory. Then specify the directory number to be changed by entering 1 and Return. The directory procedure will prompt you for the various entries. For the name, enter CompuServe and press Return. For the phone number, enter 6382762 and press Return. If you are entering a long distance number, enter the initial 1 plus the area code if required.

Next, PC-Talk asks whether you are satisfied with the communications parameters or you wish to change them from the values displayed in the directory. The parameters are displayed in the following sequence: baud rate, parity, number of data bits, and number of stop bits. The directory displays default communications parameters of 300 baud, even parity, seven data bits, and one stop bit. Change this by responding with N for no, and then enter a baud rate of 1200, E for even parity, 7 for

```
===DIALING DIRECTORY  1 ===   Modem dialing command = ATDT
                            Long distance service +# =
                                                  -# =
   Name                          Phone #    Comm Param  Echo Mesg Strip Pace
  1-----------------------   - --- --- ----   300-E-7-1    N    N    N    N
  2-----------------------   - --- --- ----   300-E-7-1    N    N    N    N
  3-----------------------   - --- --- ----   300-E-7-1    N    N    N    N
  4-----------------------   - --- --- ----   300-E-7-1    N    N    N    N
  5-----------------------   - --- --- ----   300-E-7-1    N    N    N    N
  6-----------------------   - --- --- ----   300-E-7-1    N    N    N    N
  7-----------------------   - --- --- ----   300-E-7-1    N    N    N    N
  8-----------------------   - --- --- ----   300-E-7-1    N    N    N    N
  9-----------------------   - --- --- ----   300-E-7-1    N    N    N    N
 10-----------------------   - --- --- ----   300-E-7-1    N    N    N    N
 11-----------------------   - --- --- ----   300-E-7-1    N    N    N    N
 12-----------------------   - --- --- ----   300-E-7-1    N    N    N    N
 13-----------------------   - --- --- ----   300-E-7-1    N    N    N    N
 14-----------------------   - --- --- ----   300-E-7-1    N    N    N    N
 15-----------------------   - --- --- ----   300-E-7-1    N    N    N    N

 Dial entry #:              ¦ or...     Enter: R to revise or add to directory
                                               M for manual dialing
                                           F / B to page through directory
                                               X to exit to terminal
                            ¦ For long distance service, precede entry # with +/-
```

Fig. 5-10. Initial display of the dialing directory.

the number of data bits, and 1 for the number of stop bits.

PC-Talk then asks if you are satisfied with the remaining optional parameters. These all involve rather technical matters that are best avoided for now. Answer yes by pressing Y. The final question is whether the directory changes you have entered are satisfactory. Answer yes by pressing Y, and the new entry is permanently added to your dialing directory, which will now appear as in Fig. 5-11. The dialing directory is stored in a file on the disk and will be available for your use each time you load PC-Talk.

Current directory entries can be revised using exactly the same procedure. Enter R and the number of the directory entry to be revised. PC-Talk takes you through the procedure step-by-step, asking whether or not you wish to make revisions. A single directory entry or a range of contiguous entries can be deleted using the same command. After entering the R, enter C to indicate that you wish to clear entries. PC-Talk will request the first and last entries in the block to be deleted, and then ask once more if you are certain you wish to do this.

The dialing directory can hold up to 60 entries. Fifteen are displayed on the screen at one time. By entering the commands F, for forward, and B, for backward, you can page through the four pages of directory entries. To make revisions, you must be viewing the page with the entry to be revised.

The comments on the screen regarding the long distance service refer to a feature that allows the entry of local access numbers and codes for using alternative long distance services. This had been necessary in the past to use long distance companies such as MCI and Sprint. With most of the nation now changing to the Dial 1 service, allowing the choice of a long distance company, this option is less important. If you need to use it, check the PC-Talk documentation for further details.

Dialing and Redialing Numbers

With one or more entries made in the dialing directory, you can use this feature to automatically dial remote computers. If the directory is not currently displayed on the screen, enter the Alternate-

```
===DIALING DIRECTORY  1 ===   Modem dialing command = ATDT
                           Long distance service +# =
                                                 -# =
  Name                         Phone #    Comm Param  Echo Mesg Strip Pace
 1-CompuServe                  6382762    1200-E-7-1   N    N    N     N
 2------------------------  - --- --- ----   300-E-7-1   N    N    N     N
 3------------------------  - --- --- ----   300-E-7-1   N    N    N     N
 4------------------------  - --- --- ----   300-E-7-1   N    N    N     N
 5------------------------  - --- --- ----   300-E-7-1   N    N    N     N
 6------------------------  - --- --- ----   300-E-7-1   N    N    N     N
 7------------------------  - --- --- ----   300-E-7-1   N    N    N     N
 8------------------------  - --- --- ----   300-E-7-1   N    N    N     N
 9------------------------  - --- --- ----   300-E-7-1   N    N    N     N
10------------------------  - --- --- ----   300-E-7-1   N    N    N     N
11------------------------  - --- --- ----   300-E-7-1   N    N    N     N
12------------------------  - --- --- ----   300-E-7-1   N    N    N     N
13------------------------  - --- --- ----   300-E-7-1   N    N    N     N
14------------------------  - --- --- ----   300-E-7-1   N    N    N     N
15------------------------  - --- --- ----   300-E-7-1   N    N    N     N

Revise/add entry #:1
Is entry #1 ok (y/n)?
```

Fig. 5-11. Dialing directory with the entry for dialing CompuServe.

```
===REDIALING 8732390 at 08:58:17
ATDT8732390


NO CARRIER

===REDIALING 8732390 at 08:59:14
ATDT8732390


NO CARRIER

===REDIALING 8732390 at 09:00:11
ATDT8732390


NO CARRIER






   Redialing...  *** HIT ANY KEY TO TERMINATE ***  (redial started at 08:58:17)
```

Fig. 5-12. Using the automatic redial feature to make multiple attempts to contact a remote computer.

D command to bring up the dialing directory. Simply enter the number of the directory entry to be dialed and press Return. In the example, to dial CompuServe, enter 1 and press Return. The message appears on the screen that PC-Talk and the modem are dialing CompuServe, phone number 6382762. If connection is successfully established, the message CONNECT will be displayed on the screen, and you can proceed with communications.

The dialing directory can also be employed to "manually" dial any number you specify. This is handy for calling up a computer you wish to check out without having to add the information to the directory. Begin by invoking the dialing directory function with Alternate-D. Enter M for manual dialing and press Return. You will then be asked to enter the number to be dialed. Type in the number, press Return, and the number will be dialed. Essentially this procedure saves you from having to remember or enter the modem dialing command, the ATDT for Hayes-compatible modems. It also allows you to use the automatic redialing feature.

What happens if a number is dialed and it is not answered or is busy? Instead of the CONNECT message, a NO CARRIER message is displayed by Hayes-compatible modems, indicating that it did not receive a response from a remote computer. The problem of busy signals can be especially difficult in attempting to contact computer bulletin boards, which generally have only a single incoming line. PC-Talk includes an extremely useful feature for dealing with such situations—automatic redialing. The last number dialed through the dialing directory—either a directory entry or a manually-dialed number—can be automatically redialed simply by entering the command Alternate-Q. The message appears on the screen that the number is being redialed. If a successful connection is not achieved, PC-Talk will continue to automatically redial the number approximately once each minute. This can go on indefinitely. Pressing any key on the computer terminates the automatic redialing, as indicated by the prompt at the bottom of the screen. The appearance of the screen after several attempts at redialing a number that is busy is shown in Fig. 5-12.

When a connection is established, PC-Talk sounds an audible alarm by playing a few notes on the computer's speaker. This alerts you if you have gone off to do something else while the computer redials. A message is displayed on the screen indicating that a connection has been established. You need only press any key to proceed with communications.

COMMUNICATIONS FEATURES

PC-Talk includes a number of features for printing the information resulting from communication with remote computers and saving images of the screen or longer communications sessions to a file on the disk. Other functions useful during communications include the ability to clear the screen and a timer indicating the duration of the current session.

Printing Out Information

During a communication session with another computer, it is often desirable to keep a record of the interchange. One method of doing this is to print out the information that is also being displayed on the screen. The simplest way of accomplishing this is the basic DOS screen dump, achieved with Shift-PrtSc. The entire contents of the screen is printed out on the printer. This is not a function restricted to PC-Talk, of course, but is especially useful during computer communications. The print screen command is even listed in the summary of PC-Talk commands.

A continuous record of the information going to the screen—both the information you type in and the information sent by the remote computer—can be printed out using the Control-PrtSc command. Entering this command turns on the printer, so that everything going to the screen is also printed. The message "Printout On" is displayed on the screen. Press Control-PrtSc a second time to turn off the printing function, and information is directed only to the screen. The message "Printout Off" is displayed. The printer can be toggled on and off as often as desired during a communication session using this command.

When communicating at 1200 baud, many printers will be unable to keep up if the communication is relatively continuous. PC-Talk has a buffer that can hold a certain amount of text as the printer falls behind. If you have the opportunity, slow down the interchange. For example, when the remote computer asks you for a response, pause and give the printer a chance to catch up. If the printer falls too far behind, PC-Talk will automatically turn the printer off so that communications can proceed without delay.

Saving Information on the Disk

Just as screens and continuous streams of information can be printed out, screens of information and continuous streams can be saved in files on the disk. Before using these features, be sure that you have placed a formatted data disk in the B: drive. PC-Talk defaults to the B: drive for the storage of information. This is the logical place for those with dual floppy systems. This default can be changed using the set default command, if desired, and explicit drive specifications can be given when file names are requested.

The screen save command, Alternate-S, saves the information on the current screen in a file on the B: disk with the name SCRNDUMP.PCT. The procedure is simple and automatic. Press Alternate-S, and the information is saved. Each screenful of information is added to the end of the file SCRNDUMP.PCT, so if the procedure is used several times, the information on each screen will appear sequentially in the file.

The command to receive a file, Alternate-R, can be used to record on a disk file a continuous log of the information from a communications session going to the screen. Its use is analogous to the Control-PrtSc function for directing the stream of information to the printer. In this case, the stream of information is directed to a file on the disk. Press

Alternate-R, and you are prompted for the name of the file in which the information is to be stored. Enter any valid DOS file name, such as COMPSRV1.PCT, and press Return. (The extension .PCT is being used to indicate that this is a file from PC-Talk.) The status line on the bottom of the screen changes to indicate that the information is being recorded in the file COMPSRV1.PCT. All information entered by you or sent by the remote computer is stored in that file from that point on. Figure 5-13 shows the screen as it appears after the receive function has been initiated and the first few lines of information following that have been received.

To stop the saving of the information to the file on the disk, enter the Alternate-R command a second time. You are informed that the receipt of the file has been terminated. Any further communications are not recorded on the disk.

After exiting PC-Talk, the DOS TYPE command can be used to view the files saved with the Alternate-S or Alternate-R commands. The command COPY B:filename PRN can be used to print the files out. Alternatively, the PC-Write editor can be used with these files. See Chapter 7 for more information on using these programs in conjunction with one another.

The commands to dump the contents of the screen to the printer or to the disk file would be used when some information appeared on the screen that you suddenly realized you wished to keep. Pressing Shift-PrtSc or Alternate-S saves that information to the printer or disk respectively. If you anticipate that a considerable amount of information is to be saved, using the commands to capture a continuous stream of communications is more effective. Enter Control-PrtSc to print out the information or Alternate-R to save the information in a file on the disk before the information is actually encountered. Capture the stream of information desired, and then use the same commands to turn the function off.

```
===RECEIVE A FILE===
   specification:COMPSRV1.PCT
=================================
HELP

CompuServe                    CIS-162

BRIEF COMMAND SUMMARY
Every command must end with a carriage return.  Pressing the carriage return key

(which may be marked ENTER on some keyboards) transmits the command to
CompuServe.
In online information, the carriage return key i








  Receiving B:COMPSRV1.PCT  (ALT-R to Terminate)
```

Fig. 5-13. Storing information from a communications session with CompuServe in a file named COMPSRV1.PCT.

Miscellaneous Communications Functions

PC-Talk conveniently keeps track of the time elapsed since the beginning of any communications session. To display the elapsed time, simply enter the command Alternate-Z. The time will be displayed in a box on the upper right-hand corner of the screen, as shown in Fig. 5-14. As communications continue, this information will scroll off the top of the screen. To check the elapsed time again, repeat the Alternate-Z command. This timing feature is especially useful when you are paying for the communications, either through long distance telephone charges or through connect charges with a commercial service such as CompuServe. You can always keep track of how much time—and therefore how much in charges—you have accumulated. When a communications session is terminated and you dial again, the elapsed time is reset to zero to time the new session.

Anytime you are using PC-Talk, the command Control-C can be used to clear the screen. This is useful when the screen has become cluttered from multiple commands, error messages, or whatever. If you anticipate printing the contents of the screen or saving the screen to the disk, the clear screen function can be especially useful for getting rid of extraneous material before the information you actually want to save appears on the screen.

RECEIVING AND TRANSMITTING FILES

PC-Talk includes easy-to-use functions for receiving files from and transmitting files to remote computers. When communicating with large mainframe computers, these procedures are often referred to as *downloading* files from the remote computer and *uploading* files to the remote computer. The files received and transmitted can be text files or binary files consisting of programs for the computer.

```
BRIEF COMMAND SUMMARY                   | Elapsed time this call =  2  min |
Every command must end with a carriage                                      ey

(which may be marked ENTER on some keyboards) transmits the command to
CompuServe.
In online information, the carriage return key is represented by the symbol
<CR>.  Pressing <CR> at the end of an article returns you to the previous menu.
 T - TOP menu page
 M - previous MENU
 H or ? - HELP
 GO word or GO page - GO directly to a service
 FIND topic - FIND all references to topic
 OFF or BYE - sign off
 S n - SCROLL from n
 R - RESEND a page
 F - FORWARD a page
 B - BACK a page
 N - display NEXT menu item

Press <CR> for more !
===RECEIPT OF FILE B:COMPSRV1.PCT TERMINATED===


 ^PrtSc=prnt  Alt- T=tran R=recv V=view D=dial E=echo M=mesg X=exit <Home>=Help
```

Fig. 5-14. Display of elapsed time of the current communications session.

Basic File Receiving

The receiving of a file of information from a remote computer is accomplished in exactly the same manner as the capture of a stream of communications on the disk, for that is what the file is. The Alternate-R receive command begins the process of saving all communications to a file on your disk, and the same command terminates the process. The only difference is that in receiving a file of information, you are attempting to capture just the information sent from a particular file on the remote computer. The tricky part is beginning the process of saving information to the disk at the point when the remote computer begins transmitting the file. You need to know how to get the remote computer to begin transmitting the file to your computer, and then determine the best time to turn on the file receiving function.

As an example, consider the process of downloading a file with a listing of a short, sample BASIC language computer program from a university computer to the personal computer. The program is stored in a file on the large computer, with the file name PROG1.B20 (many computer systems use file names that are similar in format to PC-/MS-DOS). When this computer is connected with a personal computer or a terminal, the file can be sent to the PC or the terminal by using the TYPE command (again, the same as in PC-/MS-DOS). Thus, issuing this command,

```
TYPE PROG1.B10<Return>
```

would cause the file to be listed on the screen.

To download this file to your computer, you would like the saving to begin just when the file listing is sent by the remote computer. This presents a problem, because immediately after you send the above command, the listing begins. You would not have time to give the Alternate-R command and enter the file name before the transmission of the file by the remote computer began. If you turned on the receiving function with Alternate-R before issuing the command to the remote computer, then the entire command would be saved as a part of the file. This might not be a problem, for you could delete this later, but a common compromise is often used. At the appropriate point in communications with the remote computer, enter this command,

```
TYPE PROG1.B20
```

but do not press the Return key. Now enter the Alternate-R command to initiate the saving of information to the file on the disk. When prompted for the file name under which the information is to be stored, enter a valid DOS file name. You might want to use a similar name for the storage of this file on your disk, so enter the following:

```
PROG1.BAS<Return>
```

PC-Talk is now set up to store all further communications in the file on the disk.

Now press Return. This Return will be sent to the remote computer, completing the command you have previously entered. Transmission of the file from the remote computer to your system will begin. The file will be listed on the screen and will be saved in the file named PROG1.BAS on your disk in the B: drive. The appearance of the screen after these commands have been entered and file transmission has commenced is shown in Fig. 5-15. The remote computer will continue sending until the entire file has been transmitted. At that point, the remote computer will display its prompt symbol, in this case @, and stop, awaiting your next command. Terminate the receiving of the file on the disk by entering the Alternate-R command

```
TYPE PROG1.B20
===RECEIVE A FILE===
   specification:PROG1.BAS
=============================

00010 REM MOVING WAVES PROGRAM
00020 REM INTERVAL
00030 S = .4
```

Fig. 5-15. Beginning the receiving of the file PROG1.BAS from a remote computer.

again. The screen at the conclusion of the process will appear as shown in Fig. 5-16.

The entire file PROG1.B20 on the main computer has now been stored in the file PROG1.BAS on the disk. Unfortunately, two extra characters have been added. After issuing the first Alternate-S, a Return was pressed to initiate the sending of the file. This extra Return character is at the beginning of the file. At the end of the transmission of the file, the remote computer sent the prompt symbol @ to indicate that it was ready to receive the next command. This @ character was sent before you had the opportunity to turn off the saving of the file on the disk and will be appended to the end of the file PROG1.B20 that was sent. If you list or print the file PROG1.BAS using the appropriate DOS command, it would appear as shown in Fig. 5-17. The extra prompt symbol, @, is visible at the end. The extra Return character at the beginning just produces a blank line and thus is not obvious on the display.

These extra characters can easily be deleted from the file using PC-Write. Edit the file PROG1.BAS with the command

```
ED B:PROG1.BAS<Return>
```

entered from DOS. With the cursor at the very beginning of the file, in the first column on the first, blank line, press Delete to erase the Return character. Now move the cursor to the very end of the file, to the offending @ prompt symbol. Shift-Grey – will move the cursor to the end. Now press Delete once more to erase this character. The resulting file is now identical to the file sent by the remote computer. Press F1 F2 to save the file and exit PC-Write. The file can now be executed just as any other BASIC program.

Is there any way of avoiding the addition of the extraneous characters to the file being received?

```
TYPE PROG1.B20
===RECEIVE A FILE===
   specification:PROG1.BAS
============================

00010 REM MOVING WAVES PROGRAM
00020 REM INTERVAL
00030 S = .4
00040 REM TOTAL NUMBER OF STEPS
00050 T = 50
00060 FOR C = 0 TO T*S STEP S
00070 PRINT TAB(30*(SIN(C)+1)+1); "*"
00080 PRINT TAB(30*(COS(C)+1)+1); "+"
00090 NEXT C
00100 END
@
===RECEIPT OF FILE B:PROG1.BAS TERMINATED===









 ^PrtSc=prnt  Alt - T=tran R=recv V=view D=dial E=echo M=mesg X=exit <Home>=help
```

Fig. 5-16. Ending the receiving of the file PROG1.BAS from a remote computer.

```
A>TYPE B:PROG1.BAS

00010 REM MOVING WAVES PROGRAM
00020 REM INTERVAL
00030 S = .4
00040 REM TOTAL NUMBER OF STEPS
00050 T = 50
00060 FOR C = 0 TO T*S STEP S
00070 PRINT TAB(30*(SIN(C)+1)+1); "*"
00080 PRINT TAB(30*(COS(C)+1)+1); "+"
00090 NEXT C
00100 END
@


A>
```

Fig. 5-17. Display of the file PROG1.BAS using the DOS TYPE command.

This depends upon the computer system with which you are communicating. If the system explicitly provides for the downloading of files, it may allow you to enter the command to download the file and then pause, allowing you time to enter the Alternate-R command and begin the data capture process before it begins sending the file. At the end of the transmission, the remote computer may again pause, allowing you time to give the second Alternate-R command to turn off the file saving. With systems that do not automatically provide such assistance for the downloading of files, avoiding one or more extra characters will be possible only if you can find ways to instruct the remote computer to pause before beginning the transmission of the file and to finish the transmission without sending its prompt character.

If you are communicating with another person using another personal computer—perhaps also using PC-Talk—then avoiding the extra characters is easier. After the operator of the other computer has agreed to send a file, ask him to pause for a while to allow you to turn on the receiving function, before sending the file. Also, have the operator wait after file transmission has been completed to allow time for you to turn off the receiving function.

Basic File Transmitting

Transmitting a file of information to a remote computer is easier, because you have control and do not have to worry about the problem of the extra characters. The command Alternate-T is used to initiate the transmission of a file on the disk to the remote computer. All that is required is that the remote computer be ready to receive the file before you begin sending it. The information in the file you send will go to the remote computer exactly as if you had typed it in through the keyboard.

For example, suppose you are sending someone a message on CompuServe using their electronic mail facility. Rather than spending the time on CompuServe typing in the message (paying for the connect time), you compose it ahead of time using PC-Write. The message is stored on the B: disk in a file named MESSAGE. Establish communications with CompuServe in the normal manner. Give the commands required to send the message. Enter the file transmission command, Alternate-T. When prompted for the name of the file, enter MESSAGE and press Return. The contents of the file will appear on your screen and it will be transmitted to CompuServe. The status line displays the name of the file being transmitted and an estimate of the number of minutes more that it will take to transmit the file. This process, and the first few lines of the message, are shown on the screen displayed in Fig. 5-18.

If for some reason you should want to terminate the transmission of the file before it is completed, enter the Alternate-T command again. When the file transmission has been completed, do whatever may be necessary to indicate to the remote computer that you are through. For example, using CompuServe's mail facility, the command /EX must be entered to indicate that you have completed the entry of a piece of mail.

To transmit (or upload) any file, you need to determine what commands you would have to give the remote computer if you were to simply type in the information from the keyboard. Enter those commands, and then give the Alternate-T command to transmit the file on the disk instead. When the transmission is complete, proceed with what-

```
  1 XMODEM (MODEM7) protocol
  2 CompuServe 'B' protocol
  3 DC2/DC4 CAPTURE protocol
  4 NO Protocol

Enter choice !4

No error detection/correction.
Do you want to be prompted for each line (Y/N)? N
Begin sending your data.  Use
/EX to indicate the end of your
data.


===TRANSMIT A FILE===
   specification:MESSAGE
===========================
Dear Ed,
This is just a short message to try out the mail service on CompuServe and to
give you the information you were requesting on low-cost programs.  I am using
PC-WRITE to write out this message.  It is a fine, powerful word processing
program, and I am very pleased with it.  PC-FILE is the user-supported data
base program I mentioned to you.  Sometimes I am just ama
  Transmitting B:MESSAGE (ALT-T to terminate)   min. remain:              0.0
```

Fig. 5-18. Transmitting the file MESSAGE to CompuServe's electronic mail facility.

ever procedures would have been required after you had entered that information from the keyboard.

The XMODEM Protocol

The basic receive and transmit functions discussed thus far work fine for transferring text files. An extraneous character at the beginning or end of the file is not a serious problem and can be readily deleted. If an error occurs in the transmission, an individual character might be garbled, but the text will still be readable, and the error can probably be corrected. For data files consisting of long lists of numbers, however, errors are not so easily detected by examination or corrected. With program files, any extra characters or an error in even a single bit can be fatal, causing the program to fail and not run.

In the early days of microcomputers, Ward Christensen developed a *protocol*, or set of procedures, for transferring files between computers with error checking. He placed a communications program using this protocol in the public domain. The program was called XMODEM. The XMODEM protocol has come to be widely used for reliably transferring files, especially program files, in personal computer communication. Some of the large information services provide support for XMODEM file transfers, and many of the computer bulletin boards do so as well. Use of the XMODEM protocol requires that both the sending and receiving computers support and use this procedure when transferring a file. With XMODEM file transfers, the odds are extremely high that the transfer will take place without any errors.

PC-Talk supports the XMODEM protocol for both receiving and transmitting files. All that is required to use the protocol is to add the designation =X to the end of the specification for the file name being received or transmitted. It is also necessary to assure that the remote computer is also using the XMODEM protocol. The XMODEM protocol uses eight data bits for the transmission of the information, so it is necessary that the communications parameters be set to eight data bits and no parity bit in order to use the XMODEM protocol. The Alternate-P command to change communications parameters can be employed to accomplish this. Simply select options 2 or 4 for 300 or 1200 baud communication respectively.

The most common use of the XMODEM protocol for most users will be the downloading of program files from remote computer systems. The following example will illustrate the receipt of a file from a computer bulletin board system. After you have logged onto a bulletin board system, you will first have to learn the procedures for using the system and discover the names of the files that are available. Assume that you then decide to download a program file named FACE.COM. The command D is given to the bulletin board system to download the file. The name of the file is entered. An X is then entered to specify the use of the XMODEM protocol. Note that all of these commands are specific to the particular bulletin board system being used for this example and can vary.

The bulletin board system replies that it is ready to transmit the file. It is now waiting for you. Enter the Alternate-R command to receive a file. When asked for the file specification, enter the following:

```
FACE.COM=X<Return>
```

This message will appear on the screen:

```
*** Holding for Start . . .
```

This indicates that the XMODEM protocol is in effect and that file transmission is ready to begin. When transmission begins, you next see this message:

```
Received block # 1 - verified
```

With the XMODEM protocol, information is sent one block at a time, each block being 128 bytes in length. When each block is received, a check is made that no errors have occurred. If the block is error-free, the receiving computer sends a message back that it is ready for the next block. This process continues, block by block, until the entire file has been transferred. The appearance of the screen after the XMODEM transfer has been initiated and file transfer begun is illustrated in Fig. 5-19. After the file has been received, the file transfer ends automatically. There is no need to enter a second Alternate-R command to stop the file receiving process. The Alternate-R command can be used to stop the file transfer before it is completed, however.

If errors occur during transmission, the receiving computer notifies the sender, and the block is retransmitted. A message to that effect is displayed. With the XMODEM protocol, the computers keep trying until they get it right. If too many errors accumulate, however, making transfer impractical or impossible, transmission may be terminated automatically.

After file transmission has been completed, a message to that effect will be displayed on the screen. At that point, you can continue with your communication with the bulletin board. After you exit PC-Talk, you can see the file FACE.COM on your B: disk and can execute the program just as you would any other.

File transmission with the XMODEM protocol works in exactly the same fashion. Give the Alternate-T command to transmit a file and add =X to the file name specification. The receiving computer must also initiate receipt of the file using the XMODEM protocol, of course, and you will have to determine the command required to instruct it to do so.

Managing Files

With all of this receiving and transmitting of files taking place, a communications session can involve the use of numerous files. PC-Talk conveniently includes a number of facilities for checking the directory of files on a disk, viewing the contents of files, and otherwise managing the files involved in communications.

Finding out what files are currently stored on the disk in the B: drive is simple. When you are

```
File Function <D,G,H,L,N,Q,U,?>? D
Enter full filename to download? FACE.COM
This is a binary file and requires XMODEM transfer
Download type <X>modem, <A>scii, <Q>uit? X
File size is 29 blocks.
Transfer time: 0 min., 40 sec.
Ready to send. Enter <Ctrl X> to abort transfer...

===RECEIVE A FILE===
   specification:FACE.COM=X
============================
===RECEIVE FILE WITH XMODEM===

***Holding for Start...
Received Block # 1 - verified
Received Block # 2 - verified
Received Block # 3 - verified
Received Block # 4 - verified
Received Block # 5 - verified
Received Block # 6 - verified
Received Block # 7 - verified
Received Block # 8 - verified

  Receiving B:FACE.COM=X  (ALT-R to Terminate)
```

Fig. 5-19. Receiving a file using the XMODEM protocol.

prompted for the file name when using the Alternate-R receive command or the Alternate-T transmit command, just enter ? and Return. The directory of the files on the disk in the B: drive is displayed on the screen, as shown in Fig. 5-20. The desired file name can then be entered in the usual fashion.

PC-Talk allows the viewing of the contents of a file while remaining in PC-Talk and in communication with a remote computer. This can be very handy for checking the contents of a file before sending it, to assure that you are sending the correct file. The view feature can also be employed to check a file that has been received to determine if the transfer has taken place properly. Only text files—the same files that can be examined with the DOS TYPE command—can be viewed. Viewing a file takes place without the information being sent to the remote computer. It is just an activity involving you, your personal computer, and PC-Talk.

Suppose you are getting ready to transmit a file named MESSAGE to CompuServe for sending by electronic mail, as illustrated above. Before initiating the transmission, check the contents of the file to make certain it is correct. To view a file, enter the command Alternate-V, type in the name of the file, and press Return. The first 20 lines of the file are displayed on the screen. Figure 5-21 shows the screen as these first lines of the file are being transmitted. The status line at the bottom of the screen indicates how you should proceed. To continue the display of more of the file, press the space bar. The Alternate-V command terminates the viewing of the file.

If the disk becomes full or you begin to accumulate too many unwanted files, PC-Talk allows the deletion of files. The delete file command is Alternate-Y. Enter that command and the name of the file to be deleted. The file is permanently erased from the disk.

Should the need arise to change the logged, default drive specification while using PC-Talk, use

```
===TRANSMIT A FILE===
   specification:?

ADDRESS .HDR ADDRESS .INX ADDRESS .DTA DIRECT   .RPT LABELS   .RPT INVEN    .HDR
INVEN   .INX INVEN   .DTA INVRPT  .RPT INVRPT2 .RPT INVEN2   .DTA INVEN2   .HDR
INVEN2  .INX FIRST   .DOC FACE    .COM SECOND  .&DO SECOND   .DOC FIRST    .&DO
LETTER  .&   FIG5-16      LETTER       COMPUTER.LST PROG1    .BAS LET
FIG5-15      SCRNDUMP.PCT HRBSTOCK.PCT COMPSRV1.PCT SCRNDUMP.&PC FIG5-13
FIG5-13 .&   MESSAGE

   specification:












 ^PrtSc=prnt  Alt- T=tran R=recv V=view D=dial E=echo M=mesg X=exit <Home>=Help
```

Fig. 5-20. Directory of files on the disk in the B: drive.

```
===VIEW A FILE===
   specification:MESSAGE
===========================



Dear Ed,
This is just a short message to try out the mail service on CompuServe and to
give you the information you were requesting on low-cost programs.  I am using
PC-WRITE to write out this message.  It is a fine, powerful word processing
program, and I am very pleased with it.  PC-FILE is the user-supported data
base program I mentioned to you.  Sometimes I am just amazed at the variety of
capabilities built into this program.  Of course, I will be sending this
message to CompuServe with PC-TALK, the original "Freeware" program.  I am
completely happy using this as my communications program.  Try out these user-
supported programs.  It will cost you nothing to experiment with them.  Then,
if you like them, pay the modest registration fees.  They are a lot cheaper
than most of the programs in the stores.  Good luck.
John



  Viewing B:MESSAGE  Press <space> to continue  (Alt-V to terminate)
```

Fig. 5-21. Display of the contents of the file MESSAGE during a communications session.

the Alternate-L command. Enter the command and the new drive specification, such as A:, and press Return. The A: drive will now be the default drive used if no drive prefix is given as part of a file name.

KEYBOARD INPUT STRINGS

During communications with remote computers, certain instructions, responses, or other strings of characters may need to be entered repeatedly. PC-Talk allows the storage of such character strings for entry with a single keystroke. The strings can be permanently stored and entered with function key combinations, or temporary assignments can be made for the current session to Alternate key combinations.

Function Key Input Strings

PC-Talk allows the permanent assignment of up to 40 strings of characters to the function keys and the combinations of the function keys with Control, Shift, and Alternate. These strings can be up to 126 characters in length. Once these strings have been assigned, they can be sent at any time by simply pressing the appropriate function key or function key combination.

One obvious application for the function-key input strings would be for storing the log-on information for various computer systems. Suppose you used CompuServe regularly and wanted to expedite logging on by defining function keys to hold your user identification number and password. Begin the assignment to the function keys by calling up the function key directory using the command Alternate-K. If this is the first time you have used the function key directory, it will be blank, as shown in Fig. 5-22.

Begin by entering the account number 76167,456 for Function key F1. Enter R to revise the function key assignments, and press F1 to indicate this is the function key to which the assignment is to be made. PC-Talk then prompts for the

```
                         ===FUNCTION KEY DIRECTORY===
                                   Func F1-10
                         F-    Input String
                          1 =
                          2 =
                          3 =
                          4 =
                          5 =
                          6 =
                          7 =
                          8 =
                          9 =
                         10 =

                         Press:  R to revise Func-F assignments
                             F / B to page through directory
                                 X to exit to terminal

^PrtSc=prnt  Alt- T=tran R=recv V=view D=dial E=echo M=mesg X=exit <Home>=Help
```

Fig. 5-22. Initial display of function key assignments.

```
                    ===FUNCTION KEY DIRECTORY===
                               Func F1-10
                    F-   Input String
                     1 = 76167,456}
                     2 =
                     3 =
                     4 =
                     5 =
                     6 =
                     7 =
                     8 =
                     9 =
                    10 =
New input string for Func-F 2:
BOAT*TOUCH}

Use } as substitute for carriage returns
       ↵ to leave key unchanged
<space>↵ to clear key

 ^PrtSc=prnt  Alt- T=tran R=recv V=view D=dial E=echo M=mesg X=exit <Home>=Help
```

Fig. 5-23. Making function key assignments with CompuServe user identification number and password.

entry of the string of characters to be assigned to that function key. You not only want the user identification number sent when you press the function key; you also want the Return entering the user identification number to be sent.

The Return key presents peculiar problems. Pressing Return does not cause anything to be displayed on the screen, and one would like the function key directory to show that a Return is included as part of the string to be sent. Furthermore, Return is used to enter the function key string, so the Return key cannot be pressed to include it within the string to be sent. PC-Talk handles this by defining the right brace ("curly bracket") symbol, }, as meaning Return in the function and Alternate key definitions. You enter the right brace wherever a Return is to be sent. This symbol is displayed in the function key directory. When the function key is pressed to send the string, however, a Return is sent in place of the right brace symbol.

Thus, to enter the CompuServe user identification number with the Return, enter the following string of characters:

76167,456}<Return>

The string is entered into the function key directory. Enter the CompuServe password for function key F2 by pressing R and F2 and entering the following:

BOAT*TOUCH}

Again, note the use of the right brace to indicate the Return at the end. (Of course, this is not my real CompuServe password, only an example.) The appearance of the directory while this second entry is being made is shown in Fig. 5-23. Press Return to enter the password into the directory for function key F2. If you make an error in entering an entry or wish to change an entry, simply revise it again. To delete an entry from the directory, enter R, press the function key to select the appropriate entry, enter one space, and press Return. The entry will be deleted.

The initial display of the function key directory shows the definitions of the function keys F1 through F10. Thirty more function key definitions can be entered for the combinations of the function keys with the Control, Shift, and Alternate keys. You can move forward or backward through the screens for the other function key combination definitions by pressing F and B. As you move, the second line in the box changes to indicate the use of the function keys with Control, Alternate, or Shift. To exit from the function key definition function, press X and you are returned to the terminal mode. The Proceed prompt appears in the bottom of the function key directory box, but the list remains on the screen for reference, until it scrolls off.

Using the strings assigned to the function keys is as easy as pressing the function keys. To illustrate, log onto CompuServe. Use Alternate-D to call up the dialing directory. Enter 1 and press Return to dial the CompuServe number. When you get the CONNECT message, press the Control-C required by CompuServe. The prompt will appear from CompuServe for your user ID. Function key F1 has been defined with this information, so press F1. The account number appears on the screen. CompuServe then prompts for your password. Press F2. Since CompuServe does not echo the password, this does not appear on the screen, but you are now logged on and receive CompuServe's opening message. The screen appears exactly as it would if you had typed in the information from the keyboard, as shown in Fig. 5-24.

You can check on the definitions of the various function keys anytime before using them by issuing the Alternate-K command. The directory appears on the screen. Page through it, if necessary, with the F or B commands and then exit back

```
===DIALING CompuServe
ATDT6382762

CONNECT
^C

User ID: 76167,456
Password:

Job 47 on CompuServe Information Service at 20:37 EST 5-Aug-86 on T14IND








 ^PrtSc=prnt  Alt- T=tran R=recv V=view D=dial E=echo M=mesg X=exit <Home>=Help
```

Fig. 5-24. Logging onto CompuServe using function keys F1 and F2 for the user identification number and password.

```
►►►►Alt- 1 ▐MESSAGE    ▌R=recv V=view D=dial E=echo M=mesg X=exit <Home>=Help
```

Fig. 5-25. Entering the Alternate-1 key definition MESSAGE.

to terminal mode with X. The directory remains on the screen, and you can consult it before pressing a function key to enter a string of characters.

Alternate Key Input Strings

The function key definitions are permanently stored on the disk and will be available each time you start PC-Talk. Sometimes you may wish to define a character string temporarily for input during the current communications session, without permanently storing it. PC-Talk allows up to 10 such strings to be stored and invoked by pressing the Alternate key in conjunction with the numerals 1 through 0. The Alternate key combinations are limited to 50 characters each.

Suppose you are involved in communications in which you are constantly using the file MESSAGE. This file specification can be temporarily assigned to the Alternate-1 combination and then can be entered at any time simply by pressing Alternate-1. To assign an input string to an Alternate key combination, enter the command Alternate – = (hold the Alternate key down and press the equals sign key). Prompting for Alternate key definition occurs on the bottom status line. You must first enter the number of the key to be used with Alternate; enter 1. Alt-1 appears on the status line, with a space for entering the characters to be assigned. This space will increase as characters are typed in. Enter the following string:

```
MESSAGE
```

The screen will now appear as shown in Fig. 5-25. No Return character is being entered this time, because the string MESSAGE may sometimes have the = X added for XMODEM file transfer. By leaving the Return off, this can be entered after the file name. If a Return is desired as part of an Alternate key input string, use the right brace in exactly the same way it is used with the Function key definitions. Press Return to enter the string as the Alternate key definition.

Whenever an Alternate key definition has been entered, the status line at the bottom of the screen changes to display the definitions of all of the Alternate key combinations as shown in Fig. 5-26. The first few characters of the string are displayed along with the number that must be pressed in conjunction with the Alternate key. To enter the string, just hold down the Alternate key and press the appropriate number key. For example, suppose you wished to examine the information currently stored in the file MESSAGE. Enter the Alternate-V command to view a file, and when prompted for the file name, press Alternate-1. The file name MESSAGE immediately is sent and appears on the screen. Since no Return was included in the string, you must then press Return to enter the file name and proceed with the viewing of the file. The appearance of the screen before Return is pressed is shown in Fig. 5-26.

To change or delete the assignment of a string of characters to an Alternate key combination, repeat the Alternate key definition procedure using the command Alternate – = and the number of the combination to be changed. Then enter the new string, or if you wish to erase the entry, enter a space and press Return. If all of the Alternate key definitions are erased, the Alternate key definitions disappear from the status line and the original information reappears.

Alternate key definitions last only until you exit the program, at which point they are lost. They are only good for the current work session. To keep special input string definitions permanently, use the function keys instead.

SPECIALIZED PC-TALK FEATURES

PC-Talk includes three additional commands

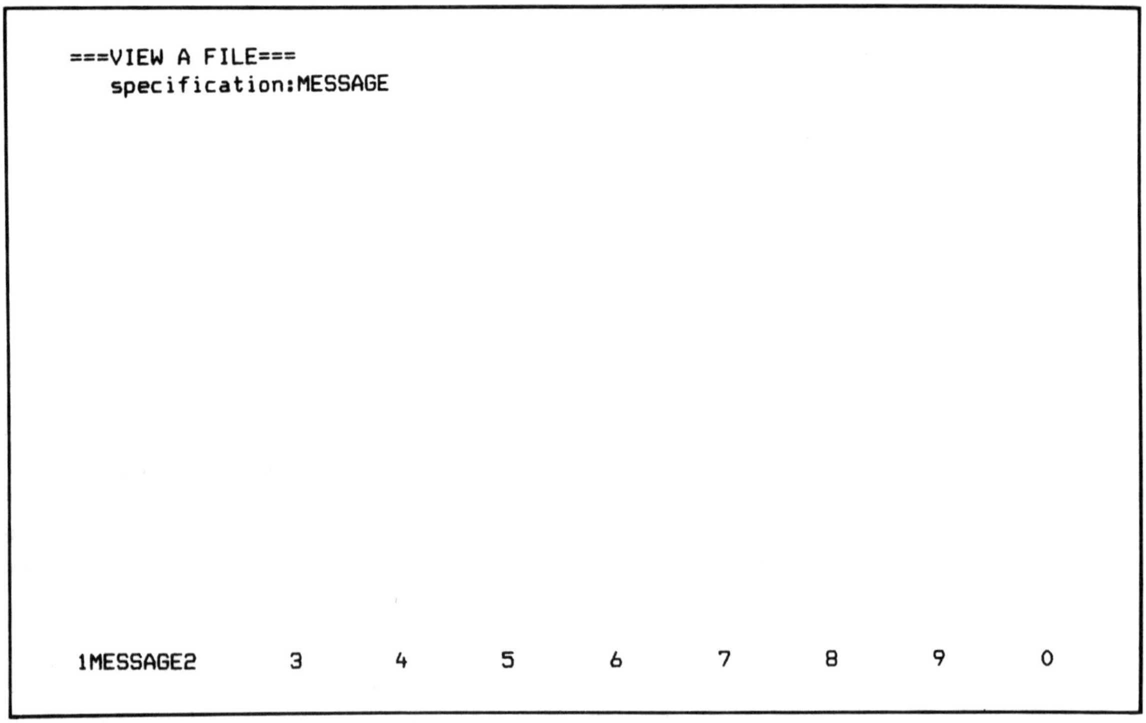

Fig. 5-26. Appearance of Alternate-1 key assignment on status line and use in viewing file.

and a number of additional options that can prove useful for specialized communications applications. The majority of users, however, should be able to use PC-Talk to meet their communications needs without having to worry about the specialized options described in this section.

Many of the remote computers with which you will be communicating will have a limit on the maximum length of lines that can be entered, often 72 or 80 characters. PC-Talk includes a width alarm that will beep at you when you reach a preset limit. The width alarm will not stop you from entering longer lines, it will only issue the warning. In its default configuration, the PC-Talk width alarm is set to 70 characters. This can be adjusted using the Alternate-W command. Simply enter the command and respond with the number of characters allowed on a line before the width alarm sounds.

For transmitting and receiving files, PC-Talk includes a function for sending a message to the remote computer to mark the start and end of transmission or reception. When transmitting a file, the message function sends START OF FILE and END OF FILE messages when transmission is begun and completed. When receiving a file, the message READY TO RECEIVE is sent when the receiving function is turned on and FILE RECEIVED is sent when the receiving function is turned off. This feature will generally be useful only when communicating with another personal computer with an operator who can read and respond to the messages. Even then, it is generally best for only the receiving computer to have the message function on. If the computer transmitting a file turns on the message function, those messages will become part of the files being received at the other end. The message function is turned on and off with the Alternate-M command.

Many remote computer systems have a special command to interrupt operations and gain their attention. One commonly used command for this purpose is Control-C. PC-Talk can send the control characters from the keyboard with no problem. Control characters can even be embedded in input strings defined for the function and Alternate keys. Some computers use a special interrupt command called "Break." Break is not an actual character, transmitted with start and stop bits, but rather a sustained signal transmitted on the line. No character on the IBM PC keyboard can produce a break signal. The break on the scroll lock key, invoked by entering Control-Scroll Lock, is completely different and is not to be used with PC-Talk. PC-Talk can send a break signal to a remote computer. This is accomplished by using the Control-End combination.

The remaining options will be discussed only briefly. Full information is provided in the documentation that comes on the PC-Talk disk. Some of these options govern the receiving and transmitting of files; they sometimes can be invoked in more than one location within PC-Talk—as an optional file specification, as a parameter in the dialing directory for a particular system, or as a default for PC-Talk.

To transmit and receive binary files without using the XMODEM protocol, add the suffix =B to the file specification. This causes the file not to be directed to the screen—where it would appear as garbage anyway. You must be communicating with eight data bits, and no parity for binary file transfer to take place. If the XMODEM protocol is available on the remote computer, use this. The error checking and automatic control provided make for much more reliable file transfer. Simple binary file transfer is available as an option, however.

When transmitting files to some mainframe systems (uploading), delays in the response of the remote system can result in some characters being lost. If this is a problem, PC-Talk can insert specified delays after the transmission of each line. This is called the pacing function, and it can be accomplished in three ways. Add the suffix =P followed by the number of seconds of delay after the file name when the transmission function is invoked. If pacing is generally required with a particular system with which you communicate, you can specify a pacing option in the entry in the dialing directory. Finally, a pacing delay can be specified as a PC-Talk default. The pacing feature also includes the option of waiting to send the next line until a specific prompt character is sent back by the remote computer.

Sometimes when information is sent from a remote computer, certain "problem" characters are sent that you do not wish to store in the file. Such characters might even prematurely indicate an end-of-file condition before the actual end. PC-Talk allows up to three different incoming characters to be examined and to be either *stripped* from the incoming information or converted to some other characters. Character stripping and conversion can be specified for particular remote systems as part of the dialing directory entries, or they can be included in the PC-Talk defaults.

Entries in the dialing directory can also indicate for each system whether characters are displayed as they are typed or only when they are received from the remote computer. This is the echo function, involving switching from full- to half-duplex communication. The message function can also be turned on or off for individual entries.

The set default command, Alternate-F, can be used to modify the way in which PC-Talk is configured when the program is started. Many of the items on the list of defaults shown in Fig. 5-27 can be altered during the use of PC-Talk using other procedures. The parameter function, Alternate-P, alters the baud rate and other communications parameters. Echo is switched on or off with Alternate-E, and the message function is switched with Alternate-M. Character stripping can be specified in the dialing directory, which can also handle all of the preceding functions and the pacing function. Pacing can also be invoked with the file name specification.

The remaining items in the second column of the program default screen shown in Fig. 5-27 can be modified only by changing the default values here. The first four are fairly obvious: the name of the file in which the screen information is stored with the Alternate-S command can be specified, the time between attempts at redialing can be altered, the prompt displayed when a connection is made can be changed, and the help line on the bottom of the screen can be turned off or on. Foreground,

```
===SET NEW DEFAULTS===

 Present program defaults:

Baud rate        1200          Screendump file B:SCRNDUMP.PCT
Parity           E             Redial delay    20
Data bits        7             Connect prompt  CONNECT
Stop bits        1             Line 25 help    Y
Echo             N             Foreground      7
Messages         N             Background      0
Strip #1         0             High inten.     15
Replace #1       0             Print port      LPT1:
Strip #2         0             Print init.
Replace #2       0             Print width     80
Strip #3         0             Comm. port      COM2:
Replace #3       0             Comm. init.     ,CS,DS
Pacing p=                      Modem init.
Logged drive     B:            C/R subst.      }
Margin width     70

 Enter ↵ to leave unchanged - <space>↵ for 'null' value - <ESC>↵ to quit
*** Enter new values
```

Fig. 5-27. List of PC-Talk defaults.

background, and intensity refer to the colors used for the screen. The defaults are white text (7) on a black background (0), with high intensity white text (15) for highlighting. This works fine for monochrome as well as color monitors. If you have a color monitor and wish PC-Talk to use other colors, enter those here. Color numbers range from 0 to 15 and can be found in the documentation received with your computer system.

The printer port is the place where the printer is connected. The first parallel port, LPT1:, is most common, but if you have a printer connected elsewhere, this can be changed. For example, a printer with a serial interface might be connected to COM1: with the modem then being connected to COM2:. The next entry is an initialization string, currently empty, that can be sent to the printer when PC-Talk is started. Such a string could switch to narrower characters, use higher-quality text, or employ any other feature of the printer desired. Printer width refers to the number of characters the printer can print on a line.

The communications port is an important default and was discussed in the first section dealing with the initial use of PC-Talk. It will be one of the serial ports, either COM1: or COM2:. The next line includes instructions for initializing the serial port being used for the modem. This is a technical matter that very, very few people should have to change. If your modem needs a string of characters at startup to configure it in the desired fashion, these can be entered on the following line. Finally, the character used in place of the Return character in specifying strings can be changed from the right brace to any other character. You might want to do this if you had a need to use the right brace itself in input strings.

CONCLUSION

PC-Talk is a very capable, usable communications program. It works well, it is easy to use, and it provides a whole host of features designed to make communications easier. If you experience some problems in the early stages of attempting to communicate with remote computers, be patient and keep trying. Remember that you are trying to learn a new activity—computer communications—while at the same time learning to operate a new program for your personal computer—PC-Talk—and also learning to operate entirely different computer systems—the remote computers. With all this going on at once, in a context involving some fairly technical matters, it is not surprising that things often do not go right at the beginning. Start off slowly, learning one thing at a time. Soon, given the capabilities of PC-Talk, you will be sitting down, hitting a few keys, and starting to communicate with remote computers. At this point, new skills, such as file downloading, can be learned one at a time.

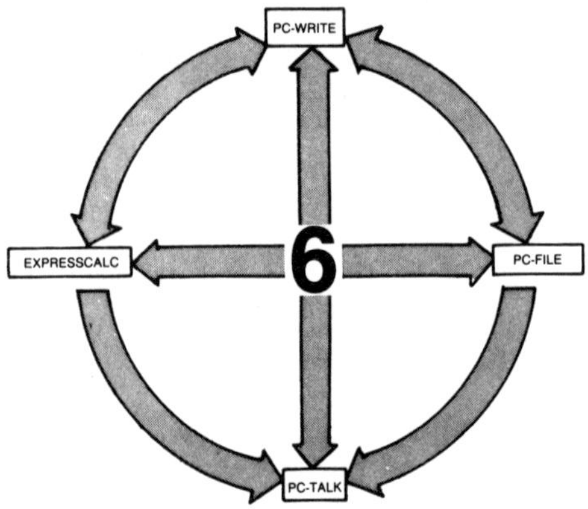

Using ExpressCalc

Electronic spreadsheet programs turn personal computers into powerful tools for performing calculations and analysis involving tables of numbers. Spreadsheet programs can be used for tasks ranging from balancing a checkbook and preparing a household budget to preparing elaborate budgets for large organizations and doing complex financial analysis. Electronic spreadsheets are easy to learn and use. The programs turn the computer into a large worksheet. Labels, numbers, and formulas are entered into the worksheet. The program performs all calculations automatically. Perhaps the most powerful and amazing feature of electronic spreadsheet programs is their ability to automatically recalculate the values displayed in the spreadsheet whenever any number is changed. This allows a user to easily make changes and experiment with different assumptions.

ExpressCalc is a representative electronic spreadsheet program, containing most of the basic features found in such programs. Compared with the more expensive commercial spreadsheet programs, ExpressCalc is not as fast, the worksheet is not as large, and fewer features are available. Nevertheless, ExpressCalc provides nearly everything that typical spreadsheet users working with most spreadsheets will require. One notable feature is the ability to use information from other ExpressCalc spreadsheets and from PC-File databases within the spreadsheet.

New users can quickly grasp the basic concepts of the operation of ExpressCalc (and other spreadsheet programs), because the programs display their operations in an intuitive fashion. Initial learning is made easier because it is possible to enter information into the spreadsheet immediately and see the results. The first section of this chapter introduces ExpressCalc and the basic operation of the electronic spreadsheet. A practical spreadsheet example—a loan amortization table—is then employed in the next two sections to illustrate all of the fundamental skills involved in creating and using an ExpressCalc spreadsheet. Some of the additional features of ExpressCalc are covered in the following section. Information on configuring ExpressCalc for specific systems and operating preferences is then presented.

All of the examples in this chapter use ExpressCalc version 3.10. This is the version of the program currently being distributed by ExpressWare, which now handles the distribution of this spreadsheet program. Up until mid-1986, this spreadsheet program was distributed by Buttonware under the name PC-Calc. If you wish to obtain the program from a computer users group or from a distributor of public domain and user-supported software, it may be listed under the name PC-Calc. PC-Calc, version 3.0, is essentially identical to ExpressCalc, version 3.10. The previous version, PC-Calc, version 2.0, has been widely distributed. Version 2.0 lacks a few of the features of the later versions, has a smaller spreadsheet, and operates somewhat more slowly. Operation of version 2.0 is very much like that of later versions, though the program has a few differences that might cause problems initially. The major differences will be pointed out in this chapter.

EXPRESSCALC FUNDAMENTALS

The best way to become familiar with ExpressCalc is to start the program and begin experimenting. Enter labels, values, and formulas and watch what happens. This section gives a basic introduction to ExpressCalc. Creation of a full-fledged, formal spreadsheet application is deferred to the following section.

Getting Started

Place the working copy of the ExpressCalc disk in the A: drive and a blank, formatted disk for the storage of spreadsheets in the B: drive. Turn on the computer; DOS should load, and you can enter the date and time. (If the computer is already on and you have the DOS A> prompt displayed on the screen, you can skip this step.) If you have either a color monitor or a monochrome monitor with the monochrome display adapter, start ExpressCalc by entering the following:

```
CALC<Enter>
```

If you are using a monochrome monitor with the color/graphics adapter card, however, you need to start ExpressCalc with the following:

```
CALC BW<Enter>
```

The BW (for black-and-white) added to the starting command tells ExpressCalc not to attempt to display the information in color. If you enter ExpressCalc without the BW when it is necessary, the display will have strange shadings and will be very difficult to read. Should this happen, simply restart ExpressCalc with the BW.

ExpressCalc first displays a title screen for a short period of time. The program then clears the screen and displays the ExpressCalc worksheet and the associated message and data entry lines, as shown in Fig. 6-1. The major part of the screen is taken up by the worksheet itself, which is simply a table in which information is entered. The rows of the worksheet are labeled with numbers at the left-hand side of the screen. When ExpressCalc is started, rows 1 through 21 are displayed. The columns are labeled with letters across the top of the screen. Columns A through G are displayed initially.

Information will be entered into the cells of the worksheet, lying at the intersections of the rows and columns. A large, highlighted (or reverse image) block appears in the upper left-hand corner of the worksheet. This block is the cell cursor, used to point to various cells in the worksheet. When ExpressCalc is started, the cursor is placed in the cell at the intersection of row 1 and column A. This cell is designated cell A1, combining the column letter and the row number.

The bottom three lines on the screen are used for messages and for the entry of information into the worksheet. The first of these lines contains the entry 441K, indicating the amount of memory currently available for the creation of the spreadsheet on the system I am using, which has 640K of random access memory (RAM). The value you will see will depend upon the amount of RAM in your personal computer. As information is entered into the spreadsheet and some of the available memory is used, this number will be reduced. During the oper-

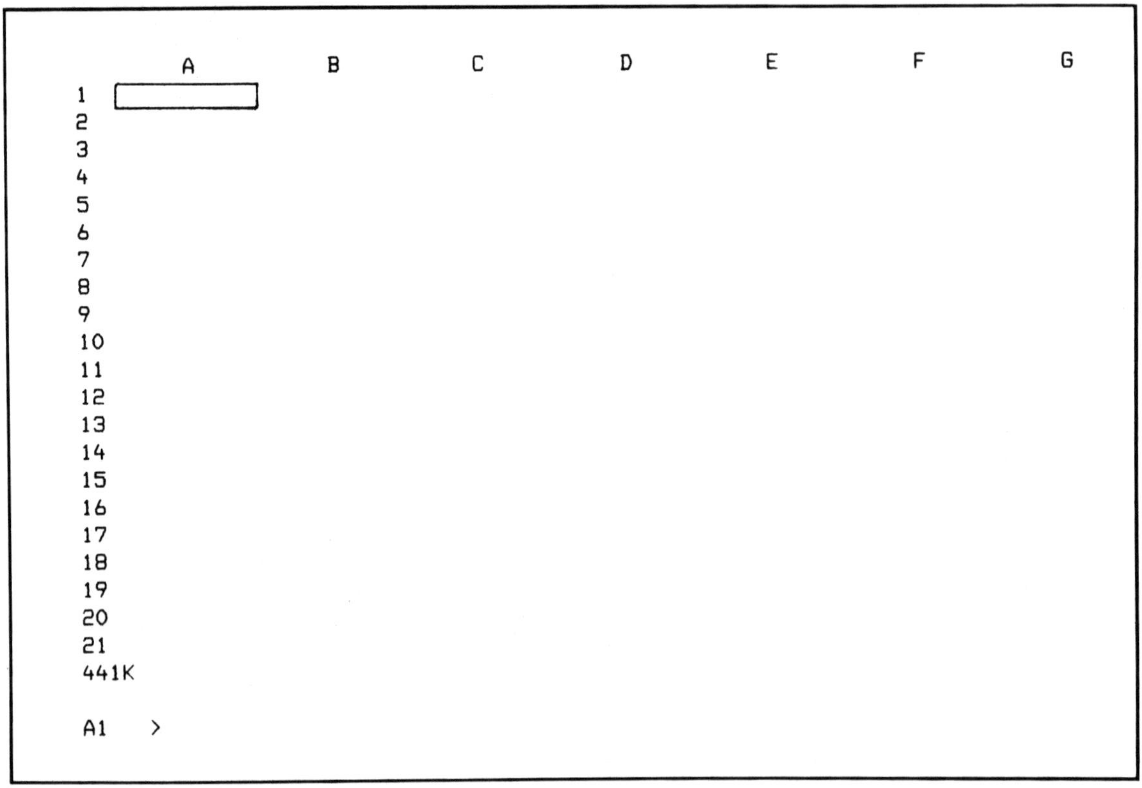

Fig. 6-1. Blank ExpressCalc display.

ation of ExpressCalc, messages and other information will be displayed on this line and the line immediately below, which is currently blank. The final line at the bottom of the screen is used for entering information into the spreadsheet and for giving commands to ExpressCalc.

Everything typed in will appear first on this line. The A1 at the far left indicates the current location of the cell cursor on the spreadsheet. This will change as the cursor is moved around the spreadsheet to other cells. The > (greater than) symbol points to the location where information is to be entered.

The ExpressCalc spreadsheet is much larger than the portion displayed on the screen. The spreadsheet contains 64 columns, designated by the letters A through Z, AA through AZ, and BA through BL. The spreadsheet also contains 255 rows, numbered 1 through 255. All of this information cannot be displayed on the screen at one time. Instead, the screen acts as a window, displaying a portion of the spreadsheet. The part of the spreadsheet displayed is determined by the location of the cell cursor. As the cursor is moved around the spreadsheet, the spreadsheet automatically shifts up or down, or right or left, to display the appropriate part.

Pressing any of the four cursor-control arrow keys moves the cell cursor one cell in the direction chosen (unless the cursor is on the border of the spreadsheet). Press the right arrow, and the cell cursor moves to cell B1. Pressing this key five more times moves the cursor to cell G1, at the right-hand edge of the screen. Press the right arrow once more, and the cell cursor moves over to cell H1, but now the spreadsheet has to scroll over to display column H. At this point, columns B through H are displayed on the screen. Continued pressing of the right arrow moves the spreadsheet over further. Pressing the left arrow key moves the cursor back toward the left. Once more, when the screen boundary is reached, the spreadsheet scrolls over. Continued pressing of the left arrow key returns the cell cursor to cell A1.

Moving up and down works in exactly the same way. The down arrow key moves the cursor down a row. Pressed repeatedly, the cursor first moves to row 20 at the bottom of the screen. Further movement down the spreadsheet forces the spreadsheet to scroll up, displaying a higher range of rows. The process is reversed using the up arrow.

The other keys on the cursor control pad can be used to move around the spreadsheet more quickly. The Home key moves the cell cursor to the upper left-hand corner of the screen. If the cell cursor is already in the upper left-hand corner, pressing Home moves the cursor to cell A1. The End key moves the cell cursor to the lower right-hand corner. The Page Down (PgDn) key moves down the spreadsheet one screenful, leaving the cell cursor in the middle row. The Page Up (PgUp) key moves the spreadsheet back in the same fashion.

For moving the cell cursor long distances quickly, ExpressCalc includes a command to jump the cursor to a specific cell. To try this out, move the cursor down and over to cell M55 using the cursor control keys. Now, to jump back to cell A1, press the = (equal sign) key. ExpressCalc will prompt you to enter the cell to which you wish to jump. Type in A1. The screen should now look like Fig. 6-2. Press Return, and the cell cursor will immediately move to cell A1 and that portion of the spreadsheet will be displayed.

Entering Information

It is now time to start entering some information into that blank spreadsheet. Three types of information can be entered into cells: text, values, and formulas. By entering such information in the appropriate combinations, very powerful applications can be generated.

Text is nothing more than strings of characters

```
          G         H         I         J         K         L         M
35
36
37
38
39
40
41
42
43
44
45
46
47
48
49
50
51
52
53
54
55
441K Go to coordinate:

M55   >=A1
```

Fig. 6-2. Jumping the cell cursor from cell M55 to cell A1.

entered into the cells. Text entries are used in spreadsheets for titles, row and column headings, and other types of labels. To enter text into any cell, first move the cell cursor to the cell desired. Type in the text and press Return. For example, to enter the column heading "Outlays" in cell C3, move the cell cursor to that cell and enter the following:

Outlays<Return>

As you type in the text, it will appear on the bottom line of the screen as shown in Fig. 6-3. Pressing Return causes the text to be entered into the cell and be displayed there. The result is shown in Fig. 6-4. When the cell cursor is pointing to a cell containing information, that information is displayed on the first line immediately below the spreadsheet display. Note in Fig. 6-4 that the information

(Text) "Outlays

is displayed on the line below the spreadsheet: this indicates that text has been stored in the current cell, C3, shown on the bottom line, and this text is "Outlays. The quotation mark is automatically entered by ExpressCalc to indicate text entry. If the string of text is longer than a cell, the information will be displayed in the cells to the right, if those cells are empty. This feature is very handy for entering longer titles. To try this out, move the cell cursor to cell B1 and enter the following

Total Outlays for September<Return>

This title will be displayed starting in cell B1 and spilling on over into cells C1 and D1. Note that if anything is entered into cell C1, for example, the entire title will no longer be displayed; you will see only those letters that fit into cell B1.

If you wish to enter a numeric value into a cell as text, you must precede the value with a quotation mark. This is required so that ExpressCalc can

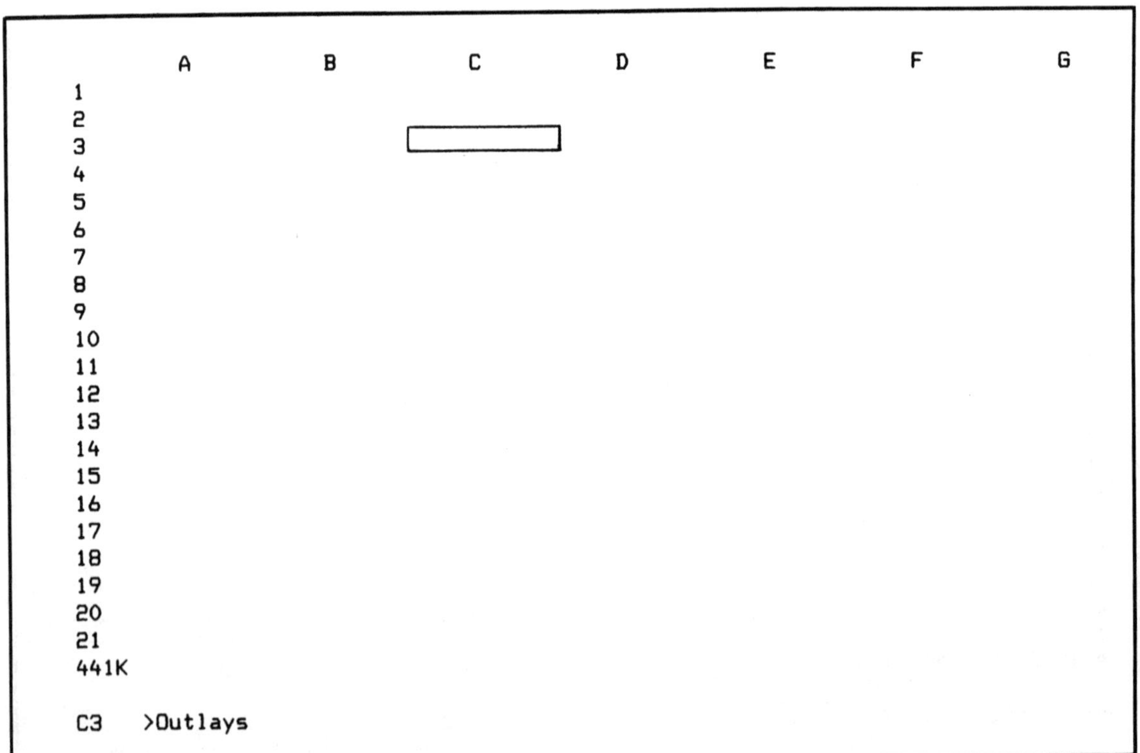

Fig. 6-3. Entering the text "Outlays" into cell C3.

```
          A         B         C         D         E         F         G
 1
 2
 3                          [Outlays   ]
 4
 5
 6
 7
 8
 9
10
11
12
13
14
15
16
17
18
19
20
21
441K (Text)  "Outlays

C3   >
```

Fig. 6-4. The text "Outlays" entered into cell C3.

distinguish the numeric text entry from a numeric value being entered into a cell. The entry of numbers as text might be desirable, for example, if years were to be used as column headings. For example, to enter the year 1986 into a cell as text, enter the following:

'1986<Return>

Users of PC-CALC, version 2.0, will need to precede all text entries with a quotation mark in this fashion.

You may already have made errors in entering information into a cell; if not yet, you will. You can always enter the erroneous information and then reenter the correct information. When new information is entered into a cell, it replaces the old information.

ExpressCalc also provides several commands for editing the information you are currently entering on the entry line before you press Return and commit the information to the cell. Once you have started entering characters on the entry line, the backspace and tab keys can be used to move the small data entry cursor (the underline) on the entry line left and right respectively. Suppose you were trying to enter "Outlays" and, being an absolutely miserable typist, managed to enter the following:

Ourrlys

Move the date entry cursor back to one of the r's and type t. The t will overtype the r, replacing it. Now you have this:

Outrlys

The remaining r should not be there either. Move the data entry cursor to the r and press the delete

(Del) key. The r will be deleted, and the line now reads:

Outlys

All that remains is to insert the letter a. Move the data entry cursor to the y. Press the Insert (Ins) key to turn on the insert mode. This will be indicated by the data entry cursor changing shape from an underline to a block. The Insert key works as a toggle, turning the insert mode on if it is off, and turning the insert mode off if it is on. Press the Insert key several times and observe the data entry cursor changing from the underline to the block shape and back. Now, with the insert mode on, enter the a, which will be inserted in the proper position, giving

Outlays

The entry is now correct, and you can press Return to enter the text into the cell.

One additional command will frequently be useful when you are entering information on the entry line. Escape is the cancel command. This cancels the complete entry, erasing everything currently on the entry line. If you make a mess of things, or get stuck while entering commands, Escape immediately clears everything and you are ready to begin a new entry. Control-C can also be used in place of Escape, and version 2.0 of PC-Calc only allows the use of Control-C as a cancel command; Escape is not supported.

The second type of information that can be entered into a cell is a value, which is any number. To make a value entry, just type the number and press Return. Move the cell cursor to cell C5 and enter the following:

1347

Now press the down arrow key. The number 1,347.00 is now displayed in cell C5, and the cell cursor is moved down to cell C6. Pressing any arrow key while entering information on the data entry line enters the information, just as Return does, and moves the cell cursor in the direction of the arrow. This feature is very handy for entering rows or columns of numbers. Rather than pressing Return and then pressing the appropriate arrow key to move the cell cursor, you can enter the value and move the cell cursor with a single keystroke.

The number in cell C5 is displayed in the cell according to the format currently in effect for displaying values. In this case, the default format with commas separating thousands and two digits after the decimal point is used. If you move the cell cursor back to cell C5, the line below the spreadsheet indicates that a value has been entered into the cell:

(Value) 1347

To provide a few more values to work with, enter the value 253.86 into cell C6 and the value 988 into cell C7.

The final type of information that can be entered into a cell is a formula, which consists of references to values in other cells, possibly combined with numbers and special ExpressCalc functions. When a formula has been entered, the values in the referenced cells are determined, the formula is evaluated, and the resulting value is displayed in the cell. To add up the values entered into the three cells and determine the total outlays, move the cell cursor to cell C9 and enter the following formula:

C5 + C6 + C7 <Return>

This formula instructs ExpressCalc to take the value displayed in cell C5, add it to the value displayed in cell C6, and add the result to the value displayed in cell C7. The resulting sum, 2,588.86, is displayed in cell C9 as shown in Fig. 6-5. Note that the contents of cell C9 are displayed on the line below the spreadsheet as follows:

(Formula) C5 + C6 + C7

How does ExpressCalc know that a formula is being entered rather than text? For every entry, ExpressCalc attempts to interpret the entry as a formula. If the entry is a correct formula, ExpressCalc

```
          A          B          C          D          E          F          G
1              Total Outlays for September
2
3                          Outlays
4
5                            1,347.00
6                              253.86
7                              988.00
8
9                            2,588.86
10
11
12
13
14
15
16
17
18
19
20
21
441K (Formula)    C5+C6+C7

C9    >
```

Fig. 6-5. The sum of the three outlays displayed in cell C9.

enters it as such. On the other hand, if the entry is not a correct formula, it is assumed to then be text and is entered as such. This means that if an error is made in entering a formula, such that the entry is not a valid ExpressCalc formula, the entire entry is placed into the cell as text. For example, had you accidentally entered the following as the formula,

C5 + C6 + + C7

ExpressCalc would enter this as a string of text into the cell. The entry of a formula as text indicates that an error has been made. Reenter the correct formula.

ExpressCalc includes a number of functions that can be used in entering formulas. One of the most useful is the SUM function, which automatically adds up a row or column of numbers. Move the cell cursor to cell D9 and try an alternative method for computing the total of the outlays. Enter the following formula:

SUM(C5:C7)<Return>

The function is entered by typing the name, SUM, and inside parentheses the range of the row or column to be totaled. To specify the range, enter the first and last cell coordinates, separated by a colon. The function computes the total, which is of course the same as that obtained using the other formula.

Formulas can be constructed using numbers, various ExpressCalc functions, and cell coordinates to reference values in other cells. These are combined using the arithmetic operators for addition (+), used in the first formula), subtraction (−), multiplication (*), division (/), and exponentiation (^). With multiple operators, exponentiation is done first, then multiplication and division, and finally addition and subtraction. These operators are summarized in Table 6-1. For example, in the following formula,

```
3*B14 + 1
```

three would be multiplied times the value in cell B14 first, and the result would be added to 1. The order in which operations are performed can be changed using parentheses. In the example, if the 1 was to be added to the value from cell B14 first, with the resulting sum to be multiplied by 3, parentheses could be used as follows:

```
3*(B14 + 1)
```

The following sections have many examples of ExpressCalc formulas that aid in making these concepts clearer. ExpressCalc version 3.10 has a number of additional operators that can be used in constructing formulas, but the operators summarized here will be used most often. For further information, see the ExpressCalc manual.

One of the most powerful features of any electronic spreadsheet program is the recalculation of the formulas when information in the spreadsheet is changed. This makes it easy to examine the implications of possible changes and alternative assumptions. The electronic spreadsheet program can be used to ask "what if" questions, quickly displaying what happens if any value is changed. Move the cell cursor to cell C5, the first value in the list of outlays, which is currently 1347. To ask "what if" this value were 2458, enter this number and press Return. The message "CALCULATING" will briefly appear, and the value of the total will change to 3,699.86. The full power of this feature will not be appreciated, however, until larger spreadsheets, such as the loan amortization table to be created below, are used.

Table 6-1. Basic Arithmetic Operators in ExpressCalc.

Operation	Operator	Precedence
Exponentiation	^	First
Multiplication	*	Second
Division	/	Second
Addition	+	Third
Subtraction	-	Third

Commands

ExpressCalc employs a series of commands to perform a variety of different operations. This section illustrates the general procedure for invoking commands and demonstrates the use of two of the simpler commands. The use of most of the ExpressCalc commands will be illustrated in this chapter, as the commands are required to accomplish various tasks. A summary of the commands is provided in Table 6-2.

To invoke any ExpressCalc command, press the slash key (/). ExpressCalc will display a list of all of the commands on the two lines below the spreadsheet and will await your selection. This display is shown in Fig. 6-6. To select any command, simply press the first letter of the command. The name of the command will appear on the data entry line, following the slash. A prompt will appear on the lines above, indicating the action that is required next. All of the commands provide as many prompts as are required to specify the action to be taken. After you have used a command once or twice, operation will be very obvious and you can quickly proceed through the various steps required.

The first command to be demonstrated clears the contents of the spreadsheet so that work can begin from scratch on a new spreadsheet. The command is rather graphically named Zap. Be careful in using this command, because if the contents of the spreadsheet have not been previously saved on the disk, zapping the spreadsheet causes all of the information to be permanently lost. The very simple example being used here is hardly worth keeping. To clear the contents, after the Slash has been entered to display the list of commands, press Z for Zap. The word Zap appears on the entry line and the prompt "Clear contents? (Y or N)" is displayed above, as shown in Fig. 6-7. Press Y, and the contents of the spreadsheet are cleared.

Table 6-2. ExpressCalc Commands.

Command	Description
Arrange	Sorts (arranges) rows or columns
Blank	Clears the contents from a cell or range
Configure	Customizes display and operation of PC-CALC
Delete	Deletes a row or column
Edit	Moves the contents of a cell to the entry line for editing
Format	Specifies the manner in which information is to be displayed in a cell, a range of cells, or the entire spreadsheet
Global	Specifies spreadsheet options
Insert	Inserts a row or column
Load	Loads a spreadsheet from a file on the disk
Print	Prints out the spreadsheet
Quit	Terminates ExpressCalc and returns to DOS
Replicate	Copies the information in a cell or group of cells to a range of cells, with the option of adjusting cell references in formulas
Save	Saves the spreadsheet currently in memory in a file on the disk
Title	Locks the top rows and/or left columns of a spreadsheet in place as the spreadsheet is scrolled
Xternal	Reads data from another ExpressCalc spreadsheet or from a FileExpress or PC-File database
Zap	Clears the contents of the spreadsheet

```
          A         B         C          D          E          F          G
1                 Total Outlays for September
2
3                           Outlays
4
5                          [2,458.00]
6                             253.86
7                             988.00
8
9                           3,699.86   3,699.86
10
11
12
13
14
15
16
17
18
19
20
21
441K  Arrange  Blank   Configure  Delete     Edit   Format   Global   Insert
      Load     Print   Quit       Replicate  Save   Title    Xternal  Zap
C5    >/
```

Fig. 6-6. Display of the selection of commands, obtained by entering Slash (/).

```
          A          B          C          D          E          F          G
1              Total Outlays for September
2
3                         Outlays
4
5                         2,458.00
6                           253.86
7                           988.00
8
9                         3,699.86   3,699.86
10
11
12
13
14
15
16
17
18
19
20
21
441K Clear contents? (Y or N).

C5   >/Zap,
```

Fig. 6-7. Using the Zap command to clear the contents of the spreadsheet.

The second command to be illustrated is Quit, which is used to terminate the operation of ExpressCalc. As with Zap, this command should be used with caution, for if the contents of the spreadsheet have not been previously saved on the disk, they will be irretrievably lost when you exit ExpressCalc. Having just cleared the spreadsheet, of course, there is currently no need for concern. To terminate operations, press the Slash and Q for Quit. If there is any new, unsaved information on the spreadsheet, ExpressCalc will then ask whether you really wish to quit. As with Zap, you will be asked to enter Y or N. If the spreadsheet has just been cleared using the Zap command or if the spreadsheet has just been saved to the disk, the question is not necessary and will not be asked. The Quit command exits ExpressCalc and returns you to the DOS prompt.

CREATING A LOAN AMORTIZATION TABLE

Calculating an amortization table listing the interest paid month-by-month on a loan and the remaining balances is not a task one would willingly undertake by hand. This problem is a natural for an electronic spreadsheet program such as ExpressCalc. This section describes the procedures to be followed in creating the loan amortization spreadsheet. The next section discusses the process of using the spreadsheet.

Statement of the Problem

A consumer loan (perhaps a car loan) is obtained for $6000. The loan is to be repaid in three years, with 36 equal monthly payments of $199.28. The interest rate on the loan is 12 percent. The problem is to produce a loan amortization table listing, for each month, the beginning balance, the amount of interest paid, the amount that goes towards reducing the principal balance owed, and the remaining balance at the end of the month.

The calculations required for this analysis are relatively straightforward. Each month, an amount must be paid in interest that is determined by multiplying the balance on the loan at the beginning of the month times the interest rate. Remember that the interest rate must be expressed in decimal form, not as a percentage, and the annual rate must be divided by 12 to yield a monthly interest rate. That portion of the monthly payment left over after paying the interest goes toward the reduction of the principal balance owed on the loan. The interest payment is subtracted from the monthly payment on the loan to determine this value. The remaining balance owed at the end of the month is the beginning balance less the payment to principal. This remaining balance at the end of each month is, of course, the beginning balance for the following month. The loan has been paid off when the balance remaining reaches zero. The final amortization table should also include the total amount of interest paid over the period of the loan, obtained by adding up the monthly interest payments.

With such an amortization table, you would always know the remaining balance owed on the loan and would have the information on the amount of interest that has been paid. Using the ExpressCalc spreadsheet, you would also be able to investigate a variety of additional questions. Perhaps you are considering an adjustable, or floating, rate loan. The interest rate could be changed, and the implications for the rate at which the loan is paid back could be determined. Perhaps the terms of the loan allow additional payments to be made toward the principal. The spreadsheet could be employed to determine the effects of such payments on reducing the number of months that payments need to be made and the total interest paid over the life of the loan.

Setting Up the Spreadsheet

Start ExpressCalc by entering CALC or CALC BW at the DOS prompt. The first task in creating

```
          A           B           C           D           E           F           G
1                                 Loan Amortization Table
2
3   Month       Beginning   Monthly     Interest    Principal   Ending
4               Balance     Payment     Paid        Paid        Balance
5
6   [          ]
7
8
9
10
11
12
13
14
15
16
17
18
19
20
21
441K

A6    >
```

Fig. 6-8. Headings for the loan amortization spreadsheet.

a spreadsheet application is generally the entry of the titles and headings. Begin by moving the cell cursor to cell C1 and entering the following text for the title:

Loan Amortization Table<Return>

Note that the text continues into the adjoining cells. Next come the column headings. In cell A3, enter "Month" and press Return. Follow the same procedures for entering all of the remaining column headings as shown in Fig. 6-8. Note that each of the other column headings requires two entries, one in row 3 and one in row 4.

Suppose that in entering these headings, you accidentally entered text into the wrong cell. Perhaps in entering the word "Interest," the cell cursor was mistakenly placed in row 2 of column D, one row up. Changing an incorrect entry in a cell is easy—just enter the correct information—but how is an incorrect entry erased from a cell? The ExpressCalc Blank command will erase, or blank, a single cell or a group of cells. To try out this command, first make the incorrect entry into cell D2. Leave the cell cursor pointing to D2 and start the Blank command by pressing Slash and B. An extended prompt is displayed, as shown in Fig. 6-9.

To blank a portion of the spreadsheet, a range of cells must be entered. In ExpressCalc, a range can be a single cell, a list of cells in a row or a column, or a rectangular block of cells. A single cell range is simply designated by entering the cell coordinates, such as A1. A list of cells is designated by entering the coordinates of the first and last cell in the list, separated by a colon. (This is the same procedure used in the SUM function described above.) For example, the list of cells in column B from B3 to B17 is indicated by entering B3:B17, and the list of cells in row 7 from C7 to H7 is indicated with C7:H7. Finally, a rectangular block of cells is designated by specifying the cells in the upper left-hand corner and the lower right-hand cor-

```
          A          B          C          D          E          F          G
1                               Loan Amortization Table
2                                          [Interest  ]
3    Month           Beginning  Monthly    Interest   Principal  Ending
4                    Balance    Payment    Paid       Paid       Balance
5
6
7
8
9
10
11
12
13
14
15
16
17
18
19
20
21
441K Enter range to be blanked; or enter ALL to blank all cells;
     or enter VALUES to blank all values, but leave text and formulas intact.
D2   >/Blank,
```

Fig. 6-9. Using the Blank command to erase the contents of a cell.

ner of the block, again separated by a colon. The range B3:F10 specifies the block with the top row of cells extending from B3 to F3 and the bottom row of cells extending from B10 to F10.

Returning to the problem at hand: to blank cell D2, you could enter D2 and press Return. Any time a command calls for a cell coordinate, however, you can automatically enter the coordinate of the cell currently selected by the cell cursor simply by pressing Return. Since the cell cursor is in cell D2, which is to be blanked, all you need to do is press Return.

Entering the Basic Values and Formulas

With the column headings in place, the initial values and formulas can be entered for the first month or two. Begin with the month. The months will be numbered from 1 to 36. Move the cursor to cell A6, enter 1, and press the right arrow key. The value will be entered and the cell cursor will be moved over to cell B6, ready for the next entry. The value will be displayed as 1.00 in the cell, hardly appropriate for the month number, but this is simply a matter of formatting and will be taken care of later.

The beginning balance in month 1 is the total amount of the loan, $6,000. With the cursor in cell B6, enter 6000 and press Return. The monthly payment is $199.29. Move the cursor to cell C6, enter 199.29, and press the right arrow key again.

The interest paid is calculated by multiplying the monthly payment by the interest rate. A formula will be required. It would be possible to place the interest rate of 12 percent in this formula, but this is not a good idea. Later on, if you would want to see the consequences of changing the interest rate, the formula itself would have to be changed, a cumbersome process. Much better would be to place the interest rate in a separate cell and then refer to the value in this cell in the interest rate formula. In creating spreadsheets, it is generally a good idea to place all values in separate cells rather than incorporating them into formulas.

In the loan amortization spreadsheet, it would make sense to place the interest rate right at the top, below the title and above the column headings. This was not planned for, however. Trying to fit the rate in row 2 would make the spreadsheet cluttered and difficult to read. What is needed are two more rows added between the title and the column headings. ExpressCalc has a command to add rows or columns—Insert. Pressing Slash and I starts the Insert command. ExpressCalc then asks whether you wish to insert a row or a column. Enter R for row, and the screen will now appear as shown in Fig. 6-10.

You are then asked to enter a row number above which the new row will be inserted. Enter 3 to place the new row above the column headings and press Return. A new row is inserted. The top row of the column headings is now in row 4. Repeat exactly the same command sequence one more time to insert a second row. Enough space has been opened for the interest rate. The current spreadsheet does not yet contain formulas. If it did, the cell references in the formulas would automatically be adjusted as rows or columns were inserted to preserve the relationships.

Now the interest rate can be entered. First move the cell cursor to B3 and enter the following text:

```
Annual Interest Rate<Return>
```

Move the cell cursor over to D3, enter the value 12, and press Return. The formula using the interest rate can now refer to the value in cell D3. If at any time you want to change the interest rate, you can simply change the single value in that cell.

Now the formula can be entered for computing the interest paid. The interest rate has been entered in cell D3 as a percentage rate. This will have to be multiplied by 0.01 to convert the rate to decimal form. Furthermore, this is an annual rate, but interest is to be charged on a monthly basis. The interest rate will have to be divided by twelve. The monthly interest rate, in decimal form, is as follows:

```
0.01*D3/12
```

The complete formula for the interest to be paid involves multiplying the beginning balance on the

```
           A          B          C          D          E          F          G
1                              Loan Amortization Table
2
3  Month          Beginning  Monthly    Interest   Principal  Ending
4                 Balance    Payment    Paid       Paid       Balance
5
6          1.00   6,000.00      199.29 [          ]
7
8
9
10
11
12
13
14
15
16
17
18
19
20
21
441K Enter line number. New line will be inserted above it.

D6   >/Insert,Row,
```

Fig. 6-10. Using the Insert command to insert a row into the spreadsheet.

loan times this interest rate. For the first month, this balance is in cell B8. Move the cell cursor to C8 and enter the following formula:

B8*0.01*D3/12<Return>

The formula will be immediately calculated using the current values in cells B8 and D3, and the resulting value of 60.00 is displayed in cell D8. The spreadsheet will appear as shown in Fig. 6-11. Note that, since the cell cursor is still located in cell D8, the formula just entered is displayed on the line immediately below the spreadsheet display.

Suppose you had made a minor error in entering the formula, perhaps entering 13 instead of 12, only to notice this after the formula had been entered. Instead of reentering the entire formula, you can edit the current entry by using the Edit command. Enter Slash, then E. You will be prompted to enter the cell to be edited. Either enter D8 and press Return, or if the cursor is currently pointing to D8, you need only press Return. The entry in the cell selected is then displayed on the data entry line, as shown in Fig. 6-12. The editing procedures described above can now be used to correct the error without retyping. Use the tab key to move the entry line cursor to the 3 at the end. Type 2, which will replace it. The formula is now correct, so press Return to enter the corrected formula into cell D8. Learning to use the command line editing techniques and the Edit command make the entry of complex formulas into a spreadsheet much easier.

The remaining formulas to be entered into the spreadsheet are relatively simple. The first task is to take care of the remaining two formulas for month 1. The principal paid—the amount by which the balance of the loan is reduced—is calculated by subtracting the interest paid from the monthly payment. The interest paid is in cell D8 and the monthly payment is in cell C8. Enter the following formula into cell E8:

C8-D8 <Return>

In a similar manner, the ending balance at the end of the month is calculated by subtracting the principal paid, in cell E8, from the beginning balance, in cell B8. Move the cursor to cell F8 and enter this formula:

B8-E8 <Return>

This completes the entry of the values and formulas for the first month. The ending balance of 5,860.71 should be displayed in the final cell in the first row.

Now proceed to month two, where three more formulas must be entered. First, a 2 is needed in the month column. The value could be entered into cell A9, but it will turn out to be easier in the long run if a formula is used to calculate the month number. The appropriate value is computed by adding 1 to the previous month number in the cell above, A8. Just enter this formula into cell A9:

A8 + 1 <Return>

Now the value 2.00 is displayed for the month. The beginning balance for month 2 is simply the ending balance for month 1, which is in cell F8. To obtain this value, just enter the reference to that cell into cell B9:

F8 <Return>

Finally, the monthly payment in month 2 is the same as the monthly payment in month 1. A reference to the cell above can be entered into cell C9:

C8 <Return>

```
          A           B           C           D           E           F           G
1                            Loan Amortization Table
2
3                Annual Interest Rate           12.00
4
5   Month        Beginning   Monthly     Interest    Principal   Ending
6                Balance     Payment     Paid        Paid        Balance
7
8          1.00    6,000.00      199.29 [     60.00]
9
10
11
12
13
14
15
16
17
18
19
20
21
441K (Formula)  B8*0.01*D3/12

D8   >
```

Fig. 6-11. Loan amortization spreadsheet with the interest rate formula entered into cell D8 for month 1.

```
          A          B          C          D          E          F          G
1                          Loan Amortization Table
2
3                Annual Interest Rate          12.00
4
5  Month         Beginning  Monthly    Interest   Principal  Ending
6                Balance    Payment    Paid       Paid       Balance
7
8         1.00   6,000.00      199.29 [    55.38]
9
10
11
12
13
14
15
16
17
18
19
20
21
441K

D8    >B8*0.01*D3/13
```

Fig. 6-12. Using the Edit command to correct a formula.

Values are now displayed for the first row and for the first half of the second row. The spreadsheet should appear as shown in Fig. 6-13.

Completing the Spreadsheet

If all of the formulas had to be individually entered into the appropriate cells for all 36 months, creating the loan amortization spreadsheet would be tedious indeed. Fortunately, ExpressCalc provides a command for replicating formulas when an identical or similar formula is required. This can be used to automatically enter formulas in the remainder of the spreadsheet.

Start with the month. Cell A9 contains the formula A8 + 1, calculating the month by adding one to the month number in the cell above. Exactly the same procedure, requiring similar formulas, will work for calculating the remaining month numbers. The formula needs to be copied to the 34 remaining cells, each time adjusting the formula so that it always refers to the cell immediately above. To accomplish this, use the Replicate command. First press the Slash and the R. ExpressCalc first prompts you to enter the range you are replicating "from"—the cell or cells from which information is to be copied. Since the formula for calculating the month number in cell A9 is to be copied, enter A9 and press Return. If the cell cursor is currently in cell A9, just pressing Return will cause A9 to be entered in the same manner.

Next, the Replicate command prompts for the entry of the range you are replicating "to"—the cell or cells into which the information is to be copied. The spreadsheet needs 34 more month numbers, in cells A10 through A43. Enter this range, with the cell coordinates separated by a colon:

A10:A43 <Return>

As you proceed through the Replicate command (and other complex commands), each entry made is displayed on the entry line.

At this point in the process, the display will appear as shown in Fig. 6-14, with the "from" and "to" ranges following the Replicate command. The line above displays this message:

Replicating cell A9. Adjust A8 Yes or No? (Or A to adjust all)

The message conveys the following information: ExpressCalc is in the process of replicating the information. It is currently working on replicating the information in cell A9. (In this example, A9 is the only cell being replicated, but it is possible to have a "from" range involving replication from several cells.) The formula in cell A9 includes a reference to cell A8. ExpressCalc is asking whether this cell reference is to be adjusted as the formula is replicated into the cells in the "to" range. You are to respond by pressing Y or N.

Whether you choose to "adjust" the cell reference or not determines the formulas that are placed in the "to" range. If the cell reference is not adjusted, each copy of the formula will include the same cell coordinate appearing in the original formula, in this case, A8. Each of the 34 formulas would be A8 + 1, each yielding a value of 2. Adjusting the cell reference, on the other hand, will change the cell coordinate each time the formula is replicated so as to preserve the relationship from the original cell. In this case, the formula A8 + 1 in cell A9 caused a 1 to be added to the value in the cell above, A8. Replicating this formula into cell A10 with adjustment changes the cell reference from A8 to A9. The formula in A10 will be A9 + 1 and will continue to refer to the cell immediately above. The 1 will be added to the value 2 in cell A9, giving 3, the correct month number. In this

```
          A          B          C          D          E          F          G
1                               Loan Amortization Table
2
3                    Annual Interest Rate        12.00
4
5   Month            Beginning  Monthly    Interest   Principal  Ending
6                    Balance    Payment    Paid       Paid       Balance
7
8           1.00     6,000.00     199.29      60.00     139.29   5,860.71
9           2.00     5,860.71   [ 199.29]
10
11
12
13
14
15
16
17
18
19
20
21
441K (Formula)  C8

C9   >
```

Fig. 6-13. Loan amortization spreadsheet with all of the basic formulas entered.

```
          A          B          C          D          E          F          G
1                           Loan Amortization Table
2
3               Annual Interest Rate          12.00
4
5  Month        Beginning  Monthly    Interest   Principal  Ending
6               Balance    Payment    Paid       Paid       Balance
7
8          1.00  6,000.00     199.29      60.00     139.29   5,860.71
9          2.00  5,860.71     199.29
10
11
12
13
14
15
16
17
18
19
20
21
441K Replicating cell A9. Adjust A8    Yes or No? (or A to adjust all)

A9   >/Replicate,A9,A10:A43,
```

Fig. 6-14. Using the Replicate command to copy the formula for displaying the month.

case, therefore, adjustment is desired, so press Y.

The formula is replicated with adjustment of the reference to cell A8, and the values are calculated and displayed for each cell. Cell A10 displays the value 3.00 and contains the formula A9 + 1; you can see this by moving the cell cursor to A10. Move all the way down to the bottom of the spreadsheet, to cell A43. The value 36 is displayed, and the formula in the cell is A42 + 1.

The replication of formulas takes a while to explain and understand, but once you understand the process, the operation is very quick. In the next step, replicate the formulas for the beginning balance and the monthly payment in cells B9 and C9. Both formulas contain references to the cells in the preceding row. These references should be adjusted when the cells are replicated. Begin by entering the Slash and Return. For the "from" range, enter the range for these two cells:

B9:C9 <Return>

When replicating multiple cells, the "to" range is the range of cells in which the replicated range *begins*. In this case, the range of cells lies in column B. Enter this for the "to" range:

B10:B43 <Return>

You will be asked whether adjustments are to be made to F8 in cell B9 and to C8 in cell C9. Press Y in each case or press A for All. The formulas will be replicated and the values will be calculated and displayed. The spreadsheet display appears as shown in Fig. 6-15. The beginning balance column shows a long list of zeros. This is because no formulas have yet been entered into the cells referred to in the ending balance column. Reference to an empty cell returns a zero. This will be taken care of as the spreadsheet is completed.

The replication of the interest calculation formula in cell D8 is slightly more complex, so this formula will be replicated by itself. Enter Slash, R, and then D8 and Return to specify the "from" range. This formula is to be replicated into cells D9 through D43, so enter this for the "to" range:

D9:D43 <Return>

The interest calculation formula in cell D8 is B8*0.01*D3/12 and includes references to two cells, B8 and D3. The reference to cell B8 is to the beginning balance for the current month. This should be adjusted as the formula is replicated, so when prompted on whether or not to adjust B8, press Y. The reference to cell D3, on the other hand, is to the value of the interest rate entered in that cell. All copies of the formula must refer to that value in that cell; the reference must not be adjusted. When asked whether to adjust D3, press N. The formula is then replicated. The correct value is displayed for month 2, because the beginning balance is available. Zeroes are again displayed for the following months, because the interest on the current beginning balance of zero is zero.

The last two formulas can now be replicated. Press Slash and R. The "from" range is E8 to F8, so enter this:

E8:F8 <Return>

The "to" range in which the replication is to begin extends down column E from rows 9 through 43:

E9:E43 <Return>

Both of the formulas, each with two cell references, refer to values in the current row and should be adjusted. The easiest way to accomplish this is to enter A to adjust all of the cell references. Otherwise, ExpressCalc would inquire four times about adjustment, and you would need to press Y each time.

This last group of formulas is replicated. All

```
          A           B          C          D          E          F          G
 1                           Loan Amortization Table
 2
 3              Annual Interest Rate        12.00
 4
 5   Month      Beginning  Monthly    Interest   Principal  Ending
 6              Balance    Payment    Paid       Paid       Balance
 7
 8         1.00  6,000.00     199.29      60.00     139.29   5,860.71
 9         2.00  5,860.71     199.29
10         3.00       .00     199.29
11         4.00       .00     199.29
12         5.00       .00     199.29
13         6.00       .00     199.29
14         7.00       .00     199.29
15         8.00       .00     199.29
16         9.00       .00     199.29
17        10.00       .00     199.29
18        11.00       .00     199.29
19        12.00       .00     199.29
20        13.00       .00     199.29
21        14.00       .00     199.29
437K (Formula)  F8

B9   >
```

Fig. 6-15. Loan amortization spreadsheet with the formulas in the first three columns replicated.

formulas in the spreadsheet are automatically recalculated, which takes a little time. Now the correct values for the loan amortization table are displayed throughout the spreadsheet. One more formula is required to complete the spreadsheet. To present the total interest paid, the monthly amounts of interest paid must be totaled. Move the cell cursor down to cell D45, under the interest paid column. Enter the following formula to add up the 36 interest payments:

```
SUM(D8:D43)<Return>
```

This totals the values in the range from D8 through D43. This total, 1,174.24, is calculated and displayed. A label should also be added to identify this total. Move the cell cursor to B45 and enter this text:

```
Total Interest Paid<Return>
```

The loan amortization table is now complete, displaying the proper values. The entire table is displayed in Fig. 6-16 as it would appear in scrolling up and down the spreadsheet. Figure 6-17 shows the contents of each cell as they have been entered, including all of the formulas in the spreadsheet. You can scroll around the screen to examine various portions of the table on your computer. The balance on the loan declines over the 36 month period, reaching a value of -.20 at the end of the final month. This might suggest that you would be overpaying the loan by twenty cents. Do not rush to the bank and complain, however. It is usually impossible to make such equal payment loans work out exactly to the penny. In addition, various banks can have slightly different procedures for computing interest. Things can get complex when considering that the number of days in a month can vary from 28 to 31, for example. Finally, differences in when and how values are rounded off to the nearest penny can also affect the outcome.

Formatting the Spreadsheet

While the numbers are all correct, the loan amortization table could stand some improvement in the way in which the information is displayed. ExpressCalc includes the Format command, which can be used to tailor the appearance of the spreadsheet in a variety of ways. It will be used here to alter column widths, the location of column headings, and the formats of some of the numbers.

As it currently stands, the spreadsheet appears a little cramped. Widening the columns just a little would put more space between the columns of figures and make the table easier to read. Start the Format command by pressing Slash and F. The first prompt asks you to enter the range to be formatted, as shown in Fig. 6-18. The Format command allows formatting of individual cells, ranges, or the entire spreadsheet. To change the widths of all of the columns in the spreadsheet, enter ALL and press Return.

The next prompt, shown in Fig. 6-19, requests the type of formatting change desired. Twelve options are listed. The decimals option allows specification of the number of digits displayed after the decimal point and allows numbers to be displayed in floating point or scientific notation. Width (to be used here) makes changes in the column widths. Justify is used to align text within columns. Commas give the option of displaying commas to separate digits into groups of three. The dollar sign format option provides for the display of a leading dollar sign. The parenthesis option is used to display negative values inside parentheses, as is commonly done in accounting, rather than with a minus sign.

The percent option is used to display a percent sign after values displayed in the cells. Protect is used to keep formulas and headings in cells from being accidentally altered. This is useful when a standard spreadsheet is being created for repeated use. The headings and formulas can be protected, so that a user can enter values without worrying about damaging the basic spreadsheet. Unprotect, as the name suggests, removes this protection. Hide can be used to prevent the information in certain cells from being displayed on the screen or on printouts of the spreadsheet. The bargraph format option can display values as horizontal bars for the creation of simple bar graphs. Finally, the zero-as-

	A	B	C	D	E	F
1			Loan Amortization Table			
2						
3		Annual Interest Rate		12.00		
4						
5	Month	Beginning	Monthly	Interest	Principal	Ending
6		Balance	Payment	Paid	Paid	Balance
7						
8	1.00	6,000.00	199.29	60.00	139.29	5,860.71
9	2.00	5,860.71	199.29	58.61	140.68	5,720.03
10	3.00	5,720.03	199.29	57.20	142.09	5,577.94
11	4.00	5,577.94	199.29	55.78	143.51	5,434.43
12	5.00	5,434.43	199.29	54.34	144.95	5,289.48
13	6.00	5,289.48	199.29	52.89	146.40	5,143.08
14	7.00	5,143.08	199.29	51.43	147.86	4,995.22
15	8.00	4,995.22	199.29	49.95	149.34	4,845.88
16	9.00	4,845.88	199.29	48.46	150.83	4,695.05
17	10.00	4,695.05	199.29	46.95	152.34	4,542.71
18	11.00	4,542.71	199.29	45.43	153.86	4,388.85
19	12.00	4,388.85	199.29	43.89	155.40	4,233.45
20	13.00	4,233.45	199.29	42.33	156.96	4,076.49
21	14.00	4,076.49	199.29	40.76	158.53	3,917.96
22	15.00	3,917.96	199.29	39.18	160.11	3,757.85
23	16.00	3,757.85	199.29	37.58	161.71	3,596.14
24	17.00	3,596.14	199.29	35.96	163.33	3,432.81
25	18.00	3,432.81	199.29	34.33	164.96	3,267.85
26	19.00	3,267.85	199.29	32.68	166.61	3,101.24
27	20.00	3,101.24	199.29	31.01	168.28	2,932.96
28	21.00	2,932.96	199.29	29.33	169.96	2,763.00
29	22.00	2,763.00	199.29	27.63	171.66	2,591.34
30	23.00	2,591.34	199.29	25.91	173.38	2,417.96
31	24.00	2,417.96	199.29	24.18	175.11	2,242.85
32	25.00	2,242.85	199.29	22.43	176.86	2,065.99
33	26.00	2,065.99	199.29	20.66	178.63	1,887.36
34	27.00	1,887.36	199.29	18.87	180.42	1,706.94
35	28.00	1,706.94	199.29	17.07	182.22	1,524.72
36	29.00	1,524.72	199.29	15.25	184.04	1,340.68
37	30.00	1,340.68	199.29	13.41	185.88	1,154.80
38	31.00	1,154.80	199.29	11.55	187.74	967.06
39	32.00	967.06	199.29	9.67	189.62	777.44
40	33.00	777.44	199.29	7.77	191.52	585.92
41	34.00	585.92	199.29	5.86	193.43	392.49
42	35.00	392.49	199.29	3.92	195.37	197.12
43	36.00	197.12	199.29	1.97	197.32	-.20
44						
45		Total Interest Paid		1,174.24		

Fig. 6-16. Loan amortization spreadsheet with all formulas entered and replicated and the correct values displayed.

	A	B	C	D	E	F
1			"Loan Amortization Table			
2						
3		"Annual Interest Rate		12		
4						
5	"Month	"Beginning	"Monthly	"Interest	"Principal	"Ending
6		"Balance	"Payment	"Paid	"Paid	"Balance
7						
8	1	6000	199.29	B8*0.01*D3/12	C8-D8	B8-E8
9	A8+1	F8	C8	B9*0.01*D3/12	C9-D9	B9-E9
10	A9+1	F9	C9	B10*0.01*D3/12	C10-D10	B10-E10
11	A10+1	F10	C10	B11*0.01*D3/12	C11-D11	B11-E11
12	A11+1	F11	C11	B12*0.01*D3/12	C12-D12	B12-E12
13	A12+1	F12	C12	B13*0.01*D3/12	C13-D13	B13-E13
14	A13+1	F13	C13	B14*0.01*D3/12	C14-D14	B14-E14
15	A14+1	F14	C14	B15*0.01*D3/12	C15-D15	B15-E15
16	A15+1	F15	C15	B16*0.01*D3/12	C16-D16	B16-E16
17	A16+1	F16	C16	B17*0.01*D3/12	C17-D17	B17-E17
18	A17+1	F17	C17	B18*0.01*D3/12	C18-D18	B18-E18
19	A18+1	F18	C18	B19*0.01*D3/12	C19-D19	B19-E19
20	A19+1	F19	C19	B20*0.01*D3/12	C20-D20	B20-E20
21	A20+1	F20	C20	B21*0.01*D3/12	C21-D21	B21-E21
22	A21+1	F21	C21	B22*0.01*D3/12	C22-D22	B22-E22
23	A22+1	F22	C22	B23*0.01*D3/12	C23-D23	B23-E23
24	A23+1	F23	C23	B24*0.01*D3/12	C24-D24	B24-E24
25	A24+1	F24	C24	B25*0.01*D3/12	C25-D25	B25-E25
26	A25+1	F25	C25	B26*0.01*D3/12	C26-D26	B26-E26
27	A26+1	F26	C26	B27*0.01*D3/12	C27-D27	B27-E27
28	A27+1	F27	C27	B28*0.01*D3/12	C28-D28	B28-E28
29	A28+1	F28	C28	B29*0.01*D3/12	C29-D29	B29-E29
30	A29+1	F29	C29	B30*0.01*D3/12	C30-D30	B30-E30
31	A30+1	F30	C30	B31*0.01*D3/12	C31-D31	B31-E31
32	A31+1	F31	C31	B32*0.01*D3/12	C32-D32	B32-E32
33	A32+1	F32	C32	B33*0.01*D3/12	C33-D33	B33-E33
34	A33+1	F33	C33	B34*0.01*D3/12	C34-D34	B34-E34
35	A34+1	F34	C34	B35*0.01*D3/12	C35-D35	B35-E35
36	A35+1	F35	C35	B36*0.01*D3/12	C36-D36	B36-E36
37	A36+1	F36	C36	B37*0.01*D3/12	C37-D37	B37-E37
38	A37+1	F37	C37	B38*0.01*D3/12	C38-D38	B38-E38
39	A38+1	F38	C38	B39*0.01*D3/12	C39-D39	B39-E39
40	A39+1	F39	C39	B40*0.01*D3/12	C40-D40	B40-E40
41	A40+1	F40	C40	B41*0.01*D3/12	C41-D41	B41-E41
42	A41+1	F41	C41	B42*0.01*D3/12	C42-D42	B42-E42
43	A42+1	F42	C42	B43*0.01*D3/12	C43-D43	B43-E43
44						
45		"Total Interest Paid		SUM(D8:D43)		

Fig. 6-17. Contents of the loan amortization spreadsheet, showing the formulas in each cell.

```
           A           B           C           D           E           F           G
1                               Loan Amortization Table
2
3                Annual Interest Rate         12.00
4
5   Month        Beginning  Monthly    Interest    Principal  Ending
6                Balance    Payment    Paid        Paid       Balance
7
8          1.00   6,000.00     199.29      60.00      139.29   5,860.71
9          2.00   5,860.71     199.29      58.61      140.68   5,720.03
10         3.00   5,720.03     199.29      57.20      142.09   5,577.94
11         4.00   5,577.94     199.29      55.78      143.51   5,434.43
12         5.00   5,434.43     199.29      54.34      144.95   5,289.48
13         6.00   5,289.48     199.29      52.89      146.40   5,143.08
14         7.00   5,143.08     199.29      51.43      147.86   4,995.22
15         8.00   4,995.22     199.29      49.95      149.34   4,845.88
16         9.00   4,845.88     199.29      48.46      150.83   4,695.05
17        10.00   4,695.05     199.29      46.95      152.34   4,542.71
18        11.00   4,542.71     199.29      45.43      153.86   4,388.85
19        12.00   4,388.85     199.29      43.89      155.40   4,233.45
20        13.00   4,233.45     199.29      42.33      156.96   4,076.49
21        14.00   4,076.49     199.29      40.76      158.53   3,917.96
432K Enter range to be formatted (or ALL)

A1    >/Format,
```

Fig. 6-18. Using the Format command: specifying the range to be formatted.

blank format can be used to display zero values in cells as blanks rather than zero. See the ExpressCalc manual for more information on the various format options.

Press the W to indicate that column widths are to be changed. ExpressCalc asks you to enter the column width, from 0 to 75. The current column width of 11 is displayed on the entry line. See Fig. 6-20. Type a new column width of 12 over the existing value and press Return. The columns are immediately widened on the screen. In fact, only six columns are now displayed on the screen at one time, because the seventh no longer fits. The format display is returned to the selection of formatting options shown before in Fig. 6-18. This allows the entry of more than one formatting change for a given range, without starting over with the Format command. Pressing Return at this point ends the operation of the Format command, and ExpressCalc is ready for the entry of information or another command.

The column headings are currently displayed flush with the left-hand edge of each column, while the numbers are right-justified. This looks awkward and makes the table difficult to read. Better would be the right-justification of those text entries, placing them directly above the columns of numbers. Press Slash and F to begin the Format command. The column headings are in rows 5 and 6 and extend from columns A through F. Specify this rectangular range by entering the upper-left and lower-right cell coordinates, as follows:

A5:F6<Return>

Select the Justify option by pressing J. The options are to right-justify, left-justify, or center. Press R to choose right justification. The column headings are immediately moved over. Pressing Return ends this Format command operation.

```
          A          B          C          D          E          F          G
1   [          ]              Loan Amortization Table
2
3               Annual Interest Rate          12.00
4
5   Month       Beginning  Monthly    Interest   Principal  Ending
6               Balance    Payment    Paid       Paid       Balance
7
8          1.00  6,000.00     199.29      60.00     139.29   5,860.71
9          2.00  5,860.71     199.29      58.61     140.68   5,720.03
10         3.00  5,720.03     199.29      57.20     142.09   5,577.94
11         4.00  5,577.94     199.29      55.78     143.51   5,434.43
12         5.00  5,434.43     199.29      54.34     144.95   5,289.48
13         6.00  5,289.48     199.29      52.89     146.40   5,143.08
14         7.00  5,143.08     199.29      51.43     147.86   4,995.22
15         8.00  4,995.22     199.29      49.95     149.34   4,845.88
16         9.00  4,845.88     199.29      48.46     150.83   4,695.05
17        10.00  4,695.05     199.29      46.95     152.34   4,542.71
18        11.00  4,542.71     199.29      45.43     153.86   4,388.85
19        12.00  4,388.85     199.29      43.89     155.40   4,233.45
20        13.00  4,233.45     199.29      42.33     156.96   4,076.49
21        14.00  4,076.49     199.29      40.76     158.53   3,917.96
432K Decimals   Width      Justify    Commas     $          (          %
     Protect    Unprotect  Hide       Bargraph   Zero-blank
A1   >/Format,ALL,
```

Fig. 6-19. Using the Format command: selecting the formatting option.

The values displayed for the months look silly with the two zeroes after the decimal point. The months should be whole numbers. Press Slash and F to begin Format. Enter the range of the month numbers:

A8:A43 <Return>

Press D for decimals to change the number of digits displayed after the decimal point. You will be asked to enter the number of decimal places, from 0 to 9. Press the zero key, and the months will be displayed as whole numbers. Return completes the operation.

A nice final touch would be the addition of a percent sign after the interest rate in cell D3. The procedure should be familiar by now: press Slash, F, D3, and Return to select the format command and specify the range. As always, if the cell cursor is located in cell D3, just pressing Return after the F will enter this current cell coordinate. From the list of formatting options, press the percent sign (%). You will be asked if you want the percent sign after the number. Press Y and then Return to complete the command.

The top portion of the spreadsheet now appears on the screen as shown in Fig. 6-21. The columns are wider, column headings are lined up above the figures, the months are now displayed as whole numbers, and a percent sign follows the value for the interest rate. The display formats can be changed as often as desired, so it is easy to experiment with any spreadsheet to obtain an attractive layout.

USING THE LOAN AMORTIZATION SPREADSHEET

The loan amortization spreadsheet is now finished. The time has come to begin doing things with this spreadsheet—saving it on the disk, printing it out, and doing some analysis.

Saving and Loading the Spreadsheet

When you are creating a spreadsheet, the information is stored only in the internal (RAM) memory of the computer. If you exit ExpressCalc or turn off the computer, the spreadsheet is lost. To keep a spreadsheet for later use, it must be saved in a file on the disk. Do this with the Save command. Press Slash and S. You will be prompted to enter the file name to be used to identify the spreadsheet file. The file name can be any valid DOS file name of up to eight characters plus an optional three character extension. To store the file on the data disk in the B: drive, the file name must include the drive designation. LOAN would make a good file name for this spreadsheet. While an extension is not required, many people find it useful to employ an extension such as .CAL to identify the file as a ExpressCalc spreadsheet file. Enter the following file name:

B:LOAN.CAL<Return>

Figure 6-22 shows the appearance of the screen just before pressing the Return key. The B: drive will operate and the spreadsheet will be stored in a file named LOAN.CAL on the B: disk.

If you later try to save this spreadsheet again using the file name LOAN.CAL, ExpressCalc will inform you that the file exists and will ask if you wish to overwrite the old file or back it up. This is for your protection. You have three options at this point. If you have improved the spreadsheet and do not wish to keep the old version, letting the new replace the old by overwriting may be appropriate. Choosing backup gives the old file the

```
           A          B          C          D          E          F          G
 1   [          ]               Loan Amortization Table
 2
 3               Annual Interest Rate         12.00
 4
 5   Month       Beginning  Monthly    Interest   Principal  Ending
 6               Balance    Payment    Paid       Paid       Balance
 7
 8         1.00    6,000.00     199.29       60.00     139.29   5,860.71
 9         2.00    5,860.71     199.29       58.61     140.68   5,720.03
10         3.00    5,720.03     199.29       57.20     142.09   5,577.94
11         4.00    5,577.94     199.29       55.78     143.51   5,434.43
12         5.00    5,434.43     199.29       54.34     144.95   5,289.48
13         6.00    5,289.48     199.29       52.89     146.40   5,143.08
14         7.00    5,143.08     199.29       51.43     147.86   4,995.22
15         8.00    4,995.22     199.29       49.95     149.34   4,845.88
16         9.00    4,845.88     199.29       48.46     150.83   4,695.05
17        10.00    4,695.05     199.29       46.95     152.34   4,542.71
18        11.00    4,542.71     199.29       45.43     153.86   4,388.85
19        12.00    4,388.85     199.29       43.89     155.40   4,233.45
20        13.00    4,233.45     199.29       42.33     156.96   4,076.49
21        14.00    4,076.49     199.29       40.76     158.53   3,917.96
432K Enter column width (0 to 75).

A1    >/Format,ALL,Width,11
```

Fig. 6-20. Using the Format command: changing the column widths.

	A	B	C	D	E	F
1			Loan Amortization Table			
2						
3		Annual Interest Rate		12.00%		
4						
5	Month	Beginning	Monthly	Interest	Principal	Ending
6		Balance	Payment	Paid	Paid	Balance
7						
8	1	6,000.00	199.29	60.00	139.29	5,860.71
9	2	5,860.71	199.29	58.61	140.68	5,720.03
10	3	5,720.03	199.29	57.20	142.09	5,577.94
11	4	5,577.94	199.29	55.78	143.51	5,434.43
12	5	5,434.43	199.29	54.34	144.95	5,289.48
13	6	5,289.48	199.29	52.89	146.40	5,143.08
14	7	5,143.08	199.29	51.43	147.86	4,995.22
15	8	4,995.22	199.29	49.95	149.34	4,845.88
16	9	4,845.88	199.29	48.46	150.83	4,695.05
17	10	4,695.05	199.29	46.95	152.34	4,542.71
18	11	4,542.71	199.29	45.43	153.86	4,388.85
19	12	4,388.85	199.29	43.89	155.40	4,233.45
20	13	4,233.45	199.29	42.33	156.96	4,076.49
21	14	4,076.49	199.29	40.76	158.53	3,917.96

432K

A1 >

Fig. 6-21. Screen display of the loan amortization spreadsheet after reformatting.

extension .BAK to indicate it is a backup file, and saves the current spreadsheet under the given file name. If you have modified the spreadsheet for a new problem you might, however, also want to retain the original spreadsheet for the old problem under the original name. Overwriting would destroy the old spreadsheet, and backing it up would leave it with the .BAK extension. In this case, you have been given the warning and the opportunity to go back and enter a new file name.

The complement of the Save command is the Load command, which reads spreadsheet files from the disk into the memory of the computer, allowing you to work with that spreadsheet. To demonstrate the use of the Load command, first clear the spreadsheet from memory with the Zap command (Slash, Z, Y). Begin the Load command with Slash and L. As with the Save command, you are prompted to enter the file name and are given the option to see the directory. Suppose you had forgotten the name used in storing the loan amortization spreadsheet—but at least you believe it is on the disk in the B: drive. Enter B: and press Return. A list of all of the files on the disk in the B: drive is displayed across the top of the screen, as shown in Fig. 6-23. Recognizing LOAN.CAL as the name used for the loan amortization spreadsheet, you can now enter it as follows:

B:LOAN.CAL <Return>

You are now given options to load all of the spreadsheet file from the disk, only a portion of the spreadsheet, or to consolidate the spreadsheet in the disk file with the one currently in memory. All is the simplest and most common option. Enter A, and the spreadsheet is read from that file on the disk, and in a few moments the loan amortization spreadsheet is displayed on the screen.

```
          A           B           C           D           E           F
1  [          ]              Loan Amortization Table
2
3            Annual Interest Rate             12.00%
4
5         Month   Beginning     Monthly    Interest   Principal      Ending
6                   Balance     Payment        Paid        Paid     Balance
7
8             1    6,000.00      199.29       60.00      139.29    5,860.71
9             2    5,860.71      199.29       58.61      140.68    5,720.03
10            3    5,720.03      199.29       57.20      142.09    5,577.94
11            4    5,577.94      199.29       55.78      143.51    5,434.43
12            5    5,434.43      199.29       54.34      144.95    5,289.48
13            6    5,289.48      199.29       52.89      146.40    5,143.08
14            7    5,143.08      199.29       51.43      147.86    4,995.22
15            8    4,995.22      199.29       49.95      149.34    4,845.88
16            9    4,845.88      199.29       48.46      150.83    4,695.05
17           10    4,695.05      199.29       46.95      152.34    4,542.71
18           11    4,542.71      199.29       45.43      153.86    4,388.85
19           12    4,388.85      199.29       43.89      155.40    4,233.45
20           13    4,233.45      199.29       42.33      156.96    4,076.49
21           14    4,076.49      199.29       40.76      158.53    3,917.96
432K Enter the file name. (Enter A:, B:, etc. for directory.)

A1    >/Save,B:LOAN.CAL
```

Fig. 6-22. Using the Save command to store the loan amortization spreadsheet in the disk file B:LOAN.CAL.

```
ADDRESS .HDR  ADDRESS .INX  ADDRESS .DTA  DIRECT  .RPT  LABELS  .RPT
INVEN   .HDR  INVEN   .INX  INVEN   .DTA  INVRPT  .RPT  INVRPT2 .RPT
INVEN2  .DTA  INVEN2  .HDR  INVEN2  .INX  FIRST   .DOC  FACE    .COM
SECOND  .&DO  SECOND  .DOC  FIRST   .&DO  LETTER  .&    FIG5-16
LETTER        COMPUTER.LST  PROG1   .BAS  LET           FIG5-15
SCRNDUMP.PCT  HRBSTOCK.PCT  COMPSRV1.PCT  SCRNDUMP.&PC  FIG5-13
FIG5-13 .&    MESSAGE       IUNET   .TXT  IUNET   .&TX  EXAMPLE .TXT
MEMO2         PCWADDR .RPT  PCWADDR .LST  FORMLET       FORMLET .&
FORMOUT       HRBSTOCK      HRBSTOCK.&    HRBORIG       HRBEDIT
HRBEDIT .&    PRINTER       PRINTER .&    HRBTEST .HDR  HRBTEST .INX
HRBTEST .DTA  TEMP          HRBSTOCK.HDR  HRBSTOCK.INX  HRBSTOCK.DTA
NEW           TEST          LOAN1         LOANFORM      LOAN    .CAL






A1    >/Load,B:
```

Fig. 6-23. Using the Load command and viewing the directory of the files on the B: drive.

Printing the Spreadsheet

Printing a simple, small spreadsheet such as the loan amortization table is easy. Be sure the printer is turned on and is ready. Use the Print command and keep on pressing Return to accept the default entries. In more detail, this is what transpires. Pressing the Slash and the P begin the Print command. The first prompt requests the range to be printed. ALL is displayed on the command line. Pressing Return indicates that the entire spreadsheet is to be printed. The next request is for the page width, with 80 columns on the entry line. This will work with virtually all printers. Pressing Return accepts this value. Likewise the page length provides a default of 58 lines, which is appropriate for 11-inch paper; you press Return once more. A list of options is displayed. Return indicates that none of the options are to be used. The last prompt asks whether the spreadsheet is to be printed to the printer or to a file on the disk. The P, for printer, is displayed. With all of the defaults selected thus far, the entry line appears as shown in Fig. 6-24. Pressing Return one last time directs the output to the printer, and the spreadsheet is printed out. The printout of the loan amortization spreadsheet is shown in Fig. 6-25.

Printing Options

Printing the loan amortization table could be accomplished with the default printing options. In other cases, various choices allowed in the Print command will be important. The possibilities are discussed here.

The first choice involves whether to print the entire spreadsheet (ALL) or a specified range. Especially with very large spreadsheets, it may be easier or more desirable to print out one portion at a time. Ranges are specified in the normal fashion by indicating the upper left-hand cell and the lower right-hand cell, separated by a colon. In deciding

	A	B	C	D	E	F
1			Loan Amortization Table			
2						
3		Annual Interest Rate		12.00%		
4						
5	Month	Beginning	Monthly	Interest	Principal	Ending
6		Balance	Payment	Paid	Paid	Balance
7						
8	1	6,000.00	199.29	60.00	139.29	5,860.71
9	2	5,860.71	199.29	58.61	140.68	5,720.03
10	3	5,720.03	199.29	57.20	142.09	5,577.94
11	4	5,577.94	199.29	55.78	143.51	5,434.43
12	5	5,434.43	199.29	54.34	144.95	5,289.48
13	6	5,289.48	199.29	52.89	146.40	5,143.08
14	7	5,143.08	199.29	51.43	147.86	4,995.22
15	8	4,995.22	199.29	49.95	149.34	4,845.88
16	9	4,845.88	199.29	48.46	150.83	4,695.05
17	10	4,695.05	199.29	46.95	152.34	4,542.71
18	11	4,542.71	199.29	45.43	153.86	4,388.85
19	12	4,388.85	199.29	43.89	155.40	4,233.45
20	13	4,233.45	199.29	42.33	156.96	4,076.49
21	14	4,076.49	199.29	40.76	158.53	3,917.96

432K Printer or Disk.

A1 >/Print,ALL,80,58,P

Fig. 6-24. Using the Print command to print out the loan amortization spreadsheet, accepting all defaults.

Loan Amortization Table

Annual Interest Rate 12.00%

Month	Beginning Balance	Monthly Payment	Interest Paid	Principal Paid	Ending Balance
1	6,000.00	199.29	60.00	139.29	5,860.71
2	5,860.71	199.29	58.61	140.68	5,720.03
3	5,720.03	199.29	57.20	142.09	5,577.94
4	5,577.94	199.29	55.78	143.51	5,434.43
5	5,434.43	199.29	54.34	144.95	5,289.48
6	5,289.48	199.29	52.89	146.40	5,143.08
7	5,143.08	199.29	51.43	147.86	4,995.22
8	4,995.22	199.29	49.95	149.34	4,845.88
9	4,845.88	199.29	48.46	150.83	4,695.05
10	4,695.05	199.29	46.95	152.34	4,542.71
11	4,542.71	199.29	45.43	153.86	4,388.85
12	4,388.85	199.29	43.89	155.40	4,233.45
13	4,233.45	199.29	42.33	156.96	4,076.49
14	4,076.49	199.29	40.76	158.53	3,917.96
15	3,917.96	199.29	39.18	160.11	3,757.85
16	3,757.85	199.29	37.58	161.71	3,596.14
17	3,596.14	199.29	35.96	163.33	3,432.81
18	3,432.81	199.29	34.33	164.96	3,267.85
19	3,267.85	199.29	32.68	166.61	3,101.24
20	3,101.24	199.29	31.01	168.28	2,932.96
21	2,932.96	199.29	29.33	169.96	2,763.00
22	2,763.00	199.29	27.63	171.66	2,591.34
23	2,591.34	199.29	25.91	173.38	2,417.96
24	2,417.96	199.29	24.18	175.11	2,242.85
25	2,242.85	199.29	22.43	176.86	2,065.99
26	2,065.99	199.29	20.66	178.63	1,887.36
27	1,887.36	199.29	18.87	180.42	1,706.94
28	1,706.94	199.29	17.07	182.22	1,524.72
29	1,524.72	199.29	15.25	184.04	1,340.68
30	1,340.68	199.29	13.41	185.88	1,154.80
31	1,154.80	199.29	11.55	187.74	967.06
32	967.06	199.29	9.67	189.62	777.44
33	777.44	199.29	7.77	191.52	585.92
34	585.92	199.29	5.86	193.43	392.49
35	392.49	199.29	3.92	195.37	197.12
36	197.12	199.29	1.97	197.32	-.20

Total Interest Paid 1,174.24

Fig. 6-25. Printout of the loan amortization spreadsheet.

upon how much of the spreadsheet is to be printed out, keep in mind the maximum number of characters that can be printed on one line with your printer. If you print out a wider spreadsheet, ExpressCalc will print out as many columns as will fit on a line. After all of the rows have been printed, ExpressCalc starts over and prints the remaining columns (or however many more will fit on the line). The result is a printout of the spreadsheet in multiple vertical pieces. You can always tape the pieces together.

The next question is the page width—the number of columns that the printer can print on one line. A typical narrow-carriage printer printing at a normal ten characters per inch can print 80 characters on a line. This is the default displayed on the entry line. Using the same size characters, a wide-carriage printer with 14-inch paper can print 132 characters per line. On either size of printer, more characters can be fit onto line using narrower characters, which most dot matrix printers can generate. The typical compressed print option prints 16.2 characters per inch, or 132 characters on a line of the narrow-carriage printer. Enter the value appropriate for your printer. Remember, however, that if you plan to use compressed printing, the printer will have to somehow be instructed to print in that mode.

The page length is probably the simplest choice. At a standard six lines per inch, a total of 66 lines can be printed on a standard 11-inch long piece of paper. To allow small margins at the top and bottom, ExpressCalc selects a default value of 58 lines per page. For most situations this will be fine, but you can enter a smaller value if you desire larger top or bottom margins.

The Print command next allows the selection of options from a list of 10, as shown in Fig. 6-26. To select any option, enter the letter and press Return. As many options can be entered in this fash-

```
                A           B            C            D            E            F
1    [          ]               Loan Amortization Table
2
3                    Annual Interest Rate          12.00%
4
5              Month   Beginning      Monthly     Interest    Principal       Ending
6                        Balance      Payment         Paid         Paid      Balance
7
8                  1    6,000.00       199.29        60.00       139.29     5,860.71
9                  2    5,860.71       199.29        58.61       140.68     5,720.03
10                 3    5,720.03       199.29        57.20       142.09     5,577.94
11                 4    5,577.94       199.29        55.78       143.51     5,434.43
12                 5    5,434.43       199.29        54.34       144.95     5,289.48
13                 6    5,289.48       199.29        52.89       146.40     5,143.08
14                 7    5,143.08       199.29        51.43       147.86     4,995.22
15                 8    4,995.22       199.29        49.95       149.34     4,845.88
16                 9    4,845.88       199.29        48.46       150.83     4,695.05
17                10    4,695.05       199.29        46.95       152.34     4,542.71
18                11    4,542.71       199.29        45.43       153.86     4,388.85
19                12    4,388.85       199.29        43.89       155.40     4,233.45
20                13    4,233.45       199.29        42.33       156.96     4,076.49
21                14    4,076.49       199.29        40.76       158.53     3,917.96
432K Options: D=double space, S=setup, P=pause, C=contents, M=Multiple copies,
     B=border, O=offset, T=Top margin, H=Heading lines, F=Footing lines
A1   >/Print,ALL,80,58,
```

Fig. 6-26. List of print options displayed by the Print command.

```
        A           B           C           D           E           F
1  [          ]            Loan Amortization Table
2
3                Annual Interest Rate            12.00%
4
5             Month    Beginning      Monthly    Interest    Principal       Ending
6                        Balance      Payment        Paid         Paid      Balance
7
8                 1     6,000.00       199.29       60.00       139.29     5,860.71
9                 2     5,860.71       199.29       58.61       140.68     5,720.03
10                3     5,720.03       199.29       57.20       142.09     5,577.94
11                4     5,577.94       199.29       55.78       143.51     5,434.43
12                5     5,434.43       199.29       54.34       144.95     5,289.48
13                6     5,289.48       199.29       52.89       146.40     5,143.08
14                7     5,143.08       199.29       51.43       147.86     4,995.22
15                8     4,995.22       199.29       49.95       149.34     4,845.88
16                9     4,845.88       199.29       48.46       150.83     4,695.05
17               10     4,695.05       199.29       46.95       152.34     4,542.71
18               11     4,542.71       199.29       45.43       153.86     4,388.85
19               12     4,388.85       199.29       43.89       155.40     4,233.45
20               13     4,233.45       199.29       42.33       156.96     4,076.49
21               14     4,076.49       199.29       40.76       158.53     3,917.96
432K Enter printer setup codes, then ENTER.
     Epson             printers: "A" = 10 cpi, "B" = 12 cpi, "C" = 17 cpi.
A1   >/Print,ALL,80,58,S,
```

Fig. 6-27. Using the setup option to send special codes to the printer.

ion as desired. Several of the choices require little explanation. D double-spaces the printed spreadsheet. P will cause printing to be paused at the end of each page, required when you are printing on single sheets that have to be individually fed into the printer. B prints the row numbers and column letters at the borders of the spreadsheet. If this is not selected, the row and column identifiers will not be printed. T sets the top margin—the bottom margin is then determined by the page length and the number of lines on the page. M prints multiple copies of the spreadsheet. Headings and footings can be added to the printout of the spreadsheet using H and F.

The offset option, O, is used to change the left margin or page offset. ExpressCalc normally includes a seven-column margin to the left of the text. This can be changed to alter the position at which the spreadsheet is printed on the page. It may have to be altered to print wide spreadsheets, since the seven-column offset takes up seven of the printing positions on the line. The contents options, C, prints out the contents of each cell—such as a formula. This output is only useful for documenting the spreadsheet; results are not displayed.

The setup option, S, is used to send special codes to the printer. The most common use of this capability is to change the widths of the characters printed, selecting alternative numbers of characters per inch. When the S option is entered, the prompt is displayed as shown in Fig. 6-27. The option works in two different ways as indicated by the two lines of the prompt. The second line lists a type of printer (Epson, in this case) and provides letter codes for the selection of printing at varying numbers of characters per inch. Several brands of printers can be selected using the Configure command, described below.

If your printer is an Epson (or whatever type is displayed), you can make the selection just by entering the appropriate letter and pressing return. Alternatively, you can follow the first line of the prompt and enter the actual code for your printer. For example, with a C.Itoh ProWriter, the code for elite (12 characters per inch) printing is Escape E. Enter the code by pressing the Escape key followed by the E. For special characters, Control key combinations will have to be employed. See the ExpressCalc manual for instructions.

The final choice to be made in printing a spreadsheet is whether it is to be printed on the printer or to a file on the disk. If you enter D to select the disk option, you will be prompted for the name of the file for the storage of the output. More information on the use of this option is provided in Chapter 7.

Spreadsheet Analysis

The flexibility and power of an electronic spreadsheet program become apparent when it is used to examine alternative assumptions and ask what-if questions. By changing just one or a few values, entirely new results can be quickly generated. This section considers two simple variations of the loan amortization spreadsheet.

Suppose the loan in question were an adjustable-rate loan that would be paid off more quickly if interest rates fell. How quickly would the loan be paid off if the interest rate immediately dropped from 12 percent to 10 percent. Simply move the cursor to cell D3 and enter the new value:

10<Return>

The spreadsheet is recalculated. Figure 6-28 is a display of the entire spreadsheet as it would appear as you moved up and down on the screen. The loan is paid off after 35 months.

The terms of the loan allows you to make additional payments on the principal balance owed that will reduce the length of time to pay off the loan and the total interest paid. Your income and the prospects for increases in the future allow you to consider paying $220 per month for the first 12 months, $240 for the next year, and $260 for the remainder of the loan. Revising the spreadsheet will require the entry of these values. First, change the value for the interest rate in cell D4 back to 12. As you enter this value, the spreadsheet again is recalculated, which takes a considerable amount of time. Waiting for these recalculations after the entry of each of the new monthly payments would be a nuisance. The automatic recalculation carried out by ExpressCalc can be turned off using the Global command, which sets certain spreadsheet-wide (global) parameters. The prompts are displayed as shown in Fig. 6-29.

The Manual option switches from automatic to manual recalculation. Press M and return. The Auto option, of course, switches back. Row and Column refer to the order in which the formulas are calculated, and Border can be used to turn the row and column numbers and letter off or on. Choosing the Formula option displays the formulas in the cells rather than the values. Zero-as-blank works like the format option, except it works for the spreadsheet as a whole. Finally, the Smart-cursor option can be used to force the cursor to move in a chosen direction when data values are entered with the Return key, useful for entering long strings of numbers with the numeric keypaid.

With the spreadsheet in manual recalculation mode, the formulas will not be recalculated each time an entry is made. To recalculate the spreadsheet, it is now necessary to enter the recalculation command ! (the exclamation point).

The plan is to pay $220 for the first 12 months. Enter this value in the monthly payment column, in cell C8. Nothing else changes, because the spreadsheet is in the manual recalculation mode. If the spreadsheet were recalculated, however, this value would be repeated down through the monthly payment column, because the formulas copy the value in the cell above.

As you move the cursor down to the lower parts of the spreadsheet, you notice the title and column headings moving off the top of the screen. It would be nice to be able to freeze these headings while you moved up and down through the spreadsheet. The Title command does just this. Move the cell cursor to the top of area to be scrolled and not locked in place, to any cell in row 8. Press Slash

	A	B	C	D	E	F
1			Loan Amortization Table			
2						
3		Annual Interest Rate		10.00%		
4						
5	Month	Beginning	Monthly	Interest	Principal	Ending
6		Balance	Payment	Paid	Paid	Balance
7						
8	1	6,000.00	199.29	50.00	149.29	5,850.71
9	2	5,850.71	199.29	48.76	150.53	5,700.18
10	3	5,700.18	199.29	47.50	151.79	5,548.39
11	4	5,548.39	199.29	46.24	153.05	5,395.34
12	5	5,395.34	199.29	44.96	154.33	5,241.01
13	6	5,241.01	199.29	43.68	155.61	5,085.40
14	7	5,085.40	199.29	42.38	156.91	4,928.49
15	8	4,928.49	199.29	41.07	158.22	4,770.27
16	9	4,770.27	199.29	39.75	159.54	4,610.73
17	10	4,610.73	199.29	38.42	160.87	4,449.86
18	11	4,449.86	199.29	37.08	162.21	4,287.65
19	12	4,287.65	199.29	35.73	163.56	4,124.09
20	13	4,124.09	199.29	34.37	164.92	3,959.17
21	14	3,959.17	199.29	32.99	166.30	3,792.87
22	15	3,792.87	199.29	31.61	167.68	3,625.19
23	16	3,625.19	199.29	30.21	169.08	3,456.11
24	17	3,456.11	199.29	28.80	170.49	3,285.62
25	18	3,285.62	199.29	27.38	171.91	3,113.71
26	19	3,113.71	199.29	25.95	173.34	2,940.37
27	20	2,940.37	199.29	24.50	174.79	2,765.58
28	21	2,765.58	199.29	23.05	176.24	2,589.34
29	22	2,589.34	199.29	21.58	177.71	2,411.63
30	23	2,411.63	199.29	20.10	179.19	2,232.44
31	24	2,232.44	199.29	18.60	180.69	2,051.75
32	25	2,051.75	199.29	17.10	182.19	1,869.56
33	26	1,869.56	199.29	15.58	183.71	1,685.85
34	27	1,685.85	199.29	14.05	185.24	1,500.61
35	28	1,500.61	199.29	12.51	186.78	1,313.83
36	29	1,313.83	199.29	10.95	188.34	1,125.49
37	30	1,125.49	199.29	9.38	189.91	935.58
38	31	935.58	199.29	7.80	191.49	744.09
39	32	744.09	199.29	6.20	193.09	551.00
40	33	551.00	199.29	4.59	194.70	356.30
41	34	356.30	199.29	2.97	196.32	159.98
42	35	159.98	199.29	1.33	197.96	-37.98
43	36	-37.98	199.29	-.32	199.61	-237.59
44						
45		Total Interest Paid		936.85		

Fig. 6-28. Loan amortization spreadsheet with the interest rate changed to 10 percent.

	A	B	C	D	E	F
1			Loan Amortization Table			
2						
3		Annual Interest Rate		12.00%		
4						
5	Month	Beginning	Monthly	Interest	Principal	Ending
6		Balance	Payment	Paid	Paid	Balance
7						
8	1	6,000.00	199.29	60.00	139.29	5,860.71
9	2	5,860.71	199.29	58.61	140.68	5,720.03
10	3	5,720.03	199.29	57.20	142.09	5,577.94
11	4	5,577.94	199.29	55.78	143.51	5,434.43
12	5	5,434.43	199.29	54.34	144.95	5,289.48
13	6	5,289.48	199.29	52.89	146.40	5,143.08
14	7	5,143.08	199.29	51.43	147.86	4,995.22
15	8	4,995.22	199.29	49.95	149.34	4,845.88
16	9	4,845.88	199.29	48.46	150.83	4,695.05
17	10	4,695.05	199.29	46.95	152.34	4,542.71
18	11	4,542.71	199.29	45.43	153.86	4,388.85
19	12	4,388.85	199.29	43.89	155.40	4,233.45
20	13	4,233.45	199.29	42.33	156.96	4,076.49
21	14	4,076.49	199.29	40.76	158.53	3,917.96

```
432K Border, Row, Column, Manual, Auto, Formula, Zero-blank, Smart-cursor

D3   >/Global,
```

Fig. 6-29. Using the Global command to change from automatic to manual recalculation.

and T. The horizontal titles across the top are to be frozen, so press H. Now, as you move to the bottom of the spreadsheet, the title and column headings remain fixed as the table itself scrolls. Use the Title command and select the None option to unlock the titles.

To provide for a monthly payment of $240 for the second year, move the cell cursor down to month 13 (row 20) and enter 240. This replaces the formula. When recalculation occurs, months below will have payment values of 240. Finally, move the cursor down to month 25 (row 32) and enter 260 to specify monthly payments at that level for the third year. Now recalculate the spreadsheet by pressing ! (the exclamation point). The spreadsheet shows that the loan would be paid off in month 30, as shown in Fig. 6-30. Note that the titles are frozen at the top of the screen, even though a lower portion of the table is being displayed.

In performing this final analysis by changing the level of monthly payments, the information in the monthly payment column was altered and the formulas in several of the cells were replaced. If you wish to get back to the original loan amortization spreadsheet, load in the version that was previously stored on the disk.

ADDITIONAL FEATURES OF EXPRESSCALC

In working through the loan amortization spreadsheet example, most features of ExpressCalc have been employed. To round out the presentation, a few additional features will be described: ExpressCalc has a wide variety of functions that can be employed in formulas while building spreadsheets. ExpressCalc also has a special capability allowing reference to values in other ExpressCalc spreadsheets and even in PC-File databases.

Functions

The loan amortization spreadsheet made use

of the SUM function to add up the interest paid. This is but one of the many functions available in ExpressCalc. The functions available in version 3.10 are summarized in Tables 6-2 and 6-3 and are discussed in this section.

The first group of ExpressCalc functions, presented in Table 6-3, are the functions of a single value. A single value is enclosed in parentheses following the function name. This value can be a number, a cell coordinate referencing the value in another cell, or a more complex formula. The function computes, or returns, a single value. A function can be the only entry in a cell in the spreadsheet, or it can be used within a more complex formula.

The SQR function, which computes the square root of a number, is used to illustrate the various possibilities. To compute the square root of the number 25, enter this function in a cell:

```
SQR(25)
```

This will be evaluated to yield the value 5, of course. The following function,

```
SQR(C8)
```

will compute the square root of whatever value is displayed in cell C8. This is an example of a function of a more complex formula:

```
SQR(B1*B1 – 4*A1*C1)
```

The value of the formula inside of the parentheses is evaluated, and then the square root is computed. (The mathematically inclined will recognize this as a part of the quadratic formula used for computing the roots of equations.) The above functions can be entered directly into cells in the spreadsheet, or

	A	B	C	D	E	F
1			Loan Amortization Table			
2						
3		Annual Interest Rate		12.00%		
4						
5	Month	Beginning	Monthly	Interest	Principal	Ending
6		Balance	Payment	Paid	Paid	Balance
7						
32	25	1,430.59	260.00	14.31	245.69	1,184.90
33	26	1,184.90	260.00	11.85	248.15	936.75
34	27	936.75	260.00	9.37	250.63	686.12
35	28	686.12	260.00	6.86	253.14	432.98
36	29	432.98	260.00	4.33	255.67	177.31
37	30	177.31	260.00	1.77	258.23	-80.92
38	31	-80.92	260.00	-.81	260.81	-341.73
39	32	-341.73	260.00	-3.42	263.42	-605.15
40	33	-605.15	260.00	-6.05	266.05	-871.20
41	34	-871.20	260.00	-8.71	268.71	-1,139.91
42	35	-1,139.91	260.00	-11.40	271.40	-1,411.31
43	36	-1,411.31	260.00	-14.11	274.11	-1,685.42
44						
45		Total Interest Paid		954.58		
432K						

A45 >

Fig. 6-30. The bottom portion of the loan amortization spreadsheet, with the titles locked, showing the results of increasing monthly payments.

Table 6-3. Functions of a Single Value.

Function	Description
	MATHEMATICAL FUNCTIONS
ATN	Computes the arctangent of the value; the result is the angle in radians
COS	Computes the cosine of the value, which must be expressed in radians
EXP	Computes the exponential of the value, which is e, the base of the natural logarithms, raised to the power of the value
LOG	Computes the natural logarithm of the value
RANDOM	Returns a random number between zero and one
SIN	Computes the sine of the value, which must be expressed in radians
SQR	Computes the square root of the value
TAN	Computes the tangent of the value, which must be expressed in radians
	SIGN AND NUMBER FUNCTIONS
ABS	Returns the absolute value of the value; the result is a positive number
FIX	Returns the integer portion of the value, truncating digits after the decimal point
INT	Returns the greatest integer less than the value, truncating digits after the decimal point
ROUND	Rounds a number to a specified number of decimal places
SGN	Returns +1 if the value is positive, 0 if the number is zeo, and − 1 if the number is negative

they can be used as a part of larger formulas. The following formula could be entered into a cell:

```
B8 + SQR(C8)
```

Formulas can thus be employed in many ways to perform nearly any type of computation desired in a spreadsheet.

The functions of a single value in Table 6-3 have been divided into two groups. ExpressCalc includes the most frequently used mathematical functions. SQR calculates the square root. SIN, COS, TAN, and ATN are the trigonometric functions for the sine, cosine, tangent, and arctangent. All refer to angles in radians. The LOG function computes the natural logarithm of a value, and the EXP function raises *e*, the base of the natural logarithms, to the power of the value. These functions will be used most frequently for science and engineering calculations on the spreadsheet. If you need them, you will know what these functions are. If you do not understand some of these functions, you probably will not need them.

The functions in the second group in Table 6-3 each alter the value of the number based on the sign, or truncate the value by dropping digits after the decimal point. ABS is the absolute value function, providing a positive value whether the value in parentheses is positive or negative. The sign function, SGN, returns a value based upon the sign of the number in parentheses— +1 if positive, 0 if zero, and −1 if negative. The FIX and INT functions both transform the value to an integer by truncating the digits after the decimal point. For positive numbers, they return the same value. They differ on how they treat negative numbers. The INT function transforms the value to the next lowest integer, so INT(−2.4) would return a value of −3. The FIX function, on the other hand, just drops the digits after the decimal point, so FIX(−2.4) would return a value of −2. The ROUND function is used to round off values to any specified number of decimal places.

The remaining ExpressCalc functions are more closely related to the idea of the spreadsheet, because they compute a value based upon multiple values in the spreadsheet. These functions of multiple values are summarized in Table 6-4.

Table 6-4. Functions of Multiple Values.

Function	Format	Description
	FUNCTIONS OF RANGES	
AVG	AVG(Range)	Computes the average of the values in a range
COUNT	COUNT(Range)	Counts the number of non-blank cells in a range
MAX	MAX(Range)	Determines the largest value in a range
MIN	MIN(Range)	Determines the smallest value in a range
STDEV	STDEV(Range)	Computes the standard deviation of the values in a range
SUM	SUM(Range)	Computes the total of the values in a range
	OTHER FUNCTIONS	
IF	IF(Relation, Expression1,Expression2)	If Relation is true, returns the value of Expression1, otherwise returns the value of Expression2
LOOKUP	LOOKUP(Search Value, List)	Finds the greatest value in an ordered list less than or equal to the search value and returns the value in the adjacent cell
NPV	NPV(Discount Rate Expression,List)	Uses the discount rate provided by the first expression to compute the net present value of the values over time provided by the list
PAYMENT	PAYMENT(Principal,Rate,Periods)	Computes the periodic payment for a loan with a given principal, interest rate, and number of periods
PERIODS	PERIODS(Principal,Payment,Rate)	Computes the number of periods for loan with a given principal, periodic payment, and interest rate
PRINCIPAL	PRINCIPAL(Payment,Rate,Periods)	Computes the principal for a loan with a given periodic payment, interest rate, and number of periods
RATE	RATE(Principal,Payment,Periods)	Computes the interest rate for loan with a given principal, period payment, and number of periods

Each of the commands in the first group return a single value that depends upon the values in a specified range. The range can be a list of cells in a column or row, or it can be a rectangular block of cells. The range is specified in the usual manner. For example, to total the values in the block comprising the first seven rows of the table from columns B through G, enter the following function:

```
SUM(B1:G7)
```

The remaining functions of ranges operate in the same manner. COUNT gives the number of non-blank cells in the range. AVG computes the average of the values of the cells in the range. This is simply the SUM divided by the COUNT. MAX and MIN return the largest and smallest values in the range. STDEV calculates the standard deviation of the values in the range.

The remaining functions are more complex. The IF function allows the selection of a value or function based upon a comparison. The first entry in the parentheses shows a relation: two expressions separated by a *relational* operator. The relational operators specify the comparison and are as follows:

=	Equal to
< >	Not equal to
<	Less than
>	Greater than
< =	Less than or equal to
> =	Greater than or equal to

The IF function makes the comparison specified. If it is true, the value of the first expression is returned. If it is false, the value of the second expression is returned.

An example using the loan amortization spreadsheet can illustrate the use that can be made of the IF function. When a lower interest rate was entered, the loan was paid off before the end of the 36-month period. The spreadsheet continues after the loan is paid off to compute negative interest payments based upon a growing negative balance owed. In effect, the loan is turned into a savings account. Adding in these negative payments results in an incorrect total interest to be paid on the loan. Figure 6-28 illustrates the problem. The IF function can be employed to compute the correct interest—a positive value if the remaining balance is positive, and zero if the balance drops below zero and the loan is paid off. The IF function should compare the beginning balance to zero. The following function can be entered in cell D8:

```
IF(B8>0,B8*0.01*D3/12,0) <Return>
```

The formula would then be replicated for cells D9 through D43 in the usual fashion, adjusting the references to cell B8 but not the reference to cell D3 with the interest rate.

The IF function then checks each month to determine whether the beginning balance, in cell B8, is greater than zero. If it is, it calculates the value of the next expression, which is the interest formula. That value is entered into the cell. On the other hand, if the beginning balance has dropped to zero or below, the IF function returns the value of the second expression, which is zero. Now, if a 10 percent interest rate is entered, the spreadsheet stops interest payments when the loan is paid off, and the correct total is reported for the interest paid. Figure 6-31 shows the results, with the titles frozen to display the titles with the bottom portion of the spreadsheet. If you want to get more elaborate, the IF function can also be used to terminate monthly payments after the loan has been paid off and even to adjust the final monthly payment to exactly pay off the loan.

The LOOKUP function can be used to determine a value from a table based upon another value. For example, in a spreadsheet to calculate income taxes, the tax rate could be determined from a table based upon the value of the taxable income. As an example, the LOOKUP function will be used to determine discounts to be applied to sales of various sizes. For the problem at hand, discounts will be applied to larger sales. There is no discount for invoice amounts of less than $50. Above $50, a discount of at least 5 percent is available, rising to a maximum of 20 percent for sales totaling over $500.

	A	B	C	D	E	F
1			Loan Amortization Table			
2						
3		Annual Interest Rate		10.00%		
4						
5	Month	Beginning	Monthly	Interest	Principal	Ending
6		Balance	Payment	Paid	Paid	Balance
7						
32	25	2,051.75	199.29	17.10	182.19	1,869.56
33	26	1,869.56	199.29	15.58	183.71	1,685.85
34	27	1,685.85	199.29	14.05	185.24	1,500.61
35	28	1,500.61	199.29	12.51	186.78	1,313.83
36	29	1,313.83	199.29	10.95	188.34	1,125.49
37	30	1,125.49	199.29	9.38	189.91	935.58
38	31	935.58	199.29	7.80	191.49	744.09
39	32	744.09	199.29	6.20	193.09	551.00
40	33	551.00	199.29	4.59	194.70	356.30
41	34	356.30	199.29	2.97	196.32	159.98
42	35	159.98	199.29	1.33	197.96	-37.98
43	36	-37.98	199.29	.00	199.29	-237.27
44						
45		Total Interest Paid		937.17		
430K						
A45 >						

Fig. 6-31. The bottom portion of the loan amortization spreadsheet with the interest rate changed to 10 percent and the IF function used to avoid interest payments when balance drops below zero.

A table listing the discounts has been entered into the top portion of the spreadsheet shown in Fig. 6-32. The invoice amount is in the left-hand column, and the applicable discount rate is in the right-hand column. The lower portion of the spreadsheet applies these discounts to sales of varying amounts using the LOOKUP function. The first column lists the invoice amounts for the various sales. In the second column is the discount rate, obtained from the table above using the LOOKUP function. For example, in row 17, the following formula is entered:

```
LOOKUP(B17,B7:B11)
```

The LOOKUP function works as follows: The first value in the parentheses is the value to be looked up. In this case, it is the invoice amount in cell B17, which currently has a value of 150.00. The range in the parentheses, B7:B11, specifies the location of the table where the lookup is to occur. In this case, the value of 150.00 from cell B17 is compared with the values in the range from B7 to B11. The LOOKUP function determines which is the greatest value in the range exceeded by the value being looked up. In this example, it is 100.00, for the invoice amount of 150.00 in cell B17 is greater than 100.00 but less than 250.00, the next value in the table.

The LOOKUP function returns the value in the cell to the right of the cell found in the range B7 to B11. In this example, it is the value in cell C9, the discount rate of 0.10, which is to the right of the invoice amount of 100.00, the minimum required to qualify for this discount rate. Thus, the discount rate of 0.10 is displayed in cell C17. The LOOKUP formula has been replicated into the cells below and is used to determine the discount rate for each of the corresponding invoice amounts.

The remaining functions in Table 4-3 are used for financial calculations. The net present value function, NPV, is used in the analysis of investments. The function takes a stream of values occurring over time and discounts these to the present value of the total. The first expression in the NPV function is the discount rate. The second expression is a range of cells in which the values occurring over time are located. This is another one of those cases in which, if you need to use the function, you will understand what is meant by the net present value. If not, do not worry.

The PAYMENT, PERIODS, PRINCIPAL, and RATE functions are related and involve the computation of the terms of loans. Each function will calculate one of the loan terms, given the other three. For example, the PAYMENT function determines the periodic payment amount required to pay off a loan, given the principal, interest rate, and number of periods. If you have the payment amount but not the number of periods required to pay off the loan, the PERIODS function can be employed to determine this. In each case, the three known values must be entered in the parentheses after the function name, and the function returns the value of the fourth.

The current version of ExpressCalc includes a number of functions for controlling the layout, display, and printing of the spreadsheet. These functions can be entered into cells to specify page breaks, characters per inch, and other print characteristics. They are summarized in Table 6-5. See the ExpressCalc manual for further details.

Using Values from Other Files

ExpressCalc includes a powerful feature for incorporating values from other spreadsheets or from PC-File databases into any spreadsheet. This can be employed to create complex applications involving several spreadsheets or databases.

The external command, Xternal, is used to enter a single value from another spreadsheet or from

```
         A          B          C          D          E          F          G
1
2                Sales Prices, with Discounts
3
4                   Invoice    Discount
5                    Amount        Rate
6
7                       .00         .00
8                     50.00         .05
9                    100.00         .10
10                   250.00         .15
11                   500.00         .20
12
13
14                  Invoice    Discount    Discount       Final
15                   Amount        Rate                  Amount
16
17                   150.00         .10       15.00      135.00
18                    35.00         .00         .00       35.00
19                   980.00         .20      196.00      784.00
20                   490.00         .15       73.50      416.50
21
440K (Formula)  LOOKUP(B17,B7:B11)

C17  >
```

Fig. 6-32. Use of LOOKUP function to determine sales discounts.

Table 6-5. Display and Printing Functions.

Function	Description
CPI	Sets the number of characters per inch at which following portions of the spreadsheet are to be printed; requires that ExpressCalc be configured for the printer
KEYWORD	Displays the date, time, or page number
LPI	Sets the number of lines per inch at which the spreadsheet will be printed
NOLF	Causes the current line to be printed without a line feed, so the following line on the spreadsheet is printed on same line
NOPRINT	Causes the current line not to be printed
PAGE	Begins the printing of the following portion of the spreadsheet at the top of a new page

a PC-File database stored on the disk. Imagine you were creating a spreadsheet with an analysis of your finances and wished to include the total interest paid on the loan analyzed above. First start a new spreadsheet by clearing with the Zap command. Enter this text in cell B8:

Interest on Loan<Return>

Move the cell cursor to D8 for the entry of the total interest on the loan. Begin the Xternal command with a Slash and X. You will be asked whether you want to enter data from a CALC spreadsheet or from a FILE database. Enter C. The next prompt is for the name of the spreadsheet to be used. Enter this:

B:LOAN.CAL<Return>

Then you are asked to enter the cell from which the value is to be obtained. Enter D45. The information on the entry line appears as shown in Fig. 6-33. Press Return to enter the final information. ExpressCalc accesses the B: disk to read the value in cell D45. That value, the interest paid, 1,174.24, is now displayed in cell D8, as shown in Fig. 6-34. Note that the two lines below the spreadsheet display both the value in cell D8 and the external reference to the loan amortization spreadsheet.

The external reference to the loan amortization spreadsheet will be updated each time the new spreadsheet is loaded from the disk. If changes are made to the loan amortization spreadsheet resulting in a new total, this new value will be brought into the new spreadsheet the next time it is loaded from the disk.

A similar procedure is employed to obtain data from PC-File databases. The Xtern command prompts for the name of the database, the field to be searched, the value to be searched for, and the field to be retrieved. The ExpressCalc manual provides further information and examples on the use of this powerful command.

CONFIGURING EXPRESSCALC

ExpressCalc includes the Configure command, which can be used to setup ExpressCalc to work with your system and match your operating preferences. Using the Configure command is comparable to using the Setup program with PC-File, except that Configure is invoked as a command from within ExpressCalc. The Configure command stores changes in a file on the disk, so the changes permanently affect the operation of ExpressCalc from then on.

If you are using a monochrome monitor with the color/graphics display adapter, the Configure command will modify ExpressCalc so you no longer have to type the BW each time you start the program. Configure will automatically save this option when it is employed to modify the program. To make this change, start the Configure command with the Slash and the C. The display will appear as shown in Fig. 6-35. You do not need to specify

```
        A         B         C         D         E         F         G
1
2
3
4
5
6
7
8              Interest on Loan       [          ]
9
10
11
12
13
14
15
16
17
18
19
20
21
441K Enter the cell to be read.
     Example:  A1
D8   >/Xternal,CALC,B:LOAN.CAL,D45
```

Fig. 6-33. Using the Xternal command to enter the total interest from the loan amortization spreadsheet into another spreadsheet.

any option to accomplish this reconfiguration. Just enter S and Return to save the new configuration. You will be asked for the name of a profile (.PRO) file in which the configuration information is to be stored. Enter CALC, as the profile file CALC.PRO is automatically used when ExpressCalc is started. ExpressCalc will save the configuration—including the information that you are using the monochrome monitor with the color/graphics display adapter. Press Escape to exit the Configuration procedure. Now the next time you start ExpressCalc, you need only enter PCCALC; you do not have to add the BW.

The prompt line for the Configure command shows the various options you can choose when you are modifying the operation of ExpressCalc. Width and Height vary the size of the screen display. Likewise, the Keys options can be used to redefine the meaning of some of the keys on the keyboard. Most users will have no occasion to make changes here.

Layout provides options on where the information is to be displayed on the screen. The default arrangement, used throughout this chapter, has the display of the spreadsheet at the top, the two message lines next, and the entry line at the bottom of the screen. You can rearrange these elements as desired. For example, the entry line can be placed at the top, followed by the two message lines and the spreadsheet display at the bottom. This is the arrangement used by some popular commercial spreadsheet programs. You may wish to try it out.

The Color option allows you to change the foreground and background colors for the border, the display, the message lines, the entry lines, and the cell cursor. If you are using a color monitor and do not like the colors ExpressCalc currently displays, use this option to experiment with other combinations. One warning: black text on a black background (or blue-on-blue, etc.) does not show up very well! You can make elements of your spreadsheet disappear.

The Printer option can be used to select a printer. When using the setup option in the Print command, codes can be automatically entered to set the characters per inch for that printer. Unfortunately, only a few brands of printers are supported in the Configure command.

Each time you select an option and make a change with the Configure command, the changes are immediately made to the operating version of ExpressCalc. No changes are permanently recorded, however, until you select the Save option and press Return. You are then asked for the name of a profile file. The file CALC.PRO is always consulted to determine configuration information each time ExpressCalc is started. Permanent reconfiguration information should be placed in that file.

Alternatively, you can store the reconfiguration information in another file for use on special occasions. This profile file is then invoked by including the main portion of the file name after CALC when ExpressCalc is started. For example, if you would like to create a special configuration of ExpressCalc with different colors only for occasional use, use the Configure command to select the new colors. Then, when you save the configuration, enter the file name NEWCOLOR. This will create a profile file named NEWCOLOR.PRO. When you wish to use ExpressCalc with the new colors, start the program with the command CALC NEWCOLOR. This causes the file NEWCOLOR.PRO to be read when ExpressCalc is started, and the new color scheme will be displayed.

The Configure command can be used, and ExpressCalc can be reconfigured as often as desired. Even more elaborate reconfiguration of ExpressCalc can be accomplished by directly editing the .PRO profile files. Among other things, this allows

```
             A         B         C         D         E         F         G
 1
 2
 3
 4
 5
 6
 7
 8                 Interest on Loan     1,174.24
 9
10
11
12
13
14
15
16
17
18
19
20
21
441K (Value)    1174.24
     (External) CALC,B:LOAN.CAL,D45
D8   >
```

Fig. 6-34. The display of the total interest paid obtained from the loan amortization spreadsheet.

```
      A        B        C        D        E        F        G
1
2
3
4
5
6
7
8              Interest on Loan    1,174.24
9
10
11
12
13
14
15
16
17
18
19
20
21
441K Enter the name of the .PRO file. The current system options will be written
     to the file. (If the .PRO extension is not entered, it will be added.)
D8   >/Configure,Save,CALC
```

Fig. 6-35. Using the Configure command to alter the default settings of ExpressCalc.

the configuration of ExpressCalc for any printer, not just those supported by the Configure command. See the ExpressCalc manual for more information on the various possibilities available for customizing the program.

CONCLUSION

In working through the creation and use of the loan amortization spreadsheet, most of the features of ExpressCalc have been employed. If you have worked through the examples presented, you will be well on your way to being a proficient user of ExpressCalc. Continued practice, combined with occasional reference to the ExpressCalc manual, will make you an expert.

The next step involves imagination—thinking of the ways in which problems of interest might be expressed on a spreadsheet. For example, if you wish to keep track of your checking account on the computer, ExpressCalc can be used to easily set up an appropriate spreadsheet. Go on from there, and you will soon be developing household budgeting tools. If you are involved in a business, budgeting and financial analysis are obvious candidates for spreadsheet applications. Even scientific and engineering calculations can often be handled effectively in the spreadsheet format. Electronic spreadsheets are powerful general-purpose tools for analysis. ExpressCalc puts this power at your disposal.

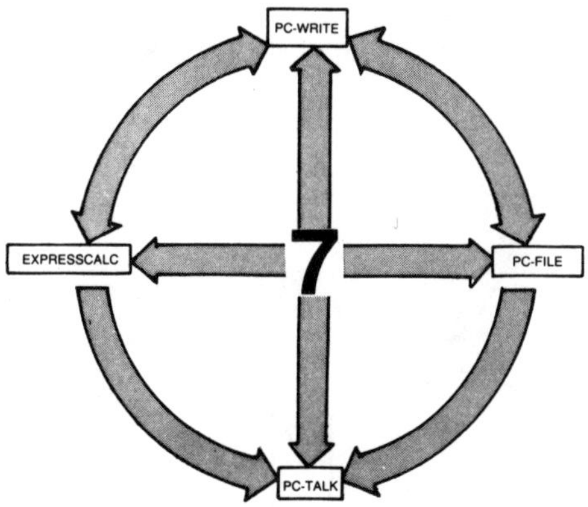

Sharing Information among the Programs

The problem-solving power of the four user-supported programs is significantly enhanced when the programs are used together. For example, reports produced by PC-File and ExpressCalc can be included in word processing documents generated with PC-Write. Information in PC-File databases can be used to produce form letters with PC-Write. Information from these three programs can be transmitted to other computers with PC-Talk.

The key to such information sharing for advanced applications is the ability of the programs to produce files of information in a format that can be used by other programs. Fortunately, the four user-supported programs can generate and use files of information in relatively standard formats. This increases their capabilities for sharing information. PC-File, PC-Write, PC-Talk, and ExpressCalc can be used together as a package of software for collectively addressing relatively sophisticated applications.

The transfer of files of information among programs is often viewed as a complex, technical activity beyond the grasp of most users. Most discussions of personal computer software give file transfer limited attention, probably because they focus on a single piece of software. While there are additional things that must be learned to move information from one applications program to another, the process is often not that difficult. As with so many aspects of personal computer use, the major task is becoming familiar with a few new concepts and procedures. After going through the process once or twice, the notion of file transfer is no longer foreign. It then becomes far easier to understand the documentation and learn new procedures for dealing with different situations.

This chapter provides examples of many of the ways in which the four user-supported programs can be used together. Figure 7-1 illustrates the varieties of file transfers that will be addressed in this chapter. As this illustrates, a great number of combinations are possible and will be considered here.

The first section of this chapter briefly discusses some of the basic principles of transferring data between programs. Specific examples involv-

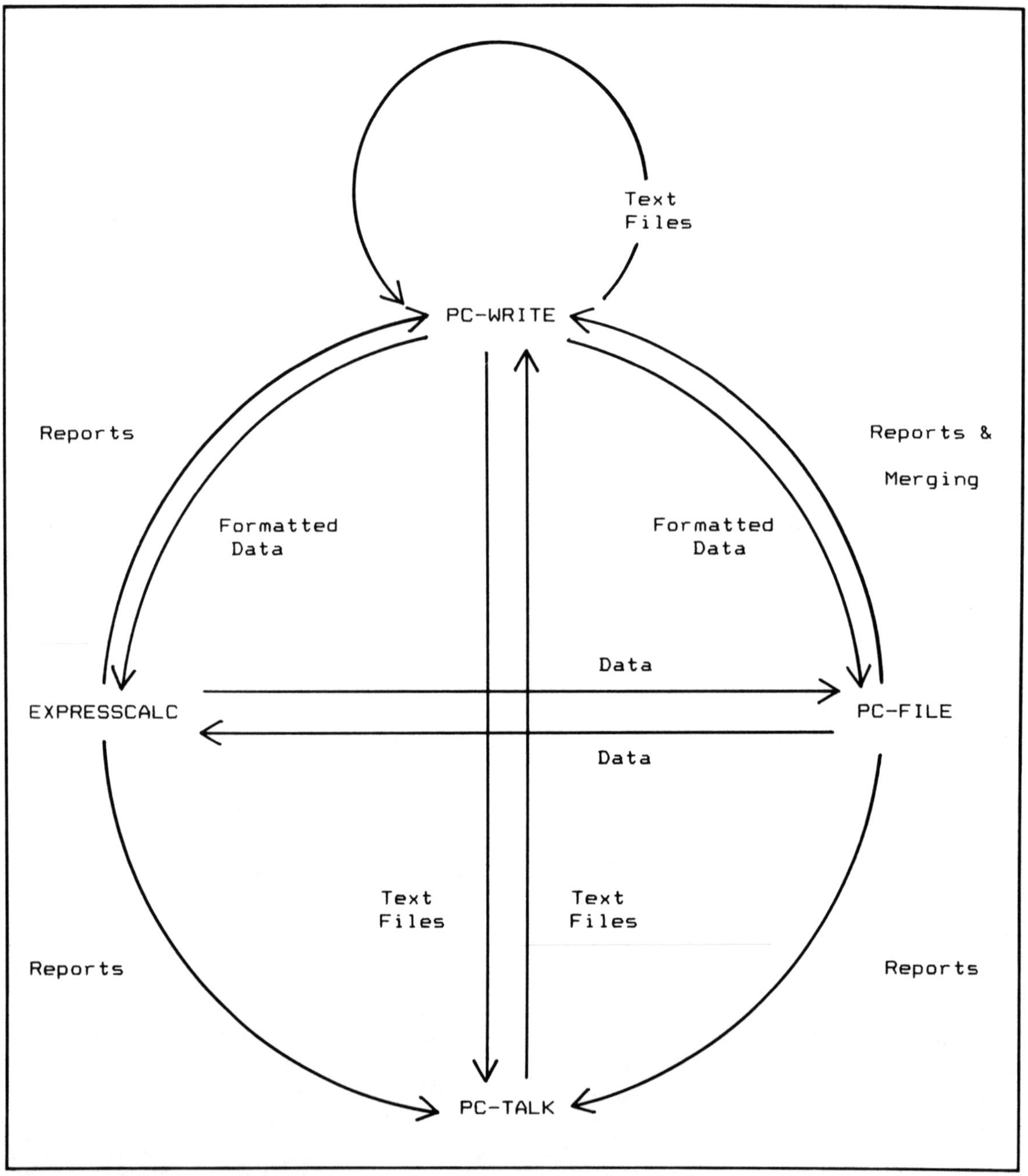

Fig. 7-1. Types of files transfers among the four user-supported programs.

ing the use of the four programs together are then considered: moving information into PC-Write, sending information with PC-Talk, and exchanging data between ExpressCalc and PC-File. A more comprehensive example involving all four of the programs is then presented. The final section briefly discusses the issues involved in exchanging data with other programs.

GENERAL PRINCIPLES OF INFORMATION SHARING

Personal computer programs generally store their information on the disks in their own unique formats. These formats are designed to be appropriate and efficient for a program's application. Because the structure of the files is unique to a single program, however, other programs cannot directly use those files. For example, a spreadsheet file stored by ExpressCalc cannot be directly used by PC-Write.

To share information among programs, it is generally necessary for one program to produce a special file in a format that can be used by a second program. These intermediate files become the vehicles for the transfer of information from one program to another. Special procedures will often be required both in using the source program to generate this intermediate file and in using the destination program to read this file. For example, to include an ExpressCalc spreadsheet within a word processing document produced by PC-Write, you would have to go through two steps. First, ExpressCalc must be directed to print the spreadsheet to a file on the disk. Then PC-Write must be directed to read this file into the document being edited.

The key to transferring information between two programs is to identify a type of file that the sending program can produce and that the receiving program can understand. In some instances, procedures are available within the sending program to produce files in the format generally used by the receiving program. In other cases, the receiving program will have capabilities for directly using the normal files produced by the sending program. More complex is the situation in which the sending program has to be used to produce a file in a special format, and special procedures must be employed by the receiving program to use the file in that format. Part of the problem in accomplishing information transfer among programs is identifying a common format that the programs can produce and use.

Most information interchange among programs makes use of what are frequently called *ASCII files*. These are files made up of characters—letters, numbers, and the standard keyboard symbols—expressed in the ASCII code. Carriage return characters (and possibly linefeed characters) are used to indicate the ends of lines. Otherwise, special codes are not used in the files. ASCII files are standard, and the information contained within these files can be generally understood without additional information. ASCII files can be displayed on the screen and printed on the printer from DOS. To examine an ASCII file on the screen, simply enter

```
TYPE filename<Return>
```

and to print the file, issue this command:

```
COPY filename PRN<Return>
```

The information will be presented and will be readable.

When it comes to transferring a file with multiple data elements, such as you would have with a spreadsheet or database manager, there is more involved than just having an ASCII file. Provisions must be made for separating or distinguishing among the individual data elements. The means for doing this becomes part of the file format that must be understood by both the sending and the receiving programs. Different possibilities will be discussed in this chapter.

PC-Write can be used to produce perfectly clean, straight ASCII files. To do this, do not include the font characters, guidelines, or any other special characters entered using the Control or Alternate keys. These special characters produce the funny graphics symbols on the screen and yield unpredictable results when the file is printed directly from DOS. They have no meaning to any program other than the PC-Write printer program, which interprets these special characters in a unique way in determining the format in which the document is to be printed.

Because PC-Write can be used to produce straight ASCII files, this program can be used for applications other than word processing. PC-Write can produce control files, such as batch files, used by DOS. It is a lot easier to use than the primitive line editor, EDLIN, included with DOS. For programmers, the PC-Write editor is an excellent choice for producing source code—the files of program statements entered by the programmer. If you do a lot of different things with your computer, you will find many applications in which PC-Write's ability to produce ASCII files will be useful.

Computer communications presents somewhat different issues in terms of file compatibility and information sharing. PC-Talk can transmit or receive files in any format. The issue is not file compatibility with PC-Talk—it is file compatibility with the remote computer and the software that will be using the files on the remote computer. In general, only ASCII files will be usable in such situations. The exception arises if you are transmitting information to another personal computer user with the same software that you are using. If the other user has ExpressCalc, for example, you can transfer a spreadsheet file saved with ExpressCalc for his or her use with ExpressCalc. You can also transmit or receive program files that are compatible with your system. For example, you could even transmit the ExpressCalc program files to another user for use with the ExpressCalc spreadsheet file. Aside from these obvious exceptions, however, most communications will involve the transfer of information in ASCII files.

MOVING INFORMATION INTO PC-WRITE DOCUMENTS

In preparing documents with PC-Write, you may wish to incorporate information generated with one of the other three programs—or even with PC-Write. This is perhaps the easiest form of information interchange between the programs. All that is required is that an ASCII text file be produced with the appropriate information. PC-Write can readily bring the information in such a file into the document being edited.

Reports from ExpressCalc

You are preparing a memo with PC-Write and wish to incorporate the information from a spreadsheet produced with ExpressCalc. Begin with ExpressCalc. Create or load the spreadsheet. The small spreadsheet used for this example is an analysis in changes in sales figures from one year to the next. The entire spreadsheet can be displayed on the screen at one time and is shown in Fig. 7-2. The first column is set to a width of 20 characters, and the remaining three columns are set to widths of 15 characters. Print this spreadsheet using the Print command. Press Return four times to accept all of the default options of printing the entire spreadsheet (ALL), at 80 columns per line, at 58 lines per page, with no options. The spreadsheet will be printed with the default offset of seven characters. ExpressCalc next asks whether it is to print the spreadsheet to the printer or the disk. Select the disk by entering D. You will be prompted for the file name. Enter B:SALES.TXT. Press Return, and an ASCII text file with the contents of the spreadsheet is stored in the file SALES.TXT on the disk in the B: drive.

This completes the work with ExpressCalc. Save the spreadsheet file on the disk if you have not done so already. Be sure to use a different name for the spreadsheet file than was used for the text file just produced. You might save the spreadsheet under the name SALES.CAL, with the .CAL extension indicating that this is a ExpressCalc file rather than a text file. The extension .TXT indicates a text file resulting from the printing of the Sales spreadsheet to a disk file. Exit from ExpressCalc and return to DOS in the usual manner.

As this is the first example of a file transfer, it is instructive to actually look at the contents of the file SALES.TXT that has been created. At the DOS A> prompt, display the file on the screen with the following command:

```
TYPE B:SALES.TXT<Return>
```

The file is displayed on the screen as shown in Fig. 7-3. This is the SALES spreadsheet, exactly as it would have been printed, without the row and column borders. SALES.TXT is a good example of an ASCII file.

```
                 A                B              C              D
 1  [          ]            Sales Report
 2
 3                  (Thousands of Dollars)
 4
 5  ---------------------------------------------------------------
 6  Region                      1985           1986        Percent
 7                             Sales          Sales         Change
 8  ---------------------------------------------------------------
 9  New England               324.00         340.00           4.94
10  Mid Atlantic              511.00         552.00           8.02
11  Great Lakes               480.00         512.00           6.67
12  Great Plains              260.00         247.00          -5.00
13  Southeast                 294.00         299.00           1.70
14  South Central             312.00         299.00          -4.17
15  Southwest                 396.00         422.00           6.57
16  Rocky Mountain            189.00         208.00          10.05
17  Pacific                   488.00         511.00           4.71
18
19  Total U.S.              3,254.00       3,390.00           4.18
20  ---------------------------------------------------------------
21
439K

A1    >
```

Fig. 7-2. Sales spreadsheet for transfer to PC-Write.

```
A>TYPE B:SALES.TXT

                              Sales Report

                         (Thousands of Dollars)

        ---------------------------------------------------------------
        Region                      1985           1986        Percent
                                   Sales          Sales         Change
        ---------------------------------------------------------------
        New England               324.00         340.00           4.94
        Mid Atlantic              511.00         552.00           8.02
        Great Lakes               480.00         512.00           6.67
        Great Plains              260.00         247.00          -5.00
        Southeast                 294.00         299.00           1.70
        South Central             312.00         299.00          -4.17
        Southwest                 396.00         422.00           6.57
        Rocky Mountain            189.00         208.00          10.05
        Pacific                   488.00         511.00           4.71

        Total U.S.              3,254.00       3,390.00           4.18
        ---------------------------------------------------------------
```

Fig. 7-3. Display of SALES.TXT file using the DOS TYPE command.

Now write the memo that will incorporate the SALES spreadsheet. Place the PC-Write working disk in the A: drive and create a new document by issuing the following command:

ED B:MEMO<Return>

Modify the ruler line with F2, to set the left margin at column 8 and the right margin at column 73. The left margin of eight was chosen to leave seven spaces to left of the text, exactly the same number of spaces included in the default ExpressCalc offset. Enter the short sample memo shown on the screen in Fig. 7-4. The space in the middle, with the three blank lines, is where the SALES spreadsheet will be inserted.

Move the cursor to the beginning of the second blank line. Press Control-F3 to insert a file. The top line will prompt for the name of the file to be inserted. Enter B:SALES.TXT. The top line will now appear as shown in Fig. 7-4. Press Return, and PC-Write will read the contents of that file from the disk and insert it at the location of the cursor. The SALES spreadsheet appears in the middle of the memo and is a part of the PC-Write document. Unmark the inserted text by pressing F5. Delete the line at the end of the insertion beginning with the female symbol, which is a form feed character. Otherwise, a new page would begin at that point. Add or delete blank lines as desired before and after the inserted text. You can continue editing the document, including the spreadsheet table, as you desire. Print out the finished memo in the usual manner by pressing F1 and then F7 and responding to the prompts. The memo, with the SALES spreadsheet incorporated within it, is shown in Fig. 7-5.

This is all that is involved in producing an ASCII file with the contents of a spreadsheet from ExpressCalc and inserting the contents of that (or any other) ASCII file into a PC-Write document. The example shows how simple and straightforward the process can be. Numbers of small problems can arise in the file transfer, however. Some hints will be given for producing the transfer files with ExpressCalc and for using such files within PC-Write.

ExpressCalc normally prints documents with a page offset of seven characters, which means that seven blank spaces are printed at the beginning of each line. The example presented here was planned to accommodate those extra spaces. These spaces

```
File to insert (Esc:cancel F8:dir): "B:SALES.TXT"

       TO:   Judith Henderson

       FROM:   Sam Smith

       SUBJECT:   Sales Figures

       You requested a comparison of 1985 and 1986 sales figures by
       region to determine the areas in which we were having problems.
       Here is the breakdown you requested:


       _

       As you can see, several regions exhibited mediocre performances or
       outright drops in sales from 1985 to 1986.  I am convening a
       meeting of the sales managers from the lagging regions in an
       attempt to determine the nature of the problems.
```

Fig. 7-4. Inserting the file SALES.TXT into the PC-Write MEMO document.

TO: Judith Henderson

FROM: Sam Smith

SUBJECT: Sales Figures

You requested a comparison of 1985 and 1986 sales figures by region to determine the areas in which we were having problems. Here is the breakdown you requested:

Sales Report

(Thousands of Dollars)

Region	1985 Sales	1986 Sales	Percent Change
New England	324.00	340.00	4.94
Mid Atlantic	511.00	552.00	8.02
Great Lakes	480.00	512.00	6.67
Great Plains	260.00	247.00	-5.00
Southeast	294.00	299.00	1.70
South Central	312.00	299.00	-4.17
Southwest	396.00	422.00	6.57
Rocky Mountain	189.00	208.00	10.05
Pacific	488.00	511.00	4.71
Total U.S.	3,254.00	3,390.00	4.18

As you can see, several regions exhibited mediocre performances or outright drops in sales from 1985 to 1986. I am convening a meeting of the sales managers from the lagging regions in an attempt to determine the nature of the problems.

Fig. 7-5. Print out of the memo with the sales spreadsheet inserted.

will often not be desired in files to be transferred to other programs. Thus, you will probably want to use the offset option to change the page offset to zero or to some other value. In this way, the correct number of extra spaces are inserted at the beginnings of lines. In some instances, you might want the spaces to indent the table from the PC-Write left margin, and the offset can be set to do this. The key is to be aware of where the ExpressCalc table is to be inserted and how you want the table to appear.

In producing a spreadsheet report file with ExpressCalc, it is important to be aware of the number of characters that will fit on a line in the destination PC-Write document. The spreadsheet may have to be printed and moved in two or more parts. If the lines of the spreadsheet are longer than the lines on the PC-Write document, the spreadsheet may be printed in the margin or lines may even wrap around to the next line. The latter produces results that are virtually unintelligible. Longer lines can be accommodated in the PC-Write document by printing with narrower characters, using the appropriate PC-Write font commands. This requires some planning and often experimentation to get things right.

The page length defaults to 58 lines when a ExpressCalc spreadsheet is being printed. When you are printing spreadsheets shorter than 58 lines, this is of no consequence. With longer spreadsheets, breaks will be placed every 58 lines to format the document vertically on the page. When transferring a spreadsheet to PC-Write, you do not want these breaks placed in the file by ExpressCalc. The report should be continuous. Any page breaks will be inserted later by PC-Write. Therefore, increase the page length when printing so that it is longer than the spreadsheet being transferred.

When inserting a file into a document with PC-Write, be sure that the margins are set appropriately to accommodate the lines in the file, such as the ExpressCalc spreadsheet file, being inserted. If the file has very long lines, it may be necessary or desirable to print the table in narrower elite or compressed print to fit it in. Use the .R: command before the spreadsheet table in the PC-Write document to shift to the appropriate font. Be sure to shift back at the end of the table with the .Q: command.

Be very careful to assure that ExpressCalc spreadsheets inserted into a PC-Write document are not reformatted. If PC-Write rearranges a table as it would a normal paragraph, the results may be extremely hard to unscramble. Turn off automatic reformatting when working with a document with inserted tables. Even better, insert guidelines with .– (dot, minus) before and .+ (dot, plus) after the insertion to prevent all reformatting, both automatic and manual.

Creating nicely formatted tables can be tedious, even when using a word processor such as PC-Write. Some people find it easier to use ExpressCalc to produce any tables that are to be used within a document, even tables that do not require the calculation capabilities of the spreadsheet program. Headings and numbers can be inserted into cells, and the table can be appropriately formatted using the ExpressCalc formatting commands. Then the table can be transferred to the PC-Write document using the procedure described above.

Reports from PC-File

The procedures for moving information from PC-File into a PC-Write document are very similar. A report is produced with PC-File in the usual fashion, but the report is printed to a file on the disk. Using PC-Write, the report can be inserted into a document following exactly the same procedures followed with ExpressCalc.

The example uses the household inventory database, INVEN, described in Chapter 3. A letter is to be written to your insurance agent checking on the coverage of your computer equipment. A list of the equipment from the INVEN database is to be included in the letter. Place the PC-File working disk in the A: drive and the data disk with the INVEN database in the B: drive. Start PC-File and work with the INVEN database.

From the main PC-File menu, press F6 to begin the file listing procedure. Select the report form INVRPT2, which will be appropriate for the current application. PC-File displays the prompt "List on Printer,Scrn,or Dsk (P,S,D)." Enter D for disk and press Return. Then you are asked whether you are cloning the database or printing to disk. Enter P to print to disk and press Return. When prompted for the output drive, enter B and Return. Finally, you are asked to enter the name for the output file. Enter COMPUTER and Return.

The remainder of the procedure involves the steps that are required each time a report is to be printed. No subtotals are needed, so to the request for the field to trigger subtotals, press Return. Since only selected records for computer equipment are to be printed, enter S in response to the question about printing all or selected records. The record selection screen appears. Enter the selection criterion for Category = "Computers" as shown in Fig. 7-6. Press F10 when you are finished. PC-File now prints the report to the file and displays

```
Item
Category
Date
Value#

________________________________________________________________________________

                                 Compare to which field     And,
 Field to             Compare    or to what value?          Or,
 search on              how?     (if value, in quotes)      End
[Category           ]  [= ]  ["Computers"               ]  [E]
[                   ]  [= ]  [                          ]  [E]
[                   ]  [= ]  [                          ]  [E]
[                   ]  [= ]  [                          ]  [E]
[                   ]  [= ]  [                          ]  [E]
[                   ]  [= ]  [                          ]  [E]
[                   ]  [= ]  [                          ]  [E]
[                   ]  [= ]  [                          ]  [E]
[                   ]  [= ]  [                          ]  [E]
[                   ]  [= ]  [                          ]  ►◄

Enter data. Press (F10) when complete.
```

Fig. 7-6. PC-File record selection screen to select records for the computer category.

a message when completed. Exit from PC-File in the usual manner.

The file COMPUTER.LST has been created on the B: drive and contains the report produced by PC-File. PC-File adds the extension .LST for all report listings printed to the disk. If you wish, you can use the DOS TYPE command to examine this file, as shown in Fig. 7-7.

Now begin PC-Write and create a document with the name B:LETTER. Set the margins to 5 and 75. Type in the short example letter shown in Fig. 7-8. The PC-File report on the computer equipment is to be inserted between the two paragraphs. Place the cursor at the beginning of the second blank line after the first paragraph and press Control-F3. Enter the file name B:COMPUTER.LST on the top line in response to the prompt, as shown in Fig. 7-8, and press Return. The report produced by PC-File is inserted into the document.

In this case, some additional editing is required after the insertion. The PC-File report heading and the title are not necessary or appropriate within the letter. They could have been eliminated by specifying a new report format in PC-File, but it is easier just to delete the lines now. Place the cursor on each of the lines to be deleted and issue the line delete command, Shift-Control-Return. Likewise, the totals, information on the records selected, and the new page symbol are not needed. Delete these lines as well.

The PC-File document has been inserted in the PC-Write document starting in column 1, while the text of the memorandum begins in column 5. The insertion must be shifted over five spaces to begin at the same left margin as the text of the memo. To shift the insertion, move the cursor to the beginning of the first line of the inserted text. Insert four spaces by pressing the insert key four times. Now press Shift-Delete to move the line back to its

```
A>TYPE B:COMPUTER.LST
                              SELECTED INVENTORY REPORT
01-01-80                                                              Page 1

Category          Item                              Date          Value
----------        ------------------------------    --------      --------
Computers         GamePro Home Computer             11-11-82        490.00
Computers         Super GT Personal Computer        09-30-85       1190.00
Computers         Telescreen Monitor                09-30-85         96.00
Computers         SuperPro Dot Matrix Printer       01-20-86        385.00
Computers         SturdyWood Computer Desk          02-14-86         93.00
Computers         Floppy Disk File                  03-30-86         25.00
Computers         CommunicationsPro Modem           05-01-86        235.00

TOTALS
----------------------------
Value                   2,514.00
Printed 7 of the 19 records.
Records were selected as follows:
Category      =  "COMPUTERS"              END
```

Fig. 7-7. Display of the file COMPUTER.LST using the DOS TYPE command.

```
 File to insert (Esc:cancel F8:dir): "B:COMPUTER.LST"
     James P. Smith
     Warm Blanket Insurance Company
     1202 North Ninth Street
     Centerville, Indiana 46333

     Dear Jim:

     As we were discussing on the phone yesterday, I am concerned about
     whether my homeowners policy covers my personal computer equipment at
     home in the even of damage, theft, or other loss.  Here is the
     inventory of the equipment that I promised:

     _

     Thank you for checking into this for me.

                               Sincerely yours,



                               John Jones
```

Fig. 7-8. Inserting the file COMPUTER.LST into the PC-Write LETTER document.

original position. Mark the block of text to be moved by placing the cursor at the beginning, pressing F3, moving the cursor to the line after the end, and pressing F3 again. Now press Shift-Insert and the entire block will be moved over, and the inserted report will begin in column 5, along with the rest of the memorandum. Press F5 to unmark the block of text.

Another problem arises because the lines of the report are longer than the lines of text in the letter. They would fit in if they were printed at 12 characters per inch. Insert a blank line before the report by pressing Return, and enter the following guideline on that line:

<Alternate – G>.R:<Alternate – E>

The .R: command changes the font for printing, and Alternate-E selects elite (12 character-per-inch) printing. Likewise, insert a blank line after the report and insert this guideline to turn off printing in this font:

<Alternate – G>.Q:<Alternate – E>

The screen image in Fig. 7-9 illustrates the changes that have been made to the document. Now the letter can be printed by pressing F1 and F7. The finished memorandum as printed is shown in Fig. 7-10. Note that the report inserted from PC-File is printed in slightly smaller characters than the rest of the letter.

As illustrated in this example, longer line lengths can be handled with PC-Write by changing the size of the characters in which the line is printed. In producing reports with PC-File for insertion into PC-Write documents, it is still important to keep track of line lengths so the lines fit and

```
Esc:MenuPush Reform-. 97% Free. 99% Thru. Read "B:LETTER"

     Dear Jim:

     As we were discussing on the phone yesterday, I am concerned about
     whether my homeowners policy covers my personal computer equipment at
     home in the even of damage, theft, or other loss.  Here is the
     inventory of the equipment that I promised:


     ♂.R:♥
     Category          Item                            Date          Value
     ----------        ------------------------------  --------     -------
     Computers         GamePro Home Computer           11-11-82       490.0
     Computers         Super GT Personal Computer      09-30-85      1190.0
     Computers         Telescreen Monitor              09-30-85        96.0
     Computers         SuperPro Dot Matrix Printer     01-20-86       385.0
     Computers         SturdyWood Computer Desk        02-14-86        93.0
     Computers         Floppy Disk File                03-30-86        25.0
     Computers         CommunicationsPro Modem         05-01-86       235.0


     ♂.Q:♥
     Thank you for checking into this for me.

                            Sincerely yours,
```

Fig. 7-9. Editing of the letter after the insertion of the report from PC-File.

James P. Smith
Warm Blanket Insurance Company
1202 North Ninth Street
Centerville, Indiana 46333

Dear Jim:

As we were discussing on the phone yesterday, I am concerned about whether my homeowners policy covers my personal computer equipment at home in the even of damage, theft, or other loss. Here is the inventory of the equipment that I promised:

Category	Item	Date	Value
Computers	GamePro Home Computer	11-11-82	490.00
Computers	Super GT Personal Computer	09-30-85	1190.00
Computers	Telescreen Monitor	09-30-85	96.00
Computers	SuperPro Dot Matrix Printer	01-20-86	385.00
Computers	SturdyWood Computer Desk	02-14-86	93.00
Computers	Floppy Disk File	03-30-86	25.00
Computers	CommunicationsPro Modem	05-01-86	235.00

Thank you for checking into this for me.

Sincerely yours,

John Jones

Fig. 7-10. Printout of the letter with the computer inventory report inserted.

so that the PC-Write document can be edited accordingly. Also, PC-Write can be used to edit the inserted report itself, as shown in the deletion of the headings and the final summary information in this case. These capabilities can be used with any insertions, not only with the reports produced using PC-File.

Text Files from PC-Talk

Information received from a remote computer using PC-Talk can be inserted into a document. For a very brief example, suppose you were writing a set of instructions on how to use the Indiana University Computing Network and wanted to include actual examples. Use PC-Talk to dial the network. After connection has been established, enter the Alternate-R command to begin receiving a file, and enter the file name IUNET.TXT. You now press Return to get the first network prompt, and then press Return once again to get additional information. Enter DECB to select that machine and press Return. The message appears indicating that a connection has been established. For an actual application, you might want to continue, but this is sufficient for the example. Press Alternate-R to terminate receiving of the file. Hang up the modem and exit PC-Talk in the normal manner.

The file IUNET.TXT contains the record of the communications. This could be inserted into a PC-Write document as was done in the preceding examples. Instead, this time editing will begin with the file that has been received, and text will be added to the file. Begin PC-Write with the command to edit the file that has just been received:

ED B:IUNET.TXT <Return>

The information captured by PC-Talk is displayed on the screen, ready for editing, as illustrated in Fig. 7-11. Place the cursor at the beginning of the document and press Return several times to place some blank lines at the top. Now, with the cursor at the top, type in the introductory paragraph describing the material that follows. This is illustrated in Fig. 7-12.

Move the cursor down to the second response for the Indiana University Network and press Return several more times to open up space for additional text. Type in a second paragraph discussing what is happening next. Follow the same procedure to add a third paragraph. The document can be printed out in the standard fashion. The print out of the resulting document, as it has been edited to this point, is illustrated in Fig. 7-13.

With a longer example downloaded using PC-Talk, this process of making insertions could be repeated numerous times. The downloaded file can be edited just as any other text file. In some cases, starting with the file transferred from another program and editing that will be the easiest way to proceed. In others, inserting the contents of the file into another PC-Write document will be more logical.

The information downloaded from remote computers is very often in the form of straight ASCII files. Thus, many files of information captured with PC-Talk can be readily used with PC-Write. They can either be edited directly or they can be inserted into other PC-Write documents.

From PC-Write to PC-Write

By this point, it goes without saying that PC-

```
Esc:MenuPush Reform-. 97% Free.  0% Thru. Edit "B:IUNET.TXT"

 Welcome to the Indiana University Computing Network - Indianapolis Node 20

 Indianapolis resources:  BBOARD, DECA, DECB, ETVAX, IBMFS0, IBMFS1, IBMCMS, IB


 Enter system name or carriage return for menu:

 Bloomington:  CDC855
               [Primes] ALPHA, BETA, GAMMA
               [Vaxes] BLUE, GOLD, GREEN, ORANGE, PURPLE, RED, WHITE, YELLOW

 Indianapolis resources:  BBOARD, DECA, DECB, ETVAX, IBMFS0, IBMFS1, IBMCMS, IB


 Enter system name or carriage return for menu: DECB
 (16) SUCCESSFUL CONNECTION

 I U P U I 2060 DECB, TOPS-20 Monitor 6.1(7030)-2
@LOGIN OTTENSMANN-JR-URBAN
 Job 11 on TTY122 5-Aug-86 20:55:49, Last Login  5-Aug-86 20:00:52
 End of PS:LOGIN.CMD.1
@
```

Fig. 7-11. The file IUNET.TXT as editing begins with PC-Write.

```
Esc:MenuPush Reform-. 96% Free. 13% Thru. Edit "B:IUNET.TXT"

This introduction describes the procedures for beginning to use one of the
Indiana University computers through the IU Computing Network.  Begin by
calling one of the IU Network numbers with your computer.  When communications
has been established, press Return and the following message will be
displayed:


 Welcome to the Indiana University Computing Network - Indianapolis Node 20

 Indianapolis resources:  BBOARD, DECA, DECB, ETVAX, IBMFS0, IBMFS1, IBMCMS, IB


 Enter system name or carriage return for menu:

 Bloomington:  CDC855
               [Primes] ALPHA, BETA, GAMMA
               [Vaxes] BLUE, GOLD, GREEN, ORANGE, PURPLE, RED, WHITE, YELLOW

 Indianapolis resources:  BBOARD, DECA, DECB, ETVAX, IBMFS0, IBMFS1, IBMCMS, IB


 Enter system name or carriage return for menu: DECB
 (16) SUCCESSFUL CONNECTION
```

Fig. 7-12. The file IUNET.TXT with the addition of an introductory paragraph of text.

Write documents can be used with other PC-Write documents. You merely need to insert one document into the other using the procedures that have already been described. When doing this, guidelines, font characters, and other special characters used in PC-Write can be included. Just make sure that what made sense in the document that is being inserted also makes sense in the context of the new document into which it is moved.

PC-Write allows you to take this one step further. A block of text within a PC-Write document can be copied to another file. This file can then be inserted into other PC-Write documents or used in other ways. Continuing the example from the preceding section, suppose you were sending someone a memo describing the set of instructions you were writing. It might be nice to include a brief excerpt from those instructions in the memo. While editing the file IUNET.TXT above, write the first paragraph and the accompanying example from the network to a separate file on the disk for transfer to the memo. What is required is a special type of block operation. Move the cursor to the beginning of the document. Press Control-F6, which is the command to copy a block of text to another file. You are now marking the text. Move the cursor to the line below the first example and press Control-F6 again. The top line now prompts for a file name. Enter B:EXAMPLE.TXT, as shown in Fig. 7-14. When you press Return, the marked block is copied to that file.

The remainder of the process should be familiar. Create a new PC-Write file, say MEMO2. Enter the text of the memorandum. Use Control-F2 to insert the contents of the file EXAMPLE.TXT into the document. Complete any further editing required, and print out the document. An example of a memorandum produced in this fashion is shown

```
This introduction describes the procedures for beginning to use one of the
Indiana Universitycomputers through the IU Computing Network.  Begin by
calling one of the IU Network numbers with your computer.  When communications
has been established, press Return and the following message will be
displayed:

Welcome to the Indiana University Computing Network - Indianapolis Node 20

Indianapolis resources:  BBOARD, DECA, DECB, ETVAX, IBMFS0, IBMFS1, IBMCMS, IB


Enter system name or carriage return for menu:


This is a listing of the computer systems available at Indianapolis.  To get a
complete listing of all of the systems on the network, simply press Return
once more:

Bloomington:   CDC855
               [Primes] ALPHA, BETA, GAMMA
               [Vaxes] BLUE, GOLD, GREEN, ORANGE, PURPLE, RED, WHITE, YELLOW

Indianapolis resources:  BBOARD, DECA, DECB, ETVAX, IBMFS0, IBMFS1, IBMCMS, IB


Enter system name or carriage return for menu: DECB


Enter the name of the computer system desired and press Return.  In this
example, DECB, one of the Indianapolis computers, has been selected.  You will
then be informed if connection is made to this computer, and the DECB displays
its introductory message followed by its @ prompt.

 (16) SUCCESSFUL CONNECTION

 I U P U I 2060 DECB, TOPS-20 Monitor 6.1(7030)-2
@


You are now ready to log onto the DECB computer.
```

Fig. 7-13. Print out of the document IUNET.TXT as received using PC-Talk and edited using PC-Write.

```
Copy mark text to file (Esc:cancel F8:dir): "B:EXAMPLE.TXT"

This introduction describes the procedures for beginning to use one of the
Indiana University computers through the IU Computing Network.  Begin by
calling one of the IU Network numbers with your computer.  When communications
has been established, press Return and the following message will be
displayed:


 Welcome to the Indiana University Computing Network - Indianapolis Node 20

 Indianapolis resources:  BBOARD, DECA, DECB, ETVAX, IBMFS0, IBMFS1, IBMCMS, IB


 Enter system name or carriage return for menu:


This is a listing of the computer systems available at Indianapolis.  To get a
complete listing of all of the systems on the network, simply press Return
once more:


 Bloomington:  CDC855
               [Primes] ALPHA, BETA, GAMMA
               [Vaxes] BLUE, GOLD, GREEN, ORANGE, PURPLE, RED, WHITE, YELLOW
```

Fig. 7-14. Writing a block from IUNET.TXT to a file named EXAMPLE.TXT using PC-Write.

in Fig. 7-15. Note that the example has been indented and printed in compressed characters to make it stand out.

The ability to copy blocks of text to files and to insert the contents of those file into other documents opens up new applications for PC-Write. In a business setting, stock paragraphs used for routine correspondence or standard contracts could be saved in files on the disk. Then, when new documents are being created, these stock paragraphs can be inserted without their having to be retyped. Some organization will be required to manage and keep track of such "boilerplate" text. If the paragraphs are reused frequently, however, these procedures can save significant amounts of retyping.

MERGING INFORMATION FROM PC-FILE INTO PC-WRITE

A more sophisticated application involves the creation of multiple documents (such as form letters) by the merging of a data file (such as a list of names and addresses) with a file containing the formatting information and the common text (the form letter). PC-Write has the capability of performing such merging of files. This greatly expands the range of potential applications of this program.

The data file to be used for such merges can be created directly with PC-Write, but PC-File is a far more effective tool for creating and managing data files. If you have an application that requires the merging of a data file with text, the best way to proceed is to use these two programs together. PC-File is employed to generate the data file, and PC-Write is used to merge this information to produce the final documents.

Suppose you wished to send letters to your acquaintances living in California informing them that you will be traveling to their state in the near future. The ADDRESS database will be used to produce a file with the list of their names and addresses. Then PC-Write can be used to type the basic letter and merge these names and addresses to produce all of the letters required.

Begin with PC-File, using the ADDRESS file created in Chapter 2. A disk file must be created in the appropriate format for use by the PC-Write merge procedure. From the main PC-File menu, press F6 to list a file. A new report format must be created, so leave the cursor on the blank field and press F10. No title is needed on the report so press Return.

Next comes the definition of the report format. The file for PC-Write is to have the information for each field on a separate line, followed by a Return. The first field will be the first name of the person. Enter

```
Firstname<Return>
```

to specify the printing of this field. Then enter

```
/<Return>
```

to indicate that the following field is to be printed on the next line. This inserts the Return character. The remainder of the report format is entered in

```
TO:  Martha Peters

FROM:  Ed Smith

SUBJECT:  IU Network Introduction


As we have discussed, I am undertaking the task of preparing
a brief introduction on the use of the computer systems in
the network.  I am approaching this task by using files of
actual communications with the system, and then inserting
text to explain what is happening.  Here is an example from
the beginning of the introduction:


        This introduction describes the procedures for beginning to use one of the
        Indiana Universitycomputers through the IU Computing Network.  Begin by
        calling one of the IU Network numbers with your computer.  When communications
        has been established, press Return and the following message will be
        displayed:


        Welcome to the Indiana University Computing Network - Indianapolis Node 20

        Indianapolis resources:  BBOARD, DECA, DECB, ETVAX, IBMFS0, IBMFS1, IBMCMS, IB


        Enter system name or carriage return for menu:

I hope that this meets your expectations, and I would
appreciate any suggestions you might wish to make.
```

Fig. 7-15. Printout of the memorandum incorporating the file EXAMPLE.TXT.

the same manner, as follows:

```
Lastname<Return>
/<Return>
Address<Return>
/<Return>
City<Return>
/<Return>
State<Return>
/<Return>
Zip<Return>
```

No Slash is required following the last field, Zip, because the next record automatically begins on a new line. After this format information has been entered, press Return to indicate that it is complete.

Enter Y and Return to save the report format for later use, and enter the file name PCWADDR, which stands for PC-Write ADDRESS format. List this report to the disk by entering D and Return. Choose the label format by entering L and Return. Indicate that a report is to be printed, P, rather than cloned, and press Return. Choose the B: drive for the file to be created on. Enter the name of the file to which the report should be written:

```
PCWADDR
```

This file name was chosen to indicate that this is a list of names and addresses for PC-Write. PC-File will append the .LST extension, as this is a report being created on the disk by the PC-File List procedure. No subtotals are required, so press Return. Since only the names of persons living in California are to be printed, enter S and Return to select records. On the selection screen, enter the selection criterion State = "CA." When finished, press F10. The report will be "printed" to the file PCWADDR.LST on the disk. When this is completed, exit PC-File.

The file PCWADDR.LST, shown in Fig. 7-16, contains the information from the three records of the persons living in California. The information from each of the fields specified in the format is listed on a separate line. This file is in a format appropriate for use by PC-Write. It is referred to by PC-Write as the *input file* for the merge procedure.

```
A>TYPE B:PCWADDR.LST
Peter
Apple
12961 W. Jonathan Way
Irvine
CA
92718
Robert
Martin
3311 Van Buren Boulevard
San Francisco
CA
94138
William
Summer
7613 Wilson Avenue
Los Angeles
CA
90042

A>
```

Fig. 7-16. Contents of the file PCWADDR.LST, produced by PC-File as an input file for the PC-Write merge procedure.

The next step is to use PC-Write to create what it refers to as the *template file* for the merge procedure. The template file consists of two sections within a single PC-Write file. The *input template* defines the structure of the information contained in the input file. The *output template* contains the text of the letter and the instructions for the merging of the information into that letter.

Use PC-Write to create a new document named FORMLET (for form letter). Starting on the first line, enter names for the fields of information contained in the input file. The same names as were used in the PC-File database might as well be used, though this is not required. The names must be entered using only lowercase letters. Each field name should be enclosed in curly brackets and should be placed on a separate line. An empty pair of curly brackets indicates the end of the input template. The information entered thus far would appear on the screen as shown in Fig. 7-17. This input template tells PC-Write that the records in the input

```
Esc:MenuPush Reform-. 99% Free. 60% Thru. Edit "B:FORMLET"
{firstname}
{lastname}
{address}
{city}
{state}
{zip}
{}
```

Fig. 7-17. Input template in the PC-Write template file FORMLET.

file each contain six fields of data, and that the information for each field is on a separate line, terminated with a carriage return character.

Following this, enter the output template, which is the form letter with the field names, again enclosed in curly brackets, in the positions where information is to be inserted from the input file. This form letter, or output template, appears on the screen as shown in Fig. 7-18. At the end of the file, at the beginning of a new line, enter the following characters:

<Alternate – G> <Alternate – T>..

This special-purpose guideline instructs PC-Write that each form letter produced is to begin on a new page.

Now that both the input file and the template file have been produced, PC-Write can be used to merge these two files to produce an output file con-

```
Esc:MenuPush Reform-. 99% Free. 99% Thru. Edit "B:FORMLET"
{}
{firstname} {lastname}
{address}
{city}, {state}  {zip}

Dear {firstname},

During the first week of October, I will have the opportunity to come out to
California for the first time in several years.  I will be attending a
convention in San Francisco for a few days, and then plan to drive down the
coast.  I will give you a call when I get out there.

I hope we can arrange to get together, at least for a little while.  It has
been a long time.

                                   Sincerely,



                                   Pete Peterson

♀☼♂..
```

Fig. 7-18. Output template (form letter) in the PC-Write template file FORMLET.

taining the actual letters. While you are still in the edit mode of PC-Write, working with the template file FORMLET, initiate the procedure to merge the files by entering the command Shift-F2. The status line changes to the merge menu, shown in Fig. 7-19. Press F9 to specify the files to be used in the merge. Press F9 to specify the input file name, and enter B:PCWADDR.LST. Press F10 to specify the name of the output file, which will receive the form letters produced as a result of the merge procedure. Enter the file name B:FORMOUT. The screen will appear as shown in Fig. 7-20. Press Return, and the merge menu reappears.

The actual merging of the input and template files to produce the output file can now begin. PC-Write gives two options: you can either merge one record at a time, producing a single document that can be examined or edited before it is stored in the output file, or you can automatically merge all of the records in the input file in one step, producing all of the documents, which are then stored in the output file. Select the second option, designated "Repeat" on the merge menu, by pressing F10. The output documents produced during the merge process will appear on the screen as they are generated and sent to the output file. PC-Write informs you that the merging process has been completed. Save the template file and exit to DOS with F1 F2.

The letters produced by the merge procedure have been stored in the output file FORMOUT. This file can now be printed. At the DOS prompt, enter the command to print this file:

PR B:FORMLET <Return>

Follow the usual procedures to print out the file. Three letters are printed. The first of these is shown in Fig. 7-21. The name and address information from the first record in the file PCWADDR.LST has been inserted in the specified places in the output template. The second and third letters incorporate the comparable information from the second and third records.

This example illustrates everything you need

```
Esc F1 F5.Edit F6.Stop F7.Input F8.Output F9:Files F10.Repeat. Next-record:1
Enter names of input and output files to use for merge
{lastname}
{address}
{city}
{state}
{zip}
{}
{firstname} {lastname}
{address}
{city}, {state}  {zip}

Dear {firstname},

During the first week of October, I will have the opportunity to come out to
California for the first time in several years.  I will be attending a
convention in San Francisco for a few days, and then plan to drive down the
coast.  I will give you a call when I get out there.

I hope we can arrange to get together, at least for a little while.  It has
been a long time.

                                        Sincerely,
```

Fig. 7-19. PC-Write merge menu.

```
Esc  F8:Dir  F9:Input "B:PCWADDR.LST"  F10:Output "B:FORMOUT"
{firstname}
{lastname}
{address}
{city}
{state}
{zip}
{}
{firstname} {lastname}
{address}
{city}, {state}  {zip}

Dear {firstname},

During the first week of October, I will have the opportunity to come out to
California for the first time in several years.  I will be attending a
convention in San Francisco for a few days, and then plan to drive down the
coast.  I will give you a call when I get out there.

I hope we can arrange to get together, at least for a little while.  It has
been a long time.

                                        Sincerely,
```

Fig. 7-20. Specification of input and output files for the PC-Write merge procedure.

to know to produce form letters using a PC-File database and PC-Write to produce, merge, and print the form letters. Remember that exactly the same procedures could be used to print not just three letters, but 300 or 3000. No additional commands or work on your part would be involved. The larger projects would just take more computer time to carry out the various tasks such as creating the

```
Peter Apple
12961 W. Jonathan Way
Irvine, CA  92718

Dear Peter,

During the first week of October, I will have the opportunity to come out to
California for the first time in several years.  I will be attending a
convention in San Francisco for a few days, and then plan to drive down the
coast.  I will give you a call when I get out there.

I hope we can arrange to get together, at least for a little while.  It has
been a long time.

                                        Sincerely,



                                        Pete Peterson
```

Fig. 7-21. Printout of the first form letter from file FORMOUT.

input file with PC-File, merging the files with the PC-Write editor, and, of course, printing out the resulting output file with the PC-Write printing program.

The merge procedure in PC-Write has a great many more options than have been covered in this example. The information in the input file can be in a variety of formats. The input template has options for specifying those different formats and for handling additional situations, such as empty data fields and the entry of information into fields directly from the keyboard. The positioning of the information can be specified in a variety of ways in the output format, and provisions can be included for reformatting paragraphs as information of various lengths is inserted. Merging can be automatic or one record at a time, information can be entered into fields from the keyboard, and output documents can be edited before they are saved to the output file. All of these features are well-documented in the PC-Write manual.

The procedures suggested for using the listing function in PC-File to produce the input data file are probably the easiest way to proceed in many situations. The range of input file data formats handled by PC-Write do allow the use of a PC-File database directly, without going through the report generation procedure. The procedure is somewhat more complex, and you lose some of the options such as record selection provided by the List procedure. You can also output the PC-File database in different formats using the Utility procedure and the export function. For some repetitive, high-volume applications, one of these latter approaches might be more efficient than the procedure described here.

Form letters are the obvious application for merging information from PC-File databases into PC-Write documents. Many other uses are possible, ranging from the generation of invoices for a small business to the printing of formatted bibliographies from a database listing literature references. In one sense, the combination can be viewed as providing PC-File databases with the ultimate in reporting capabilities. The types of reports that can be produced are no longer limited to the formats provided by the PC-File List function. Instead, the information in the database can be merged into a PC-Write document that can print out the information in virtually any format desired.

SENDING INFORMATION WITH PC-TALK

PC-Talk can send any type of file to another computer. Assuming that the file is being sent so that someone else can read the contents of the file directly, standard ASCII files must be sent. Appropriate files can be produced using PC-Write, PC-File, and ExpressCalc, using the procedures described above.

The most commonly used adjunct for data communications with PC-Talk will be the PC-Write program. PC-Write can be used to produce text files that are then sent by PC-Talk using the Alternate-T command. Messages can be prepared off-line using PC-Write and then can be transferred far more quickly than you could enter the same information from the keyboard. This method can be employed to send electronic mail. In addition, if you have longer, detailed messages that you wish to communicate in an on-line conference, the message can be prepared ahead of time and transmitted as if you were entering it from the keyboard.

Preparing text for transmission in advance using PC-Write has several advantages. Since you are entering the text off-line, before you establish communications, you will not be incurring communications or connect charges. The time required to transmit the file using Alternate-T will be far less than the time required to enter the text from the keyboard, especially if you are communicating at 1200 baud or if you are a slow typist. Furthermore, the editors provided for the entry of text with most online services are relatively crude, being limited by the transmission medium and the need to work with a large variety of terminals and computer systems. The full-screen editing capabilities of PC-Write are far more flexible and easier to use than the line editors commonly available on-line. Finally, by entering the text off-line with PC-Write, you have the opportunity to edit the text and correct errors, producing a more presentable message.

In using PC-Write to create text files for transmission by PC-Talk, be careful to produce pure ASCII files without the special PC-Write formatting characters. Do not include guidelines, either ruler lines or dot commands, and do not enter any other special symbols using the Alternate or Control keys. These entries only make sense to either the PC-Write editor program or its printer program. They would have no meaning to other users, and the special characters might cause problems in transmitting or receiving the files.

Reports printed by PC-File and ExpressCalc to disk files can be transmitted in a similar fashion to other users with PC-Talk. The files are generated in exactly the same manner described earlier in this chapter for use by PC-Write. These ASCII files can be read by anyone. For example, the file SALES.TXT produced with ExpressCalc earlier in this chapter for use with PC-Write can just as easily be sent to a remote computer. Using PC-Talk, enter the Alternate-T command to transfer a file, and then enter the file name SALES.TXT. The contents of the file will be transmitted as if you had entered the same information from the keyboard.

More elaborate possibilities arise when files of information are being transmitted by PC-Talk for further use by the person on the other end. This situation will generally occur when you are communicating with another individual personal computer user rather than with an on-line information service. If the other user is using the same programs, the files stored by the programs can be transmitted directly and used at the other end. For example, you might have created an elaborate spreadsheet using ExpressCalc, saving it under the file name ELAB.CAL. This file can be transmitted to another ExpressCalc user, who can then load that file and work with it directly. If the other user does not have the ExpressCalc program, you can also transmit the program itself (since ExpressCalc is user-supported software, this is legitimate). When sending the programs, be sure to transmit all of the program files on the disk, as these are necessary for the proper operation of the program. The documentation for the program should also be transmitted.

In performing such transfers, it is advisable to use the XMODEM protocol to assure file transfer without error and to avoid the addition of extraneous characters to the beginning or end of the file. This should generally be possible, since an ardent shareware user will probably also be using PC-Talk as his communications program and will thus have the XMODEM file transfer capabilities available. When transmitting PC-File databases, remember that every database has three files on the disk. The main portion of the file names is the name of the database; the extensions are .HDR, .DTA, and .INX. Report formats defined to work with a database have the extension .RPT, and you may wish to transmit these as well.

If the other user wishes to use the data from a PC-File or ExpressCalc file with another program, it is necessary to transmit the data in a format that can be understood by that program. PC-File includes many options for writing the information from a database to files in a variety of formats. You will have to determine which format can be used by the remote system. See the final section of this chapter on exchanging information with other programs for further information. This is also relevant if you wish to receive data from another program for use by PC-File or ExpressCalc.

At least one additional possibility is the transmission of a PC-Write word processing document with complete formatting information for printing by the receiver. To do this, the person receiving the file must either have the same kind of printer you do, or you will have to reconfigure PC-Write to work with the other person's printer. Prepare the document in the normal fashion, including any formatting information desired. Print out the document, but choose to have it printed to a disk file rather than to the printer, say TEXT.PRT. This file will include all of the codes to be sent to the printer to print the document in the intended fashion. The file will make sense only to the type of printer for which PC-Write is currently configured. Transmit the file to the remote computer using the Alternate-T command. The use of the XMODEM protocol would be preferred if available. The receiver can then print out the file by using the DOS command COPY B:TEXT.PRT PRN.

This last application is not likely to be the most common application, but it does illustrate the fundamental rule in transmitting information with PC-Talk. The file transmitted must be in a format that can be understood by the user of the file. In this case, the user is the printer, so the file must be printed to a disk file with PC-Write having been configured for the desired printer. If the file is to be read by the user, it must be an ASCII text file, and if the file is to be used by another program, it must be in a format usable by that program.

EXCHANGING DATA BETWEEN PC-FILE AND EXPRESSCALC

Data stored in a PC-File database can be transferred to ExpressCalc for spreadsheet analysis. The information generated by an ExpressCalc spreadsheet can be moved into a PC-File database. The capabilities for making such transfers are provided by the two programs. ExpressCalc can read a PC-File database directly into an ExpressCalc spreadsheet. Transferring the information from an ExpressCalc spreadsheet to a PC-File database is slightly more involved. ExpressCalc must be used to create a file in a special interchange format, which can then be imported by PC-File.

Suppose you wished to move the information in the PC-File household inventory database INVEN into ExpressCalc in order to do some analysis. Start ExpressCalc and give the command to load a file by pressing Slash and L. When you are prompted for the file name, enter the following:

```
B:INVEN.HDR
```

The main part of the file name, INVEN, is the name of the PC-File database to be loaded. The extension .HDR specifies the header file associated with that database and tells ExpressCalc that a database is to be loaded. ExpressCalc will then prompt for

```
            A              B              C              D              E              F              G
  1   [          ]
  2
  3
  4
  5
  6
  7
  8
  9
 10
 11
 12
 13
 14
 15
 16
 17
 18
 19
 20
 21
441K Enter R to load by Rows, C to load by columns.

A1    >/Load,B:INVEN.HDR,A1,R
```

Fig. 7-22. Loading the PC-File INVEN database into ExpressCalc.

	A	B	C	D	E
1	Audio Deluxe Receiver	Audio	10-10-82	340.00	
2	Ecstacy Turntable	Audio	12-25-82	135.00	
3	Excelsior Speakers (2)	Audio	12-01-83	280.00	
4	FineSound Compact Audio Player	Audio	12-25-85	260.00	
5	FineSound Equalizer	Audio	12-25-85	189.00	
6	New Wave Car Stereo	Audio	01-01-86	190.00	
7	GamePro Home Computer	Computers	11-11-82	490.00	
8	Super GT Personal Computer	Computers	09-30-85	1,190.00	
9	Telescreen Monitor	Computers	09-30-85	96.00	
10	SuperPro Dot Matrix Printer	Computers	01-20-86	385.00	
11	SturdyWood Computer Desk	Computers	02-14-86	93.00	
12	Floppy Disk File	Computers	03-30-86	25.00	
13	CommunicationsPro Modem	Computers	05-01-86	235.00	
14	Waxless X-Country Skis	Recreation	01-20-83	88.00	
15	X-Country Ski Poles	Recreation	01-20-83	19.00	
16	X-Country Ski Boots	Recreation	01-20-83	54.00	
17	SuperLite Tent	Recreation	03-20-84	94.00	
18	SuperWarm Down Sleeping Bag	Recreation	08-15-84	72.00	
19	SuperLite Backpack	Recreation	12-25-84	45.00	
20					
21					

439K (Text) "Audio Deluxe Receiver

A1 >

Fig. 7-23. Information from the INVEN database in ExpressCalc spreadsheet.

the starting cell into which the database is to be loaded. To place the information into the upper left-hand corner of the spreadsheet, enter A1 and press Return. Next, ExpressCalc asks whether the database is to be entered by rows or by columns. Row entry places each PC-File database record in a single row with the fields in separate columns. Column entry places each record into a column, with the fields going down in separate rows. Select row entry by pressing R. The ExpressCalc screen with the command to load the PC-File INVEN database is shown in Figure 7-22. Press Return, and the database is now loaded into the spreadsheet.

With the default ExpressCalc column widths, only the first part of the information in the Item field in column A can be displayed. Use the Format command to increase the width of column A to 33 characters. Press Slash and F, enter A1 and press Return, enter W for column width and 33 and press Return. The spreadsheet now appears as shown in Figure 7-23, with the complete information from the INVEN database displayed.

The reverse procedure, moving data from ExpressCalc to PC-File, is slightly more complicated. For this example, the information in the ExpressCalc spreadsheet on sales, SALES.CAL, used in an earlier example in this chapter, will be moved into a PC-File database. Begin by preparing the source spreadsheet and creating the file for transfer. Start ExpressCalc and load the sales spreadsheet with the /L command, entering the file name B:SALES.CAL. This is shown in Fig. 7-24.

The information for the sales in the various regions is to be entered into a PC-File database. The fields in the database will be Region, 1985 Sales, 1986 Sales, and Percent Change. Each category will be one record. Only the information that will go into the actual PC-File records can be transferred. The title and column headings cannot be transferred, so delete the first eight rows in the

```
            A                   B               C               D           E
1  [                ]          Sales Report
2
3                    (Thousands of Dollars)
4
5  ---------------------------------------------------------------
6  Region                          1985            1986        Percent
7                                 Sales           Sales         Change
8  ---------------------------------------------------------------
9  New England                   324.00          340.00           4.94
10 Mid Atlantic                  511.00          552.00           8.02
11 Great Lakes                   480.00          512.00           6.67
12 Great Plains                  260.00          247.00          -5.00
13 Southeast                     294.00          299.00           1.70
14 South Central                 312.00          299.00          -4.17
15 Southwest                     396.00          422.00           6.57
16 Rocky Mountain                189.00          208.00          10.05
17 Pacific                       488.00          511.00           4.71
18
19 Total U.S.                  3,254.00        3,390.00           4.18
20 ---------------------------------------------------------------
21
439K

A1    >
```

Fig. 7-24. The ExpressCalc spreadsheet SALES.CAL.

spreadsheet. Likewise, the total category should not be transferred. This is not information that should go into a PC-File record; PC-File can produce its own totals. So delete the final rows. The modified spreadsheet now appears as shown in Fig. 7-25. It is possible to do the transfer without modifying the SALES.CAL spreadsheet in this fashion; you can just specify the appropriate range to be transferred. Making the modifications makes the information that is to be transferred clearer.

The information in the SALES spreadsheet will be transferred to PC-File using a file in a special format called a *DIF* file. DIF stands for *Data Interchange Format* and is a standardized format used by many programs for the interchange of information. The information from the SALES spreadsheet is saved in a DIF file by using the Save command. Enter Slash and S to begin the save procedure. When prompted for the file name, enter the following:

B:SALES.DIF <Return>

Including the extension .DIF instructs ExpressCalc that the spreadsheet is to be saved as a DIF file. You are next prompted for the cell range to be saved. Since all extraneous information has been deleted, accept the ALL by press Return. The final prompt asks whether the information is to be saved by rows or columns. Since the records in the spreadsheet appear as rows, enter R. The command line appears as shown in Figure 7-25. Press Return. The information is saved in the file SALES.DIF in the Data Interchange Format.

When data is imported into PC-File, it must be brought into an existing database. A database with the appropriate format must be defined before proceeding with the importation. The information will be added to the database like any records. The database need not have any information entered into it before the information is imported, however.

The database that is defined must have one field for each column in the ExpressCalc spreadsheet being transferred. Columns with text should be defined as regular character fields, while columns with values or formulas should be defined as numeric fields. Field sizes must be sufficient for the information being transferred.

Begin PC-File by defining a new database, SALES, to receive the information from the spreadsheet. Enter the following for field names and corresponding field lengths:

Region	20
Sales1985#	15
Sales1986#	15
PercentChange#	15

Note the number symbol, #, at the end of the last three field names, designating these as numeric fields. The data definition screen should appear as shown in Fig. 7-26. Press F10 to enter the definition after you have checked it.

From the PC-File main menu, choose option F8 to invoke the Utilities procedure. The main menu for the Utilities procedures is illustrated in Fig. 7-27. Option 6 is to import a database. Enter 6 and press Return. Indicate the drive with the import file by entering B and Return. A directory of the files on the B: disk is displayed at the top of the screen, and you are prompted for the name of the input file. Enter SALES.DIF and Return. Next you need to select the name of the database to receive the information. Use the cursor control keys to select SALES and press F10.

Now the menu of formats that are available for importing data is presented as shown in Fig. 7-28. Enter 3 to select the DIF format and press Return. PC-File proceeds to read information from the file SALES.DIF into the SALES database.

When the process has been completed, return

```
              A                      B             C             D         E
1  New England                  324.00        340.00          4.94
2  Mid Atlantic                 511.00        552.00          8.02
3  Great Lakes                  480.00        512.00          6.67
4  Great Plains                 260.00        247.00         -5.00
5  Southeast                    294.00        299.00          1.70
6  South Central                312.00        299.00         -4.17
7  Southwest                    396.00        422.00          6.57
8  Rocky Mountain               189.00        208.00         10.05
9  Pacific                      488.00        511.00          4.71
10
11
12
13
14
15
16
17
18
19
20
21
440K Enter R to save by Rows, C to save by columns.

A1    >/Save,B:SALES.DIF,ALL,R
```

Fig. 7-25. Modified Sales spreadsheet for transfer to PC-File using DIF format.

```
(Alt)H for help.  Define the database.
 FIELD NAME        LENGTH                      FIELD NAME        LENGTH
[Region        ]   [20  ]                     [             ]   [    ]
[Sales1985#    ]   [15  ]                     [             ]   [    ]
[Sales1986#    ]   [15  ]                     [             ]   [    ]
[PercentChng#]     [15  ]                     [             ]   [    ]
[              ]   [    ]                     [             ]   [    ]
[              ]   [    ]                     [             ]   [    ]
[              ]   [    ]                     [             ]   [    ]
[              ]   [    ]                     [             ]   [    ]
[              ]   [    ]                     [             ]   [    ]
[              ]   [    ]                     [             ]   [    ]
[              ]   [    ]                     [             ]   [    ]
[              ]   [    ]                     [             ]   [    ]
[              ]   [    ]                     [             ]   [    ]
[              ]   [    ]                     [             ]   [    ]
[              ]   [    ]                     [             ]   [    ]
[              ]   [    ]                     [             ]   [    ]
[              ]   [    ]                     [             ]   [    ]
[              ]   [    ]                     [             ]   [    ]
[              ]   [    ]                     [             ]   [    ]
[              ]   [    ]                     [             ]   [    ]
[              ]   [    ]                     [             ]   ►    ◄

Enter data. Press (F10) when complete.
```

Fig. 7-26. Data definition screen for PC-File SALES database to accept data from ExpressCalc.

```
                         DATABASE UTILITIES                         UTI
-----------------------------------------------------------------------

                         1. Copy (backup a database)

                         2. Rename a database

                         3. Delete a database

                         4. Delete a report format

                         5. Export a database

                         6. Import a database

                         7. Merge 2 databases together

                         8. Return to PC-File



Select a number from the menu►6◄
```

Fig. 7-27. Menu for the Utilities procedure in PC-File.

```
Checking the database header file...
O.K.

1) Mailmerge     (comma delimited    )
2) Text editor   (fixed length, c/r  )
3) DIF           (visicalc, etc.     )
4) Fixed Length  ('random' files     )
5) PC-Calc       (by Jim Button      )
6) PeachText     (1 field per record)
7) Word Perfect                      )
8) Compressed    (by PC-File export  )

What is the format of the input file?




Answer 1-8: ►3◄
```

Fig. 7-28. Menu of PC-File import formats.

to the main PC-File menu (the F option) to check on the success of the transfer. The quickest way to view the contents of a database is to use the browse option of the Display command. Press F4 to begin the Display procedure, and then press the page down key to shift into the browse mode. The four columns of information transferred from the ExpressCalc spreadsheet are displayed, as shown in Fig. 7-29. This information is now in the PC-File database named SALES, which can be used like any database. Searches can be performed, reports can be generated, and information can be added or changed.

With these capabilities for moving data back and forth between PC-File and ExpressCalc, interesting applications for data analysis and management can be developed. As a simple example, a checkbook register can be kept with ExpressCalc. Each month, the information can be added to a PC-File database that will provide a continuing record of household income and expenditure. As you develop experience in using the two programs to-

```
 RCD.|                                                           DIS
=================================================================
    1|New England    | 324      | 340      | 4.94    |
    2|Mid Atlantic   | 511      | 552      | 8.02    |
    3|Great Lakes    | 480      | 512      | 6.67    |
    4|Great Plains   | 260      | 247      |-5       |
    5|Southeast      | 294      | 299      | 1.7     |
    6|South Central  | 312      | 299      |-4.17    |
    7|Southwest      | 396      | 422      | 6.57    |
    8|Rocky Mountain | 189      | 208      | 10.05   |
    9|Pacific        | 488      | 511      | 4.71    |
***  end of file  ***




To cancel, just press (Enter) with no response.
Supply the KEY, or #nn, or +(nxt rcd), -(prior), \(last), PgUp, PgDn
►               ◄
```

Fig. 7-29. Information in the SALES database displayed using the browse option.

gether, situations will arise when you are using PC-File and think, "I wish I had more capabilities for analyzing this information." You will be using ExpressCalc and likewise wish for the ability to store more information, perform searches, and generate reports. Moving the information over to the other program may provide exactly the answer to your needs.

DOWNLOADING DATA FOR EXPRESSCALC

The final example of data transfer in this chapter is more complex. Performing the required transfer will ultimately require the use of all four of the programs. This example serves as a capstone to the consideration of data transfer. If you can follow and carry out the procedures described here, you should be able to undertake just about any task involving the sharing of data among the four programs.

The problem can be described simply. PC-Talk will be used to download historical stock price information from CompuServe. This information is to be moved into a ExpressCalc spreadsheet for analysis. The complexities arise from the limitations on various types of information transfers, requiring several steps to accomplish this process. ExpressCalc is limited in the types of external files it can use, but it can directly read PC-File databases. The data can be imported into PC-File if it is in one of the formats that PC-File is capable of importing. The information downloaded using PC-Talk will not be in an appropriate format, but with some editing with PC-Write, the information can be made suitable for PC-File. Thus, the procedure is (1) download with PC-Talk, (2) edit with PC-Write, (3) import to PC-File, and (4) read into ExpressCalc.

Downloading with PC-Talk

PC-Talk is used to access CompuServe and the stock price information. Stock prices for the past month are requested for H & R Block Corporation, symbol HRB. This company was chosen because CompuServe allows access to this information without charge to allow experimentation with the database. Additional charges are assessed for all other stock price information retrieved.

When you are ready to receive the stock price data, enter the Alternate-R command to begin the process. Enter the file name HRBSTOCK. Proceed to obtain the information from Compuserve. When the desired information has been received, terminate the process by entering Alternate-R a second time. Log off CompuServe, hang up the modem, and exit PC-Talk.

The information received in the file HRBSTOCK is shown in Fig. 7-30. This is exactly the information sent by CompuServe. This file serves as the source for the activities that follow.

Editing with PC-Write

Of the various file formats that can be imported by PC-File, the so-called text editor format with fixed field lengths and a carriage return at the end of each record is probably the easiest to use for the information in the HRBSTOCK file downloaded with PC-Talk. The information for each day represents a record in the file, with the date, the volume, and the high, low, and closing prices being the fields. Each record is already on a separate line, so the records are separated with Return characters. The information is in the same position on each line (in each record), so fixed field lengths are appropriate. To make the file appropriate for importing by PC-File, it is only necessary to remove the extraneous information and convert the information into appropriate formats, producing a pure data file with the records of stock price information.

Use PC-Write to edit the file HRBSTOCK. Delete the heading that comes before the stock prices so that the first stock price record is the first line in the file. Delete the interruption transmitted by CompuServe in the middle of the data and the second set of column headings. Delete the concluding information at the end of the file. The final line of stock price information should be the last line of the file. Now delete the blank lines within the table of the stock price information and delete the holiday line for July 4 with no stock price information. After this editing has been completed, the file should appear as illustrated in Fig. 7-31.

Two additional problems with the file

BLOCK H & R INC

Cusip: 9367110 Exchange: N Ticker: HRB

Date	Volume	High/Ask	Low/Bid	Close/Avg
7/01/86	55,700	41 1/4	39 7/8	41
7/02/86	47,900	41 3/4	40 5/8	41
7/03/86	21,000	41 3/4	41	41 3/8
7/04/86	0	HOL	HOL	HOL
7/07/86	36,800	41 1/2	40 5/8	40 3/4
7/08/86	62,400	40 1/4	39 1/4	39 5/8
7/09/86	80,300	39 3/8	39	39 1/8
7/10/86	45,300	39 1/4	38 5/8	39
7/11/86	68,200	39	38 1/4	38 5/8
7/14/86	118,800	38 1/2	38	38
7/15/86	94,500	38 1/4	37 3/4	37 7/8
7/16/86	66,800	38 1/2	38	38 3/8

Press <CR> for more !

Date	Volume	High/Ask	Low/Bid	Close/Avg
7/17/86	26,800	38 3/4	38	38 3/4
7/18/86	31,700	38 1/2	38	38 3/8
7/21/86	11,600	38 1/2	38	38 1/4
7/22/86	20,900	39	38 3/8	39
7/23/86	20,100	39 1/4	38 1/2	39
7/24/86	35,400	39 1/4	38 1/2	38 1/2
7/25/86	23,200	38 3/4	38 3/8	38 3/4
7/28/86	28,300	38 3/4	38 1/2	38 1/2
7/29/86	13,800	38 7/8	38 1/2	38 5/8
7/30/86	86,300	38 3/4	38	38 1/8
7/31/86	42,500	38 3/4	38	38 1/4

Prices Available: 12/31/73 through 8/04/86
You are not charged for
no-price days.
No surcharge assessed for H&R Block.
Enter a ticker symbol (ie. HRB), the first
6 digits of a cusip, or <CR> when finished.
You may enter a valid nagivational command
preceded by a slash (ie. /M).

Issue:

Fig. 7-30. Information in the file HRBSTOCK received from CompuServe by PC-Talk.

```
Esc  F9:Find ","  F10:Replace ""
```

7/01/86	55,700	41 1/4	39 7/8	41
7/02/86	47,900	41 3/4	40 5/8	41
7/03/86	21,000	41 3/4	41	41 3/8
7/07/86	36,800	41 1/2	40 5/8	40 3/4
7/08/86	62,400	40 1/4	39 1/4	39 5/8
7/09/86	80,300	39 3/8	39	39 1/8
7/10/86	45,300	39 1/4	38 5/8	39
7/11/86	68,200	39	38 1/4	38 5/8
7/14/86	118,800	38 1/2	38	38
7/15/86	94,500	38 1/4	37 3/4	37 7/8
7/16/86	66,800	38 1/2	38	38 3/8
7/17/86	26,800	38 3/4	38	38 3/4
7/18/86	31,700	38 1/2	38	38 3/8
7/21/86	11,600	38 1/2	38	38 1/4
7/22/86	20,900	39	38 3/8	39
7/23/86	20,100	39 1/4	38 1/2	39
7/24/86	35,400	39 1/4	38 1/2	38 1/2
7/25/86	23,200	38 3/4	38 3/8	38 3/4
7/28/86	28,300	38 3/4	38 1/2	38 1/2
7/29/86	13,800	38 7/8	38 1/2	38 5/8
7/30/86	86,300	38 3/4	38	38 1/8
7/31/86	42,500	38 3/4	38	38 1/4

Fig. 7-31. Using the find and replace procedure to eliminate commas.

HRBSTOCK must be corrected before it is ready for transfer to PC-File. The volume numbers have commas, which must be deleted. The stock prices are expressed in fractions, which must be converted into decimal values. While these changes can be made manually, one at a time, it is far easier to use PC-Write's search and replace capabilities to make the necessary changes.

To eliminate the commas, move the cursor to the beginning of the file and press F9 to initiate the search and replace procedure. Enter the comma in the search field. Then press F10 to enter the replacement field. Press the delete key to delete the default period, so that the comma is replaced with nothing. The screen will appear as shown in Fig. 7-31, with the search and replace prompt on the top line. Press Alternate-F10 and then F9 to automatically search for all of the commas and eliminate them, replacing them with nothing.

The fractions can be changed to decimals using the search and replace function as well. Begin by changing 1/2 to .5. Move the cursor to the beginning of the file and press F9. For the text to be found, enter a space and 1/2. Then press F10 and enter the replacement text, .5 and two spaces. The two spaces are included so that the total number of spaces is not changed and so the columns are not thrown out of alignment. The prompt line for the search and replace is shown in Fig. 7-32. Press Alternate-F10 and F9 and all of the 1/2 fractions are changed to .5.

Replace each of the other fractions with the corresponding decimal values in the same manner. Move the cursor to the beginning of the file. Press F9 and edit the fraction to reflect the next value to be changed. Press F10 and edit the decimal value to the new value to be replaced. Alternate-F10 and F9 will do the replacement. Making all of these changes will take a few minutes, but this procedure is faster than making the changes by hand. Once you get into the rhythm of the procedure, it goes pretty quickly. After all of the fractions have been

Esc F9:Find " 1/2" F10:Replace ".5 "

7/01/86	55700	41 1/4	39 7/8	41
7/02/86	47900	41 3/4	40 5/8	41
7/03/86	21000	41 3/4	41	41 3/8
7/07/86	36800	41 1/2	40 5/8	40 3/4
7/08/86	62400	40 1/4	39 1/4	39 5/8
7/09/86	80300	39 3/8	39	39 1/8
7/10/86	45300	39 1/4	38 5/8	39
7/11/86	68200	39	38 1/4	38 5/8
7/14/86	118800	38 1/2	38	38
7/15/86	94500	38 1/4	37 3/4	37 7/8
7/16/86	66800	38 1/2	38	38 3/8
7/17/86	26800	38 3/4	38	38 3/4
7/18/86	31700	38 1/2	38	38 3/8
7/21/86	11600	38 1/2	38	38 1/4
7/22/86	20900	39	38 3/8	39
7/23/86	20100	39 1/4	38 1/2	39
7/24/86	35400	39 1/4	38 1/2	38 1/2
7/25/86	23200	38 3/4	38 3/8	38 3/4
7/28/86	28300	38 3/4	38 1/2	38 1/2
7/29/86	13800	38 7/8	38 1/2	38 5/8
7/30/86	86300	38 3/4	38	38 1/8
7/31/86	42500	38 3/4	38	38 1/4

Fig. 7-32. Using the find and replace procedure to change 1/2 to .5.

Esc:MenuPush Reform-. 97% Free. 1% Thru. Edit "B:HRBSTOCK"

7/01/86	55700	41.25	39.875	41
7/02/86	47900	41.75	40.625	41
7/03/86	21000	41.75	41	41.375
7/07/86	36800	41.5	40.625	40.75
7/08/86	62400	40.25	39.25	39.625
7/09/86	80300	39.375	39	39.125
7/10/86	45300	39.25	38.625	39
7/11/86	68200	39	38.25	38.625
7/14/86	118800	38.5	38	38
7/15/86	94500	38.25	37.75	37.875
7/16/86	66800	38.5	38	38.375
7/17/86	26800	38.75	38	38.75
7/18/86	31700	38.5	38	38.375
7/21/86	11600	38.5	38	38.25
7/22/86	20900	39	38.375	39
7/23/86	20100	39.25	38.5	39
7/24/86	35400	39.25	38.5	38.5
7/25/86	23200	38.75	38.375	38.75
7/28/86	28300	38.75	38.5	38.5
7/29/86	13800	38.875	38.5	38.625
7/30/86	86300	38.75	38	38.125
7/31/86	42500	38.75	38	38.25

Fig. 7-33. The file HRBSTOCK after editing with PC-Write.

changed to decimal values, the file appears as shown in Fig. 7-33. Save the file HRBSTOCK and exit PC-Write.

Importing into PC-File

The next procedure is the importing of the information into a PC-File database. The first step is the definition of the database. The database will have five fields. These can be named Date, Volume#, High#, Low#, and Close#. The number signs must be used to indicate the numeric fields.

More critical is the determination of the field lengths, for these will determine the manner in which PC-File interprets the information in the file being imported. It is necessary to count the number of characters in a line in the HRBSTOCK file and to determine how many of these characters are used for each field of information. To do this, you will either need to use PC-Write, move the cursor around, and check the column positions, or use a printout of the file and a ruler, preferable marked in tenths of an inch (assuming you have printed the file at 10 characters per inch).

Several spaces separate the data elements in the various fields. The field boundaries can be placed anywhere within these blank areas. It is best to place the boundaries near the middle, so if a slight error is made, the information will still be in the proper fields. Figure 7-34 shows how you would identify the field boundaries and determine the number of columns in each field. The field lengths are 10 characters for the date, 13 for the volume, 11 for the high, 12 for the low, and 12 for the closing stock price.

Now define the PC-File database named HRBSTOCK. The database definition screen is shown in Fig. 7-35. After the database has been defined, import the file. From the main menu, select the Utilities procedure with F8 and then enter 6 and Return to import a file. The drive with the input file is B; the file name is HRBSTOCK. Select the

7/01/86	55700	41.25	39.875	41
7/02/86	47900	41.75	40.625	41
7/03/86	21000	41.75	41	41.375
7/07/86	36800	41.5	40.625	40.75
7/08/86	62400	40.25	39.25	39.625
7/09/86	80300	39.375	39	39.125
7/10/86	45300	39.25	38.625	39
7/11/86	68200	39	38.25	38.625
7/14/86	118800	38.5	38	38
7/15/86	94500	38.25	37.75	37.875
7/16/86	66800	38.5	38	38.375
7/17/86	26800	38.75	38	38.75
7/18/86	31700	38.5	38	38.375
7/21/86	11600	38.5	38	38.25
7/22/86	20900	39	38.375	39
7/23/86	20100	39.25	38.5	39
7/24/86	35400	39.25	38.5	38.5
7/25/86	23200	38.75	38.375	38.75
7/28/86	28300	38.75	38.5	38.5
7/29/86	13800	38.875	38.5	38.625
7/30/86	86300	38.75	38	38.125
7/31/86	42500	38.75	38	38.25

Field boundaries: 10 23 34 46 58

Ruler: 0 10 20 30 40 50 60

Fig. 7-34. Determining field boundaries and widths in the HRBSTOCK file.

```
(Alt)H for help.  Define the database.
 FIELD NAME        LENGTH                        FIELD NAME         LENGTH
[Date          ]   [10  ]                        [              ]   [    ]
[Volume#       ]   [13  ]                        [              ]   [    ]
[High#         ]   [11  ]                        [              ]   [    ]
[Low#          ]   [12  ]                        [              ]   [    ]
[Close#        ]   [12  ]                        [              ]   [    ]
[              ]   [    ]                        [              ]   [    ]
[              ]   [    ]                        [              ]   [    ]
[              ]   [    ]                        [              ]   [    ]
[              ]   [    ]                        [              ]   [    ]
[              ]   [    ]                        [              ]   [    ]
[              ]   [    ]                        [              ]   [    ]
[              ]   [    ]                        [              ]   [    ]
[              ]   [    ]                        [              ]   [    ]
[              ]   [    ]                        [              ]   [    ]
[              ]   [    ]                        [              ]   [    ]
[              ]   [    ]                        [              ]   [    ]
[              ]   [    ]                        [              ]   [    ]
[              ]   [    ]                        [              ]   [    ]
[              ]   [    ]                        [              ]   [    ]
[              ]   [    ]                        [              ]   [    ]
[              ]   [    ]                        [              ]   ▶    ◀

Enter data. Press (F10) when complete.
```

Fig. 7-35. Data definition screen for the PC-File HRBSTOCK database.

HRBSTOCK database and press F10. From the import format menu, select the text editor format, entering 2 and Return. The information in the file is now added to the PC-File database HRBSTOCK. To check the information that has been transferred, return to the main menu, press F4 to begin the Display procedure, and press Page Down to display the first 20 records in the browse mode. The screen will appear as shown in Fig. 7-36. By pressing Page Down, you can move through the database and make sure that all of the information has been transferred.

Importing into ExpressCalc

The information in the PC-File HRBSTOCK database can now be loaded into an ExpressCalc spreadsheet. Start ExpressCalc and give the Load command by entering Slash and L. Enter the file name B:HRBSTOCK.HDR to load the PC-File database. Enter A1 as the starting cell, and enter R to load the database by rows. Press Return, and the HRBSTOCK database is loaded into the ExpressCalc spreadsheet. The display of the spreadsheet is illustrated in Fig. 7-37. You can now perform any analysis desired on the stock price data.

Seldom will information transfers be this involved. Nevertheless, the process actually does not take all that long to do. Once you are familiar with the procedures that are required, the multistep transfer is not that difficult. If similar tasks are to be undertaken on a repetitive basis, not only will the procedures become more and more familiar, but the database definition in PC-File can be reused. For example, if one intends to download historical price information from CompuServe on numbers of different stocks, all of the information can be transferred through the same PC-File database.

Of course different data transfer problems will require different procedures. The general approach

RCD.						DIS
1	7/01/86	55700	41.25	39.875	41	
2	7/02/86	47900	41.75	40.625	41	
3	7/03/86	21000	41.75	41	41.375	
4	7/07/86	36800	41.5	40.625	40.75	
5	7/08/86	62400	40.25	39.25	39.625	
6	7/09/86	80300	39.375	39	39.125	
7	7/10/86	45300	39.25	38.625	39	
8	7/11/86	68200	39	38.25	38.625	
9	7/14/86	118800	38.5	38	38	
10	7/15/86	94500	38.25	37.75	37.875	
11	7/16/86	66800	38.5	38	38.375	
12	7/17/86	26800	38.75	38	38.75	
13	7/18/86	31700	38.5	38	38.375	
14	7/21/86	11600	38.5	38	38.25	
15	7/22/86	20900	39	38.375	39	
16	7/23/86	20100	39.25	38.5	39	
17	7/24/86	35400	39.25	38.5	38.5	
18	7/25/86	23200	38.75	38.375	38.75	
19	7/28/86	28300	38.75	38.5	38.5	
20	7/29/86	13800	38.875	38.5	38.625	

To cancel, just press (Enter) with no response.
Supply the KEY, or #nn, or +(nxt rcd), -(prior), \(last), PgUp, PgDn
▶ ◀

Fig. 7-36. Information in the HRBSTOCK database displayed using the browse option.

is the same, however. If a transfer cannot be accomplished directly, try to determine if it can be done either by using a third program as an intermediary or by using PC-Write to edit the file into a format acceptable to another program. In this example, both techniques had to be employed. With a little imagination and detective work, it is usually possible to find a method for transferring information. Even if it does take a little time and get a little involved, it is nearly always easier than retyping the information, especially for large files.

EXCHANGING INFORMATION WITH OTHER PROGRAMS

The examples in this chapter have naturally involved the transfer of information among the four programs that are the focus of this book. Personal computer users do make use of other programs, of course. Situations will arise when you wish to move information from one of the user-supported programs to another piece of software, or vice versa.

Exchanging information among word processing programs can usually be accomplished using straight ASCII text files, though all special formatting information will necessarily be lost. Reports produced by other programs as ASCII files can likewise be transferred easily. Most word processing programs can read in text from ASCII files, so there should be no problem in transferring information from PC-Write. For that matter, reports printed with ExpressCalc and PC-File to disk files can likewise be read by most word processors. The information produced by word processors that can create ASCII text files can be readily used by PC-Write. Many spreadsheets, database managers, and other kinds of programs can print their output reports to disk files. Such files should be directly usable by PC-Write.

WordStar, the most widely used personal computer word processing program, stores its documents in a nonstandard format. PC-Write includes a feature for directly using WordStar document files. Simply start the PC-Write editor to load the WordStar file. The result will look strange, but a single command will convert the file to standard ASCII format ready for editing by PC-Write. The manual gives the details.

PC-Write offers great flexibility in its use of data files for input to its merge procedure. The commands for creating the input template provide multiple options for specifying the format of the input file. In this respect, PC-Write is better than many word processing programs, which are restricted to a single format. Users of most database programs should be able to find a format that they can use to output information from their database in such a way that it can be read by PC-Write. The process may take a bit of experimentation, but given the flexibility of PC-Write, there are likely to be several different solutions to the problem.

Data may also need to be moved among different database or spreadsheet programs. PC-File is a very flexible program for such transfers, as it provides a variety of import and export options. The menu of PC-File import formats was shown above in Fig. 7-28. The menu of formats available for the export of data from PC-File is shown in Fig. 7-38. Usually transfers between database programs and spreadsheets must take place using an intermediate file format that can be exported by the other program or imported by that program, depending upon the direction of the transfer desired. PC-File may also be used to produce files for merging operations with a variety of other word processors. ExpressCalc can load and save files in the DIF format and in the WordStar format, with fields separated by commas. It can also read PC-File databases, so files can be imported via PC-File.

For the transfer of data between PC-File and other spreadsheet programs, three file formats are of primary interest. The Lotus PRN format can be used to transfer files to and from Lotus 1-2-3

	A	B	C	D	E	F	G
1	7/01/86	55,700.00	41.25	39.87	41.00		
2	7/02/86	47,900.00	41.75	40.62	41.00		
3	7/03/86	21,000.00	41.75	41.00	41.37		
4	7/07/86	36,800.00	41.50	40.62	40.75		
5	7/08/86	62,400.00	40.25	39.25	39.62		
6	7/09/86	80,300.00	39.37	39.00	39.12		
7	7/10/86	45,300.00	39.25	38.62	39.00		
8	7/11/86	68,200.00	39.00	38.25	38.62		
9	7/14/86	118,800.00	38.50	38.00	38.00		
10	7/15/86	94,500.00	38.25	37.75	37.87		
11	7/16/86	66,800.00	38.50	38.00	38.37		
12	7/17/86	26,800.00	38.75	38.00	38.75		
13	7/18/86	31,700.00	38.50	38.00	38.37		
14	7/21/86	11,600.00	38.50	38.00	38.25		
15	7/22/86	20,900.00	39.00	38.37	39.00		
16	7/23/86	20,100.00	39.25	38.50	39.00		
17	7/24/86	35,400.00	39.25	38.50	38.50		
18	7/25/86	23,200.00	38.75	38.37	38.75		
19	7/28/86	28,300.00	38.75	38.50	38.50		
20	7/29/86	13,800.00	38.87	38.50	38.62		
21	7/30/86	86,300.00	38.75	38.00	38.12		

436K (Text) " 7/01/86

A1 >

Fig. 7-37. HRBSTOCK.CAL spreadsheet as displayed by ExpressCalc.

```
Export to which format?
  C) PC-Calc
  D) DIF
  L) Lotus PRN
  M) MailMerge or WORD
  P) PeachText
  S) SYLK (Microsoft)
  T) Text editor
  V) VisiCalc
  W) Word Perfect
  X) Compressed




Select  C,D,L,M,P,S,T,V,W,X:►X◄
```

Fig. 7-38. Menu of PC-File export formats.

spreadsheets. The SYLK format can be used to transfer information to a MicroSoft MultiPlan spreadsheet and to certain other programs from MicroSoft. This transfer is only one way, however. PC-File cannot import SYLK files. The DIF format is used by many spreadsheet programs, as well as some database programs, graphics program, and other data analysis software. PC-File can import and export DIF files, as can ExpressCalc.

To move information to and from other database programs, the text editor and fixed length formats will often be appropriate. In some cases DIF files can be used. Do not overlook some of the word processing-oriented formats, such as MailMerge and PeachText, as some database programs have the capability to export or import information in these formats. Unfortunately, the names of these formats are far from standardized. The database program may have the capability for using one of these formats but refers to it by a very different name. For example, the MailMerge format is sometimes referred to as the WordStar format (the name used by ExpressCalc), as the comma-delimited format, or as the comma-separated-value (CSV) format. To determine the possibilities, it is necessary to carefully study the appropriate documentation. In the PC-File manual, read the descriptions of the various import and export formats, and then read the comparable descriptions in the manual for the program with which you wish to exchange information. Attempt to find formats with a common description.

In exchanging files between database programs, experiment first with a small sample file. Get the procedures down and make sure they work with a simple file before trying to move a large database with many fields and hundreds or thousands of records. Otherwise, you may end up spending a great deal of time defining a database and making a transfer, only to see the transfer fail or produce garbage. When that happens, you are not sure whether the approach you have taken is fundamentally flawed or whether a minor error was made in going through the process. By checking the process out with a small sample file, you can determine whether the procedure you are attempting will work and learn the steps that need to be followed for a successful transfer.

PC-File includes three import/export formats specifically intended for producing files for use by word processors in their merge functions. The MailMerge format produces files for the merge program with that name used by WordStar. This format is also appropriate for use with MicroSoft Word. The PeachText and WordPerfect formats are intended for use with those word processors. For other word processing programs, one of these formats, or possibly one of the other export formats provided by PC-File, is likely to be usable. It may also be possible to use the list function of PC-File to produce a report that is printed to the disk in a format that will work with some word processors and other programs. This was the approach taken in the PC-Write merge example presented earlier.

For programmers, the MailMerge format produces files that can be easily read by many BASIC programs. The text editor, fixed length, and PeachText formats are also good candidates for data interchange with programs written in a variety of languages.

This section on information interchange with other programs hardly presents sufficient information to enable the immediate transfer of files. Rather, it is intended as a brief guide to what is possible. Effort will be required to study the documentation of the other programs and determine the procedures required to accomplish the transfer.

PC-Write and PC-File are above average in their capabilities for sharing information with other programs. PC-Write can readily produce and read pure ASCII text files. Its merge function allows the specification of the format of the input file in a variety of ways, rather than restricting the input file to a single format as do many word processors. PC-File has an excellent selection of formats in which it can import and export data. This choice allows PC-File to exchange information with all but the most introverted, unfriendly programs.

CONCLUSION

A wider range of applications is opened when the sharing of information among the four programs is considered. All types of information can be inserted into documents produced using PC-Write. Form letters are but one example of the possibilities available when you are merging information from a PC-File database into multiple documents with PC-Write. PC-Talk can transmit the information created by the programs to other computers, and the information captured by PC-Talk can be used by those programs. PC-File and ExpressCalc can directly and easily exchange information.

Once these capabilities have been learned, the four programs, taken as a package, provide capabilities that rival the very expensive integrated packages. The methods of data transfer described in this chapter may sometimes be tedious and cumbersome, but they can get the job done. Given the low prices for the four programs, the power provided by the package of the four programs is really quite amazing.

The transferring of information among programs is not one of the easiest or most obvious of personal computer tasks. Many users never attempt it, and thus miss out on the substantial benefits to be gained. Remember that the first time is always the hardest. After working through several of the examples presented above and after using a procedure a few times, the process will cease to be so difficult. You will be on your way to the most efficient use of your software.

Appendix A

More Low-Cost Computing

Experience with the four programs dealt with in this book shows that low-cost software can be very powerful and useful. Using low-cost software does not necessarily require compromise, foregoing either ease of use or advanced features. Learning and using PC-File, PC-Write, PC-Talk, and ExpressCalc should have whet your appetite for what you can do with your personal computer on a budget. This appendix provides suggestions for how to proceed. Since the four programs work on IBM Personal Computers and compatibles, we will focus on low-cost software for these systems.

Public domain and user-supported software represent low-cost alternatives to traditional commercial software. Personal computer users on a budget need to learn about these options and how to obtain the software. Well-developed user supported programs, such as the ones addressed in this book, represent an especially attractive option. This appendix describes a number of additional possibilities.

Those on a budget should not overlook commercial software. A growing trend has been the marketing of programs commercially at low prices, often under $100. Some of these are programs designed to work like far more expensive commercial programs. A selection of the available low-cost commercial programs is described. Names, addresses, and telephone numbers of all of the software publishers and distributors mentioned in this appendix are listed at the end.

For those without their own computers already, the question of low-cost computing extends to the acquisition of the computer systems themselves. Fortunately, prices for IBM PCs and compatibles have been dropping rapidly. Compatible systems from other manufacturers often represent especially good values. These machines are gaining increasing acceptance and should be given serious consideration by those on a budget.

THREE TYPES OF SOFTWARE

Public domain software, user-supported software, and commercial software represent the three categories of programs available to personal computer owners. Prices range from zero for public domain software to many hundreds of dollars for some of the most popular commercial programs. The software can be obtained by copying it from a friend or downloading it from a computer bulletin board, or the software can come in a fancy package purchased in a computer store. Needless to say, the differences can be very important to those on a budget.

For this reason, it is important to understand the nature of these three types of software. In theory, public domain, user-supported, and commercial software might be considered to be three distinct categories. In practice, however, the boundaries are not so clear.

First, a note on the copyright law will be helpful for understanding the discussion that follows. The copyright law provides protection to the authors of various works, ranging from books to musical scores to computer programs. Copies cannot be made of copyrighted works without the permission of the copyright holder, except in extremely limited circumstances. (Owners of computer programs are allowed by the copyright law to make backup copies for archival purposes.) To copyright a work, a notice of copyright (e.g., Copyright 1986) must be included when the work is first published or distributed.

Public domain software refers to those situations where the author of a program relinquishes his or her rights to the program, allowing others to freely make copies with few or no restrictions. The author of the program is frequently a computer hobbyist who may genuinely wish to share his or her creation with others. The author may have no desire to improve the program to commercial standards or no desire to get involved in the activity of marketing the program. The author may simply believe that no significant commercial market for the program exists. For whatever reason, the author "gives" the program away to the rest of the world, allowing free copying and distribution.

With much public domain software, the author simply distributes the program with no claim of copyright. In such cases, no restrictions are placed on any use made of the program by others. Since the program has been distributed without a claim of copyright, it is truly in the public domain in the legal sense. A commercial software firm can even package and sell the program for a profit. There have been numerous instances of this happening. The original author of the program has relinquished all rights to the program and has no legal claim on any profits made from the sale of the program. You might wonder—like me—about the ethical implications of making money off of someone else's work in such a manner. The author of the program, however, has relinquished all rights to the program by distributing it without a copyright.

To avoid such commercial exploitation of public domain programs, some authors will copyright the program but will grant others the right to make copies for noncommercial purposes. From the perspective of computer users, these are public domain programs that can be freely copied and shared. The only difference is the restriction preventing the commercial marketing of the programs.

Public domain software is provided "as is," with no guarantees, no promises of support or updates. Documentation, if any, will be limited to a usually brief text file on the disk. A public domain program is not a "product" in the sense of other forms of software.

At the other extreme, traditional commercial software is always copyrighted. It is not permissible to make copies of such programs for others to use. Doing so is a violation of the copyright laws. In addition, many producers of commercial software include licensing agreements that further restrict the use of particular programs. Some commercial software is copy protected, meaning that the program has been recorded on the disk in such a way that the standard DOS commands cannot be used for making copies. Making copies of commercial software and giving the copies to others is often referred to as *software piracy.* It is wrong; it deprives the authors and publishers of the programs of the return to which they are entitled.

Commercial software generally comes with printed documentation, which is often extensive. Many software publishers have telephone help lines for providing assistance to the purchasers of their programs. The programs are often improved and updated on a regular basis. Prior purchasers are often given the opportunity to upgrade to the newer versions for far less than the full price. Of course, no publisher of commercial software is obligated to provide any of these benefits. The market, however, has come to expect such benefits with the purchase of expensive programs.

User-supported software represents an alternative method for distributing personal computer programs that falls somewhere between public domain software and traditional commercial software. The programs are copyrighted, but users are explicitly granted permission to make copies to share with others. With the program comes a request that a user send a specified contribution to the program's author if the program is found to be useful. The contribution is entirely voluntary. Making it represents a moral obligation on the part of the user.

User-supported programs generally come with fairly extensive documentation in a text file on the disk. Many—though not all—of the authors of the better user-supported software provide printed copies of the documentation when a contribution is made and the software is registered. Registered users may also be entitled to telephone support and may be given the opportunity to obtain updated versions of the programs at little or no cost. User-supported programs are often updated more frequently than commercial programs. This is possible because the author of the user-supported software does not have inventories of software at distributors and in computer stores that would be made obsolete by an update.

All this seems to suggest that the three categories of software are quite distinct. In practice, however, the differences are not necessarily that clear. Programs sometimes seem to fall between two categories, having some of the characteristics of each. With the success of the user-supported concept, many programs that might have previously been placed in the public domain now include requests for nominal contributions, often ten or twenty dollars. These user-supported programs do not necessarily come with the extensive documentation, support, updating, and printed manuals typical of many of the major user-supported programs. This does not mean that these are not good, useful programs; many are. The distinction between public domain and user-supported software has, however, become blurred.

Several of the producers of user-supported software have begun to market their programs more like traditional commercial software. The programs are being advertised in computer magazines. In at least a few cases, user-supported programs are being sold in retail stores just like commercial software. The programs are still user-supported, in that they can be freely copied and shared. The request is still made for the contribution from those receiving free copies of the programs. At least some users, however, are acquiring the software exactly like other commercial software.

ACQUIRING PUBLIC DOMAIN AND USER-SUPPORTED SOFTWARE

The greatest bargains for those interested in low-cost computing are the public domain and user-supported programs. The programs can be obtained for free (or at a very low cost). With user-supported software, the request is made for the contribution if you are satisfied with and use the program. These contributions are still quite modest—far less than the prices of most comparable commercial programs.

For many personal computer users, the idea of using public domain and user-supported software presents two problems. First, they cannot believe that any program obtained for free or for such a modest contribution can really be any good. The idea that "you get what you pay for" is deeply ingrained. I hope that the descriptions of the four user-supported programs addressed in this book have helped to disabuse you of this notion. Excellent software can be obtained very economically. Not every public domain and user-supported program is great. Neither is every commercial program. Some very good and useful software is available among the public domain and user-supported programs.

The second problem for users considering public domain and user-supported software is learning where to obtain the programs. Commercial software can be purchased in retail stores—no special knowledge is required to do that. The public domain and user-supported programs can be freely copied, but from whom? Acquiring this software is more complicated, involving very different channels of distribution. Four major options are available for the acquisition of public domain and user-supported programs: users groups, computer bulletin boards, online information services, and mail order distributors.

The growth in the use of personal computers has spawned the development of users groups for the sharing of information. Personal computers are complex, pose novel problems for users, and open up tremendous possibilities for new applications. This has led users to come together, forming organizations for the sharing of information. Often such users groups are devoted to particular types of systems. Readers of this book would be interested in users groups devoted to the IBM Personal Computer and compatible systems.

Users groups offer great opportunities for getting answers to those difficult questions and for learning about new possibilities for personal computer use. If you are seriously interested in personal computers, try to join a group and attend the meetings. You will likely learn more about personal computing doing that than from any other source.

Users groups are also good sources for obtaining public domain and user-supported software. Most users groups have established libraries of such programs. Members can make copies of any of the programs contained in the library. In addition to providing access to the programs, participation in a users group can give you information about the various programs. Other members will have tried the programs and will be able to tell you which programs are especially good and which will be most useful for your particular needs. Incidentally, most IBM PC users groups will have copies of PC-File, PC-Write, PC-Talk, and ExpressCalc (possibly under the name PC-Calc). They represent a convenient way to obtain these programs.

How do you find a users group in your area? Some computer magazines have listings. The easiest way, however, is to ask someone working in a computer store. They often have information on the users groups for the systems they sell. Find the name of a contact for any users group, even if it is not for your type of computer system. You can then call that person, and they are likely to have information about other users groups in your area.

A second source for public domain and user-support software is the network of computer bulletin boards. Bulletin boards are an interesting phenomenon. An individual or an organization sets up a personal computer system with a modem and appropriate software for public use. Individuals can call the bulletin board, read and post messages, and upload and download software. Using the bulletin boards requires that you have a modem and a communications program, such as PC-Talk. The XMODEM protocol is very commonly employed in the transfer of program files.

Bulletin board systems will have a selection of public domain or user-supported programs available for downloading to your own computer. The number and nature of the programs available will vary widely from one bulletin board to the next. You need to look around.

How do you find out about and use these bulletin boards? Computer users groups will have information about local bulletin board systems. Some groups even operate their own bulletin boards. Magazines sometimes have listings. The key is finding the first one. Most bulletin boards have information about other systems in the area. Once you are into the network, finding out about others is not too difficult.

Using a bulletin board system is not difficult. Just dial up the telephone number with your computer. The opening message will instruct you on how to proceed. Most systems have help information available for newcomers. With a little patience, you will be able to figure out how to use the various features of the bulletin board system, learn about the programs available, and learn how to download these programs to your own systems. Do not be intimidated. After a few encounters, using the bulletin boards will become quite easy and enjoyable.

The online computer information services, such as CompuServe and The Source, represent another option for obtaining public domain and user-supported software. Large numbers of programs are stored on these systems and are available for downloading by users. The key to obtaining this software lies in learning how to find it among the large numbers of services offered. On CompuServe, for example, Special Interest Groups focusing on various computer-related topics are the repositories for much of the public domain and user-supported software. The IBM PC Special Interest Group will have many of the programs of interest to the users of IBM Personal Computers and compatibles.

Mail order suppliers of public domain and user-supported software are the fourth major source for such programs. Various organizations sell disks with these programs. The organizations collect the software, prepare catalogs listing their offerings, sometimes advertise in computer magazines, and sell the disks by mail. The software is most often sold by the disk. The contents of a disk can consist of a single elaborate program, such as PC-File, or numbers of smaller programs. Since the programs themselves are free, the only cost is the disk itself, the duplication , and the postage and handling. A typical charge for the programs from the mail order distributors is $6 per disk, plus an additional charge for postage and handling.

One of the major sources for the public domain and user-supported software by mail is the PC Software Interest Group, PC-SIG. They have assembled over 500 disks of programs, with the numbers growing steadily. Their catalog comes close to being the definitive reference for public domain and user-supported software for the IBM Personal Computer and compatibles. It includes detailed descriptions of some of the most significant software in their collection. This volume, *The PC-SIG Library*, is published as a softcover book and is now being sold by bookstores.

The PC-SIG collection includes PC-File, PC-Write, and ExpressCalc. (The latter may still be listed under the name PC-Calc.) PC-Talk is not included because the limitations placed on making copies of the program do not allow copying if the disks are to be sold (even for $6).

For a great deal of additional useful information on all of these sources of public domain and user-supported software, see the book *How to Get Free Software* by Alfred Glossbrenner (St. Martin's Press, New York, 1984). This book is especially useful as a guide to obtaining programs from information services and bulletin boards. It is already slightly dated. More emphasis is placed on earlier types of computer systems than IBM PCs and compatibles. Nevertheless, the book provides a great deal of otherwise hard-to-get information and is recommended.

TYPES OF PUBLIC DOMAIN AND USER-SUPPORTED SOFTWARE

Nearly any type of program can be obtained from the vast collections of public domain and user-supported software. These programs may not make commercial software obsolete, but they represent genuine alternatives for personal computer users on a budget.

Without doubt, PC-File, PC-Write, PC-Talk, and ExpressCalc are the most prominent user-supported programs. Each is a leader in its application area. Taken as a package, they constitute a useful collection that can meet most of the needs of many personal computer users, whether on a budget or not.

Additional user-supported programs are available from several of the publishers of the "big four." Jim Button, of Buttonware, provides the widest selection of user-supported software. In addition to PC-File, Buttonware has programs for word processing, communications, graphics, and even rudimentary style checking for word-processed documents. PC-Type is the word processor. Some consider it easier to learn and use than PC-Write. The program operates quickly—like PC-Write—and has a variety of features, though not the full range of features and the power of PC-Write. PC-Dial is the communications program. The program has virtually all of the standard features for communications that are included in PC-Talk, plus limited editing capabilities and the ability to define "scripts" to automate portions of the communications process such as logging onto a remote computer. PC-Graph is a basic program for producing line graphs of information. The program can use data from PC-File and provides a variety of options for adding text and customizing the appearance of the graphs, which may be printed out on IBM or Epson printers. PC-Style provides a simple analysis of the writing style of word-processed documents. It produces counts of words and sentences and their lengths, and information on particular words. Buttonware is providing alternatives for those using user-supported software as well as extending the range of applications available.

File Express is a user-supported database program from ExpressWare, the publishers of ExpressCalc. File Express is a fast, menu driven database program like PC-File. Both programs are flexible, though PC-File, perhaps, has a few more features. Choosing between the two is likely to be a matter of personal preference. ExpressWare also distributes a graphics program, ExpressGraph, with a wide range of capabilities.

PC-Outline is a more recent addition to the collection of major user-supported programs with significant support from their publishers. The program is distributed by a firm called Softworks Development. PC-Outline falls into the class of programs called *outline processors*, or *idea processors*. The first program of this kind was ThinkTank, a commercial product that has been very successful. Outline processors allow you to enter ideas and structure your thoughts in the form of an outline, with headings, subheadings, and so forth. Ideas can be readily added, changed, and rearranged as you attempt to organize your thoughts. While the concept is somewhat difficult to explain, many find outline processors to be extremely useful. PC-Outline has received very good reviews and appears to be a worthy addition to the selection of major user-supported programs.

The range of public domain and user-supported programs reaches far beyond these traditional applications. With educational programs, you can learn things ranging from BASIC programming to touch typing. The public domain includes large numbers of games—high-quality arcade-type games, adventure games, and many others. For programmers, there are a number of different languages and many different programming aids.

The public domain is perhaps richest in utility programs—small, special purpose programs that can make using a computer easier. Some utility programs make it possible to utilize all of the specialized features of your printer. Others help in organizing the files on your disks and in displaying the information in more usable ways. Programs can recover files that have been accidentally deleted from a disk. A keyboard utility allows the reconfiguration of your keyboard and the assignment of strings of characters to particular keys for use with other applications. Print spoolers can print out documents while you are working with another program. Still other programs provide enhanced versions of some of the standard DOS commands. This is just a sampling of the types of utility programs that are available. Few of these programs are earth-shattering. You can do your computing just fine without such utilities, but they can make your work easier and solve problems that occasionally arise.

The only way to truly appreciate the possibilities of public domain and user-supported software is to explore them. Look through listings and descriptions of the programs. Try some of them. Many of the programs will appear silly and useless to you. Among the large numbers of programs, however, will be a number that are likely to do exactly what you need to have done. Try them out. More than likely, you will find programs that meet your needs and that you will use on a regular basis. Remember, the price is right. You can get the programs at little or no cost. With public domain programs, nothing more is expected. For programs offered on a user-supported basis, you can try them with no obligation. If the program is truly useful to you, then consider making the modest contribution that is requested.

LOW-COST COMMERCIAL SOFTWARE

Personal computer users on a budget can also benefit from the increasing quantity of low-cost software that is being made available commercially. The expensive programs are facing increasing competition from programs being sold at far lower prices. Often, these low-cost alternatives are good quality programs—as good, or nearly as good, as their more expensive competitors. Some elements of the software may be different: manuals may be provided as cheap paperbacks rather than in fancy, expensive binders with slipcases. There may not be a toll-free hotline for assistance. Indeed, some publishers of low-cost programs may charge for their help. These are often small prices to pay if you can obtain programs that meet your needs at a fraction of the cost of the more expensive alternatives. Once more, you do not necessarily get only what you pay for.

The movement toward low-cost software for IBM PCs and compatibles can be traced to a program called Turbo Pascal, which is published by Borland International. During the first few years of the IBM Personal Computer, software for computer programming was generally very expensive. The software allowing the writing of programs in a particular computer language often cost several hundred dollars or more. Along came Turbo Pascal, software for writing programs in the Pascal language. Turbo Pascal is in many respects superior to other implementations of Pascal. It is faster and easier to use. The program was first sold, only by mail order, at a price of $49.95. It became an instant hit. Hundreds of thousands of copies were sold. This was a far greater number than anyone had imagined the market for a Pascal compiler to be.

Borland had demonstrated that by offering good software at a low price the market is expanded and large sales volumes are possible. The large volumes make up for the low price, generating very substantial profits. Software producers were forced to reconsider their pricing strategies. From the standpoint of making the greatest profit, the best outcome is to be able to sell very large volumes at a high price, like Lotus 1-2-3. Few programs will be anywhere near this successful. A choice may have to be made between selling fewer programs at a higher price or more programs at a lower price. At least some software publishers are following Borland's example with Turbo Pascal by offering their programs at low prices.

One hundred dollars (actually $99.95) seems to be the maximum price for software that is being marketed as low-cost software. An increasing variety of very powerful programs is becoming available at these modest prices. Many are great bargains. At less than $100, the prices of these low-cost programs are comparable to the contributions/registration fees of the better user-supported software. A selection of low-cost commercial software is described in this section. Since prices change frequently, they are not given below, but all of the programs currently carry suggested retail prices of less than $100, placing them in the low-cost category. All of the programs described have received positive notice in one or more computer magazines. This listing of low-cost software is hardly comprehensive. With the increased interest in this segment of the market, it is predictable that even more low-cost programs will be forthcoming.

One class of low-cost software is the type of program that attempts to duplicate the functions of a popular expensive program. These "work-alikes" or "clones" attempt to provide all of the features of the original and sometimes add additional capabilities. They seek to be compatible with files or programs used by the original. Such copies are never 100-percent faithful. Nevertheless, they can represent tremendous bargains for computer users on a budget, especially since such users are less frequently concerned about compatibility with the original programs.

The communications program Mirror, published by Softklone Distributing Corporation, is perhaps the most blatant in announcing itself as a direct substitute for a more expensive program. Mirror has the same screen displays and the same features as the more expensive CrossTalk XVI communications programs. In addition to duplicating the features of CrossTalk, Mirror includes several added features such as a built-in editor and the ability to perform file transfers as a background task while working with other programs. For those who do a lot of computer communications and desire the features of a sophisticated communications program, Mirror is an excellent value.

Lotus 1-2-3, the combination spreadsheet, graphics, and database program, is the most popular personal computer program of all time. With a list price of $495, it is too expensive for many personal computer users on a budget. Because of its popularity, Lotus 1-2-3 has attracted the largest number of low-cost work-alike programs. Three competitors, Twin, Farsight, and VP-Planner, are each available for less than $100. Each program provides most of the functions of Lotus 1-2-3. All three are somewhat slower and use more memory than the original. None is an exact clone that can always duplicate every Lotus 1-2-3 capability and use every Lotus 1-2-3 file. All three of the programs come very close, however, and each adds at least a few capabilities not found in the original. For users on a budget, these programs are great values.

The program Twin, published by Mosaic Software, appears to be the closest clone of Lotus 1-2-3, duplicating the features of the original most faithfully. The program provides some enhancements to the graphics, including the welcome addition of the capability for printing out the graph directly from the spreadsheet. Lotus 1-2-3 requires that graphs be saved to a disk file and printed out by a separate program.

Farsight, from Integrated Technologies Corporation, presents the most different appearance from Lotus 1-2-3. Farsight can display multiple windows on the screen. The program includes a word processor along with the Lotus 1-2-3 spreadsheet and expanded data management capabilities. The major limitation in the current version lies in the area of graphics, which are not supported.

Paperback Software International publishes VP-Planner, which extends the analytical capabilities of Lotus 1-2-3. The distinguishing feature of VP-Planner is the capability to analyze multidimensional spreadsheets or databases, in addition to the standard two-dimensional spreadsheet. A related feature is the ability to directly read information from and write information to files used by dBASE, the most popular of the high-powered relational database programs.

The dBASE II program has attracted its own low-cost alternative, Practibase, published by Practicorp International. Both dBASE II and Practibase are programmable relational database programs that allow the simultaneous use of multiple data files and the design of sophisticated applications. Practibase uses dBASE II files, has similar commands, and adds menus to the rather spartan command-driven interface of dBASE II. For users with serious, heavy-duty data management requirements that go beyond PC-File, Practibase represents an economical alternative. On the other hand, prospective users should be aware that the latest version in the dBASE series is dBASE III +, which adds a great deal to the original dBASE II program.

Other personal computer applications have not been neglected by the producers of low-cost software. Accounting programs for small businesses have traditionally been one of the more expensive forms of personal computer software. Many of the programs are sold as separate modules, each costing several hundred dollars. Dac Easy Accounting, from Dac Software, combines seven functions in a single integrated program. The program handles the general ledger, accounts receivable, accounts payable, purchase orders, billing, inventory, and forecasting, covering all of the standard functions except payroll. A separate low-cost payroll program designed to work with the main program is now available. Reviews of Dac Easy Accounting have been very positive. Not every personal computer user will need an accounting program, but for those who do, Dac Easy Accounting represents a very low-cost alternative.

Another specialized application is computer-aided design, CAD, which allows the use of the computer for sophisticated drawing. Most CAD programs have cost hundreds or even thousands of dollars. Generic CADD, from Generic Software, offers computer-aided design capabilities at a low cost. The program allows precision two-dimensional drafting and provides many of the features of the more expensive CAD packages. It is definitely not a toy. Even with a low-cost program, computer-aided design is not cheap, for specialized input and output devices such as digitizing tablets and plotters are required for serious use. Nevertheless, Generic CADD dramatically reduces the costs of getting started.

For programming, Turbo Pascal from Borland International continues to represent a real bargain. This program has become a de facto standard for Pascal programming on the IBM PC and compatibles. The success of Turbo Pascal has encouraged other publishers of programming language software to offer their products at low prices. Ads in computer magazines illustrate the range of alternatives available.

Several of the publishers of low-cost software have multiple program offerings. Dac, the publisher of the accounting program, also sells Dac Easy Word. Paperback Software, of course, is a name intended to suggest low prices. In addition to VP-Planner, Paperback Software sells Executive Writer and Executive Filer, both low-cost programs.

Personal computer users on a budget should also be aware that it is seldom necessary to pay the full retail price for most commercial software. Programs can be purchased from mail order distributors at a substantial discount. For example, Lotus 1-2-3 has a retail price of $495, which at least some computer stores charge. Lotus 1-2-3 can be purchased by mail for around $300. Comparable savings can be obtained for many other programs. A price of $300 does not place Lotus 1-2-3 into the low-cost category, of course, but it does make the program far more reasonable. Ads for mail order software distributors can be found in most computer magazines.

The purchase of personal computer software from mail order distributors is well established. If, however, you feel uneasy about making such major purchases by mail, two things can be done to reduce the risk. First, check back issues of the magazines to see if the distributor has been advertising for a number of months. If they have, chances are increased that the distributor is responsible and legitimate. Also, pay for your purchase with a credit card. Most distributors accept MasterCard and VISA. In that way, if you do not receive the programs ordered, you can notify the credit card company and will not have to pay the bill.

LOW-COST PERSONAL COMPUTERS

For those on a budget planning on the acquisition of a personal computer system, finding low-cost alternatives for the purchase of the hardware is especially important. Fortunately for those interested in IBM PC compatible computers, prices continue to fall and new, less expensive alternatives are becoming available. Complete personal computer systems compatible with the IBM Personal Computer can now be purchased at a fraction of the cost of comparable systems just a few years ago. To understand the possibilities provided by low-cost alternatives, you need to understand the phenomenon of IBM PC compatibility.

The IBM Personal Computer has become the dominant standard for personal computing. Millions of IBM Personal Computers have been sold. A wider assortment of software—many thousands of programs—is available for IBM PCs than for any other type of computer system. It is this software base, more than anything else, that establishes the IBM PC as the standard. With an IBM PC or a compatible system, you can use these programs. With other personal computers, you cannot.

Soon after the introduction of the IBM Personal Computer, other manufacturers sought to capitalize on the popularity of those machines by offering compatible systems, sometimes with additional features, at lower prices. The goal of the manufacturers of compatibles was to offer computers that could accept the same accessories, especially the plug-in boards, and that could run the same software as the IBM PC.

Achieving software compatibility posed the greatest problems. Inside the IBM PC is a chip (read-only memory, or ROM) containing instructions for the computer that are copyrighted by IBM. Making a system compatible with the IBM PC requires the development of instructions that perform the same functions but are not a copy of IBM's instructions. During the first several years of IBM PC compatibles, the degree of software compatibility was a major issue. Reviews of machines would note which programs would and would not run on the systems.

More recently, however, manufacturers have learned how to design systems that are nearly completely compatible with the IBM PC. Most current compatibles can run almost all of the software available for the IBM system. No non-IBM machine can be an exact duplicate of the IBM PC and be 100-percent compatible. For that matter, even different IBM Personal Computers are not completely compatible with one another. Most of the compatibles do come extremely close. For low-cost hardware alternatives, you would look to the possibilities offered by the compatibles.

IBM PC compatibles can be roughly grouped into three categories: enhanced systems from major manufacturers, lower-cost systems distributed through regular retail channels, and the generic clones distributed by mail. Some of the major manufacturers have attempted to add improvements to the basic design of the IBM PC in personal computers priced slightly less than IBM's comparable models. Compaq and AT&T computers are representative of the systems available in this first category. These are systems that people may choose to purchase instead of IBM PCs even when the price is not the major item of concern.

Other systems available in retail computer stores are competing with the IBM PC more explicitly on the basis of price. The Leading Edge Model D, Radio Shack's Tandy 1000, and the Epson Equity I are representative of such computers. Leading Edge caused something of a sensation when it introduced its Model D in 1985, offering a complete personal computer system for $1495, and this price has since been lowered. Several chains of computer stores have joined the competition by introducing their own private brands of IBM PC compatibles.

By far the lowest priced IBM PC compatibles are the generic clones available by mail order. These systems are generally assembled from components manufactured in the Far East and typically carry no recognizable brand name—and sometimes no name at all. They are advertised in many computer magazines. Most of the systems attempt to be straight clones of the IBM PC, with few added features. The documentation that comes with the machines may not be the best, especially for beginners. Obtaining service requires that the system be shipped back to the seller, obviously an inconvenience.

The IBM PC has increasingly come to be viewed as a standardized commodity by many personal computer purchasers. As such, less emphasis is being placed on brand names, and more concern is being focused on the price. The compatibles have been capturing an increasing share of the market from IBM. Even some large corporate purchasers, who have traditionally purchased their personal computers from IBM, are now buying the less-expensive clones. They see these machines as providing comparable computing capabilities at far lower costs.

If you are purchasing a personal computer on a tight budget, the primary alternatives will probably be the low-cost compatibles offered by retail computer stores and the generic clones that can be purchased from mail order distributors. This can be a difficult choice. The mail-order clones are less expensive. On the other hand, if you encounter any problems in setting up the machine and getting it operating correctly, you will not have a local dealer to turn to. Getting service will necessarily be a nuisance. With a low-cost, though somewhat more expensive system purchased from a local dealer, such basic support will be available.

Purchasing a computer from a recognized company also seems to be less risky than purchasing a no-name clone. Especially for new, inexperienced personal computer users, the advantages of the support gained by acquiring a system from a local retail store may well outweigh the price break associated with purchasing a mail-order generic clone. On the other hand, if you have some experience with computers or if a very limited budget allows no other options, the mail order clones may be the alternative to go with. A compromise might be the purchase of a name-brand system from a mail order distributor. Often the same machines can be obtained at a significantly lower price by mail. In doing so, you are still foregoing the advantages of local support, but you gain the reassurance of acquiring a known machine.

The highest-price alternative is usually the purchase of an IBM PC from a local authorized dealer. In doing so, you get the original, with guaranteed software compatibility (by definition), local support, and the confidence that a very large company will continue to stand behind it. To get all this, you have to pay for it. To acquire an IBM PC compatible system at a lower cost requires foregoing at least some of these advantages. The key to making the choice lies in deciding what you really require and which advantages you can safely do without.

One final note on shopping for a personal computer system on a budget: personal computers are often sold at substantial discounts from the suggested list prices. These discounts can vary from one dealer to another, so it definitely pays to shop around. The "street price" at which a particular system can actually be purchased is often hundreds of dollars less than the list price.

CONCLUSION

Low-cost computing requires a little extra effort, but for anyone on a budget, the results can be very worthwhile. The easiest way to get started in IBM-compatible personal computing is to go out and purchase an IBM PC and buy the most popular commercial software packages, such as Lotus 1-2-3 and dBase III Plus. This is also the most expensive way to proceed, and may not be necessary for many users.

Less expensive alternatives are available if you take the time to look for them. PC-File, PC-Write, PC-Talk, and ExpressCalc provide a package of software for the basic personal computer functions at a very low cost. These are very powerful, very usable programs that will adequately meet the needs of very many users. You are sacrificing little in using these programs.

As software is needed for additional applications, keep in mind the tremendous variety of programs available as public domain and user-supported software. You may be able to find a program that meets your needs exactly. The price is right, since you can obtain the programs free or at very low cost. With user-supported software, there is no obligation to make a contribution until you find the program worthwhile and decide to use it. If such a program does meet your needs, the modest contribution is a tremendous bargain.

With more and more low-cost commercial software being marketed, you may well be able to find programs that meet your needs for less than 100 dollars. Do not automatically assume that more expensive means better. Read the reviews in computer magazines to determine where the true values lie. Remember, too, that no one program—even the popular, expensive best-seller—is best for everyone. Identify what you need and find the software to meet that need. With luck, that software may not be very expensive.

In purchasing an IBM PC-compatible system, identify your real needs and determine what systems will meet those needs at the lowest price. Figure out what benefits of going with IBM you may be willing to forego, and what risks associated with other alternatives make sense. By all means, get a system with the support you need, but be willing to save money by not paying for reassurance.

Low-cost computing can be fun. It is exciting to discover a public domain, user-supported, or low-cost commercial program that meets your needs as effectively as some more-expensive program. User-supported software, especially PC-File, PC-Write, PC-Talk, and ExpressCalc, has played an important role in making low-cost computing possible. Support the shareware concept. If you find any of these programs valuable and choose to use them, please make your contributions and register the programs.

The benefits of getting the printed documentation, support, and updates are worth the cost, but more importantly, you will feel that you have done the right thing.

SOFTWARE SOURCES

Dac Easy Accounting, Dac Easy Word
Dac Software
4801 Spring Valley Road
Building 110-B
Dallas, TX 75244
Telephone: (214) 458-0038, (800) 992-7779

Farsight
Integrated Technologies Corporation
3336 Richmond, Suite 200
Houston, TX 77098
Telephone: (713) 523-8422

File Express, ExpressGraph
ExpressWare
P.O. Box 230
Redmond, WA 98073
Telephone: (206) 481-3040

Generic CADD
Generic Software Inc.
West Willows Technology Center
8763 148th Avenue N.E.
Redmond, WA 98052
Telephone: (800) 228-3601,
(800) 885-5307 (in Washington)

Mirror
Softklone Distributing Corporation
1210 East Park Avenue
Tallahassee, FL 32301
Telephone: (904) 878-8564

PC-Dial, PC-Style, PC-Type
Jim Button
Buttonware, Inc.
P.O. Box 5786
Bellevue, WA 98006
Telephone: (206) 454-0479
Orders: (800) 528-8866

PC-Outline
Softworks Development
750 Stierlin Road, Suite 142
Mountain View, CA 94043
Telephone: (800) 538-8157 (ext. 844), (800) 672-3470 (ext. 844, in California)

PC-Software Interest Group (PC-SIG)
1030-D East Duane Avenue
Sunnyvale, CA 94806
Telephone: (408) 730-9291
Orders: (800) 245-6717, (800) 222-2996 (in California)

Practibase
Practicorp International Inc.
The Silk Mill
44 Oak Street
Newton Upper Falls, MA 02164
Telephone: (617) 965-9870

Turbo Pascal
Borland International
4585 Scotts Valley Drive
Scotts Valley, CA 95066
Telephone: (408) 438-8400
Orders: (800) 255-8008, (800) 742-1133 (in California)

Twin
Mosaic Software
1972 Massachusetts Avenue
Cambridge, MA 02141
Telephone: (617) 491-2434

VP-Planner, Executive Filer, Executive Writer
Paperback Software International
2830 Ninth Street
Berkeley, CA 94710
Telephone: (415) 644-2116

Appendix B

Using the Programs on Different Systems

All four of the programs discussed in this book will work as described on the standard system outlined in Chapter 2. The standard system is an IBM Personal Computer or compatible with 256K bytes of random-access-memory (RAM) and two double-sided floppy disk drives. Those with personal computer systems that differ from these standards may still be able to use some or all of the programs, but doing so may require special procedures. This appendix outlines the operation of the programs on different personal computer systems.

USE OF OTHER MS-DOS MACHINES

The four programs were written for the IBM Personal Computer. They will operate without problems or the need for special procedures on the IBM Personal Computer, the IBM Personal Computer XT, and the IBM Personal Computer AT. Many other personal computers are highly compatible with the IBM PC and can likewise use the programs without problems. For example, all of the work for this book was done not on an IBM PC but on Zenith Z-158 and Z-161 computers.

A major reason for the incompatibility of some machines with programs written for the IBM Personal Computer are the differences in the video display systems. Some programs that write to the IBM PC video display directly, to achieve the most efficient operation, will not work with computers that are not completely compatible. Fortunately, several of the programs addressed in this book provide options for operation with other video display systems. If the programs do not work on your computer system, try the procedures described below. They *may* allow the programs to operate on your computer.

ExpressCalc provides the easiest option. Simply start the program with the following command:

```
CALC SL
```

The SL specifies that ExpressCalc is to be started using the profile file SL.PRO, which employs special "slow" routines for writing to the screen (hence the SL). The use of these routines may allow ExpressCalc to operate on computers that would otherwise be unusable. The special routines will slow down the display of information on the screen compared with the normal routines. If the choice is between a slower display and no display at all, the use of the special routines can be the key to making ExpressCalc work on your machine.

PC-File provides for reconfiguration for less-compatible machines with the PCSETUP program. Run PCSETUP as described in Chapter 3. The first question asks about IBM PC compatibility. If option 1, for IBM PCs and compatibles does not work, try option 2 for mostly compatible machines. This employs the same ROM BIOS approach used by the ExpressCalc SL option. If this does not work, PC-File offers a third option for other less-compatible MS-DOS machines. Using PCSETUP, specify option 3, which uses the ANSI device driver. If you use this option, you will have to copy the file ANSI.SYS from your DOS disk to your PC-File work disk. In addition, the disk will have to include a file named CONFIG.SYS with the following command line:

```
DEVICE = ANSI.SYS
```

If the file CONFIG.SYS does not already exist with this command, the file can be created or the command can be added to the file using PC-Write.

PC-Write can accommodate certain nonstandard video display options by including special commands in the edit control file. See the PC-Write manual for the details concerning the commands required.

Another type of video display incompatibility is faced by users limited to 40-column video displays. This would be most common with those using a color television set as the video display, perhaps with an IBM PCJr. ExpressCalc can be used with 40-column displays by starting the program with the command

```
CALC 40
```

With a monochrome display and 40 columns, use CALC BW40. Again, PC-Write can be configured for use with a 40-column display by placing the appropriate commands in the edit control file. The current version (4.0) of PC-File III no longer supports 40 column displays, but earlier versions did. You might try to locate an older version of the program.

Another area of possible incompatibility lies with the keyboards. Some computers do not have all of the keys included on the IBM PC keyboard, or the keys do not work in exactly the same manner, especially the multiple key combinations. This is not likely to be a fatal problem, for most program operations will still be possible. PC-File even provides an option for those using computers with no function keys. Only function key F10 is absolutely required for the operation of PC-File, and the program will recognize Control-A as an alternative.

Several of the programs have alternative keystroke combinations for some of the commands. For example, PC-Write includes Control key combinations mimicking many of the WordStar commands for a large number of basic operations. If the standard key combinations do not work, try these alternate combinations. PC-Write even includes a special edit control file for making the editing program perform better with the keyboard of the Tandy 1000 computer.

LIMITED RAM MEMORY

All of the programs will perform fine with the 256K bytes of random-access-memory (RAM) specified for the standard system. ExpressCalc, version 3.10 requires the full 256K of RAM. If you have less, the only option is to attempt to obtain a copy of version 2.0 of PC-Calc, which can run in 128K of RAM.

PC-File can operate with 128K of RAM. Any additional RAM will be used by the program, however. With more RAM, sorting and searching operations on large databases will proceed more quickly, as more of the information will be held in memory and fewer disk accesses will be required.

PC-Write can operate in as little as 128K of RAM, though on such systems, the size of the documents you can create is limited. With 192K of RAM, PC-Write is able to edit documents of about 60K, the maximum size it can handle. Additional RAM is not used by PC-Write.

PC-Talk will work fine with a minimum of 128K of RAM. The PC-Talk disk even includes an interpreted BASIC version of the program (not described in this book), which can operate with as little as 64K of RAM on an IBM Personal Computer, which has a major portion of BASIC in ROM. On compatible machines, the entire BASIC interpreter must be loaded into RAM, negating the space savings associated with the use of the interpreted BASIC version of PC-Talk. On these machines, 128K of RAM is needed, and the procedures for using the compiled version of PC-Talk described in this book should be followed.

In summary, those with systems having at least 128K of RAM can use all of the programs except ExpressCalc, though with limits on the size of documents that can be created with PC-Write. Moving up to 192K of RAM eliminates these limitations. The full 256K of RAM in the standard system is required for ExpressCalc.

ONE FLOPPY DISK DRIVE

All four of the programs can be used on computers with a single floppy disk drive. DOS can simulate two floppy disk drives. You can specify that a file is to be stored on the B: disk, and DOS will prompt you to swap disks at the appropriate times. This procedure will work with all of the programs, so that data files can still be stored on a separate B: disk.

The alternative for users with a single floppy disk drive is to store the data on the same disk with the programs. The program files for PC-Write and PC-Talk are sufficiently small that adequate space is available on the program disks. Indeed, even users with two floppy disk drives may find this single-disk operating procedure to be more convenient than using separate disks for program and data storage. When more disk storage is required for files of information, create additional working disks.

With PC-File, modest databases can be stored on the program disk. The amount of space taken up by the program files severely limits the size of the databases that can be accommodated in this fashion, however. Given the large sizes of the program files on the ExpressCalc disk, spreadsheets of any reasonable size must be stored on separate B: disks, even though they must be swapped in and out on a single floppy disk drive system.

HARD DISK DRIVES

As hard disk drives represent a more expensive option for personal computing, typical users of the four programs covered in this book are less likely than others to be using hard disks. Nevertheless, the four programs can all be used with hard disks. The faster disk access provided by a hard disk will especially enhance the operation of PC-File and ExpressCalc, programs that frequently access the disk to load different program segments.

Using a hard disk drive effectively requires the use of special DOS capabilities to create and use subdirectories. The subdirectories are needed to manage the large volume of files that are normally stored on a hard disk. It is assumed that hard disk users will be familiar with these procedures, including the DOS commands to make and change directories and the concept of path names.

Perhaps the simplest way to use any of the four programs with a hard disk is to create and use a single subdirectory for the storage of both program and data files. For each program, make a subdirectory for that program and copy the program files to that subdirectory. Then, when you wish to use the program, issue the DOS command to use that subdirectory. Start the program in the usual fashion. The files created and used by the program will be stored in the same subdirectory as the program files.

PC-File and PC-Write can also use files stored in other subdirectories on the hard disk. This will enable you to further organize the storage of information on the hard disk when you are using these programs. When you start PC-File, you are asked to provide an optional path name to provide access to the databases. With this feature, databases can be stored in and used from any subdirectory on the hard disk. With PC-Write, the path name can be specified when you start the editor, as follows:

```
ED \pathname\filename<Return>
```

In this way, files in any subdirectory on the hard disk can be edited with PC-Write.

When you are sharing information among the programs, as described in Chapter 7, it may be necessary to occasionally copy files of information from one subdirectory to another. PC-File and PC-Write can directly access information from the subdirectories you will have created for PC-Talk and ExpressCalc. Without copying the information into other subdirectories, however, you may end up with a very confusing organization of your hard disk, with PC-Write documents in your ExpressCalc subdirectory, and so forth.

PRINTERS

Those with printers connected to a serial port rather than to the parallel port need only issue a DOS command to redirect printer output prior to starting any of the programs. This involves the use of the following DOS MODE command:

```
MODE LPT1: = COM1
```

assuming that the printer is connected to the COM1: port. You may also have to send a prior MODE command to configure the serial port for your printer. You will probably want to include these commands in an AUTOEXEC.BAT file, so that the printer setup takes place automatically every time DOS is booted.

Index

Index